# ESSENTIALS OF
# HUMAN
# COMMUNICATION

# ESSENTIALS OF HUMAN COMMUNICATION

*Joseph A. DeVito*

*Hunter College of the City University
of New York*

HarperCollins*CollegePublishers*

*Acquisitions Editor:* Daniel F. Pipp

*Developmental Editor:* Sid Zimmerman

*Project Coordination, Text and Cover Design:* PC&F, Inc.

*Cover Photo:* The Stock Market, Gabe Palmer

*Photo Researcher:* Carol Parden

*Production Manager:* Willie Lane

*Compositor:* PC&F, Inc.

*Art Supervision:* John Callahan

*Art Preparation:* LaToya Wigfall

*Printer and Binder:* R.R. Donnelley & Sons Company

*Cover Printer:* The Lehigh Press, Inc.

ESSENTIALS OF HUMAN COMMUNICATION

LIBRARY OF CONGRESS CATALOGING-IN-PUBLICATION DATA

DeVito, Joseph A.
    Essentials of human communication / Joseph A. DeVito.
       p.   cm.
    Includes bibliographical references and index.
    ISBN 0-06-500454-X
    1. Communication.  I. Title
P90.D483        1992                    92-5395
302.2--dc20                                 CIP

93 94 95 9 8 7 6 5 4 3 2

# ABOUT THE AUTHOR

Joseph A. DeVito is Professor of Communications at Hunter College of the City University of New York. He earned his M.A. at Temple University and his Ph.D. at the University of Illinois. He has taught a wide variety of communication courses for more than 20 years. Dr. DeVito has written widely for major scholarly journals such as the *Quarterly Journal of Speech, Communication Monographs,* the *Journal of Communication, Communication Education,* and many others. He is the author of a number of textbooks, including *The Interpersonal Communication Book, The Elements of Public Speaking, Messages,* and *Human Communication,* all available from HarperCollins.

## *Books by the Author*

*The Psychology of Speech and Language: An Introduction to Psycholinguistics*

*Communication: Concepts and Processes (Third Edition)*

*General Semantics: Nine Lectures*

*General Semantics: Guide and Workbook (Revised Edition)*

*Language: Concepts and Processes*

*Psycholinguistics*

*Articulation and Voice: Effective Communication*

*The Interpersonal Communication Book (Sixth Edition)*

*The Elements of Public Speaking (Fourth Edition)*

*The Nonverbal Communication Workbook*

*The Nonverbal Communication Reader*

*Messages: Building Interpersonal Communication Skills (Second Edition)*

*Human Communication: The Basic Course (Fifth Edition)*

# CONTENTS

# PREFACE

*Essentials of Human Communication* and *Human Communication*, from which it grew, are similar and yet very different. Each serves a particular classroom need. *Essentials* focuses primarily on developing practical communication skills in interpersonal, small group, and public speaking. *Human Communication* also covers skills, but focuses primarily on understanding theory and research. It also covers a wider spectrum of communication: interpersonal, small group, organizational, public speaking, intercultural, and mass communication. Both books explore the nature and principles of human communication, perception, listening, and verbal and nonverbal messages.

*Essentials of Human Communication* introduces the student to the elements and forms of communication. It is designed for the fundamentals course that covers several communication contexts.

*Essentials* is divided into two parts. Part One—Foundations of Human Communication—covers the nature of communication, the self, perception and listening, verbal and nonverbal messages. The objective is to provide the necessary groundwork to master the three major communication forms covered in Part Two.

Part Two—Contexts of Human Communication—covers interpersonal communication (including interpersonal relationships and interviewing), small group communication, and public speaking.

## Three Major Themes

This book's uniqueness can best be explained by identifying its three major themes.

### Communication Skills Development

Focusing on communication skills, this book provides the reader with the essentials in three areas:

■ INTERPERSONAL COMMUNICATION
the skills for interacting one-on-one, for establishing and maintaining relationships, and for interviewing

■ SMALL GROUP COMMUNICATION
the skills for interacting in and leading small groups: for problem-solving, generating ideas, learning, and gaining self-awareness

■ PUBLIC SPEAKING
the skills for preparing and delivering informative and persuasive speeches

Although it is impossible to present skills without some theory and research, the emphasis here is clearly on skill development. This focus is seen throughout the text—in the emphasis given the various topics, in the self-tests designed for assessing one's skills, and in the frequent practical suggestions. This emphasis is also seen in the Skill Development Experiences that conclude each chapter.

Varying from the relatively simple to the relatively complex, these skills range from how to open or close a conversation to how to engage in productive rather than destructive conflict, how to solve a problem in a group, and how to inform and persuade an audience.

## Intercultural Perspectives

In the United States, and throughout much of the world, communication is intercultural. Every day we communicate with people from cultures noticeably different from our own. Because of this, intercultural examples are integrated throughout. There are frequent reminders that the principles that work for one culture will not work in another, that the meanings of nonverbal gestures will vary from one culture to another, and that such common communication experiences as asking questions, self-disclosing, and giving feedback, for example, will take on markedly different values depending on the participants' culture.

## Critical Thinking Skills

The skills of critical thinking are incorporated throughout the text. In addition, at the end of each part, the nature of critical thinking is discussed and the skills covered are highlighted. Quotations and probes in the margins will stimulate students to use their critical thinking skills and to question, reflect upon, extend, and challenge what we say about communication. Even the photo captions and cartoons are designed to stimulate critical thinking.

The critical thinking skills are both specific and general. They are specific in that they are presented in a communication context and illustrated with examples from interpersonal, small group, and public communication. They are general, however, in that they apply to all subjects and situations that require clear and critical thinking. Thus they are eminently transferable to other forms of communication as well as to situations and contexts other than communication. Put differently, the goal of this critical thinking emphasis is not only to make the reader a better thinker about communication, but simply a better thinker.

---

## Features of Essentials of Human Communication

In addition to the communication skills, the intercultural perspectives, and the critical thinking skills emphases, this book has a variety of features designed to make learning the material more effective and enjoyable.

### Learning Goals

Each chapter opens with goals that spell out what the student should learn from the chapter. These goals highlight the chapter's essential content and should be reread after completing the chapter to make sure they can be accomplished.

### Feedback Summaries

At the end of each chapter is a summary (called "feedback") that highlights the major elements *and* skills. The skill summary serves as a checklist to allow the student to determine his or her current level of mastery. In this way, those skills requiring further effort can be highlighted.

### Self-Tests

Sixteen self-tests are integrated throughout. Although these tests are interesting and fun to do, their primary purpose is to encourage self analysis, an essential prerequisite for learning human communication skills.

### Skill Development Experiences

Exercises at the end of each chapter provide opportunities to learn human communication skills in an enjoyable way and in a supportive atmosphere.

### Quotations and Probes

As already noted, the marginal quotations and probes (including those in the photo captions) will provide frequent opportunities to interact with the text and to extend the principles discussed to other situations.

---

## Supplementary Materials

*Essentials* comes with a wide variety of supplementary materials to make this book an efficient and effective learning and teaching tool. Instructors should consult their HarperCollins representative for further information on any of these materials.

### Instructor's Manual and Test Bank with Transparency Masters

*Essentials* comes with a detailed Instructor's Manual prepared by Joseph Giordano of the University of Wisconsin, Eau Claire. This manual contains Unit Planners for each chapter, sample syllabi, guidelines for using the Skill Development Experiences, suggestions for additional exercises, 124 transparency masters, and a detailed glossary. In addition, a test bank, containing hundreds of test questions and organized by chapter, is included. The test bank is also available on TestMaster.

### TestMaster

The complete test bank is contained on diskette for IBM PC and compatibles. TestMaster comes with a word-processing program that allows complete customizing capabilities.

### Grades

A grade-keeping and classroom management software program for IBM PC and compatibles that can maintain data for up to 200 students.

### The Interpersonal Challenge

A card game for use with such topics as perception, interpersonal relationships, ethics, and self-disclosure is also available. This game, constructed by the author, contains 150 questions designed to encourage self analysis and critical thinking.

### The HarperCollins Communication Video Library

Numerous videos are available to users and cover such topics as effective listening, interpersonal relationships, interviewing, small group communication, and public speaking.

## Acknowledgments

I would like to thank the many reviewers who read the manuscript at various stages of development, gave graciously of their time and experience, and offered suggestions that resulted in many significant improvements. To all these colleagues I am most thankful. I especially wish to express my appreciation to the following:

- Edward M. Brown, Abilene Christian University
- Kelly L. Burns, Indiana-Purdue University at Fort Wayne
- Charles F. Cline, Tacoma Community College
- Ray Collins, San Jose City College
- Robert Dixon, St. Louis Community College, Meramec
- Mary C. Forestieri, Lane Community College
- Laurie W. Hodge, Bergen Community College
- Elaine S. Klein, Westchester Community College
- Donald Loeffler, Western Carolina University
- Weslynn Martin, Rockhurst College
- William L. Robinson, Purdue University, Calumet
- Patricia Rochelt, Western Wisconsin Technical Institute
- Chris R. Sawyer, Tarrant County Junior College, Northwest
- James S. Taylor, Houston Baptist University
- Stella Ting-Toomey, California State University, Fullerton
- Donald E. Williams, University of Florida

For their reviews of the critical thinking material throughout this text, I am grateful to:

- Rachel Lauer, director of the Straus Thinking and Learning Center, Pace University
- Robert J. Sternberg, IBM Professor of Psychology and Education, Yale University

I also wish to thank Sid Zimmerman who coordinated and summarized reviews and who made content, style, and design suggestions that contributed greatly to the strength of the completed text. I also wish to acknowledge the contributions of the many writers and teachers I have drawn on, for example, the teachings of Harry Weinberg and the writings of William Haney.

The staff at HarperCollins likewise helped in important ways. Communication editors Melissa Rosati and currently Dan Pipp supported the project from its inception to its publication. Carla Samodulski, developmental editor, intelligently supervised the review and revision process and contributed to all stages of production. I am also grateful to Carol Parden photo researcher, who located the very photos needed to amplify the text and to Kewal Sharma and Willie Lane for their effective and efficient guidance of the production and manufacturing processes.

The people at PC&F were a pleasure to work with. Elaine Hall served admirably as copyeditor and is responsible for significant improvements too numerous to identify. I also wish to thank the text designer, Margaret Saunders, who gave this text a most appealing yet functional design that will serve as a model for future textbooks.

Joseph A. DeVito

I am not an Athenian or a Greek, but a citizen of the world.

—SOCRATES

# FOUNDATIONS OF HUMAN COMMUNICATION

*In this part we explain what human communication is and how it works. We look at the central part of human communication—yourself—and examine self-awareness, self-esteem, and self-disclosure and how these relate to your own communication effectiveness. We then consider perception and listening and especially how you might improve the accuracy of your judgments of others and the efficiency of your listening. The last two chapters in this part focus on messages—verbal and nonverbal. We concentrate on the way in which these systems work and how you can use them more effectively—as sender and as receiver.*

*Throughout these five chapters, we have integrated a variety of critical thinking skills. At the end of these five chapters, we discuss critical thinking directly and highlight and summarize the critical thinking principles covered so far.*

*In this part we try to answer a number of questions that you probably have already asked yourself. Here is just a brief sampling:*

## 1. INTRODUCTION TO HUMAN COMMUNICATION

*How will communication skills figure into my personal, social, and professional life? Can I really learn more effective methods of communication in just one course?*

## 2. THE SELF IN COMMUNICATION

*How can I improve my self esteem and how will this influence my everyday communications? Should I reveal who I really am and what I really think? If so, to whom?*

## 3. PERCEPTION AND LISTENING

*How do people judge me? How do I judge others? Can I improve my accuracy? How important is listening? Is it worth the effort to try to improve my listening habits?*

## 4. VERBAL MESSAGES

*How can I avoid the common barriers to effective communication? Can I make my speech more effective?*

## 5. NONVERBAL MESSAGES

*Can I make my nonverbal messages more effective? How can I read the nonverbal messages of others more accurately?*

## CRITICAL THINKING PERSPECTIVES AND REVIEW

*How can I make more accurate judgments? How can I listen more critically? How can I more critically analyze verbal and nonverbal messages?*

# CHAPTER 1

# Introduction to Human Communication

## COMMUNICATION: A DEFINITION
- *Communication Context*
- *Sources-Receivers*
- *Encoding-Decoding*
- *Communicative Competence*
- *Messages and Channels*
- *Feedback and Feedforward*
- *Noise*
- *Effects*
- *Ethics*

## PRINCIPLES OF COMMUNICATION
- *Communication Is a Package of Signals*
- *Communication Is a Process of Adjustment*
- *Communication Involves Content and Relationship Dimensions*
- *Communication Involves Symmetrical and Complementary Transactions*
- *Communication Sequences Are Punctuated for Processing*
- *Communication Is a Transactional Process*
- *Communication Is Inevitable*
- *Communication Is Purposeful*
- *Communication Is Irreversible*

## FEEDBACK

## SKILL DEVELOPMENT EXPERIENCES

## Goals

*After completing this chapter, you should be able to*

1. *define* communication *and its components*
2. *explain why communication is a package of signals*
3. *explain why communication depends on adjustment*
4. *distinguish between the content and the relationship dimensions of communication and between symmetrical and complementary transactions*
5. *define* punctuation
6. *explain why communication is transactional, inevitable, purposeful, and irreversible*

*■ How might you profit from the study of communication? ■ In what areas of your personal, social, and professional lives can communication make you more effective? ■ What kind of a speaker and listener are you now? ■ What kind of a communicator would you like to become? ■ What communication goals would you like to set for yourself? ■ How might you reach these goals?*

These are some of the questions we explore in this first chapter as we begin our study of human communication.

Of all the knowledge and skills you have, those concerning communication are among the most important and useful. Human communication involves sending and receiving messages. You communicate when you send messages as in speaking, writing, and smiling and receive messages by listening, reading, and seeing the messages of others. You can even communicate with yourself. Through **intrapersonal communication** you talk with, learn about, and judge yourself. You persuade yourself of this or that, reason about possible decisions to make, and rehearse

> When Aristotle was asked how much educated men were superior to the uneducated, he replied, 'As much as the living are to the dead.'
> —DIONYSIUS OF HALICARNASSUS

**Table 1.1** *Areas of Communication*

| Areas of Human Communication | Some Common Purposes | A Few Theory-related Concerns | A Few Skill-related Concerns |
|---|---|---|---|
| Intrapersonal: communication with oneself | To think, reason, analyze, reflect | How does one's self-concept develop? How does one's self-concept influence communication? How can problem-solving and analyzing abilities be improved and taught? What is the relationships between personality and communication? | Enhancing self-esteem, increasing self-awareness improving problem-solving and analyzing abilities; increasing self-control; reducing stress; managing interpersonal conflict |
| Interpersonal: communication between two persons | To learn, relate, influence, play, help | What is interpersonal effectiveness? Why do people develop relationships? What holds friends, lovers, and families together? What tears them apart? How can relationships be repaired? | Increasing effectiveness in one-to-one communication, developing and maintaining effective relationships (friendship, love, family), improving conflict resolution abilities |
| Small group: communication within a small group of persons | To share information, generate ideas, solve problems, help | What makes a leader? What type of leadership works best? What roles do members serve in groups? What do groups do well and what do they fail to do well? How can groups be made more effective? | Increasing effectiveness as a group member, improving leadership abilities, using groups to achieve specific purposes (for example, solving problems, generating ideas) |
| Public: communication of speaker to audience | To inform, persuade, entertain | What kinds of organizational structures work best in informative and persuasive speaking? How can audiences be most effectively analyzed and adapted to? How can ideas be best developed for communication to an audience? | Communicating information more effectively; increasing persuasive abilities; developing, organizing, styling, and delivering messages with greater effectiveness |

messages that you plan to send to others. Through **interpersonal communication** you interact with others, learn about them and yourself, and reveal yourself to others. Whether with new acquaintances, old friends, lovers, or family members, it is through interpersonal communication that you establish, maintain, sometimes destroy (and sometimes repair) personal relationships. Interpersonal communication also occurs during interviews—in, for example, applying for a job, gathering information, and counseling. Through **interviewing** you exchange information, persuade, and evaluate.

Through **small group communication** you interact with others. You solve problems, develop new ideas, and share knowledge and experiences. You live your work and social life largely in groups. From the employment interview to the executive board meeting, from the informal social group having coffee to the formal meeting discussing issues of international concern, you interact in small groups. Through **public communication**, others inform and persuade you. And you, in turn, inform and persuade others—to do, to buy, or to think in a particular way, or to change an attitude, opinion, or value. This book, then, is about these communications and it is about you—as speaker and listener.

It seeks to accomplish three goals:

1. to explain the *theories and concepts* important to the many forms of communication;
2. to improve your own *skills and abilities* as speaker and listener; and
3. to enhance your ability to *think critically* about communication.

Table 1.1 summarizes these areas of communication and their corresponding communication skills that you will focus on in this course.

## TEST YOURSELF:

### *What Do You Know About Communication?*

Respond to each of the following statements with T (true) if you think the statement is usually true and F (false) if you think the statement is usually false.

_____ 1. Good communicators are born, not made.
_____ 2. The more we communicate, the better that communication will be.
_____ 3. Unlike effective speaking, effective listening really cannot be taught.
_____ 4. Opening lines such as "Hello, how are you?" or "Fine weather today" or "Have you got a light?" serve no useful communication purpose.
_____ 5. In interpreting the meanings of another person's communication, you should focus exclusively on the words used.
_____ 6. When verbal and nonverbal messages contradict each other, people believe the verbal message.
_____ 7. Complete openness should be the goal of any meaningful interpersonal relationship.
_____ 8. Interpersonal conflict is a reliable sign that your relationship is in trouble.
_____ 9. Like good communicators, leaders are born, not made.
_____ 10. Fear of speaking is detrimental and must be eliminated.

*Scoring:* All ten statements are false. As you read this book, you'll discover not only why these statements are false but some problems that arise when people act on the basis of such misconceptions.

# Communication: A Definition

*Communication* occurs when you send or receive messages, and when you assign meaning to another person's signals. Human communication always is distorted by noise, occurs within a context, has some effect, and involves some opportunity for feedback (Figure 1.1). Let's look at each of these essential elements.

## Communication Context

How would you describe the communication context (physical, cultural, social-psychological, and temporal) in which you find yourself right now?

Communication always takes place in a specific setting or environment—a context. The context influences both what you say and how you say it. Contexts have at least four aspects: physical, cultural, social-psychological, and temporal (Table 1.2).

These four aspects interact—each influences and is influenced by the others. For example, arriving late for a date (temporal context) may lead to changes in the degree of friendliness (social-psychological context), which would depend on the cultures of you and your date (cultural context), and which may lead to changes in where you go on the date (physical context).

**Figure 1.1** *A Model of Human Communication*

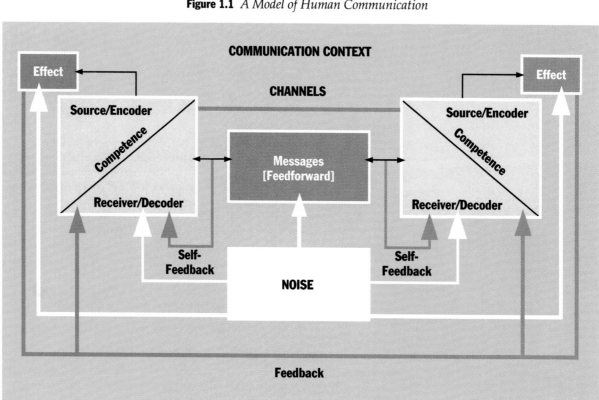

| | |
|---|---|
| **Physical Context** | The tangible or concrete environment, the room, park, or auditorium; we don't talk the same way at a football game as at a funeral. |
| **Cultural Context** | The lifestyles, beliefs, values, behavior and communication, rules of a group of people for considering something right or wrong. |
| **Social-Psychological Context** | The status relationships among the participants, the cultural rules of the society, the formality-informality of the situation; we don't talk the same way in the cafeteria as we would at a formal dinner at our boss's house. |
| **Temporal (time) Context** | The position in which a message fits into a sequence of events; we don't talk the same way after someone tells us of the death of a close relative as we do after someone tells us of winning the lottery. |

**Table 1.2** *Communication Contexts*

> No culture can live, if it attempts to be exclusive.
> —MAHATMA GANDHI

## Sources-Receivers

Each person involved in communication is both a source (or speaker) and a receiver (or listener). To emphasize this dual function we hyphenate these terms. You send messages when you speak, write, gesture, or smile. You receive messages by listening, reading, smelling, and so on. As you send messages, however, you also receive messages. You receive your own (you hear yourself, you feel your own movements), as well as the messages of the other person—visually, auditorily, or through touch or smell. For example, as you speak, you look for responses—for approval, understanding, sympathy, agreement, and so on. As you decipher these nonverbal signals, you are a receiver.

> Communication . . . the process of assigning meaning and intention to the acts of others.
> —PHILIP TOMPKINS

## Encoding-Decoding

*Encoding* is the act of producing messages—such as speaking, writing, or gesturing. When you put your thoughts and feelings into words, marks on paper, or gestures, you are putting them into a code, hence you are encoding your ideas. *Decoding* is the act of receiving-and-interpreting messages—for example, listening, reading, or seeing. When you translate sound waves, words on paper, or gestures into ideas, you are taking the ideas out of the code (the language or gestural code, for example), hence *decoding*. Thus, we refer to speakers, writers, those who gesture or otherwise communicate nonverbally as *encoders;* and listeners, readers, and those who interpret the meanings of the nonverbal behaviors as *decoders.*

As with *source-receiver,* we hyphenate *encoding-decoding* to emphasize that you perform these functions *simultaneously.* As you speak (encode), you also decipher (decode) the responses of the listener.

> Communication is the exchange of information between two or more minds.
> —JOHN C. LILLY

## Communicative Competence

Your ability to communicate effectively is your *communicative competence* (Spitzberg and Cupach 1989). It includes your knowledge of the

> Communication is power. Those who have mastered its effective use can change their own experience of the world and the world's experience of them.
> —ANTHONY ROBBINS

*In interpersonal and small group communication, it is relatively easy to appreciate the interconnectedness of source and receiver—of encoding and decoding. In public speaking, however, we often assume that the speaker is the only source and the audience is the receiver. In what ways does the public speaker receive messages from the audience? In what ways does the audience send messages to the speaker? In what ways do audience members send and receive messages to each other?*

**What noted personality would you nominate for the "Communication Competence Hall of Fame"? Why?**

**Most of us are born with the potential to learn communication; whether or not we acquire *effective* communication skills is up to us. Through careful instruction, personal observation, experience, and practice an individual can learn many of the communication skills needed to be a better communicator.**
**—Virginia P. Richmond and James C. McCroskey**

role the context plays in influencing the content and form of communication. For example, your competence includes the knowledge that in certain contexts and with certain listeners one topic is appropriate and another is not. Knowledge about the rules of nonverbal behavior—the appropriateness of touching, vocal volume, and physical closeness—is also part of your communication competence. One of the major goals of this text and course is to spell out the nature of communication competence; thereby increasing your communication competence and effectiveness in interpersonal, small group, and public situations. The process goes like this:

knowledge of communication
*leads to*
↓
greater communication competence
*leads to*
↓
greater number of available choices or options for communicating
*leads to*
↓
greater likelihood of communicating effectively in any situation

## Culture and Competence

Competence is specific to a given culture. The principles of effective communication will vary from one culture to another; what will prove effective in one culture may prove ineffective in another. For example, U.S. business executives will discuss business during the first several minutes of a meeting. However, Japanese business executives interact socially for an extended period of time in order to find out about each other. Thus, the small group communication principle influenced by U.S. culture would advise the participants to attend to the meeting's agenda during the first five or ten minutes. The principle influenced by Japanese culture would advise participants to avoid dealing with business until all have socialized sufficiently and feel they know each other well enough to begin business negotiations.

Note that neither principle is right nor wrong. Each is effective within its own culture and ineffective outside its own culture.

## Messages and Channels

Communication *messages* take many forms and are transmitted or received through one or a combination of sensory organs. We communicate verbally (with words) and nonverbally (without words). Our meanings or intentions are conveyed with words (Chapter 4) and with the clothes we wear, the way we walk, and the way we smile (Chapter 5). Everything about us communicates.

The communication *channel* is the medium through which messages pass. Communication rarely takes place over only one channel. Rather, we use two, three, or four different channels simultaneously. In face-to-face conversations, for example, we speak and listen (vocal channel), but we also gesture and receive these signals visually (visual channel). We also emit and smell odors (olfactory channel) and often we touch one another, and this, too, is a communication (tactile channel).

It [communication] is that which links any organism together.
—E. Colin Cherry

Communication means that information is passed from one place to another.
—George A. Miller

"How can I learn communication skills if you keep telling me to be quiet?"

From The Wall Street Journal—Permission, Cartoon Features Syndicate

"*I don't understand. Eddie Murphy uses the word and makes a million dollars. I use the same word and lose a month's allowance.*"

CARTOON BY WILLIAM CANTY

Can you explain—using communication terms—the differences between this boy's and Eddie Murphy's use of the "same" word?

### Feedback and Feedforward

*Feedback* is information that is sent back to the source (Clement and Frandsen 1976). Feedback may come from yourself or from others. When you send a message—say, in speaking to another person—you also hear yourself. That is, you get feedback from your own messages; you hear what you say, you feel how you move, you see what you write.

In addition to this self-feedback, you also get feedback from others. This feedback may take many forms. A frown or a smile, a yea or a nay, a pat on the back or a punch in the mouth, an audience asleep or in wild applause are all types of feedback.

*Feedforward* is information about messages that are to be sent in the future (Richards 1951). We frequently preface our messages with such

What kinds of feedback are you receiving right now?

statements as "I may be wrong about this but . . . ," "I want you to know exactly what happened . . . ," or "Don't get the wrong idea, but . . . ." These messages tell the listener something about future messages.

## Noise

*Noise* interferes with your getting a message someone is sending. The noise may be physical (others talking loudly, cars honking), psychological (preconceived ideas, wandering thoughts), or semantic (misunderstood meanings). To the extent that the message is interfered with—how much it differs from what is sent—noise is present. Technically, noise is described as a disturbance in communication that distorts the message. It prevents the receiver from receiving the message the source is sending.

How might the concept of noise apply to written communications?

Note that since messages may be visual as well as spoken, noise too may be visual. Thus, the sunglasses that prevent someone from seeing the messages from your eyes would be considered noise as would blurred type on a printed page. Table 1.3 identifies these three major types of noise in more detail.

Noise is inevitable. All communications contain noise of some kind. You cannot eliminate noise completely. You can, however, reduce noise and its effects. Making your language more precise, sharpening your skills for sending and receiving nonverbal messages, and improving your listening and feedback skills are some ways to combat the interference of noise.

## Effects

'Communication,' in its broadest interpretation, may be defined as the eliciting of a response.
—FRANK E. X. DANCE

Communication *always* has some effect on those involved in the communication act. For every communication act, there is some consequence. For example, you may gain knowledge or learn how to analyze, synthesize, or evaluate something. These are intellectual or cognitive effects. Second, you may acquire new attitudes or beliefs or change existing ones. These are affective consequences. Third, you may learn new bodily movements such as how to throw a curve ball, paint a picture, give a compliment, or express surprise. These are psychomotor effects.

**Table 1.3** *Three Types of Noise*

| Type | Definition | Example |
|------|------------|---------|
| Physical | Interferes with the physical transmission of the signal or message | Screeching of passing cars, hum of computer, sunglasses |
| Psychological | Cognitive or mental interference | Biases and prejudices in senders and receivers, closed-mindedness |
| Semantic | Speaker and listener assigning different meanings | People speaking different languages, use of jargon or overly complex terms not understood by listener |

## Ethics

Because communication has effects, it also involves questions of *ethics*. There is a right-versus-wrong aspect to any communication act (Jaksa and Pritchard 1988; Bok 1978). For example, while it may be effective to lie in selling a product, it would not be ethical. The decisions you make concerning communication are guided by what you consider right as well as effective.

Whether communications are ethical or unethical is grounded in the notion of choice and the assumption that people have a right to make their own choices. Communications are ethical when they facilitate the receiver's freedom of choice by presenting that person with accurate information or bases for choice. Communications are unethical when they interfere with the receiver's freedom of choice by preventing that person from securing information relevant to the choice.

Ethical issues are integral to all forms and functions of communication. Here are a few questions which deal with issues we will consider throughout this text:

- Would it be ethical to lie to your partner to avoid an argument and ill-feelings?
- Would it be ethical to reveal another person's secrets?
- Would it be ethical to exaggerate your virtues and minimize your vices to win someone's approval? To get a job? To what extent can a person exaggerate before it is considered unethical?
- Would it be ethical to assume leadership of a group to get the group to do as you wish?
- Would it be ethical to present another's research as your own in a public speech?
- Would it be ethical to persuade an audience to do something by scaring them? By threatening them?

## Principles of Communication

In this section, we elaborate on the nature of communication by presenting nine principles that are essential to an understanding of communication in all its forms and functions.

### Communication Is a Package of Signals

Communication normally occurs in "packages" of verbal and nonverbal behaviors or messages (Pittenger, Hockett, and Danehy 1960). Usually, verbal and nonverbal behaviors reinforce or support each other. We do not usually express fear with words while the rest of our body relaxes. We do not normally express anger with our bodily posture while our face smiles. The entire person works as a whole—verbally and nonverbally—to express thoughts and feelings.

Usually, we pay little attention to the packaged nature of communication. It goes unnoticed. But when the messages contradict each other—when the weak handshake belies the verbal greeting, when the nervous posture belies the focused stare—we take notice. Invariably we begin to question the sincerity and honesty of the person.

> It is these four 'moralities': the duty of search and inquiry, allegiance to accuracy, fairness, and justice in the selection and treatment of ideas and arguments, the willingness to submit private motivations to public scrutiny, and the toleration of dissent—which provide the ethic of communication in a free society.
> —Karl R. Wallace

> At times, others might have to make decisions for small children or those who are mentally unable to make safe and sensible decisions for themselves. Are there other exceptions to the notion of choice explained here?

> Important principles may and must be flexible.
> —Abraham Lincoln

> What do you say to a friend who says that he or she is feeling fine after a recent romantic breakup but walks with head down, cries without apparent reason, and avoids any social activities with friends?

## Communication Is a Process of Adjustment

All truly wise thoughts have been thought already thousands of times; but to make them truly ours, we must think them over again honestly, til they take root in our personal experience.
—GOETHE

Effective communication takes place only to the extent that the people understand one another's system of signals (Pittenger, Hockett, and Danehy 1960). When people speak different languages, for example, communication is difficult because they cannot grasp what the signals are intended to mean. As a general principle, to the degree that language systems differ, communication is reduced. This becomes especially clear when we realize that no two people use identical signal systems. Parents and children not only have largely different vocabularies but also different meanings for the terms they do share. Different cultures, even those with a common language, often have greatly different nonverbal communication systems. To the extent that these systems differ, effective communication will not take place.

Part of your communication effectiveness depends on your ability to identify the other person's signals, to learn how they are used, and to understand what they mean. Think of your close relationships. It probably took you time, effort, and patience to learn the other person's signals. If you want to understand what another person means (by a smile, by saying "I love you," by arguing about trivia, by self-deprecating comments), rather than simply hearing what the other person says, you have to learn that person's system of communicating.

With whom are you most effective in communicating? Why? With whom are you least effective? Why?

"If you don't want me to borrow the car,
just say so. Don't tell me you've lost it."

CARTOON BY JIM M'GUINNESS

## Communication Involves Content and Relationship Dimensions

Communications, to some extent, refers to something external to both speaker and hearer—the weather, yesterday's political events, or a television program. At the same time, however, communications also refer to the relationships between the persons (Watzlawick, Beavin, and Jackson 1967). For example, an employer may say to a worker, "See me after the meeting." This simple message has a *content aspect* and a *relational aspect*.

The content aspect refers to the behavioral responses expected—namely, that the worker see the employer after the meeting. The relationship aspect refers to the relationship between the employer and the worker; it states how the communication is to be dealt with. For example, the use of the command indicates a status difference between the two parties: the employer can command the worker. If the worker commanded the employer, it would appear awkward and out of place simply because it would violate the normal relationship between employer and worker.

Many problems between people result from the failure to distinguish between the content and the relationship levels of communication. Consider an engaged couple arguing over the fact that Pat made plans to study with friends during the weekend without first asking Chris. Probably both would have agreed that to study over the weekend was the right choice to make. Thus, the argument is not at all related to the content level. The argument centers on the relationship level. Chris expected to be consulted about plans for the weekend. Pat, in not doing this, rejected this definition of the relationship.

Examine the following interchange and note how relationship considerations are ignored.

PAUL: *I'm going bowling tomorrow. The guys at the plant are starting a team. [He focuses on the content and ignores any relational implications of the message.]*

JUDY: *Why can't we ever do anything together? [She responds primarily on a relational level and ignores the content implications of the message, expressing her displeasure at being ignored in his decision.]*

PAUL: *We can do something together anytime; tomorrow's the day they're organizing the team. [Again, he focuses almost exclusviely on the content.]*

Here is essentially the same situation, but with something added: sensitivity to relationship messsages.

PAUL: *The guys at the plant are organizing a bowling team. I'd sure like to be on the team. Would it be all right if I went to the organizational meeting tomorrow? [Although he focuses on content, he shows awareness of the relational dimensions by asking if this would be a problem. He also shows this in expressing his desire rather than his decision to attend this meeting.]*

JUDY: *That sounds great but I'd really like to do something together tomorrow. [She focuses on the relational dimension but also acknowledges his content orientation. Note too that she does not respond defensively, as if she has to defend herself or her emphasis on relational aspects.]*

PAUL: *How about your meeting me at Luigi's for dinner after the organizational meeting? [He responds to the relational aspect—without abandoning*

> Speech is civilization itself. The word, even the most contradictory word, preserves contact. It is silence which isolates.
> —THOMAS MANN

> The only way to speak the truth is to speak lovingly.
> —HENRY DAVID THOREAU

> How would you respond to a friend who says, "I just can't go to that club and be ignored again all night"?

Recall a recent interpersonal, small group, or public communication situation. What were the major content messages communicated? The major relationship messages? Can you think of a communication transaction in which only content messages were communicated? Only relationship messages?

his desire to join the bowling team—and seeks to include it into his communications. He tries to negotiate a solution that will meet both Judy's and his needs and desires.]

JUDY: That sounds great. I'm dying for spaghetti and meatballs. [She responds to both messages, approving of both his joining the team and also of their dinner date.]

Arguments over content are relatively easy to resolve: it is fairly easy to verify disputed facts. For instance, we may look up something in a book or ask someone what actually took place. Arguments on the relationship level, however, are much more difficult to resolve, in part because we seldom recognize that the argument is in fact a relationship one.

## Communication Involves Symmetrical and Complementary Transactions

Relationships are either symmetrical or complementary (Watzlawick, Beavin, and Jackson 1967). In a *symmetrical relationship* the two people mirror each other's behavior. The behavior of one person mirrors or imitates the behavior of the other. If one member nags, the other member responds in a similar way. If one member expresses jealousy, the other expresses jealousy. If one member is passive, the other is passive. The relationship is one of equality, with the emphasis on minimizing the differences between the two individuals.

With whom do you have a symmetrical relationship?

Note, however, the problems that can arise in this type of relationship. Consider the situation of a husband and wife, both of whom are very aggressive. The aggressiveness of the husband fosters aggressiveness in the wife; the aggressiveness of the wife fosters aggressiveness in the husband. As this escalates, the aggressiveness can no longer be contained, and the relationship is consumed by the aggression.

In a *complementary relationship* the two individuals engage in different behaviors. The behavior of one serves as the stimulus for the complementary behavior of the other. In complementary relationships the differences between the parties are maximized. The people occupy different positions, one superior and the other inferior, one passive and the other active, one strong and the other weak. At times cultures establish such relationships—as the complementary relationship between teacher and student or between employer and employee.

A problem in complementary relationships, familiar to many college students, is one created by extreme rigidity. When young, the complementary relationship between a nurturing and protective mother and a dependent child is appropriate and essential to the life of the child. When the child is older, however, that same relationship becomes a handicap to further development. The change so essential to growth is not allowed to occur.

## Communication Sequences Are Punctuated for Processing

Communication events are continuous transactions with no clear-cut beginning or ending. As participants in or observers of communication, we divide this continuous, circular process into causes and effects, or stimuli and responses. That is, we segment or *punctuate* this continuous stream of communication into smaller pieces (Watzlawick, Beavin, and Jackson 1967). Some of these we label causes, or stimuli, and others effects, or responses. Most often we punctuate communication in ways that allow us to look good and that are consistent with our own self-image.

Consider this example: The manager lacks interest in the employees, seldom offering any suggestions for improvement or any praise for jobs well done. The employees are apathetic and morale is low. Figure 1.2(a) illustrates the sequence of events in which there is no absolute beginning and no absolute end. Each action (the manager's lack of involvement and the employees' low morale) stimulates the other. Each serves as the stimulus for the other but there is no initial stimulus. Each event may be seen as a stimulus *or* as a response. There is no way to determine which is which.

Figure 1.2(b) illustrates how the manager might divide this continuous transaction. From this point of view, the manager sees the employees' apathy as the stimulus and his or her lack of interest and involvement as the response. Figure 1.2(c) shows how the employees might divide the transaction. They might see the manager's lack of involvement as the stimulus (or cause) and their own apathy as the response (or effect).

---

With whom do you have a complementary relationship?

---

When John was a child his parents made all decisions for him. As John grew up, however, his parents continued to make his decisions and he has continued to depend on their doing so. Using the concepts of symmetrical and complementary relationships, how would you explain this situation?

---

People don't care how much we know until they know how much we care.
—DUTCH BOLING

**Figure 1.2**
*The Sequence of Events*

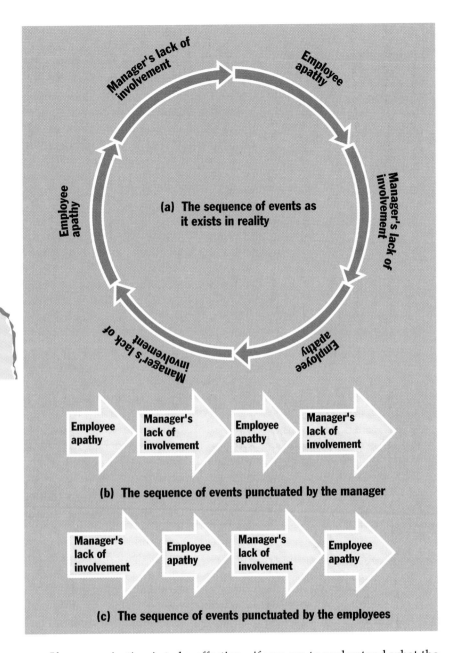

(a) The sequence of events as it exists in reality

Manager's lack of involvement

Employee apathy

Manager's lack of involvement

Employee apathy

Manager's lack of involvement

Employee apathy

| Employee apathy | Manager's lack of involvement | Employee apathy | Manager's lack of involvement |

(b) The sequence of events punctuated by the manager

| Manager's lack of involvement | Employee apathy | Manager's lack of involvement | Employee apathy |

(c) The sequence of events punctuated by the employees

Can you identify another example to illustrate differences in punctuation?

How would you use the principle of punctuation to explain this familiar argument? Pat: Of course, I don't help you with the dishes. Do you help me with the lawn? Do you help me at my job?

If communication is to be effective—if you are to understand what the other person means from his or her point of view,—then you have to see the sequence of events as punctuated by the other person. Further, you need to recognize that your punctuation does not reflect what exists in reality. Rather, it reflects your own unique, subjective, and fallible perception.

## Communication Is a Transactional Process

Communication is a transaction—a simultaneous sending-and-receiving of messages. In a transactional view of communication, all parts are interrelated and always in motion (Watzlawick, Beavin, and Jackson 1967; Watzlawick 1977, 1978; Barnlund 1970; Wilmot 1987).

COMPONENTS ARE INTERRELATED. In any transactional process, each element relates integrally to every other element. The elements of communication are *inter*dependent (never independent). Each exists in relation to the others. For example, there can be no source without a receiver. There can be no message without a source. There can be no feedback without a receiver. Because of this interdependence, a change in any one element produces changes in the other elements. Say that you are talking with a group of your friends and your mother enters the group. This change in audience will lead to other changes. Perhaps you or your friends will change what you are saying or how you are saying it. Regardless of what change occurs, other changes will follow.

COMMUNICATION IS A PROCESS. Communication is always in motion; it is a process, an activity. Everything in communication is in a state of constant change. We are constantly changing, the people with whom we are communicating are changing, and our environment is changing. Nothing in communication ever remains static.

## Communication Is Inevitable

Communication often takes place even though a person does not intend or want to communicate. Take, for example, a student sitting in the back of the room with an expressionless face, perhaps staring out the window. Although the student might claim not to be communicating with the teacher, the teacher may derive any of a variety of messages from this behavior. Perhaps the teacher assumes that the student lacks interest, is bored, or is worried about something. In any event, the teacher is receiving messages even though the student might not intend to be sending any. In an interactional situation, you cannot *not* communicate (Watzlawick, Beavin, and Jackson 1967). This does not mean that all behavior is communication. For instance, if the student looked out the window and the teacher did not notice, no communication would have taken place. The two people must be in an interactional situation for the principle of inevitability to operate.

Further, when you are in an interactional situation you cannot *not* respond to the messages of others. For example, if you notice someone winking at you, you must respond in some way. Even if you do not respond actively or openly, that lack of response is itself a response, and it communicates. You cannot *not* respond. Again, if you don't notice the winking, then obviously there was no communication.

## Communication Is Purposeful

You communicate for a purpose. When you speak or write or paint, you are trying to send some message to another and trying to accomplish some goal. Four purposes may be emphasized: to discover, to relate, to persuade, and to play. Table 1.4 presents a classification of these purposes with examples.

| To Discover | • To learn about ourselves, our strengths and our weaknesses<br>• To learn about the outside world, about objects, events, and other people<br>• To compare ourselves to others to see how we fare in strengths and weaknesses<br>• To secure feedback on our own behaviors for self improvement |
| --- | --- |
| To Relate | • To establish, maintain, and repair close relationships with others<br>• To express friendship, love, and caring |
| To Persuade | • To change the attitudes and behaviors of others<br>• To influence the beliefs of others |
| To Play | • To enjoy comedians, speeches, songs, and movies<br>• To tell jokes, say clever things, and relate interesting stories |

**Table 1.4** *The Purposes of Human Communication*

When we compare ourselves to others, we engage in a process called *social comparison.* In what ways do you compare yourself with others? Do you generally find this a pleasant or an unpleasant process? Identify a typical comparison and explain what you did as a result of the comparison.

## Communication Is Irreversible

You can reverse the processes of only some systems. For example, you can turn water into ice and then turn the ice back into water. And you can repeat this reversal process as many times as you wish. Other systems, however, are irreversible. You can turn grapes into wine but you cannot turn the wine back into grapes. The process can go in only one direction. Communication is also an irreversible process. Once you communicate something, you cannot uncommunicate it. You can, of course, try to reduce the effects of your message. You can say, for example, "I really didn't mean what I said." Regardless of how hard you try to negate or reduce the effects of your message, the message itself, once it has been sent and received, cannot be taken back. In a public speaking situation in which the speech is recorded or broadcast, inappropriate messages may have national or even international effects. Here, attempts to reverse what one has said (in, say, trying to offer clarification) often have the effect of further publicizing the original statement.

Will the new communication technologies—electronic mail, working at computer terminals, and telecommuting, for example—change the basic purposes of communication identified here?

This principle has several important implications for communication. In interpersonal interactions you need to be careful not to say things you may be sorry for later. Especially in conflict situations, when tempers run high, you need to avoid saying things you may wish to withdraw. Commitment messages—the "I love you" messages and their variants—need also to be monitored. Otherwise, you might commit yourself to a position you may not be happy with later. In public and in mass communication situations, when the messages are heard by hundreds, thousands, and even millions of people, it is especially crucial to recognize the irreversibility of communications.

Without thinking and with very good intentions, you tell your partner "I guess you'll just never learn how to dress." To your surprise your partner becomes extremely offended. Although you know you can't take the statement back (communication really is irreversible), you want to lessen its negative tone and its effect on your partner. What do you say?

# FEEDBACK

In this chapter we explained what communication is, its major components, and nine communication principles.

**1. Communication** is the act, by one or more persons, of sending and receiving messages that are distorted by noise, occur within a context, have some effect (and some ethical dimension), and provide some opportunity for feedback.

**2.** The universals of communication—the elements present in every communication act—are: **context (physical, cultural, social-psychological,** and **temporal), source-receiver, message, channel, noise (physical, psychological,** and **semantic), sending** or **encoding processes, receiving** or **decoding processes, feedback** and **feedforward, effect** and **ethics.**

**3. Communication competence** is the ability to communicate effectively

**4.** Communication **messages** may be of varied forms and may be sent and received through any combination of sensory organs. The communication **channel** is the medium through which the messages are sent.

**5. Feedback** refers to messages or information that is sent back to the source. It may come from the source itself or from the receiver. **Feedforward** refers to messages that preface other messages.

**6. Noise** is anything that distorts the message; it is present to some degree in every communication.

**7.** Communication always has an **effect.** Effects may be cognitive, affective, or psychomotor.

**8. Communication ethics** refers to the moral rightness or wrongness of a message and is an integral part of every effort to communicate.

**9. Normally, communication is a package of signals,** each reinforcing the other. When these signals oppose each other, we have contradictory messages.

**10. The process of adjustment** is central to communication but takes place only to the extent that individuals use the same system of signals.

**11. Communication** involves both content **dimensions** and relationship dimensions.

**12. Communication involves symmetrical and complementary transactions.**

**13. Communication sequences are punctuated** for processing. Individuals divide the communication sequence into stimuli and responses in different ways.

**14. Communication is transactional.** Communication is a process of interrelated parts.

**15.** In any interactional situation, **communication is inevitable;** we cannot *not* communicate nor can we *not* respond to communication.

**16. Communication is purposeful.** Through communication, we discover, relate, persuade, and play.

**17. Communication is irreversible.** We cannot take back the message we have sent.

Several important communication skills, emphasized in this chapter, are presented here in summary form (as they are in every chapter). Check your ability to apply these skills. You will gain most from this brief experience if you think carefully about each skill and try to identify instances from your recent communications in which you did or did not act on the basis of the specific skill. Use a rating scale such as the following: (1) = almost always, (2) = often, (3) = sometimes, (4) = rarely, (5) = hardly ever.

_____ 1. I'm sensitive to **contexts** of communication. I recognize that changes in the physical, cultural, social-psychological, and temporal contexts will alter meaning.

_____ 2. I look for **meaning** not only in words but in nonverbal behaviors as well.

_____ 3. I am sensitive to the **feedback** that I give to others and that others give to me.

_____ 4. I combat the effects of physical, psychological, and semantic **noise** that distort messages.

_____ 5. Because communication is a **package of signals**, I use my verbal and nonverbal messages to reinforce rather than contradict each other and I respond to **contradictory messages** by identifying and openly discussing the dual meanings communicated.

_____ 6. I listen to the **relational messages** that I and others send, and respond to the relational messages of others to increase meaningful interaction.

_____ 7. I actively look for the **punctuation** pattern that I and others use in order to better understand the meanings communicated.

_____ 8. Because **communication is inevitable,** I look carefully for hidden meanings.

_____ 9. Because **communication is purposeful,** I look carefully at both the speaker's and the listener's purposes.

_____ 10. Because **communication is irreversible,** I am especially cautious in communicating messages that I may later wish to withdraw.

# SKILL DEVELOPMENT EXPERIENCES

### 1.1 OPENING A CONVERSATION

Listed here are several ways to open a conversation based on the communication process you have just studied.

1. Self-references. Say something about yourself. Such references may be of the name, rank, and serial number variety. For example: "My name is Joe, I'm from Omaha." On the first day of class, students might say "I'm worried about this class" or "I took this instructor last semester; she was excellent."

2. Other references. Say something about the other person or ask a question: "I like that sweater," "Didn't we meet at Charlie's?"

3. Relational references. Say something about the two of you, "May I buy you a drink?" "Would you like to dance?" or simply "May I join you?"

4. Context references. Say something about the physical, social-psychological, or temporal context. The familiar "Do you have the time?" is of this type. But, you can be more creative, such as, "This place seems real friendly" or "That painting is just great."

Keep in mind two general rules. First, lead off with something positive rather than something negative. Say, "I really enjoy coming here" instead of "Don't you just hate this place?" Second, do not be too revealing; don't disclose too intimately, too early in an interaction. If you do, people will think you're strange.

This exercise should help clarify the essential elements of communication and also provide experience in starting a conversation. Working individually, think of at least two ways in which you might begin a conversation with the persons described in each of the situations below. Then, in small groups or with the class as a whole, discuss your responses. Which approaches seem favored? Which approaches seem frowned upon?

1. On the first day of class, you and another student are the first to come into the classroom and are seated in the room alone.

2. You are a guest at a friend's party. You are one of the first guests to arrive and are now seated in a living room with several other people whom you have never met. Your friend, the host, is busy with other matters.

3. You have just started a new job as one of several computer operators in a large office. Most of the other operators know each other.

4. You are at a college dance and notice someone who you would like to meet. When you glance over at this person, who is with three other people, your glance is returned showing a clear sign of interest.

### 1.2 USING RELATIONAL MESSAGES

The following sample dialogue focuses too much on content and not enough on relationships. Read it over and note how both Harry and Diane avoid dealing with the relationship implications of what they are saying.

Rewrite the dialogue with a greater emphasis on relational messages. Show how Harry can get his needs met without stepping on Diane's needs and Diane can get her needs met without stepping on Harry's needs.

HARRY: *I'm staying glued to the TV this weekend. There are six great movies on cable and I'm going to watch them all.*

DIANE: *But I want to have the people from the office over this weekend. Remember I told you three weeks ago?*

HARRY: *Have them over. I'm watching my movies.*

DIANE: *Harry, you're acting like a selfish slob.*

HARRY: *Look, you dislike every one of the people you work with; you tell me so every day. So, forget them. Anyway, I'm watching TV.*

DIANE: *You are not. I'll throw a brick through the set before I let you ruin my party.*

HARRY: [Blasts the TV and falls onto the couch.]

## 1.3 CLOSING A CONVERSATION

Closing a conversation is almost as difficult as opening one. It is frequently awkward and uncomfortable. Working individually, indicate at least two ways in which you might close each of the conversations in the situations below.

Then, in small groups or with the entire class, share your closings. What types seem most effective? Which seem least effective? You might consider the following:

1. Reflect back on and briefly summarize the conversation to bring it to a close. For example, "I'm glad I ran into you and found out what happened at that union meeting. I'll probably be seeing you at the meetings."
2. State the desire to end the conversation directly and to get on with other things. "I'd like to continue talking but I really have to run. I'll see you around."
3. Refer to future interaction. "Let's get together next week sometime and continue this discussion."
4. Ask for closure. "Have I explained what you wanted to know?"
5. State that you enjoyed the interaction. "I really liked talking to you."

With each of these closings, it should be clear to the other person that you want to end the conversation. Obviously, you will have to use more direct methods with those who don't take subtle hints—those who don't realize that *both* persons are responsible for the interpersonal interaction.

1. You and a friend have been talking on the phone for the last hour but not much new is being said. You have a great deal of work to do and would like to close the conversation. Your friend just doesn't seem to take your hints.
2. You are on a plane, seated next to a person who just talks and talks without allowing any openings for you to join in. If you don't end the conversation, you will not have time to go over an important proposal you must make. You do not want to insult this person and yet you must close the conversation.
3. You are at a party and having a lot of fun. But it's late and you need to get home because you have an early class the next morning. When you say good night to the young couple throwing the party, they say the night's young and implore you to stay.
4. You just have had a conference with your professor, which has been very helpful. It has clarified several issues and you have learned a number of important things. Now it's time for you to leave.

## 1.4 ANALYZING COMMUNICATION

The nine principles of human communication discussed in this chapter should prove useful in analyzing any communication interaction. To help understand these principles and to gain some practice, apply them to this representation of a family dinner. Carefully study the interaction of the family members and identify each of the nine principles of communication that follow.

**Dinner with Margaret and Fred**

*Cast of Characters:*

Margaret: mother, housewife, junior high school history teacher; 41 years old
Fred: father, gas station attendant; 46 years old
Diane: daughter, receptionist at an art gallery; 22 years old
Stephen: son, college freshman; 18 years old

Margaret is in the kitchen finishing the preparation of dinner—lamb chops, Fred's favorite, though she does not care much for them. Diane is going through some records. Stephen is reading one of his textbooks. Fred comes in from work and throws his jacket over the couch; it falls to the floor.

FRED: [bored but angry, looking at Stephen] *What did you do with the car last night? It stunk like rotten eggs. And you left your school papers all over the back seat.*

STEPHEN: [as if expecting the angry remarks] *What did I do now?*

FRED: *You stunk up the car with your pot or whatever you kids smoke, and you left the car a mess. Can't you hear?*

STEPHEN: [says nothing; goes back to looking at his book but without really reading]

MARGARET: *Alright everybody, dinner's ready. Come on. Wash up and sit down.*

[At dinner]

DIANE: *Mom, I'm going to the shore for the weekend with some friends from work.*

MARGARET: *Okay. When will you be leaving?*

DIANE: *Friday afternoon, right after work.*

FRED: *Like hell you're going. No more going to the shore with that group.*

MARGARET: *Fred, they're nice people. Why shouldn't she go?*

FRED: *Because I said so, okay? Finished. Closed.*

DIANE: [mumbling] *I'm 22 years old and he gives me problems.* [Turning to Fred] *You make me feel like a kid, like some stupid little kid.*

FRED: *Get married. Then you can tell your husband what to do.*

DIANE: *I wish I could.*

STEPHEN: *But nobody'll ask her.*

MARGARET: *Why should she get married? She's got a good life—good job, nice friends, good home. Listen, I was talking with Elizabeth and Cara this morning and they both feel they've just wasted their lives. They raised a family and what have they got? They got* nothing. [To Diane] *And don't think sex is so great either; it isn't, believe me.*

FRED: *Well, they're idiots.*

MARGARET: [snidely] *They're idiots? Yeah, I guess they are.*

DIANE: *Joanne's getting married.*

MARGARET: *Who's Joanne?*

STEPHEN: *That creature who lives with that guy Michael.*

FRED: *Watch your mouth, Stephen. Don't be disrespectful to your mother or I'll teach you how to act right.*

Margaret: *Well, how do you like the dinner?*

[Prolonged silence]

DIANE: *Do you think I should be in the wedding party if Joanne asks me? I think she will; we always said we'd be in each other's wedding.*

MARGARET: *Sure, why not. It'll be nice.*

FRED: *I'm not going to no wedding, no matter who's in it.*

STEPHEN: *Me neither.*

DIANE: *I hope you'll both feel that way when I get married.*

STEPHEN: *By then I'll be too old to remember I got a sister.*

MARGARET: *How's school?*

STEPHEN: *I hate it. It's so big. Nobody knows anybody. You sit in these big lecture halls and listen to some creep talk. I really feel lonely and isolated, like nobody knows I'm alive.*

Fred: *Listen to that college talk. Get yourself a woman and you won't feel lonely, instead of hanging out with those potheads.*

DIANE: [looking to Margaret, giving a sigh as if to say, "Here we go again"]

MARGARET: [to Diane, in whisper] *I know.*

DIANE: *Mom? Do you think I'm getting fat?*

STEPHEN: *Yes.*

FRED: *Just don't get fat in the stomach or you'll get thrown out of here.*

MARGARET: *No, I don't notice it.*

DIANE: *Well, I just thought I might be.*

STEPHEN: [pushing his plate away] *I'm finished; I'm going out.*

FRED: *Sit down and finish your supper. You think I work all day for you to throw the food away? You wanna go smoke your dope?*

STEPHEN: *No. I just want to get away from you—forever.*

MARGARET: *You mean we both work all day; it's just that I earn a lot more than you do.*

FRED: *No, I mean I work and you baby-sit.*

MARGARET: *Teaching junior high school history isn't baby-sitting.*

FRED: *Well, what is it then? You don't teach them anything.*

MARGARET: [to Diane] *You see? You're better off single. I should've stayed single. Instead . . . . Oh, well. I was young and stupid. It was my own fault for getting involved with a loser. Just don't you make the same mistake.*

FRED: [to Stephen] *Go ahead. Leave the table. Leave the house. Who cares what you do?*

1. Communication is a package of signals.

    a. What instances show communication as a package of signals?

    b. Are there any examples of mixed or contradictory messages?

    c. What effects do you suppose these messages will have on subsequent interactions?

2. Communication is a process of adjustment.

    a. Can any of the failures to communicate be traced to the lack of adjustment?

    b. Throughout the interaction, how do the characters adjust to one another?

    c. What suggestions would you offer this family to increase their abilities to adjust to one another?

3. Communication involves both content and relationship dimensions.

    a. How do each of the characters deal with the self-definitions of the other characters? For example, how does Fred deal with the self-definition of Margaret? How does Margaret deal with the self-definition of Fred?

    b. Are any problems caused by the failure to recognize the distinction between the content and the relationship levels of communication?

    c. Select one topic of conversation and identify both the content and the relationship messages communicated.

4. Communication involves symmetrical and complementary transactions.

    a. What type of relationship do you suppose exists between Fred and Margaret? Between Fred and Diane? Between Fred and Stephen? Between Diane and Stephen? Between Margaret and Stephen?

    b. Can you find any instances of rigid complementarity? What problems might rigid complementarity cause this particular family?

5. Communication sequences are punctuated for processing.

    a. Select any two characters and indicate how they differ in their punctuation of any specific sequence of events. Do the characters realize that they are each arbitrarily dividing the sequence of events differently?

    b. What problems might a failure to recognize the arbitrary nature of punctuation create?

6. Communication is transactional.

    a. How is the process nature of communication illustrated in this interaction? For example, why is it impossible to identify specific beginnings and endings for any of the varied interactions? Are there instances in which individual characters attempt to deny the process nature of interactions?

    b. In what ways are the messages of the different characters interdependent?

    c. In what ways do the characters act and react as wholes?

7. Communication is inevitable.

    a. Do the characters communicate significant messages, even though they may attempt not to?

    b. In what ways do the characters communicate simply by their physical presence or by the role they occupy in the family?

    c. What attempts do the characters make not to communicate? Why are these attempts unsuccessful?

8. Communication is purposeful.

    a. Do the characters seem to realize the number of different purposes their messages are communicating?

    b. How many different purposes of communication can you identify from the dialogue?

9. Communication is irreversible.

    a. Are any messages communicated that you think the characters would have (at a later date) wished they had not communicated? Why?

    b. Do any of the characters attempt to reverse the communication process— that is, to "uncommunicate"?

As an alternative to analyzing this interaction, the entire class may watch a situation comedy, television drama, or film and explore the nine communication principles in these presentations. Use the questions in this exercise to formulate parallel questions for the television program or film.

Another way to approach this topic is to have all students watch the same television programs for an entire evening and have groups of students concentrate on the way different principles operate. Thus, one group might focus on the impossibility of not communicating, one group on the content and relationship dimensions of messages, and so on. Each group can then report its findings and insights to the entire class.

# CHAPTER 2

# The Self in Communication

## SELF-AWARENESS
- *The Johari Window*
- *Increasing Self-Awareness*

## SELF-ESTEEM

## SELF-DISCLOSURE
- *Factors Influencing Self-Disclosure*
- *Thinking Critically About Self-Disclosure*

## SELF-DISCLOSURE GUIDELINES

## FEEDBACK

## SKILL DEVELOPMENT EXPERIENCES

## Goals

*After completing this chapter, you should be able to*

1. *explain self-awareness and the Johari Window*
2. *explain how you can increase self-awareness and self-esteem*
3. *define* self-disclosure *and explain its major rewards and dangers*
4. *explain the factors that influence self-disclosure and why people avoid self-disclosing*
5. *explain the guidelines for self-disclosing and for responding to the disclosures of others*

*■ How well do you know yourself? ■ In what ways can you learn more about yourself? ■ Do you think you're a valuable person? ■ How high is your self-esteem? ■ Can you compare your self-esteem to that of your friends? ■ Would it be helpful to increase your self-esteem? ■ How might you increase self-esteem? ■ Do you have many secrets? ■ Under what circumstances and to whom would you reveal these secrets?*

In all communications, the most important part is the self. Who you are and how you see yourself influence the way you communicate and how you respond to others. In this chapter, we explore three aspects of the self. First, we look at self-awareness and our several selves. Our aim is to suggest ways to increase self-awareness. Second, we consider self-esteem; again, with the aim of suggesting ways to increase self-esteem. Third, we look at self-disclosure, that form of communication in which you reveal something of who you are. Our aim is to identify how you can regulate self-disclosure for greatest effectiveness.

## Self-Awareness

Self-awareness is basic to all communication (Kleinke 1978). We can explain self-awareness by examining the several aspects of ourselves as they might appear to others as well as to ourselves. A commonly used tool for this examination is a metaphoric division of the self into four areas and called the *Johari Window* (Figure 2.1, Luft 1969, 1984). The window gets its name from its inventors, Joseph Luft and Harry Ingham.

> No matter what else human beings may be communicating about, or may think they are communicating about, *they are always communicating about themselves, about one another, and about the immediate context of the communication.*
> —R. Pittinger, Charles Hockett, and John Danehy

> . . . many of the communication difficulties between persons are the by-product of communication barriers within the person.
> —Abraham H. Maslow

> Some research evidence (for example, Swann 1984, 1987) shows that people adapt strategies and enter relationships that will confirm their self-concepts, even when these self-concepts are negative (Jones 1990). People, Swann (1987) notes, "gravitate toward social relationships in which they are apt to receive self-confirmatory feedback." Do you do this? Do those you know also do this?

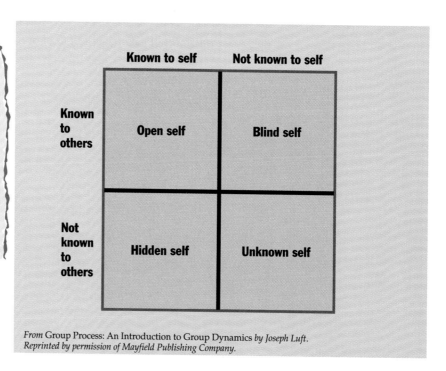

From Group Process: An Introduction to Group Dynamics *by Joseph Luft.*
*Reprinted by permission of Mayfield Publishing Company.*

**Figure 2.1** *The Johari Window*

Only the shallow know themselves.
—OSCAR WILDE

I am an invisible man. . . . I am a man of substance, of flesh and bone, fiber and liquids—and I might even be said to possess a mind. I am invisible, understand, simply because people refuse to see me.
—RALPH ELLISON

## *The Johari Window*

Divided into four areas or "panes," the window pictures different aspects or versions of the self. The four versions are: the *open self, blind self, hidden self,* and *unknown self*. These areas are not separate from one another, but rather, interdependent. As one dominates, the others recede to a greater or lesser degree; or, to stay with our metaphor, as one window pane becomes larger, one or another becomes smaller (Figure 2.2). The four window panes can be defined in the following way.

The *open self* represents all the information, behaviors, attitudes, and feelings about yourself that you and others know. This could include your name, skin color, sex, age, religion, and political beliefs among other matters. The "size" of the open self varies according to your personality and according to whom you are relating. With some people you may be open and with others not. Probably you are selectively open—open about some things and not about others.

The *blind self* represents knowledge about you that others have but you do not. This might include your habit of saying "you know" or finishing other peoples' sentences or rubbing your nose when you become anxious. It may also include your tendency to overreact to imagined insults or to compete for attention. Your blind self also might include

**Figure 2.2** *Johari Windows of Varying Sizes*

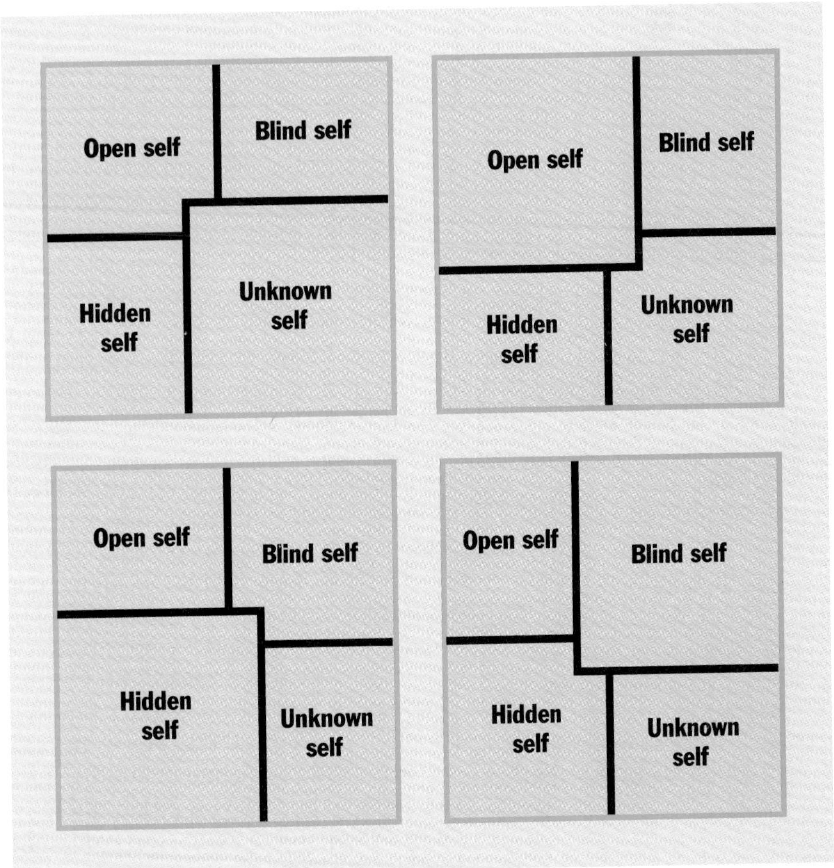


Do your close friends see you as essentially the same person that you see yourself to be? What conclusions are you willing to draw on the basis of the degrees of similarity-difference?

*"Walter—am I a New Year's resolution?"*

past experiences that you were never told or that you may have forgotten—your grandmother's affection for you, your conflicts with your kindergarten classmates, and your first tries at riding a bicycle. Blind areas—like famous blind spots—interfere with communication, so it is important to reduce your blind self as much as possible.

The *unknown self* represents those parts of yourself that neither you nor others know. This is information that is buried in your subconscious or that has somehow escaped awareness. You gain insight into the unknown self from several ways. Sometimes this area is revealed through hypnosis, dreams, or psychological tests, like the ink-blot test devised by the Swiss psychiatrist Hermann Rorschach. Another way is to explore yourself in an open, honest, and understanding way with those whom you trust—parents, lovers, and friends.

The *hidden self* represents all the knowledge you have of yourself but keep from others. This window pane includes all your successfully kept secrets. It may include your dreams and fantasies, experiences about which you are embarrassed, and attitudes, beliefs, and values of which you may be ashamed. Of course, most of us keep secrets from some people and not from others. For example, you might not tell your parents you are dating someone of another race or religion, but you might tell a close friend. So too, you might not let your friends know you have difficulty asking for a date, but you might discuss this problem with a brother or sister.

> I am sufficiently proud of my knowing something to be modest about my not knowing everything.
> —Vladimir Nabokov

> How would you draw your own Johari Window when you are interacting with your friends at school? With your parents? With your primary relational partner?

## Increasing Self-Awareness

Because self-awareness is so important in communication you should make every effort to increase your awareness of your needs, desires, habits, beliefs, and attitudes. One way to do this is to make a list of those things important to you. Also make a list of qualities that you think are characteristic of you. Then observe your own behavior with both lists in mind. Think of this as a sort of internal dialogue.

Another way is to thoughtfully listen to and observe the responses of those with whom you are interacting. Both verbal and nonverbal forms of communication can provide clues into yourself. Also, asking direct questions about your behavior can help reduce your blind self. And, looking at yourself through the eyes of your friends and acquaintances, may provide new and valuable perspectives. Most of all, open yourself to others. It is through such openness that you best get to know yourself.

## Self-Esteem

Self-esteem refers to the way you feel about yourself. How much do you like yourself? How valuable a person do you think you are? How competent? The answers to these questions reflect your self-esteem—the value that you place on yourself.

How would you describe your own level of self-awareness? What might you do to increase your self-awareness?

What level of self-esteem do you have? How comfortable are you with this level?

"It's Kevin Costner! Let me in!"

Reprinted with special permission of King Features, Inc.

Nothing can stop you from achieving self-confidence, if you really want to.
—ROBERT ANTHONY

If you wish in this world to advance
Your merits you're bound to enhance;
You must stir it and stump it.
You blow your own trumpet,
Or, trust me, you haven't a chance.
—W. S. GILBERT

Good people are good because they've come to wisdom through failure. We get very little wisdom from success.
—WILLIAM SAROYAN

What other means might you use to increase self-esteem?

*What kinds of communication situations seem to enhance your self-esteem? What kinds seem to decrease your self-esteem? What kinds of messages would you use to enhance a child's self-esteem? What kinds would you avoid?*

The major reason why self-esteem is so important is simply that success breeds success. When you feel good about yourself—about who you are and what you are capable of doing—you will perform more effectively. When you think like a success, you are more likely to act like a success. When you think you're a failure, you're more likely to act like a failure. Increasing self-esteem will, therefore, help you to function more effectively in school, in your interpersonal relationships, and in your careers. Here are a few ways to increase your self-esteem:

ENGAGE IN SELF-AFFIRMATION. Remind yourself of your successes from time to time. Focus on your good deeds, positive qualities, strengths, and virtues. Also, look carefully at the good relationships you have with friends and relatives. Concentrate on your potential, not your limitations (Brody 1991).

SEEK OUT NOURISHING PEOPLE. Seek out positive people who are optimistic and make you feel good about yourself. Avoid those who find fault with just about everything. Seek to build a network of supportive others (Brody 1991).

WORK ON PROJECTS THAT WILL RESULT IN SUCCESS. Success builds self-esteem. Each success will make achieving the next success a little easier. When a project does fail, remember it does not mean that you are a failure. Everyone fails sometime. Successful people know how to deal with failure—they know failure is something that happens, not something inside you. Further, your failing once does not mean that you will fail the next time. Put failure in perspective; do not make it an excuse for not trying again.

YOU DO NOT HAVE TO BE LOVED BY EVERYONE. No one is. Many, however, believe that everyone should love them. The problem with this is that it leads you to believe that you must always please others.

# Self-Disclosure

Ideally, growing communicators self-disclose to one another their many changing faces.
—STEPHEN LITTLEJOHN

*Self-disclosure* is a type of communication in which you reveal information about yourself (Jourard 1968, 1971a, 1971b).

*Self-disclosure is a type of communication.* Thus, overt statements about the self as well as slips of the tongue, unconscious nonverbal movements, and public confessions would all be considered forms of self-disclosure. Usually, however, the term *self-disclosure* is used to refer to the conscious revealing of information, such as the statements, "I'm afraid to compete; I guess I'm afraid I'll lose" or "I love you" or "I finally saved enough and I'm buying a car this week."

*Self-disclosure is "information"*—something previously unknown by the receiver. This may vary from the relatively commonplace ("I'm really afraid of that French exam") to the extremely significant ("I'm so depressed, I feel like committing suicide"). Often, when we think of self-disclosure, we think of information that is in our hidden self that we actively keep others from learning.

In addition to disclosing *information about yourself*, you might also disclose information about those close to you, if it has a significant bearing on your life, social status, or professional capabilities. Thus, self-disclosure could refer to your own actions or the actions of, say, your parents or children, since these have a direct relationship to who you are.

*Self-disclosure involves at least one other individual.* For self-disclosure to occur, the communication must involve at least two persons. It cannot be an *intra*personal act—the information must be received and understood by another individual.

To whom do you disclose most about your inner feelings? Your financial situation? Your fears? Your loves? Your goals and ambitions? Your fantasies?

## TEST YOURSELF:
### *How Willing to Self-Disclose Are You?*

Respond to each of the following statements by indicating the likelihood that you would disclose such items of information to, say, other members of this class. Use the following scale:

    1 = would definitely self-disclose
    2 = would probably self-disclose
    3 = don't know
    4 = would probably not self-disclose
    5 = would definitely not self-disclose

_____ 1. My religious beliefs.
_____ 2. My attitudes toward other religions, nationalities, and races.
_____ 3. My economic status.
_____ 4. My parents' attitudes toward other religions, races, and nationalities.
_____ 5. My feelings about my parents.
_____ 6. My sexual fantasies.
_____ 7. My past sexual experiences.
_____ 8. My physical condition and mental health.
_____ 9. My ideal mate.
_____10. My drinking and/or drug-taking behavior.

*Continued*

_____ 11. My most embarrassing moment.
_____ 12. My unfulfilled desires.
_____ 13. My major weaknesses and worries.
_____ 14. My general self-concept.
_____ 15. My feelings about the people in this group.

After all the questionnaires are completed, in groups of five or six or with the class as a whole, discuss the responses, self-disclosing or not disclosing what you wish. Discussion might center on such issues as the following:

1. Are there discrepancies between what you said you would disclose and what you actually choose to disclose? Why?
2. Can you classify the types of information that people are reluctant to disclose? What does this tell you about self-disclosure?
3. Self-disclosure is usually a two-way process having what is called the dyadic effect—what one person does, the other does. One person's disclosures stimulate the other person's disclosures which stimulate the first person's further disclosures, and so on. Did this dyadic effect occur in this group? Why? Why not?
4. Would the results of this questionnaire have differed if the target audience was your parents? A stranger you would never see again? A best friend or lover? A teacher or counselor?
5. Do you notice sex differences in self-disclosing behavior? Are there cultural differences? Do some cultures reward self-disclosure more than others? Can you give specific examples of cultural variation?

> Would you consider yourself a high, mid, or low self-discloser (in general)? Are you satisfied with this level? If not, how might you go about changing this?

## Factors Influencing Self-Disclosure

Self-disclosure occurs more readily under certain circumstances. For example, it occurs more in _small groups_ than in large groups. Dyads (groups of two people) are the most hospitable setting for self-disclosure. With one listener, you can attend to the responses carefully. You can monitor the disclosures, continuing if there is support and stopping if there is not. With more than one listener, such monitoring becomes difficult since the responses are sure to vary among the listeners.

Sometimes self-disclosure takes place in group and public speaking situations. In consciousness-raising groups and in meetings like those of Alcoholics Anonymous, members may disclose their most intimate problems to ten or perhaps hundreds of people at the same time. In these situations, group members are pledged to be totally supportive. These and similar groups are devoted specifically to encouraging self-disclosure and to giving each other support for the disclosures.

> How would you describe the disclosures of such public figures as Jim Bakker or Jimmy Swaggert? In what ways are these situations the same as disclosures in dyads? In what ways are they different?

> Trust, the essence of which is emotional safety, serves as the foundation for self-disclosure.
> —KATHLEEN M. GALVIN AND BERNARD J. BROMMEL

Since we disclose ourselves on the basis of support we receive, we generally disclose to _people we like_ (Derlega, Winstead, Wong, and Greenspan 1987) and to people we trust (Wheeless and Grotz 1977). We also come to like those to whom we disclose (Berg and Archer 1983). At times self-disclosure occurs more in temporary than permanent relationships—for example, between strangers on a train or plane, a kind of "in-flight intimacy" (McGill 1985). In this situation, two people set up an intimate self-disclosing relationship during a brief travel period, but they do not pursue it beyond that point.

We also disclose when the person we are with discloses. This *dyadic effect* probably leads us to feel more secure and, in fact, reinforces our own self-disclosing behavior. Disclosures are also more intimate when they are made in response to the disclosures of others (Berg and Archer 1983).

*Competent people* engage in self-disclosure more than less competent people. Perhaps competent people have greater self-confidence and more positive things to reveal. Similarly, their self-confidence may make them more willing to risk possible negative reactions (McCroskey and Wheeless 1976).

Not surprisingly, *personality* influences self-disclosure. Highly sociable and extroverted people self-disclose more than those who are less sociable and more introverted. People who are apprehensive about talking in general also self-disclose less than do those who are more comfortable in communicating.

We are more likely to disclose about some *topics* than others. For example, we are more likely to self-disclose information about our jobs or hobbies than about our sex lives or financial situations (Jourard 1968, 1971a). We also disclose favorable information more readily than unfavorable information. Generally, the more personal and negative the topic, the less likely we are to self-disclose.

> If I can talk, I can sing.
> If I can walk, I can dance.
> —AFRICAN PROVERB

> About what topics are you least likely to self-disclose to your close friends? To your colleagues at work? To your family?

*Here is an Alanon meeting. In keeping with the group's anonymity policy, no faces are revealed. How does self-disclosure in such a public setting differ from self-disclosure with one or a few trusted friends?*

COPYRIGHT 1990, LOS ANGELES TIMES SYNDICATE.
REPRINTED WITH PERMISSION.

Research (Brody 1991) shows that girls and boys as young as two years old respond differently to success and failure. For example, boys show more pride in their successes than do girls. Girls, on the other hand, react to failure with greater shame. Girls also allow a single failure to affect the way they feel about themselves more than do boys. Do you find this to be true of young children? Of young adults? Of mature adults? What do you think causes this? How might these differences influence communication between the sexes?

What factors others than those mentioned here do you think influence your own self-disclosures? How would you describe the ideal receiver of your most intimate self-disclosures?

The popular stereotype of *gender* differences in self-disclosure—aptly illustrated in the "Single Slices" cartoon—emphasizes the male reluctance to speak about himself, especially his feelings. For the most part, research supports this generally accepted view. One notable exception occurs in initial encounters. Here men will disclose more intimately than women, perhaps "in order to control the relationship's development" (Derlega, Winstead, Wong, and Hunter 1985).

Judy Pearson (1980) has argued that it is sex role, not biological gender, that accounts for the differences in self-disclosure. "Masculine women," for example, self-disclosed to a lesser extent than did women who scored low on masculinity scales. Further, "feminine men" self-disclosed to a greater extent than those who scored low on femininity scales. Men and women also give different reasons for their avoidance of self-disclosure, as illustrated in Table 2.1 (Rosenfeld 1979). Note that the first reason, "fear of projecting the wrong image," is identified by both men and women.

The *culture* also influences the amount of self-disclosure. For example, people in the United States disclose more than those in Great Britain, Germany, Japan, or Puerto Rico (Gudykunst 1984). American students also disclose more than students from nine different Middle East countries (Jourard 1971).

There are also important similarities across cultures. For example, subjects from Great Britain, Germany, the United States, and Puerto Rico are more apt to disclose personal information such as hobbies and interests and attitudes and opinions on politics and religion. Similarly, they are less apt to disclose information on finances, sex, personality, and interpersonal relationships (Jourard 1971a).

| Reasons men give for avoiding self-disclosure: | Reasons women give for avoiding self-disclosure: |
|---|---|
| "If I disclose, I might project an image I do not want to project." | "If I disclose, I might project an image I do not want to project." |
| "If I self-disclose, I might give information that makes me appear inconsistent." | " Self-disclosure would give the other person information that he or she might use against me at some time." |
| "If I self-disclose, I might lose control over the other person." | "Self-disclosure is a sign of some emotional disturbance." |
| "Self-disclosure might threaten relationships I have with people other than close aquaintances." | "Self-disclosure might hurt our relationship." |

**Table 2.1** *Reasons for Self Disclosure Avoidance*

## Thinking Critically About Self-Disclosure

What are your major reasons for avoiding self-disclosure?

Whether or not you self-disclose will depend on your assessment of the possible rewards and dangers. Some of the most important of these rewards and risks are:

### The Rewards of Self-Disclosure

We can identify at least four rewards of self-disclosure. First, self-disclosure contributes to *self-knowledge;* it helps you gain a new perspective on yourself and a deeper understanding of your own behavior. In therapy, for example, insight often comes while you are disclosing. Through self-disclosure, then, you may come to understand yourself more thoroughly.

The easiest person to deceive is one's self.
—EDWARD BULWER-LYTTON

Self-disclosure improves your *coping abilities;* it helps you to deal with problems, especially guilt. You may fear that you will not be accepted because of something you have done or because of some feeling or attitude you have. Because you feel these things are a basis for rejection, you may develop guilt. By self-disclosing such a feeling and receiving support rather than rejection, you may be better able to deal with guilt, perhaps reducing or even eliminating it.

Self-disclosure *improves communication.* You understand the messages of others largely to the extent that you understand the individuals. You can better understand what someone says if you know that individual well. You can tell what certain nuances mean, when the person is serious or joking, and when the person is being sarcastic out of fear or out of resentment. You might study a person's behavior or even live together for years, but if that person rarely self-discloses, you are far from understanding that individual as a complete person.

What happens to a dream deferred?
Does it dry up
Like a raisin in the sun?
Or does it explode?
—LANGSTON HUGHES

Self-disclosure helps you *establish meaningful relationships.* Without self-disclosure, relationships of any meaningful depth seem impossible. By self-disclosing, you tell others that you trust, respect, and care enough about them and your relationship to reveal yourself. This in turn leads the other individual to self-disclose and forms at least the start of a meaningful relationship, one that is honest and open and goes beyond trivialities.

## The Dangers of Self-Disclosure

The many advantages of self-disclosure should not blind us to its very real risks (Bochner 1984). When you self-disclose you risk *personal and social rejection.* You usually self-disclose to a person you expect will be supportive. Of course, the person you think will be supportive may turn out to reject you. Parents, normally the most supportive of all interpersonal relations, frequently reject children who self-disclose their homosexuality, their plans to marry someone of a different race, or their belief in another faith. Your best friends, your closest intimates, may reject you for similar self-disclosures.

Sometimes, self-disclosures result in *material losses.* Politicians who disclose that they have seen a psychiatrist may lose the support of their own political party and find that voters are unwilling to vote for them. Teachers who disclose disagreement with the school administrators may find themselves denied tenure, teaching undesirable schedules, and victims of "budget cuts." In the business world, self-disclosures of alcoholism or drug addiction are often met with dismissal, demotion, or transfer.

Remember that self-disclosure, like any communication, is *irreversible* (see Chapter 1). You cannot self-disclose and then take it back. Nor can you erase the conclusions and inferences listeners have made on the basis of your disclosures.

## Rewards and Dangers in Cultural Perspective

Recall our earlier model of communication and the importance of culture (Chapter 1). Not all societies and cultures view self-disclosure in the same way. In some cultures, disclosing one's inner feelings is considered a weakness. Among Anglo-Saxon Americans, for example, it would be considered "out of place" for a man to cry at a happy occasion like a wedding while that same crying would go unnoticed in some Latin cultures. Similarly, in Japan it is considered undesirable to reveal personal information whereas in the United States it is considered desirable and is even expected (Barnlund 1989; Hall and Hall 1987).

The potential rewards and dangers of self-disclosure, then, must be examined in terms of the particular cultural rules. As with all cultural rules, following them brings approval and violating them brings disapproval.

## Self-Disclosure Guidelines

Each person has to make his or her own decisions concerning self-disclosure. As we noted earlier, attitudes toward self-disclosure vary from culture to culture and these must be considered in deciding whether to, and how to, self-disclose. Moreover, decisions to self-disclose will also be based on several other factors. Among these is your concern for your relationship with the person or persons to whom you are self-disclosing (Will this add tension to the relationship? Might it place an unfair burden on the friendship?). You would also probably consider: the appropriateness of the context in which you are self-disclosing (Is this the right time, place, and circumstance? Should you disclose interpersonally, in a small

| In Self-Disclosing: | In Responding to the Self-Disclosing of Others: |
|---|---|
| 1. Is the motivation to improve the relationship? | 1. Are you trying to feel what the other person is feeling? |
| 2. Does the self-disclosure impose burdens on your listener? | 2. Are you using effective and active listening skills? |
| 3. Is the self-disclosure appropriate to the context and the relationship between yourself and your listener? | 3. Are you communicating supportiveness (verbally and nonverbally) to the discloser? |
| 4. Is the other person disclosing also? If not, might this be a sign of disinterest? | 4. Are you refraining from criticism and evaluation? |
| 5. Might the self-disclosure place too heavy a burden on you? | 5. Will you maintain confidentiality? |

**Table 2.2** *A Summary of Self-Disclosure Guidelines*

**Would you recommend other guidelines for responding to self-disclosures?**

**What do you think of "outing"—the process of making public that a noted personality is gay or lesbian?**

group, or more publicly?); the way in which the person to whom you are self-disclosing responds (sympathetically and supportively or indifferently, perhaps even hostilely?); the consequences of your self-disclosure (Can you afford to lose your job? Might it cause your friend some pain?).

Then, of course, there are times when you may be on the receiving end of self-disclosure. Here, too, you need to consider the cultural rules and customs. In addition, remember that when someone is disclosing to you, he or she is simultaneously seeking your support and placing enormous trust in you. Try to imagine yourself in that person's place and situation. Listen attentively, not only to what is said, but also to the feelings that underlie the words. Paraphrase the speaker so that you show both sympathy and understanding. Openly express your support during and after the disclosures with both words and gestures. Refrain from criticizing or passing judgments on the speaker. Do not betray the trust of the person making the disclosures by telling others or using the information against that person. This last might, depending on the disclosure, create a moral dilemma for you. If your friend reveals that he or she intends to commit suicide, you would probably want to reveal this to appropriate professionals who can provide help to your friend.

Table 2.2 summarizes some of these guidelines.

# FEEDBACK

In this chapter we looked at the most important part of the communication process: the self. We discussed (1) self-awareness and how to increase it, (2) self-esteem and how to increase it, and (3) self-disclosure and how we might be more effective disclosers.

**1.** In the Johari Window model of the self, there are four major areas: the **open self,** the **blind self,** the **hidden self,** and the **unknown self.**

**2.** To increase **self-awareness** analyze yourself, listen to others to see yourself as they do, actively seek information from others about yourself, see yourself from different perspectives, and increase your open self.

**3. Self-esteem** refers to the value a person puts on himself or herself.

**4.** Among the **ways to increase self-esteem** are: engage in self-affirmation, seek out nourishing people, work on projects that result in success, and recognize that you do not have to be loved by everyone.

**5. Self-disclosure** refers to a form of communication in which information about the self that is normally kept hidden is communicated to another person.

**6.** Self-disclosure is more likely to occur when the potential discloser is with one other person, when the discloser likes or loves the listener, when the listener also discloses, when the discloser feels competent, when the discloser is highly sociable and extroverted, and when the topic of disclosure is fairly impersonal and is also positive.

**7.** The **rewards of self-disclosure** include increases in self-knowledge, in the ability to cope with difficult situations and guilt, in communication efficiency, and in the chances for a meaningful relationship.

**8.** The **dangers of self-disclosure** include personal and social rejection, material loss, and intrapersonal difficulties.

**9.** Before self-disclosing, consider the cultural rules operating, the motivation for the self-disclosure, the possible burdens you might impose on your listener, the appropriateness of the self-disclosure, the disclosures of the other person, and the possible burdens that your self-disclosure might impose on you.

**10.** When **listening to disclosures,** take into consideration the cultural rules governing the communication situation, try to feel what the discloser is feeling, practice the skills of effective and active listening, support the discloser, refrain from criticism and evaluation, and keep the disclosures confidential.

The skills for increasing self-awareness and self-esteem and for effective self-disclosure are critical to effective communication in all its forms. Check your ability to apply these skills. If you wish, use the following rating scale:   (1) = almost always,   (2) = often,   (3) = sometimes,   (4) = rarely,   (5) = hardly ever.

_____ 1. I actively seek to increase **self-awareness** by talking with myself, listening to others, reducing my blind self, seeing myself from different perspectives, and increasing my open self.

_____ 2. I seek to increase my **self-esteem** by engaging in self-affirmation, seeking out nourishing people, working on projects that will likely succeed, and recognizing that I do not have to be loved by everyone.

_____ 3. I regulate my disclosures on the basis of the unique communication situation.

_____ 4. In deciding whether or not to **self-disclose** I take into consideration (1) the cultural rules, (2) my motivation, (3) the possible burdens on my listener, (4) the appropriateness to the other person and the context, (5) the other person's disclosures, and (6) the possible burdens the disclosures may impose on me.

_____ 5. I **respond to the disclosures of others** by trying to feel what the other person is feeling, using effective and active listening skills, expressing supportiveness, refraining from criticism and evaluation, and keeping the disclosures confidential.

# SKILL DEVELOPMENT EXPERIENCES

## 2.1 HEARING SELF-EVALUATIONS

Listen to both the good and the bad things that you say to yourself. The way you talk to yourself about yourself influences what you think of yourself. You will surely think little of yourself if you consistently talk negatively about yourself. If you tell yourself you are a failure, that others do not like you, that you will fail the next test, or that you will be rejected when asking for a date, you will soon feel negatively about yourself.

On the other hand, if you talk positively about yourself you will feel more positively about yourself. If you tell yourself you are a success, that people like you, that you will succeed on the next test, and that you will be welcomed when asking for a date you will soon feel positively about yourself.

Most often we tell ourselves these things in subtle ways, often without verbalizing them fully. It is possible, though not easy, to hear ourselves making these judgments. Learning to listen for such judgments will help you control them and your own self-evaluations.

For the next week, write down any instances of self-evaluation that you hear yourself making. Record negative and positive judgments separately. Record each occurrence of each statement, regardless of how many times the judgment is made.

You may form small groups of five or six to share the insights gained from this experience. No one should feel pressure to reveal any statements that he or she does not wish to reveal. Disclose only what you want to disclose. Group discussions may focus on some or all of the following:

1. What kinds of negative and positive statements occur most often?
2. Where do these negative and positive statements come from? That is, can you trace these statements to early experiences? Can you "hear" your mother or your father telling you any of these statements? Your employer? Your teachers? Your friends or lovers?
3. Do the negative and the positive statements make you feel differently about yourself? In what way?
4. Can you control these statements? Can you, for example, increase the frequency of one type of statement and decrease the frequency of another type?
5. What will you do as a result of this listening-to-yourself experience?

## 2.2 APPLYING THE GUIDELINES TO SELF-DISCLOSURE

Should you self-disclose or not? Here are several instances of impending self-disclosure. For each, indicate whether or not you think the self-disclosure would be appropriate. Specify your reasons for each of your judgments. In making your decision, consider each of the guidelines identified in this chapter.

1. A mother of two teenaged children (a boy and a girl) has been feeling guilty for the past year over a romantic affair she had with her brother-in-law while her husband was in prison. The mother, divorced for the last few months, wants to disclose this affair and her guilt to her children.
2. A student plagiarized a term paper in anthropology. He is sorry, especially since the plagiarized paper only earned a grade of C+. He wants to disclose to his instructor and re-do the paper.
3. Tom has fallen in love with another woman and wants to end his relationship with Cathy. He wants to call Cathy on the phone, break his engagement, and disclose his new relationship.
4. Sam is 27 years old and has been living in a romantic relationship with another man for the past several years. Sam wants to tell his parents, with whom he has been very close throughout his life, but can't seem to get up the courage. He decides to tell them in a long letter.
5. Mary and Jim have been married for 12 years. Mary has been honest about most things and has disclosed a great deal to Jim—about her past romantic encounters, fears, insecurities, ambitions, and so on. Yet, Jim doesn't seem to reciprocate. He almost never shares his feelings and has told Mary almost nothing about his life before they met. Mary wonders if she should begin to limit her disclosures.

## 2.3 I'D PREFER TO BE

This exercise should enable members of the class to get to know one another better and at the same time get to know themselves better. The questions should encourage each individual to increase awareness of some facet(s) of his or her thoughts or behaviors.

### Rules of the Game

The "I'd Prefer to Be" game is played in a group of four to six people, using the following category listing. General procedure is as follows:

1. Each person individually rank-orders each of the 15 clusters of preferences using 1 for the most-preferred and 3 for the least-preferred choice.
2. The players then consider each of the 15 categories in turn, with each member giving his or her rank order.
3. Members may refuse to reveal their rankings for any category by saying, "I pass." The group is not permitted to question the reasons for any member's passing.
4. When a member has revealed his or her rankings for a category, group members may ask questions relevant to that category. These questions may be asked after any individual member's account or may be reserved until all members have given their rankings for a particular category.
5. In addition to these general procedures, the group may establish any additional rules it wishes—appointing a leader, establishing time limits, and so forth.

### "I'd Prefer to Be"

1. _____ intelligent
   _____ wealthy
   _____ physically attractive
2. _____ movie star
   _____ senator
   _____ successful businessperson
3. _____ blind
   _____ deaf
   _____ mute
4. _____ on a date
   _____ reading a book
   _____ watching television
5. _____ loved
   _____ feared
   _____ respected
6. _____ alone
   _____ with a group of people
   _____ with one person
7. _____ brave
   _____ reliable
   _____ insightful
8. _____ communicating by phone
   _____ communicating by letter
   _____ communicating face-to-face
9. _____ traitor to a friend
   _____ traitor to my country
   _____ traitor to myself
10. _____ bisexual
    _____ heterosexual
    _____ homosexual
11. _____ the loved
    _____ the lover
    _____ the good friend
12. _____ introvert
    _____ extrovert
    _____ ambivert
13. _____ a tree
    _____ a rock
    _____ a flower
14. _____ a leader
    _____ a follower
    _____ a loner
15. _____ (Ten years from now)
    _____ married
    _____ single
    _____ living with someone but unmarried

### Areas for Discussion

Here are some areas for discussion that might prove of value:

1. What are the reasons for the individual choices? Note that the reasons for the least-preferred choice may often be as important or even more important than the reasons for the most-preferred choice.
2. What do the choices reveal about the individual? Can persons be differentiated on the basis of their choices to these and similar alternatives?
3. What is the degree of similarity of the group as a whole? Do the members show relatively similar choices or wide differences? What does this mean in terms of the members' ability to communicate with one another?

4. Do the members accept/reject the choices of other members? Are some members disturbed by the choices other members make? If so, why? Are some apathetic? Why? Did hearing the choices of one or more members make you want to get to know them better?
5. Did any of the choices make you aware of preferences you were not aware of before?

## 2.4  A SELF-DISCLOSURE EXPERIENCE

On an index card write a statement of information that is currently in your hidden self. Do not put your names on these cards; the statements are to be dealt with anonymously. These cards will be collected and read aloud to the entire group.*

**Discussion of Statements and Model**

1. Classify the statements into categories—for example, sexual problems, attitudes toward family, self-doubts, and so forth.

2. Why do you suppose this type of information is kept hidden? What advantages might hiding this information have? What disadvantages?
3. How would you react to people who disclosed such statements to you? For example, what difference, if any, would it make in your relationship?
4. What type of person is likely to have a large hidden self and a small open self? A large open self and a small hidden self?
5. Would your open self be larger than that of other group members? Smaller? The same size? Would your hidden self be larger? Smaller? The same size?

---

*The general idea for this exercise comes from Gerard Egan, *Encounter* (Belmont, Calif.: Brooks/Cole, 1970)

# Perception and Listening

## Goals

*After completing this chapter, you should be able to*

1. *define* perception *and describe the three stages in the perception process*
2. *explain how* implicit personality theory, self-fulfilling prophecy, primacy-recency, stereotyping *and* attribution *influence perception*
3. *define* listening, *its major types, and its major barriers*
4. *explain the five steps in the listening process*
5. *define* active listening, *its functions, and its techniques*
6. *explain* feedback *and identify ways to give and respond to feedback effectively*
7. *define* feedforward *and describe its phatic, preview, disclaiming, and altercasting functions*

*■ Out of all the things in the world, why do you focus on some things and ignore others? ■ What makes you notice the good qualities in people you like and the bad qualities in people you don't like? ■ On what basis do you form judgments about others? ■ How can you improve your ability to judge others more accurately? ■ Why do others so often not understand the importance of what you say? ■ Why do you so often misunderstand what others say? ■ Why do others so often misunderstand you? ■ How can you improve your ability to listen more effectively? ■ What can you do to encourage others to share their thoughts and feelings?*

In this chapter we look at the way we receive messages, focusing on perception and listening Here we consider how perception works, the processes that influence perception, and how we can make our perceptions more accurate. In our discussion of listening, we consider the process of listening and how listening may be made more effective. We also examine feedback and feedforward and how these contribute to effective communication.

## Perception

*Perception* is the process of becoming aware of the many stimuli impinging on your senses. It influences what stimuli or messages you take in *and* what meaning you give them. Perception is therefore central to the study of communication in all its forms. Here we look at (1) how perception works and (2) the processes that influence it.

*Perception* is complex. There is no one-to-one relationship between the messages that occur—in the sounds of the voice, the writings on paper—and the messages that eventually reach your brain. What occurs may differ greatly from what reaches your brain. The three steps involved in the process explain how perception works. These stages are not separate; they are continuous and blend into and overlap one another (see Figure 3.1).

### Stage One: Sensation

In the first stage, one or another of your five senses responds to a stimulus: you hear, see, smell, taste, feel, or all of these at the same time. For example, when you hold a slice of pizza, you feel it, see it, taste and smell it, and at the same time hear the sounds around you.

### Stage Two: Organization

At the second stage, you organize the sensory stimulations according to various principles. One frequently used principle is that of *proximity:* you perceive people or messages that are physically close to one another as a unit. For example, you perceive people you often see together as a unit (such as a couple). Similarly, you perceive messages

We must always tell what we see. Above all, and this is more difficult, we must always see what we see.
—CHARLES PEGUY

A fool sees not the same truth that a wise man sees.
—WILLIAM BLAKE

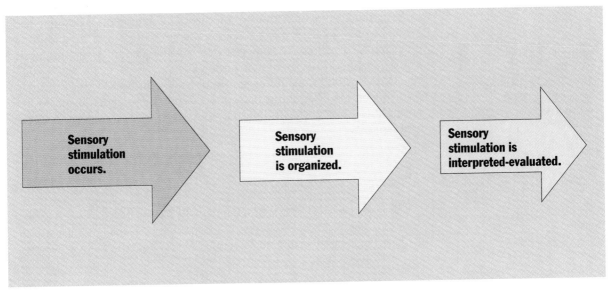

**Figure 3.1** *The Stages of Perception*

uttered one immediately after the other as a unit, assuming they are in some way related. You also assume that verbal and nonverbal signals sent at about the same time are related and constitute a unified whole.

Another such principle is *closure:* you perceive as closed, or complete, a figure or message that is actually unclosed or incomplete. For example, you perceive a broken circle as complete even though part of it is missing. You would even perceive a series of dots or dashes arranged in a circular pattern as a circle. Similarly, you fill in messages you hear with parts that seem to complete the messages.

Proximity and closure are just two of many organizing principles. In thinking about these principles, remember that whatever you perceive, you organize into a pattern meaningful to you. It is not necessarily a pattern true or logical in any objective sense.

> **What other organizing principles might be useful in illustrating this second stage of perception?**

### Stage Three: Interpretation-Evaluation

At the third stage you *interpret-evaluate* the stimulus. We hyphenate these terms to emphasize that they cannot be separated. This third step is a subjective process involving the perceiver's evaluations. Your interpretations-evaluations are not based solely on external stimulus. They are greatly influenced by your experiences, needs, wants, value systems, beliefs about the way things are or should be, current physical or emotional states, expectations, and so on. Similarly, they are influenced by cultural factors—your cultural training and values. Two men walking arm-in-arm, young children competing in school and on the sports field, and a woman in a leopard-skin coat will all be evaluated differently depending on your cultural values.

> **Can you identify a specific behavior that is permissible in one culture and frowned on in another?**

There is obviously much room for personal interpretation and disagreement. Although we may all be exposed to the same message, the way each of us interprets-evaluates it will differ. It will also differ for the same person from one time to another. The sound of a popular rock group may be heard by one person as terrible noise and by another as great music. The sight of someone one has not seen for years may bring joy to one person and anxiety to another.

These individual differences should not blind us to the validity of some generalizations about perception. While these generalizations may not hold for any *specific* individual, they seem true enough for a significant majority.

## TEST YOURSELF:

## *How Accurate Are You at People Perception?*

Respond to each of the following statements with *T* (true) if the statement is usually accurate in describing your behavior, *F* (false) if the statement is usually inaccurate.

_____ 1. I base most of my impressions of people on the first few minutes of our meeting.

_____ 2. When I know some things about another person, I fill in what I don't know.

_____ 3. I make predictions about people's behaviors that generally prove to be true.

_____ 4. I have clear ideas of what people of different national, racial, and religious groups are really like.

_____ 5. I reserve making judgments about people until I learn a great deal about them and see them in a variety of situations.

_____ 6. On the basis of my observations of people, I formulate guesses (that I am willing to revise), rather than firmly held conclusions.

_____ 7. I pay special attention to people's behaviors that might contradict my initial impressions.

_____ 8. I delay formulating conclusions about people until I have lots of evidence.

_____ 9. I avoid making assumptions about what is going on in someone else's head on the basis of their behaviors.

_____10. I recognize that people are different and don't assume that everyone is like me.

*Scoring:* This brief perception test was designed to raise questions we will consider in this chapter and not to provide you with a specific perception score. The first four questions refer to our tendencies to judge others on the basis of first impressions (Question 1), implicit personality theories (2), prophecies (3), and stereotypes (4). Ideally you would have answered "false" to these four questions since they represent sources of distortion. These processes are covered in "People (Interpersonal) Perception." Questions 5 through 10 refer to specific guidelines for increasing accuracy in people perception: looking for a variety of cues (5), formulating hypotheses rather than conclusions (6), being especially alert to contradictory cues (7), delaying conclusions until more evidence is in (8), avoiding the tendency to mind read (9), and recognizing the diversity in people (10). Ideally you would have answered "true" to these six questions since they represent suggestions for increased accuracy in perception. They are covered in "Increasing Accuracy in Interpersonal Perception: Specific Guidelines."

# Processes Influencing Perception

Between the occurrence of the stimulation (the uttering of the message, presence of the person, smile, or wink of the eye) and its interpretation-evaluation, perception is influenced by several psychological processes. Here we identify five major ones (Cook 1971; Rubin 1973; Rubin and McNeil 1985): implicit personality theory, the self-fulfilling prophecy, primacy-recency, stereotyping, and attribution.

These processes influence what you see and fail to see; what you assume to be true or false about another person. These processes help to explain why you make some predictions and decline to make others about people. Note, however, that each process also contains potential barriers to accurate perception. These barriers can exert significant influence on both your perceptions and your interpersonal interactions. We discuss these potential barriers along with the psychological processes.

## Implicit Personality Theory

Consider the following brief statements. Note the characteristic in parentheses that best seems to complete the sentence:

John is energetic, eager, and (intelligent, unintelligent).

Mary is bold, defiant, and (extroverted, introverted).

Joe is bright, lively, and (thin, fat).

Jane is attractive, intelligent, and (likable, unlikable).

Susan is cheerful, positive, and (attractive, unattractive).

Jim is handsome, tall, and (interesting, boring).

Certain choices seem right and others, wrong. What makes some seem right is the *implicit personality theory*, a system of rules that tells you which characteristics go with each other. Most people's rules tell them that a person who is energetic and eager is also intelligent. Of course, there is no logical reason an unintelligent person could not be energetic and eager.

The culture in which you were raised greatly influenced the specific theories you now hold. So, remember that your theories may not be held by others.

> It is with our judgments as with our watches; no two go just alike, yet each believes his own.
> —ALEXANDER POPE

> What implicit personality theory do others have of you? How do the theories held by your close friends differ from those held by your casual acquaintances? Who has the most accurate theory? Why?

BY PERMISSION OF JOHNNY HART AND NAS, INC.

The widely documented "halo effect" is a function of this implicit personality theory. If you believe an individual has several positive qualities, you may conclude that she or he has other positive qualities. The "reverse halo effect" operates similarly. If you know a person has several negative qualities, you might conclude the person also has other negative qualities.

BEWARE: POTENTIAL BARRIERS. The tendency to develop a personality theory and then to perceive an individual as conforming to the theory can lead you to:

- perceive qualities in an individual that your "theory" tells you should be present when they actually are not. For example, you see "goodwill" in the "charitable" acts of a friend when tax reduction may be the real motive.

- ignore or distort qualities or characteristics that do not conform to your theory. For example, you may ignore negative qualities in your friends that you would easily perceive in your enemies.

## The Self-Fulfilling Prophecy

A *self-fulfilling prophecy* occurs when you make a prediction or formulate a belief that comes true *because* you made the prediction and acted as if it were true (Merton 1957; Insel and Jacobson 1975). There are four basic steps in the self-fulfilling prophecy:

1. You make a prediction or formulate a belief about someone (often, ourselves) or a situation. For example, you predict that Pat is awkward in interpersonal situations.
2. You act toward that person or situation as if the prediction or belief is true. For example, you act toward Pat as if she were in fact awkward.
3. Because you act as if the belief were true, it becomes true. Because of the way you act toward Pat, she becomes tense and manifests awkwardness.
4. Your effect on the person or the resulting situation strengthens your beliefs. Seeing Pat's awkwardness reinforces your belief that Pat is in fact awkward.

If you expect people to act in a certain way, your predictions will frequently come true because of the self-fulfilling prophecy. Consider, for instance, people who enter a group situation convinced that other members will dislike them. Almost invariably they are proved right, perhaps because they act in a way that encourages people to respond negatively. Such people fulfill their own prophecies.

A widely known example of the self-fulfilling prophecy is the *Pygmalion effect* (Rosenthal and Jacobson 1968). In one study, teachers were told that certain pupils were expected to do exceptionally well, that they were late bloomers. The experimenters actually selected the names at random. The students did perform at a higher level than the other students. The teacher's expectations probably generated extra attention to the students, thereby positively affecting their performance.

Have you ever made a prophecy about someone? Did the prophecy have any effect on your attitudes and behaviors toward this other person? Was it a self-fulfilling prophecy?

BEWARE: POTENTIAL BARRIERS. The tendency to fulfill your own prophecies can lead you to:

- influence another's behavior to conform to your prophecy.
- see what you predicted rather than what really is. For example, it can lead you to perceive yourself as a failure because you made this prediction rather than because of any actual failures.

### Primacy-Recency

If what comes first exerts the most influence, we have a *primacy effect*. If what comes last (or is the most recent) exerts the most influence, we have a *recency effect*. In an early study on primacy-recency effects in interpersonal perception, Solomon Asch (1946) read a list of adjectives describing a person to a group and found that the effects of order were significant. Students more positively evaluated a person described as "intelligent, industrious, impulsive, critical, stubborn, and envious" than a person described as "envious, stubborn, critical, impulsive, industrious, and intelligent." The implication is that we use early information to provide a general idea of what a person is like, then later information to make the general idea more specific. The obvious practical implication of primacy-recency is that the first impression you make is likely to be the most important. Through this first impression, others filter additional information to formulate a picture of who they perceive you to be.

Primacy-recency provides the public speaker with guidance as to how to arrange the arguments in a speech. If you have three arguments, for example, put the weakest one in the middle—the position least likely to be remembered. If your listeners have no real conviction about your position, lead off with your strongest argument to get the listeners on your side. Public speaking audiences—like interpersonal ones—also form a general impression of the speaker and then filter everything else through this initial impression.

BEWARE: POTENTIAL BARRIERS. Your tendency to give greater weight to early information and to interpret later information in light of these early impressions can lead you to:

- formulate a "total" picture of an individual on the basis of initial impressions that may not be typical or accurate. For example, you might form an image of someone as socially ill at ease. If you based this impression on watching the person at a stressful job interview or during the first few minutes of a long political campaign, it is likely to be wrong.
- discount or distort later perceptions to avoid disrupting your initial impression. For instance, you may fail to see signs of deceit in someone who made a good first impression.

### Stereotyping

A frequently used shortcut in perception is stereotyping. The term *stereotype* originated in printing, it referred to the plate that printed the same image over and over. A sociological or psychological stereotype is

What is the first impression that people—say fellow classmates—form of you? On what do they base these first impressions? Do men and women develop essentially the same first impressions of you?

Manage every second of a first meeting. Do not delude yourself that a bad impression can be easily corrected. Putting things right is a lot harder than getting them right first time.
—DAVID LEWIS

Assume that you are taking a course in which half the classes are extremely dull and half are extremely exciting. At the end of the semester, you evaluate the course and the instructor. Would your evaluation be more favorable if the dull classes came during the first half of the semester and the exciting classes during the second half? Or would it be more favorable if the order were reversed?

a fixed impression of a group of people. We all have attitudinal stereotypes—of national, religious, and racial groups, and of criminals, prostitutes, teachers, or plumbers.

If you have these fixed impressions, you might, upon meeting a member of a particular group, see that person primarily as a member of that group. When you apply all the characteristics you assign to members of that group, you run the risk of missing a great deal that is unique to the individual. If you meet someone who is a draft-resistor, for example, you might have a host of characteristics for draft-resistors that you are ready to apply. Also, you may see various characteristics in this person's behavior that you would not see if you did not know this person was a draft-resistor. Stereotypes prevent you from seeing an individual.

BEWARE: POTENTIAL BARRIERS. Grouping people into classes and then responding to individuals primarily as members of that class can lead you to:

- perceive someone as having those qualities (usually negative) that you believe characterize the particular group (for example, all Venusians are lazy) and, therefore, fail to appreciate the multifaceted nature of all people and all groups.

- ignore the unique characteristics of an individual and, therefore, fail to benefit from the special contributions each can bring to an encounter.

### Attribution

*Attribution* is a process by which we try to explain the motivation for a person's behavior. One way to do this is to ask if the person was in control of the behavior. For example, say you invited your friend Desmond to dinner for seven o'clock and he arrives at nine. Consider how you would respond to each of these reasons:

Reason No. 1: I just couldn't tear myself away from the beach. I really wanted to get a great tan.

Reason No. 2: I was driving here when I saw some young kids mugging an old couple. I broke it up and took the couple home. They were so frightened that I had to stay with them until their children arrived. Their phone was out of order, so I had no way of calling to tell you I'd be late.

Reason No. 3: I got in a car accident and was taken to the hospital.

Assuming you believe all three explanations, you would attribute very different motives to Desmond's behavior. With Reasons 1 and 2, you would conclude that Desmond was in control of his behavior; with Reason 3, that he was not. Further, you would probably respond negatively to Reason 1 (Desmond was selfish and inconsiderate) and positively to Reason 2 (Desmond was a good Samaritan). Because Desmond was not in control of his behavior in Reason 3, you would probably not attribute either positive or negative motivation to his behavior. Instead you would probably feel sorry that he got into an accident.

You probably make similar judgments based on controllability in numerous situations. Consider, for example, how you would respond to the following situations:

- Doris fails her history midterm exam.
- Sidney's car is repossessed because he failed to keep up the payments.
- Margie is 150 pounds overweight and is complaining that she feels awful.
- Thomas's wife has just filed for divorce and he is feeling depressed.

Very probably you would be sympathetic to each of these people if you feel that they were *not* in control of what happened. For example, if the examination was unfair, if Sidney lost his job because of employee discrimination, if Margie has a glandular problem, and if Thomas's wife wants to leave him for a wealthy drug dealer. On the other hand, you probably would not be sympathetic toward these people if you felt they were in control of what happened. For example, if Doris partied instead of studied, if Sidney gambled his payments away, if Margie ate nothing but junk food and refused to exercise, and if Thomas has been repeatedly unfaithful and his wife finally gave up trying to reform him.

In perceiving, and especially in evaluating, other people's behavior, we frequently ask if they were in control of the behavior. Generally, research shows that if we feel a person was in control of negative behaviors, we will come to dislike him or her. If we believe the person was not in control of negative behaviors, we will come to feel sorry and not blame the person.

BEWARE: POTENTIAL BARRIERS. Of course, the obvious problem is that we can only make guesses about another person's behaviors. Can we really know if Doris deserved to pass or fail the history exam? Can we really know if Sidney deserved to have his car repossessed? Our inability to discover the absolute truth, however, does not discourage us from making such judgments, from trying to *mind read* the motives of another person. But, if we realize that our judgments are based on guesses, we might be more apt to seek further information before acting as if they were facts.

We see this tendency to mind read in a wide variety of situations: You forgot my birthday; *you don't love me.* You don't want to go to my parents for dinner; *you've never liked my parents.* You don't want to go for that interview; *you lack self-confidence.* The italicized words represent attempts to get inside a person's head, to mind read.

Another potential problem is the *self-serving bias* which operates when we evaluate our own behaviors. It leads us to take credit for the positive and to deny responsibility for the negative. Thus, you are more likely to attribute your own negative behaviors to uncontrollable factors. For example, after getting a D on an exam, you are more likely to attribute it to the difficulty or unfairness of the test.

However, you are likely to attribute your positive behaviors to controllable factors, to your own strength, intelligence or personality. After getting an A on an exam, you are more likely to attribute it to your ability or hard work (Bernstein, Stephan, and Davis 1979). So, this self-serving bias may distort your attributions.

We judge ourselves by what we feel capable of doing; others judge us by what we have done.
—HENRY WADSWORTH LONGFELLOW

Other men's sins are before our eyes; our own are behind our backs.
—SENECA

*How do the processes influencing your perception of others (implicit personality theory, self-fulfilling prophecy, primacy-recency, stereotyping, and attribution) also influence the way you see yourself?*

The self-serving bias, however, has at least one benefit—it helps protect our self-esteem. Our self-esteem is enhanced by attributing negative behaviors to outside, uncontrollable forces and positive behaviors to internal, controllable forces.

Another problem is the tendency of *overattribution*—attributing everything a person does to one or two obvious characteristics. For example, attributing a person's behavior to alcoholic parents or to being born blind or into great wealth. And so we say, Sally has difficulty forming meaningful relationships because she grew up in a home of alcoholics, Alex overeats because he's blind, and Lillian is irresponsible because she never had to work for her money. Most behaviors and personality characteristics are the product of a wide variety of factors; it is almost always a mistake to select one factor and attribute everything to it.

> To understand one's self is the classic form of consolation; to delude one's self is the romantic.
> —GEORGE SANTAYANA

## Critical Perception: Making Perceptions More Accurate

Communication and relational effectiveness depend in great part on our perception accuracy or what we might call "critical perception." You can improve your accuracy by (1) using strategies for reducing uncertainty, and (2) following some suggested guidelines or principles.

### Strategies for Reducing Uncertainty

The general assumption made here is that communication is a gradual process during which people reduce uncertainty about each other. With each interaction, you learn more and gradually come to know another person on a more meaningful level. Three major strategies for reducing uncertainty have been identified: passive, active, and interactive strategies (Berger and Bradac 1982.)

> Seeing is deceiving. It's eating that's believing.
> —JAMES THURBER

PASSIVE STRATEGIES. When you observe another person without their being aware, you are employing *passive* strategies. Most useful is to observe the person in some active task, for example, talking with friends in the cafeteria, working on a small group task, or giving a public speech.

ACTIVE STRATEGIES. When you actively seek information about a person in any way other than interacting, you are employing *active* strategies. For example, you can ask others about the person ("What is she like?" "Does he work out?" "Does she date guys younger than she is?"). You can also manipulate the environment so you can observe the individual in more specific and revealing contexts. Employment interviews, theatrical auditions, and student teaching are ways in which people manipulate situations to see how someone might act and react and hence reduce uncertainty about the person.

INTERACTIVE STRATEGIES. When you interact with the individual, you are employing *interactive* strategies, the most revealing strategy. For example, you can ask questions ("Do you enjoy sports?" "What did you think of that computer science course?" "What would you do if you got fired?").

You also gain knowledge of another by disclosing information about yourself. Thus, if you disclose difficulties with your parents, the other person is likely to disclose feelings about his or her parents. Self-disclosure creates a relaxed environment that encourages disclosures from the person about whom you wish to learn more (see Chapter 2).

In addition to avoiding the potential barriers in the various perceptual processes and to using all three uncertainty reduction strategies, here are a few more suggestions to help you increase the accuracy of your interpersonal perceptions.

- **Look for a variety of cues** pointing in the same direction. The more perceptual cues pointing to the same conclusion, the more likely that your conclusion will be correct.
- On the basis of your observations of behaviors, **formulate hypotheses** or guesses as to what the person is like. Check these against additional information and evidence; don't draw conclusions you then seek to confirm.
- **Be especially alert to contradictory cues,** cues that will disprove your initial guesses. It is easier to perceive cues that confirm your initial guesses than to perceive contradictory evidence.
- **Delay drawing conclusions** until you have had a chance to process a wide variety of cues.
- Remember that regardless of how many behaviors you observe and how carefully you examine these behaviors, you can only *guess* what is going on in another person's mind. A person's motives, attitudes, or values are not open to outside inspection. You can only make assumptions based on overt behaviors. **Avoid mind reading** ("You forgot my birthday because you don't really love me").
- **Beware of your own biases,** for example, perceiving only the positive in people you like and only the negative in people you don't.
- Do not assume that others are like you, or that they think like you, or that they would act as you would. **Recognize the diversity in people and especially the diversity that comes from cultural differences.** The failure to recognize diversity is one of the major barriers to intercultural communication.

> The heart has eyes which the brain knows nothing of.
> —CHARLES H. PARKHURST

Which of these suggestions for improving accuracy in perception are you most likely to violate? What effects do such violations have?

# Listening

There can be little doubt that we all listen a great deal. Upon awakening you listen to the radio. On the way to school you listen to friends, people around you, screeching cars, singing birds, or falling rain. In school you listen to the teacher, to other students, and sometimes even to yourself. We listen to friends at lunch and return to class to listen to more teachers. We arrive home and again listen to family and friends. We listen to records, radio, or television. All in all, we listen for a good part of our waking day.

Before reading about this area of human communication, examine your own listening habits by taking the "Listening Test."

> Listening can be distinguished from hearing because listening is a conscious process that takes place in the brain. Listening is something we do because we want to.
> —CAROL A. ROACH AND NANCY J. WYATT

> To have great poets, there must be great audiences too.
> —WALT WHITMAN

## TEST YOURSELF:

### How Good a Listener Are You?

Before you read about the barriers to listening and the guides to effective listening, examine your own listening habits and tendencies. Respond to each question with the following scale:

    1 = always
    2 = frequently
    3 = sometimes
    4 = seldom
    5 = never

_____ 1. I focus on my own performance during an interaction which results in my missing some of what the speaker has said.

_____ 2. I allow my mind to wander away from what the speaker is talking about.

_____ 3. I try to simplify messages I hear by omitting details.

_____ 4. I focus on a particular detail of what the speaker is saying instead of the general meanings the speaker wishes to communicate.

_____ 5. I allow my attitudes toward the topic or speaker to influence my evaluation of the message.

_____ 6. I hear what I expect to hear instead of what is actually said.

_____ 7. I listen passively, letting the speaker do the work while I relax.

_____ 8. I listen to what others say but I don't feel what they are feeling.

_____ 9. I judge and evaluate what the speaker is saying before I fully understand the meanings intended.

_____10. I listen to the literal meanings that a speaker communicates but do not look for hidden or underlying meanings.

_Scoring:_ All statements describe ineffective listening tendencies. High scores, therefore, reflect effective listening and low scores reflect ineffective listening. If you scored significantly higher than 30, you probably have better-than-average listening skills. Scores significantly below 30 represent lower-than-average listening skills. Regardless of your score, however, most people can significantly improve their listening skills. Each of the questions in this listening test refers to an obstacle or effectiveness principle we discuss in this unit.

> They [higher management] believe more and more that listening skills are crucial to job performance and are demanding that managers do something about it. Listening can no longer be sloughed off as just one more item in the vocabulary of communication.
> —WARREN REED

**Figure 3.2**
*Diagrams of Listening Studies*

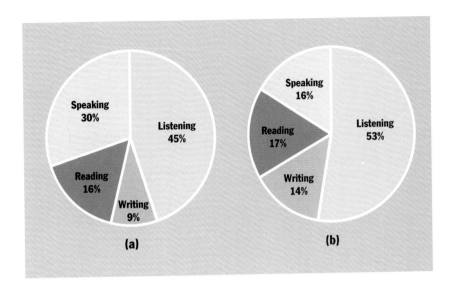

(a)  (b)

> Since we learn listening skills first and use listening skills more than any other communications skill, we might think that there would be formal training in listening during the educational process. Right?
> —Lyman Steil, Larry Barker, and Kittie Watson

If we measured importance by the time we spend on an activity, then listening would be our most important communication activity. A glance at Figure 3.2, which diagrams the results of two studies, illustrates this point. Note that in both studies (one [a] conducted in 1929 [Rankin], using adults as subjects and the other [b] in 1980 [Barker, Edwards, Gaines, Gladney, and Holley] with college students), listening occupied the most time.

Since we spend so much time listening, we would do well to improve our skills. Effective listening is not easy, however; it takes time and energy.

Because listening is often only vaguely and sometimes inaccurately understood, we need to examine the nature of this important activity.

## The Listening Process

Listening can be described as a series of five steps: receiving, understanding, remembering, evaluating, and responding. The process is visualized in Figure 3.3. Note that the listening process is a circular one. The responses of Person A serve as the stimuli for Person B whose responses, in turn, serve as the stimuli for Person A, and so on.

This five-step model draws on a variety of previous models that listening researchers have developed (for example, Barker 1990; Steil, Barker, and Watson 1983; Brownell 1987; Alessandra 1986).

### Receiving

> If you value rewarding interpersonal relationships, you need to listen effectively.
> —James Floyd

Hearing begins and ends with the first stage—receiving. Hearing just happens when we open our ears or get within earshot of some auditory stimuli. Listening, on the other hand, is quite different. Listening begins (but does not end) with receiving messages the speaker sends. Messages are both verbal and nonverbal; they consist of words as well as gestures, facial expressions, variations in volume and rate, and more as we will see when we discuss them in Chapters 4 and 5.

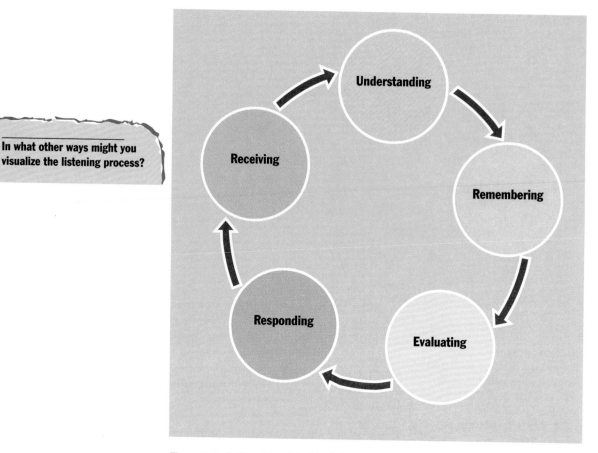

In what other ways might you visualize the listening process?

**Figure 3.3** *A Five Step Model of the Listening Process*

At this stage we note not only what is said (verbally and nonverbally) but also what is omitted. We not only receive the politician's summary of accomplishments in education, but also the omission of failure's in improved health care programs.

In **receiving** try to:

Which of these suggestions do you find most difficult to follow? Why?

- focus your attention on the speaker's verbal and nonverbal messages, on what is said and not said;
- avoid distractions in the environment;
- focus your attention on the speaker, not on what you will say next;
- maintain your role as listener; avoid interrupting the speaker until he or she is finished.

## Understanding

Understanding is when you learn what the speaker means. To understand, you must consider both the thoughts that are expressed as well as the emotional tone that accompanies them, for example, the urgency or the joy or sorrow expressed in the message.

In **understanding,** try to:

- relate the speaker's new information to what you already know (In what way will this new proposal change our present health care?);

- see the speaker's messages from the speaker's point of view; avoid judging the message until it is fully understood as the speaker intended it;

- ask questions for clarification, if necessary; ask for additional details or examples if needed; and

- rephrase (paraphrase) the speaker's ideas.

### Remembering

Messages that we receive and understand need to be retained at least for some period of time. In some small group and public speaking situations we can augment our memory by taking notes or by taping the messages. In most interpersonal communication situations, however, such note taking would be considered inappropriate, although we often do write down a phone number or an appointment or directions.

What you remember is not what was actually said, but what you think (or remember) was said. Memory for speech is not reproductive; you don't simply reproduce in your memory what the speaker said. Rather, memory is reconstructive; you actually reconstruct the messages you hear into a system that makes sense to you—a concept we noted in our discussion of perception. To illustrate this important concept, try to memorize the list of 12 words presented below (Glucksberg and Danks 1975). Don't worry about the order; only the number remembered counts. Don't read any further until you have tried to memorize the list. Take about 20 seconds to memorize as many words as possible.

**Word List**

| | |
|---|---|
| BED | AWAKE |
| DREAM | NIGHT |
| COMFORT | SLUMBER |
| REST | TIRED |
| WAKE | EAT |
| SOUND | SNORE |

Now close the book and write down as many words from the list as you can remember. Don't read any further until you have tested your own memory. If you are like my students, you not only remembered most of the words, but also added at least one word: "sleep." Most people recall "sleep" being on the list, but, as you can see, it wasn't. What happens is that you do not simply reproduce the list, but reconstruct it. In this case you gave the list meaning by including the word "sleep." We do this with all types of messages; reconstructing them into a meaningful whole and in the process often remembering a distorted version.

In **remembering,** try to:

- identify the central ideas and the major support advanced;

- summarize the message in an easier to retain form but do not ignore crucial details or qualifications;

- repeat names and key concepts to yourself or, if appropriate, aloud; and

- if this is a formal talk with a recognizable organizational structure, identify this pattern and use it (see it in your mind) to organize what the speaker is saying.

## Evaluating

Evaluating consists of judging the messages. At times you may try to evaluate the speaker's underlying intent, often without much conscious awareness. For example, Elaine tells you she is up for a promotion and is really excited about it. You may then try to judge her intention. Does she want you to use your influence with the company president? Is she preoccupied with the possible promotion, thus telling everyone? Is she looking for a pat on the back? Generally, if you know the person well, you will be able to identify the intention and respond appropriately.

In other situations, the evaluation is more of a critical analysis. For example, you would evaluate proposals advanced in a business meeting while listening to them. Are they practical? Will they increase productivity? Is there evidence to show this; is there contradictory evidence? Are there more practical and more productive alternative proposals?

In **evaluating,** try to:

- resist evaluation until you fully understand the speaker's point of view;

- assume that the speaker is a person of goodwill and give the speaker the benefit of any doubt by asking for clarification on issues you object to (Are there any other reasons for accepting this new proposal?);

- distinguish facts from inferences (see Chapter 5), opinions, and personal interpretations by the speaker; and

- identify any biases, self-interests, or prejudices that may lead the speaker to unfairly slant information presented.

## Responding

Responding occurs in two phases: (1) responses you make while the speaker is talking and (2) responses you make after the speaker has stopped talking. Responses made while the speaker is talking should be supportive and should acknowledge that you are listening. These include what nonverbal researchers call **backchanneling cues,** such as "I see," "yes," "uh-huh," that let the speaker know you are paying attention.

Have you ever stopped someone in mid-sentence to say, 'I know just what you are going to say.' Well, guess what? you don't know.
—MARY LYNNE HELDMANN

Have you ever been evaluated before being fully understood? How did this make you feel?

The ultimate in bad manners is to look at your watch while someone is talking.
—FORBES MAGAZINE

Responses after the speaker has stopped talking are generally more elaborate and might include empathy ("I know how you must feel"); asking for clarification ("Do you mean this new health plan will replace the old one or will it be just a supplement?); challenging ("I think your evidence is weak"); and agreeing ("You're absolutely right and I'll support your proposal when it comes up for a vote").

In **responding,** try to:

- be supportive of the speaker throughout the talk by using varied backchanneling cues; using only one—for example, saying "uh-huh" throughout—will make it appear that you are not listening but are merely on automatic pilot;

- express support for the speaker in your final responses; and

- own your own responses; state your thoughts and feelings as your own; use "I" messages (say "I think the new proposal will entail greater expense than you outlined" rather than "Everyone will object to the plan's cost.").

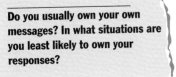

Do you usually own your own messages? In what situations are you least likely to own your responses?

*In what ways are listening in public speaking and listening interpersonally the same? In what ways are they different? Does the five-stage model adequately describe both types of listening? If not, how might you revise the model to better describe all kinds of listening?*

## Why We Listen

Listen to information on subjects you are unacquainted with, instead of always striving to lead the conversation to some favorite one of your own. By the last method you will shine, but will not improve.
—WILLIAM HAZLITT

Just as we speak for a variety of purposes, we also listen for different purposes. *Listening for enjoyment* occupies a good deal of our listening time. We listen to music, sports broadcasts, or television shows basically for enjoyment. When listening for enjoyment, you suspend your critical faculties, rid yourself of competing stimuli, relax, and enjoy the stimulation.

As a student, you are mainly *listening to gain information.* In class, you listen to the instructor and to other students. In small group and interpersonal situations, much of your time is spent listening for information—what happened to Joanne and Helen last weekend, what friends are planning to do over the holiday, what happened in the sociology class you missed. At times, you listen to learn a new skill or improve an existing one—to operate a computer, throw a curve, or prepare a particular dinner.

*Listening to help* is a crucial function and one to which we turn repeatedly. When you listen to someone complain, talk about their problems, or try to make a decision, you are often listening to help. Often the help is simply providing a receptive and supportive audience. At other times, it may be more direct, such as making suggestions or offering advice.

What type of listening are you best at? What type of listening are you poorest at? Why?

Another way to look at why we listen is to examine the benefits from effective listening. Six of these benefits are summarized in Table 3.1.

**Table 3.1** *Six Benefits of Effective Listening*

| Effective listening increases: | Examples: |
|---|---|
| 1. your ability to help others—you'll hear more, empathize more, and understand others more deeply. | 1. If you listen to your child's complaints about her teacher (instead of responding with "Now what did you do wrong?") you'll be better able to help your child cope with school and with her teacher. |
| 2. your ability to make more reasoned and more reasonable decisions—you'll acquire more information for decisions you'll have to make in business or in your personal life. | 2. Listening to the difficulties your sales staff has selling Widgets (instead of responding with "You're just not trying hard enough.") may help you design a more effective advertising campaign or offer more pertinent sales training. |
| 3. your power and influence—people are more likely to respect and follow those who have listened to them and who understand them. | 3. Workers are more likely to follow your advice once they feel you have really listened to their points of view, concerns, and insights. |
| 4. your social acceptance and popularity—people like those who are attentive and supportive. | 4. Jack and Jill will like you better if they feel you have a genuine concern for them—a concern readily communicated through attentive and supportive listening. |
| 5. your knowledge of others, the world, and yourself—you'll profit from the insights, experiences, and perceptions of others. | 5. Listening to Peter talk of his travels to Moscow will help you understand more about Peter as well as about Russian life. |
| 6. your ability to avoid problems and difficulties—you'll be able to respond to warnings of impending problems before they develop or escalate beyond control. | 6. Listening to student reactions (instead of responding with "Students just don't want to work hard.") will help the teacher plan more effective, relevant classes and respond better to real student needs and concerns. |

## Obstacles to Effective Listening

The first step in improving listening abilities is to recognize and combat the various obstacles to effective listening (Nichols and Stevens 1957; Nichols 1961). Probably the most serious and most damaging obstacle to effective listening is the *tendency to become preoccupied with ourselves*. For example, in a job interview situation, you might focus on your own performance, on whether you are communicating the right image and miss much of what the interviewer is saying.

Sometimes the preoccupation with yourself centers on assuming the role of speaker. You begin to rehearse your responses, to think of what you will say to answer the speaker or perhaps a question you want to ask the public speaker. While focusing on yourself, you inevitably miss what the speaker is saying.

In a similar way, you may become *preoccupied with external issues* that are irrelevant to what is being said. You think about what you did last Saturday or your plans for this evening or a movie you saw. Of course, the more you entertain these thoughts of external matters, the less effectively you listen.

Another obstacle is *assimilation:* the tendency to reconstruct messages so they reflect your own attitudes, prejudices, needs, and values. The tendency is to hear relatively neutral messages ("Management to institute drastic changes in scheduling.") as supporting your own attitudes and beliefs ("Management is going to foul up our schedules again.").

You may also distort messages because of the *friend-or-foe factor;* listening for positive qualities about friends and negative qualities about enemies. For example, if you dislike Freddy, then it will take added effort to listen objectively to Freddy's messages or messages about Freddy—especially if those messages reflect positively on Freddy.

CALVIN AND HOBBES © 1986 UNIVERSAL PRESS SYNDICATE.

Another obstacle is to fail to hear what the speaker is saying and instead *hear what you expect*. You know that Lin frequently complains about grades. So, when Lin tells you about problems with a teacher, you almost automatically "hear" Lin complaining (again!) about grades.

Table 3.2 presents additional guidelines for effective listening. Review the table periodically, checking off listening behaviors as you master them. By the end of the course, you should have the entire list checked and easily under your control.

**Table 3.2** *Ten Guidelines for Listening Effectively*

_____ Listening is hard work, so prepare to participate actively. Don't expect simply to be entertained.

_____ Engage in dialogue, not monologue. Communication is a two-way process. Assume there is value in what the speaker is saying. Resist assuming that what you have to say is more valuable than the speaker's remarks.

_____ Try to understand both thoughts and feelings. Listen until you understand what the speaker is feeling and thinking as well as saying.

_____ Avoid "offensive listening"—listening to bits and pieces of information that will help you find fault with the speaker or the message.

_____ Keep an open mind. Delay your judgments until you fully understand the speaker's intention and content.

_____ Recognize your own biases since these may interfere with accurate listening and distort what you hear. For example, are your ethnic, national, or religious biases preventing you from appreciating a speaker's point of view?

_____ Focus on both verbal and nonverbal messages. Recognize both consistent and inconsistent "packages" of messages and use them as guides for drawing inferences about the speaker's meaning. When in doubt, ask questions.

_____ Listen also to what the speaker omits. Remember that people communicate by what they leave out as well as include. Listen, therefore, for omissions that may give you a clue to the speaker's meanings.

_____ Listen for both content and relational messages. You need to understand both to deal effectively with any message.

_____ Listen to the personal and self-references that speakers invariably include. Whatever a person says is, in part, a reflection of who that person is.

# Active Listening

Active listening owes its development to Thomas Gordon (1975) who made it a cornerstone of his P-E-T (Parent-Effectiveness-Training) technique. Consider the following exchange:

SPEAKER: *I got a C on that paper! I really worked on that project and I get a miserable C.*

LISTENER 1: *That's not too bad; most people got around the same grade. I got a C too.*

LISTENER 2: *So what? This is your last semester. Who cares about grades anyway?*

LISTENER 3: *You should be pleased with a C. Peggy and Michael both failed and John and Judy got Ds.*

LISTENER 4: *You got a C on that paper you were working on for the last three weeks? You sound really angry and hurt.*

Which of these responses would you be most likely to give?

All four listeners are probably anxious to make the speaker feel better. But they go about it in very different ways and, we can be sure, with very different results. Listeners 1 and 2 try to lessen the significance of a C grade. This response is extremely common and may be well-intended but it does little to promote meaningful communication and understanding. Listener 3 tries to give the grade a more positive meaning. By their responses, however, these listeners are also saying that the speaker should not be feeling as he or she does. They are also saying the speaker's feelings are not legitimate and should be replaced with more logical feelings.

Listener 4, however, is different. Listener 4 uses *active listening;* a process of sending back to the speaker what you as a listener think the speaker meant—both in content and in feelings. Active listening is not merely repeating the speaker's exact words, but rather putting together into some meaningful whole your understanding of the speaker's total message.

*Listening, not imitation, may be the sincerest form of flattery.*
—JOYCE BROTHERS

## The Functions of Active Listening

Active listening serves several important functions. First, it helps you, as a listener, check your understanding of what the speaker said and, more important, meant. Reflecting back perceived meanings to the speaker gives the speaker an opportunity to offer clarification. In this way, future messages will have a better chance of being relevant.

Second, through active listening you express acceptance of the speaker's feelings. Note that in the sample responses given, the first three listeners challenged the speaker's feelings. The active listener (Listener 4), who reflected back to the speaker what he or she thought was said, gave the speaker acceptance. Rather than challenging the speaker's feelings, they were echoed in a caring manner. In addition to accepting the speaker's feelings, Listener 4 also identifies them explicitly ("You sound angry and hurt"), again allowing an opportunity for correction.

*Active listening is a remarkable way to involve the "sender" with the "receiver."*
—THOMAS GORDON

Third, active listening stimulates the speaker to explore feelings and thoughts. The response of Listener 4 encourages the speaker to elaborate on his or her feelings. This further exploration also encourages the speaker to solve his or her own problems by providing the opportunity to talk them through.

## The Techniques of Active Listening

Three simple techniques may prove useful in learning the process of active listening.

PARAPHRASE THE SPEAKER'S THOUGHTS. State in your own words what you think the speaker meant. This helps ensure understanding and also shows the speaker you are interested.

The paraphrase also gives the speaker a chance to elaborate on or extend what was originally said. Thus, when Listener 4 echoes the speaker's thought, the speaker may next elaborate on why that C was an important one. Perhaps the speaker fears that his or her history paper will receive a similar grade.

Finally, in your paraphrase, be especially careful not to lead the speaker in the direction you think he or she should go. Paraphrases should be objective descriptions.

EXPRESS UNDERSTANDING OF THE SPEAKER'S FEELINGS. In addition to paraphrasing the content, echo the feelings the speaker expressed or implied ("I can imagine how you must have felt. You must have felt horrible.") Just as the paraphrase helps you check your perception of the content, the expression of feelings will help you check your perception of the speaker's feelings. This will also allow the speaker to see his or her feelings more objectively. This is especially helpful when the speaker feels angry, hurt, or depressed.

When you echo the speaker's feelings, you also stimulate the speaker to elaborate. Most of us hold back our feelings until we are certain they (and we) will be accepted. When we feel acceptance, we then feel free to go into more detail. Active listening gives the speaker this important opportunity. In echoing feelings, be careful not to over- or understate the speaker's feelings. Try to echo as accurately as you can: "You sound determined" or "You seem really pleased."

ASK QUESTIONS. Asking questions ensures your own understanding of the speaker's thoughts and feelings and secures additional information ("How did you feel when you read your job appraisal report?"). The questions should provide just enough stimulation and support for the speaker to express his or her thoughts and feelings. These questions will further confirm your interest and concern for the speaker. Be careful not to pry into unrelated areas or challenge the speaker in any way.

## A Note on Critical Listening

Throughout this discussion, we have emphasized listening for understanding. There is also, however, critical listening (see the end of the part summary). Critical listening depends not only on the skills

Understanding is a two-way street.
—ELEANOR ROOSEVELT

What do you find to be the hardest part of active listening? Why? What suggestions can you offer to make active listening easier?

noted but also on the truth and accuracy of the information as well as on the honesty and motivation of the speaker. Thus, in addition to keeping an open mind and delaying judgments, it is necessary to focus on other issues as well:

> Silence gives consent, or a horrible feeling that nobody's listening.
> —FRANKLIN P. JONES

- Is what the speaker says the truth as far as you understand it? For example, is this car really that great? Are there any disadvantages to this particular car?

- Has the speaker presented the information in enough detail? Have crucial parts been left out? For example, has the speaker identified all the costs?

- Is the speaker being honest? Is the speaker's motivation merely self-gain? For example, might this speaker be distorting the facts merely to make a sale and earn a commission?

## Feedback

> Feedback is a method of controlling a system by reinserting into it the results of its past performance.
> —NORBERT WIENER

Throughout the listening process, listeners give the speaker *feedback*—the messages we send back to the speaker concerning our reactions to what is said. On the basis of this feedback, the speaker may adjust the message's content or form.

What is and is not appropriate feedback will depend in large part on the culture you are in. For example, a friend of mind gave a lecture in Beijing. No one asked any questions, either during or after the lecture. My friend was sure the lack of feedback meant that what she said was unclear or irrelevant. Later she learned that in China, it is considered impolite to ask questions; it would imply that the speaker was not clear and would therefore be insulting.

> How is feedback used in this class in human communication? What specific functions is it designed to serve? How might it be made more effective?

The following suggestions for giving and receiving feedback will prove useful in most contexts. Like all suggestions offered, these should be modified on the basis of the specific culture and its norms and rules.

### Giving Feedback Effectively

Effective feedback is immediate, honest, and appropriate. The most effective feedback is *immediate*. Ideally, feedback is sent immediately after you receive the message. It loses its effectiveness with time. The longer you wait to praise or punish, for example, the less effect it will have.

Feedback should be an *honest* reaction to communication. But feedback should not be merely a series of messages to build up the speaker's ego. Feedback about your understanding of and agreement with the message should be honest. Do not be afraid to admit you did not understand a message. Nor should you hesitate to disagree.

> Admonish your friends privately, but praise them openly.
> —SYRUS

Feedback should be *appropriate* to the communication situation. Remember, however, that appropriateness is a learned concept. So, what is appropriate in your culture is not necessarily appropriate in another.

What other suggestions might you offer for giving feedback effectively? [Look through the characteristics of effective interpersonal communication in Chapter 6 for suggestions. How might these be applied to giving feedback?]

In the United States, for example, it is considered appropriate to signal interest in a public speaker by maintaining focused eye contact with the speaker throughout the speech. In Japan, that same interest is signaled by closing one's eyes to aid concentration.

Further, distinguish between feedback to the *message* and feedback to the *speaker*. Make clear when disagreeing with speakers, for example, that you are disagreeing with what they say, not rejecting them as people.

## Receiving Feedback Effectively

It probably takes as much effort and ingenuity to respond appropriately to feedback as to give it to others. Receiving feedback effectively requires sensitivity, supportiveness, and open-mindedness.

Develop a *sensitivity* to feedback—one that will enable you to see feedback in situations where it often goes unnoticed. Most feedback comes in the form of nonverbal messages—a puzzled face, a wide smile, an avoidance of eye contact. These are feedback examples to which we must become sensitive. And, of course, verbal feedback also comes in many forms. At times it is obvious: "You walk like an elephant." "When you look at me that way, I want to kiss you." But most often it comes in more subtle ways—a quick, almost throwaway remark or a slow, belabored effort to say something good about your newly decorated apartment.

Can you give examples of receiving feedback supportively and defensively?

Your own *supportiveness* to feedback influences the kind of feedback you receive. People usually take defensiveness as a sign to stop giving feedback. If the feedback stops, however, you may lose much insight. For example, in hearing negative feedback you may respond in kind and criticize the other person and this will probably stop the feedback. If you assume that the person giving the feedback has your welfare in mind, your defensiveness should be lessened.

What other suggestions might you offer for responding to the feedback from others?

Listen to feedback with an *open mind*. If the feedback is negative, and especially if it deals with a sensitive issue, it becomes particularly difficult to accept ("That haircut makes your nose look even larger."). We tend to block it out even before we hear the entire message. Instead, evaluate what is said, accept what seems reasonable, and reject what seems unreasonable. But make these decisions only after listening carefully and fully understanding what the individual is saying.

## Feedforward

I am not sure I have learned anything else as important. I have been able to realize what a prime role what I have come to call 'feedforward' has in all our doings.
—I.A. RICHARDS

*Feedforward* is information that comes before the primary message. Feedforward tells us something about the messages to come. It includes such diverse examples as the preface or table of contents of a book, the opening paragraph of a chapter, a movie preview, a magazine cover, and the introduction to a speech.

Feedforward messages are examples of *metamessages*—messages that communicate about other messages. Such information may be verbal ("Wait until you hear this one.") or nonverbal (a prolonged pause or hands motioning for silence to signal that an important message is about to be spoken). Or, as is most often the case, some combination of verbal and nonverbal. Feedforward may refer to the content of the message to follow ("I'll tell you exactly what they said to each other.") or to the form ("I won't spare you the gory details.").

Feedforward has four major functions: (1) to open the channels of communication, (2) to preview the message, (3) to disclaim, and (4) to altercast.

### To Open the Channels of Communication: Phatic Communion.
Phatic communion is a perfect example of feedforward. It is information that tells you that the normal, expected, and accepted rules of interaction will be in effect. It tells you another person is willing to communicate.

Why are "opening lines" so difficult to say? Why are they so difficult to respond to?

Phatic messages are essential in initiating interactions, especially with strangers. The famous "opening line" ("Have you got a match?" or "Haven't we met before?") is a good example of phatic communion and is an essential part of the interpersonal interaction. When such phatic messages do not precede an initial exchange, you sense that something is wrong. In small group communication, phatic messages may be used to establish rapport among members. In public speaking, phatic messages are often used to establish a connection between the speaker and the audience ("It's a real pleasure speaking with you today.") When the communication "rule" demanding the use of phatic messages to open communication is broken, the speaker is thought to lack communication competence.

### To Preview Future Messages.
Feedforward messages frequently preview other messages. Feedforward may, for example, preview the content ("I'm afraid I have bad news for you."), the importance ("Listen to this before you make a move."), the form or style ("I'll tell you word-for-word what she said."), and the positive or negative quality of later messages ("You're not going to like this, but here's what I heard.").

### To Disclaim.
The *disclaimer* is a statement that aims to ensure that your message will be understood and not reflect negatively on you (Hewitt and Stokes 1975). Table 3.3 presents disclaimers with definitions and examples. As you can see, disclaimers try to persuade the listener to hear your message as you wish it to be heard.

Have you heard any disclaimers in the last day or so? What effect did they have?

### To Altercast.
In this feedforward, you place the receiver in a specific role and request that the receiver respond to you in this assumed role. This process is known as *altercasting*. It asks the receiver to approach your message from a particular role or even as someone else (Weinstein and Deutschberger 1963; McLaughlin 1984). For example, you might ask a friend, "As an advertising executive, what do you think of corrective advertising?" This question casts your friend into the role of advertising executive (rather than parent, Democrat, or Baptist, for example). It asks your friend to answer from a particular perspective.

Have you been "altercasted" in the last few days? Have you used altercasting in the last few days?

| Disclaimer | Definition /Function | Examples |
|---|---|---|
| Hedging | Speaker disclaims the importance of the message to his or her own identity; speaker makes it clear that listeners may reject the message without rejecting the speaker. | I didn't read the entire report, but…. I'm no physiologist, but that irregularity seems…. I may be wrong here but…. |
| Credentialing | Speaker knows that the message may be poorly received, but will say it nevertheless; speaker attempts to avoid any undesirable inference that may be drawn by listeners; speaker seeks to establish special qualifications. | Don't get the wrong idea; I'm not sexist, but…. I'm not homophobic…. Some of my best friends are…. |
| Sin Licenses | Speaker announces that he or she will commit a violation of some social or cultural role but should be "forgiven" in advance (a "license to sin"). | I realize that this may not be the time to talk about money, but…. I know you'll think this suggestion is out of order, but do consider…. |
| Cognitive Disclaimers | Speaker seeks to reaffirm his or her cognitive abilities in anticipation of listeners' doubts. | You'll probably think I'm crazy but let me explain the logic of the case. I know you think I'm drunk but I'm as sober and as lucid as anyone here. |
| Appeals for the Suspension of Judgment | Speaker asks the listeners to delay making judgments until a more complete account is presented. | Don't hang up on me until you hear my side of the story. Don't say anything until I explain what really happened. If you promise not to laugh I'll tell you exactly what happened on that first date. |

**Table 3.3** *Disclaimers*

How is feedforward used in this class? What specific functions does such feedforward serve? How might you use it more effectively?

We might also ask people to assume roles foreign to them, for example:

- If money were no object, what would you buy?
- What would you do if you were her father?
- If you won the lottery, what's the first thing you would do?
- If you were the author of this book, how would you explain alter-casting?

*Guidelines in Using Feedforward*

In using feedforward, keep in mind the following guidelines:

- Remember that communication is a transactional process. So, others are sending feedforward messages in their responses to your feedforward messages. The returned smile, expression of anger, or the response to your "hello" are also feedforward messages. They, too, tell you something about future communications.
- In responding to disclaimers, respond to both the disclaimer and the content message to let the speaker know that you heard the disclaimer and retain a favorable impression of him or her. For example, appropriate responses might be: "I know you're no sexist

but I don't agree that . . . ." "Well, perhaps we should discuss the money now even if it doesn't seem quite right."

■ Be brief. Feedforward that is overly detailed or contains unnecessary information is usually inappropriate. Use feedforward (especially disclaimers) sparingly. Overuse will probably weaken the impact of your messages. This is especially true of hedging.

■ Recognize that inappropriate disclaimers and disclaimers that your listeners do not accept may raise doubts about your message. The disclaimer may, in fact, create the very impression you want to avoid. For example, to preface remarks with "I'm no liar" may lead listeners to think that maybe you are a liar.

■ Consider using disclaimers when you think you might offend your listeners. Disclaimers may create a more positive impression. For example, speakers who use disclaimers before telling a potentially offensive joke are judged less insensitive than those who do not use disclaimers.

# FEEDBACK

In this chapter we discussed the way we receive messages through perception and listening.

1. **Perception** refers to the process by which we become aware of the many stimuli impinging on our senses.
2. **Perception** occurs in three stages: **sensory stimulation occurs, sensory stimulation is organized,** and **sensory stimulation is interpreted-evaluated.**
3. The following processes influence perception: (1) **implicit personality theory,** (2) **self-fulfilling prophecy,** (3) **primacy-recency,** (4) **stereotyping,** and (5) **attribution.**
4. **Implicit personality theory** refers to the private personality theory that individuals hold and that influence how they perceive other people.
5. The **self-fulfilling prophecy** occurs when you make a prediction or formulate a belief that comes true *because* you have made the prediction and acted as if it were true.
6. **Primacy-recency** refers to the relative influence of stimuli as a result of their order. If what occurs first exerts greater influence, we have a primacy effect. If what occurs last exerts greater influence, we have a recency effect.
7. **Stereotyping** refers to the tendency to develop and maintain fixed, unchanging perceptions of groups of people and to use these perceptions to evaluate individual members, ignoring their individual, unique characteristics.
8. **Attribution** refers to the process by which we try to explain the motivation for a person's behavior. Whether or not the person was in control of the behavior will influence how we evaluate the behavior.
9. **Listening** is a five-step process consisting of receiving, understanding, remembering, evaluating, and responding.
10. We listen for a variety of reasons: for enjoyment, for information, and to help.
11. **Active listening** is listening in which you send back to the speaker what you think the speaker said and felt. Active listening enables the listener to check understanding, express acceptance, and stimulate the speaker to explore his or her feelings and thoughts.
12. Three major **techniques for active listening** are: (1) paraphrase the speaker's thoughts, (2) express understanding of the speaker's feelings, (3) ask relevant questions.
13. **Feedback** refers to the messages receivers send back to the speaker concerning their reactions to what is said.
14. **Feedforward** refers to information sent before the primary message that tells receivers something about future messages.

Throughout this discussion of perception and listening, a variety of skills were identified and are presented here in summary. Check your ability to apply these skills:   (1) = almost always,   (2) = often,   (3) = sometimes,   (4) = rarely,   (5) = hardly ever.

_____ 1. Recognizing how **primacy-recency** works, I actively guard against first impressions that might prevent accurate perceptions of future events.

_____ 2. To guard against the **self-fulfilling prophecy,** I take a second look at my perceptions when they conform too closely to my expectations.

_____ 3. I bring to consciousness my **implicit personality theories.**

_____ 4. I avoid **stereotyping.**

_____ 5. I am aware of and am careful to avoid mind reading, the self-serving bias, and overattribution in trying to account for another person's behavior.

_____ 6. I am especially careful to avoid the major obstacles to effective listening: **preoccupation with self, preoccupation with external issues, assimilation, the friend-or-foe factor,** and **hearing what's expected.**

_____ 7. I use the skills of **active listening** when appropriate.

_____ 8. I use **feedback** that is immediate, honest, appropriate, and clear. As a receiver, I am sensitive and responsive to others' feedback.

_____ 9. I use **feedforward** to open the channels of communication, to preview future messages, to disclaim, and to altercast as appropriate.

# SKILL DEVELOPMENT EXPERIENCES

## 3.1 HEARING THE BARRIERS TO PERCEPTION

Learning to hear the barriers to accurate perception in ourselves and in others will help us avoid or counteract them. For the next several days, record all personal examples of the four barriers to accurate perception. Record also the specific context in which they occurred.

After you have identified the various barriers, share your findings in groups of five or six or with the entire class. As always, only disclose what you wish to disclose. You may find it worthwhile to discuss some or all of these questions:

1. What barrier seems most frequent?
2. What problems did the barrier cause?
3. What advantages do we gain when we avoid making first impressions? When we avoid using implicit theories? When we avoid making prophecies? When we avoid stereotyping?
4. What disadvantages are there in avoiding these shortcuts to people perception?

## 3.2 PARAPHRASING TO ENSURE UNDERSTANDING

For each of the messages presented below, write an acceptable paraphrase. After you complete the paraphrases, ask another person if he or she would accept them as objective restatements of thoughts and feelings. Rework the paraphrases until the other person agrees that they are accurate.

1. I can't deal with my parents' constant fighting. I've seen it for the last ten years and I really can't stand it anymore.
   *Paraphrase:* You have trouble dealing with their fighting. You seem really upset by this last fight.
2. Did you hear I got engaged to Jerry? I'm the happiest person in the world.
3. I got a C on that paper. That's the worst grade I've ever received. I just can't believe that I got a C. This is my major. What am I going to do?
4. I really had a scare with the kids the other night. They went out to the night game at the high school. They didn't walk in till 2 A.M. I thought I'd die.
5. That rotten, inconsiderate pig just up and left. He never even said goodbye. We were together for six months and after one small argument he leaves without a word. And he even took my bathrobe—that expensive one he bought for my last birthday.
6. I'm just not sure what to do. I really love Chris. She's the sweetest kid I've ever known. I mean she'd do anything for me. But, she really wants to get married. I do too and yet I don't want to make such a commitment. I mean that's a long term thing. And, much as I hate to admit it, I don't want the responsibility of a wife, a family, a house. I really don't need that kind of pressure.

## 3.3 ACTIVE LISTENING

For each of the situations described below, supply at least one appropriate active listening response.

1. Your friend Phil has just broken up a love affair and is telling you about it. *I can't seem to get Chris out of my mind. All I do is daydream about what we used to do and all the fun we used to have.*
2. You and your friend are discussing the recent chemistry examination. Your friend says: *I didn't get an A. I got a B+. What am I going to do now? I feel like a failure.*
3. A young nephew tells you that he cannot talk with his parents. No matter how hard he tries, they just don't listen. *I tried to tell them that I can't play baseball and I don't want to play baseball. But they ignore me and tell me that all I need is practice.*
4. A friend just won $20,000 on a quiz show but is depressed because she lost the championship and the chance to compete for the grand prize of $150,000. *I knew the answer, but I just couldn't think fast enough. That money could have solved all my problems.*
5. Your mother has been having a difficult time at work. She was recently passed up for a promotion and received one of the lowest merit raises given in the company. *I'm not sure what I did wrong. I do my work, mind my own business, don't take my sick days like everyone else. How could they give that promotion to Helen Sandez who's only been with the company for two years. I've given them seven years. Maybe I should just quit and try to find something else.*

## 3.4 GIVING FEEDBACK EFFECTIVELY

The following exercise provides practice in giving feedback effectively. For each of the following situations, respond with feedback that is immediate, honest, and appropriate.

1. Your friend has gained 20 pounds over the summer and asks you if it shows. It does.
2. A fellow student gives a speech that you thought was not very good. He asks you what you thought of it.
3. Your teacher has just given a pretty awful lecture—it was not particularly relevant to the course, it was disorganized, it was much too complex, it contained no human interest material, and it did not attempt to involve any of the class members—and asks you for some honest feedback.
4. Your primary relational partner asks you what you dislike most about him or her. What you dislike the most is your partner's constant focusing on himself or herself—illustrated even in the asking of this question.
5. While in a clothing store, a customer asks you what you think of a particular outfit he or she is trying on. You think it is awful.

## 3.5 WHO?

The purpose of this exercise is to explore some of the verbal and nonverbal cues that people give and that others receive and use in formulating inferences about the knowledge, abilities, and personality of these others. The exercise should serve as a useful summary of the concepts and principles of verbal and nonverbal communication and of interpersonal perception.

The entire class should form a circle so that each member may see each other member without straining. If members do not know all the names of their classmates, name tags should be used.

Each student should examine the following list of phrases and should write the name of one student to whom he or she feels each statement applies in the column marked "Who." Be certain to respond to all statements. Although one name may be used more than once, the experience will prove more effective if a wide variety of names are chosen. Unless the class is very small, no name should be used more than two times.

Next to each student's name, record a *certainty rating* in the column labeled "CR," indicating how sure you are of your choices. Use a five-point scale with 5 indicating great certainty and 1 indicating great uncertainty.

After the names and certainty ratings have been written for *each* statement by *each* student, the following procedure may prove useful. The instructor or group leader selects a statement (there is no need to tackle the statements in the order they are given here), and asks someone specifically, or the class generally, what names were put down. Before the person whose name was put down is asked if the phrase is correctly or incorrectly attributed to him or her, some or all of the following questions should be considered.

1. Why did you select the name you did? What was there about this person that led you to think that this phrase applied to him or her? What *specific* verbal or nonverbal cues led you to your conclusion?
2. What additional verbal and/or nonverbal cues would you need to raise your degree of certainty?
3. Is your response at all a function of a stereotype you might have of this individual's ethnic, religious, racial, or sexual identification? For example, how many women's names were put down for the questions or phrases about the saws or pistons? How many men's names were put down for the statements pertaining to cooking or using a sewing machine?
4. Did anyone give apparently contradictory cues? Explain the nature of these contradictory cues.
5. How pleased or disappointed are the people whose names have been proposed? Why? Were there any surprises? Why were some of these guesses unexpected?
6. How do you communicate your "self" to others? How do you communicate what you know, think, feel, and do to your peers?

| Who | CR | |
| --- | --- | --- |
| ___ | ___ | 1. Goes to the professional theater a few times a year |
| ___ | ___ | 2. Has taken a vacation out side the country in the last 12 months |
| ___ | ___ | 3. Likes to cook |

_____  _____  4. Watches soap operas on a fairly
               regular basis

_____  _____  5. Knows the function of a car's
               pistons

_____  _____  6. Attends sporting events with a
               fair degree of regularity

_____  _____  7. Has seen a pornographic (XXX-
               rated) movie within the last
               three months

_____  _____  8. Has been to an opera

_____  _____  9. Knows how to use a sewing
               machine

_____  _____ 10. Is a member of an organized
               sports team

_____  _____ 11. Watches television for an aver-
               age of three or more hours per
               day

_____  _____ 12. Has cried over a movie in the
               last few months

_____  _____ 13. Fluently speaks a foreign lan-
               guage

_____  _____ 14. Has many close friends

_____  _____ 15. Knows how potatoes should be
               planted

_____  _____ 16. Knows the difference between a
               hacksaw, and a jigsaw or a cop-
               ing saw

_____  _____ 17. Knows the ingredients of a
               bloody Mary

_____  _____ 18. Knows how to make a hol-
               landaise sauce

_____  _____ 19. Can name all 12 signs of the
               zodiac

_____  _____ 20. Has a car in his or her immedi-
               ate family costing more than
               $30,000

_____  _____ 21. Would come to the aid of a
               friend even at great personal
               sacrifice

_____  _____ 22. Has read a book on the best-
               seller list in the last year

_____  _____ 23. Is frequently infatuated (or in
               love)

_____  _____ 24. Would like, perhaps secretly, to
               be a movie star

_____  _____ 25. Writes poetry

_____  _____ 26. Could name the last 12 U.S.
               presidents

_____  _____ 27. Knows where Liechtenstein is

_____  _____ 28. Knows the political status of
               Puerto Rico

_____  _____ 29. Keeps a diary or a journal

_____  _____ 30. Knows what *prime rate* means

_____  _____ 31. Was a member of the Boy Scouts
               or Girl Scouts

_____  _____ 32. Is very religious

_____  _____ 33. Would describe himself or her-
               self as a political activist

_____  _____ 34. Wants to go to graduate, law, or
               medical school

_____  _____ 35. Would vote in favor of gay
               rights legislation

_____  _____ 36. Is planning to get married
               within the next 12 months

_____  _____ 37. Is going to make a significant
               contribution to society

_____  _____ 38. Is going to be a millionaire

_____  _____ 39. Is a real romantic

_____  _____ 40. Would emerge as a leader in a
               small group situation

# CHAPTER 4

# Verbal Messages

## LANGUAGE AS A MEANING SYSTEM
- *Meanings Are Both Denotative and Connotative*
- *Meanings Are in People*
- *Meanings Need Referents*
- *Meanings Are Infinite in Number*
- *Meanings Are Communicated Only Partially*

## BARRIERS IN THINKING AND COMMUNICATING
- *Polarization*
- *Intensional Orientation*
- *Fact-Inference Confusion*
- *Bypassing*
- *Static Evaluation*
- *Allness*
- *Indiscrimination*

## BARRIERS IN TALKING WITH OTHERS
- *In-Group Talk*
- *Self-Talk and Other-Talk*
- *Gossip*
- *Disconfirmation*
- *Racism*
- *Sexism*
- *Heterosexism*

## FEEDBACK

## SKILL DEVELOPMENT EXPERIENCES

## Goals

*After completing this chapter, you should be able to*

1. *identify the characteristics of meaning and their implications for human communication*
2. *define the barriers to thinking and communicating and ways to avoid them*
3. *explain the barriers in talking with others*

■ *Why are some people so clear in expressing themselves and others so unclear?*

■ *How can your use of language get you into trouble?* ■ *In what ways can you use language to more accurately reflect reality?* ■ *Why do people so often misunderstand each other?* ■ *When does language prove offensive?*

## Language As a Meaning System

Of all the functions of language, the communication of meaning from one person to another is surely the most significant. We need, then, to put meaning at the center of our discussion of verbal messages and ask how meaning works. The principles we present will identify the characteristics of meaning and should help to erase some common misconceptions.

### Meanings Are Both Denotative and Connotative

Two general types of meaning are essential to identify: denotation and connotation. Denotation refers to the meaning you would find in a dictionary; it is the meaning that members of the culture assign to a word. Connotation refers to the emotional meaning that specific speakers-listeners give to a word. Take as an example the word *death*. To a doctor this word might mean (or denote) the time when the heart stops. This is an objective description of a particular event. On the other hand, to the dead person's mother (upon being informed of her son's death), the word means (or connotes) much more. It recalls her son's youth, ambition, family, illness, and so on. To her it is a highly emotional, subjective, and personal word. These emotional, subjective, or personal reactions are the word's connotative meaning. The *denotation* of a word is its objective definition. The *connotation* of a word is its subjective or emotional meaning.

SNARL WORDS AND PURR WORDS. Semanticist S. I. Hayakawa (Hayakawa and Hayakawa 1990) coined the terms *snarl words* and *purr words* to further clarify the distinction between denotation and connotation. Snarl words are highly negative ("She's an idiot." "He's a pig." "They're a bunch of losers."). Purr words are highly positive ("She's a real sweetheart." "He's a dream." "They're the greatest.").

Snarl and purr words, although they may sometimes seem to have denotative meaning and to refer to the "real world," are actually connotative in meaning. These terms do not describe people or events in the real world but rather, the speaker's feelings about these people or events.

### Meanings Are in People

If you wanted to know the meaning of the word "love," you would probably turn to a dictionary. There you would find, according to *Webster's:* "the attraction, desire, or affection felt for a person who arouses delight or admiration or elicits tenderness, sympathetic interest, or benevolence." This is the denotative meaning.

Why is it relatively easy for two people to agree on a word's denotative meaning and so difficult for the same two people to agree on its connotative meaning? For example, consider securing agreement on the connotative meaning of *religion, democracy, wealth,* and *freedom.*

How would a dictionary entry for the connotative meaning of a word look? Can you construct a connotative dictionary entry for a word such as *gold* or *school* or *professor*? What factors or characteristics does your connotative meaning entry include?

A good catchword can obscure analysis for 50 years.
—WENDELL L. WILKIE

But where would you turn if you wanted to know what Pedro means when he says "I'm in love?" Of course, you'd turn to Pedro to discover his meaning. It is in this sense that meanings are not in words but in people. Consequently, to uncover meaning, we need to look into people and not merely into words.

An example of the confusion that can result when this relatively simple fact is not taken into consideration is provided by Ronald D. Laing, H. Phillipson, and A. Russell Lee in *Interpersonal Perception* (1966) and analyzed with insight by Paul Watzlawick in *How Real Is Real?* (1977). A couple on the second night of their honeymoon are sitting at a hotel bar. The woman strikes up a conversation with the couple next to her. The husband refuses to communicate with the couple and becomes antagonistic toward his wife and the couple. The wife then grows angry because he has created such an awkward and unpleasant situation. Each becomes increasingly disturbed, and the evening ends in a bitter conflict with each convinced of the other's lack of consideration. Eight years later, they analyze this argument. Apparently *honeymoon* had meant different things to each. To the husband it was a "golden opportunity to ignore the rest of the world and simply explore each other." He felt his wife's interaction with the other couple implied there was something lacking in him. To the wife *honeymoon* meant an opportunity to try out her new role as wife. "I had never had a conversation with another couple as a wife before," she said. "Previous to this I had always been a 'girl friend' or 'fiancee' or 'daughter' or 'sister.'"

This principle takes on special importance in intercultural communication. Consider the differences in meaning for such words as *woman* to an American and an Iranian, *religion* to a born-again Christian and an atheist, and *lunch* to a Chinese rice farmer and a Wall Street executive. Thus, even though the same word is used, its connotative meanings will vary greatly depending on the listeners' cultural definitions.

### Meanings Need Referents

Although not all communication makes reference to the real world, it makes sense only when it relates in some way to the external world. Meanings need to be linked to events and people in the real world.

Communication problems can arise if you use high-order abstractions (highly general terms) without linking them to observable, concrete referents. For example, when we talk of love, friendship, happiness, goodness, evil, and similar abstract concepts without linking them to specifics, we will fail to achieve a sharing of meaning. Telling a child to "be good" can mean different things. Abstractions need to be connected to objects, events, and behaviors in the real world: "Be good and play by yourself while daddy cooks dinner." When you have done this, you will be able to share what *you* mean by these terms and not leave the entire communication act to chance.

Consider the term "animal." What comes to mind? Very likely, a different image will come to each person. Notice that as we get more specific—from animal to domestic animal, dog, poodle, toy poodle, white toy poodle, pampered white toy poodle, the image becomes more specific. The more specific we are with our language—using "pampered

For what types of words is this principle that meaning is in people most important? Are there words for which this principle would be irrelevant?

Words, like eyeglasses, blur everything that they do not make more clear.
—JOSEPH JOURBERT

white toy poodle" instead of "animal"—the closer we will bring the listener to the meaning in our heads.

## Meanings Are Infinite in Number

At any given time, the words of language are finite in number, but the meanings are infinite. Most words, therefore, have more than one meaning. Communication problems arise when the same word is given different meanings by two people. For example, consider the possible differences in meaning between a dating couple for such words as "commitment," "fidelity," and "I love you." When in doubt about meanings, inquire rather than assume; disagreements may well evaporate when each person's meaning is identified.

## Meanings Are Communicated Only Partially

When you communicate, you describe only a small part of your meanings. Much of your meaning remains in your head. Consequently,

Can you apply the five principles of meaning (meanings are denotative and connotative, are in people, need referents, are infinite in number, and are communicated only partially) to describe the talk between lovers? How might the talk of lovers vary from one culture to another?

true understanding—a complete sharing of meaning—is probably an unattainable ideal. When we assume that we know "exactly what you mean," we violate this important principle of meaning.

## Barriers in Thinking and Communicating

There is a close connection between thinking and communicating—a theme we have emphasized throughout this book. Consequently, the barriers we identify here relate to both problems in thinking and in communication. The connection is simple: Distortions in thought lead to distortions in language; distortions in language (because we think in and with our language) further distort our thinking.

Let's look at seven possible barriers to thinking and communicating (Haney 1973; DeVito 1974; Rothwell 1982). These barriers may appear in interpersonal, small group, and public speaking.

### Polarization

*Polarization* is the tendency to look at the world in terms of opposites and to describe it in extremes—good or bad, positive or negative, healthy or sick, intelligent or stupid. It is often referred to as the fallacy of "either-or" or "black and white." Most people exist somewhere between the extremes. Yet we have a strong tendency to view only the extremes and to categorize people, objects, and events in terms of these polar opposites.

We create problems when we use the absolute form in inappropriate situations. For example, "The politician is either for us or against us." These options do *not* include all possibilities. The politician may be for us in some things and against us in other things, or may be neutral. During the Vietnam War, people were categorized as either hawks or doves. But clearly many people were neither and many were hawks on certain issues and doves on others.

CORRECTING POLARIZATION. In correcting this tendency to polarize, beware of implying (and believing) that two extreme classes include all possible classes—that an individual must be one or the other, with no alternatives. Most people, most events, most qualities exist between polar extremes. When others imply that there are only two sides or alternatives, look for the middle ground.

### Intensional Orientation

Have you ever reacted to the way something was labeled or described rather than to the actual item? Have you ever bought something because of its name rather than because of the actual object? If so, you were probably responding intensionally.

*Intensional orientation* (the *s* in *intensional* is intentional) refers to the tendency to view people, objects, and events in the way they are talked about—the way they are labeled. For example, if Sally is labeled

---

It is not only true that the language we use puts words in our mouths; it also puts notions in our heads.
—WENDELL JOHNSON

---

How would you describe the close connection between language and thought?

---

If thought corrupts language, language can also corrupt thought.
—GEORGE ORWELL

---

My doctor is wonderful. Once, in 1955, when I couldn't afford an operation, he touched up the x-rays.
—JOEY BISHOP

"uninteresting" you would, responding intensionally, evaluate her as uninteresting before listening to what she had to say. The tendency would be to see Sally through a filter imposed by the label "uninteresting." *Extensional orientation,* on the other hand, is the tendency to look first at the actual people, objects, and events and only afterwards at their labels. In this case, it would mean looking at Sally without any preconceived labels, guided by what she says and does, not by the words used to label her.

Intensional orientation occurs when you act as if the labels are more important than what they represent—as if the map is more important than the territory. An extreme form of intensional orientation in the person who, afraid of dogs, begins to sweat when shown a picture of a dog or hears people talking about dogs. This person is responding to the label (a picture or verbal description) as if it were the actual thing (a dog).

CORRECTING INTENSIONAL ORIENTATION. The way to avoid intensional orientation is to extensionalize. Give your main attention to the people, things, and events in the world as you see them and not as they are presented in words. For example, when you meet Jack and Jill, observe and interact with them. Then form your impressions. Don't respond to them as "greedy, money-grubbing landlords" because Harry

*"Now remember — if you want that new doll, look pathetic! And the magic words are 'quality time.'"*

© 1988, REPRINTED BY PERMISSION OF THE NATIONAL ENQUIRER AND BRENDA BURBANK labeled them this way. Don't respond to Carmen as "lazy and inconsiderate" because Elaine told you she was.

## Fact-Inference Confusion

In what ways do you respond intensionally? [Note that we make the assumption that most people respond intensionally at some time and in some situations.] What consequences did this intensional orientation have?

Often, when we listen or speak, we don't distinguish between statements of fact and those of inference. Yet, there are great differences between the two. We create barriers to clear thinking when we treat inferences (guesses, opinions) as if they are facts.

For example, you can say, "She is wearing a blue jacket," as well as "He is harboring an illogical hatred." Although the sentences have similar structures, they are different. You can observe the jacket and the blue color, but how do you observe "illogical hatred"? Obviously, this is not a descriptive but an inferential statement. One you make on the basis of what you observe and what you infer. Table 4.1 summarizes the differences between factual and inferential statements (cf. Haney 1973).

There is nothing wrong with making inferential statements. You must make them to talk about much that is meaningful to you. The problem arises when you act *as if* those inferential statements are factual. Consider the following anecdote (Maynard 1963): A woman went for a walk one day and met a friend whom she had not seen, heard from, or heard of in ten years. After an exchange of greetings, the woman said: "Is this your little boy?" and her friend replied, "Yes, I got married about six years ago." The woman then asked the child, "What is your name?" and the little boy replied, "Same as my father's." "Oh," said the woman, "then it must be Peter."

> It is the spirit of the age to believe that any fact, no matter how suspect, is superior to any imaginative exercise, no matter how true.
> —GORE VIDAL

How did the woman know the boy's father's name when she had no contact with her friend in the last ten years? The answer is obvious, but only after we recognize that in reading this short passage we have made an unconscious inference. Specifically, we have inferred that the woman's friend is a woman. Actually, the friend is a man named Peter.

Do you ever confuse facts with inferences? What created the confusion? What effects did the confusion have?

You may test your ability to distinguish facts from inferences by taking the accompanying fact-inference test.

**Table 4.1** *Differences Between Factual and Inferential Statements*

| Factual Statements: | Inferential Statements: |
|---|---|
| 1. may be made only after observation | 1. may be made at any time |
| 2. are limited to what has been observed through our senses | 2. go beyond what has been observed |
| 3. may be made only by the observer | 3. may be made by anyone |
| 4. may only be about the past or the present | 4. may be about any time—past, present, or future |
| 5. approach certainty | 5. involve varying degrees of probability |
| 6. are subject to verifiable standards | 6. are not subject to verifiable standards |

TEST YOURSELF:

## Can You Distinguish Facts from Inferences?

Carefully read the following report and the observations based on it. Indicate whether you think the observations are true, false, or doubtful on the basis of the information presented in the report. Write *T* if the observation is definitely true, *F* if the observation is definitely false, and *?* if the observation may be either true or false. Judge each observation in order. Do not reread the observations after you have indicated your judgment, and do not change any of your answers.

*A well-liked college teacher had just completed making up the final examinations and had turned off the lights in the office. Just then a tall, broad figure with dark glasses appeared and demanded the examination. The professor opened the drawer. Everything in the drawer was picked up and the individual ran down the corridor. The dean was notified immediately.*

_____ 1. The thief was tall, broad, and wore dark glasses.
_____ 2. The professor turned off the lights.
_____ 3. A tall figure demanded the examination.
_____ 4. The examination was picked up by someone.
_____ 5. The examination was picked up by the professor.
_____ 6. A tall, broad figure appeared after the professor
          turned off the lights in the office
_____ 7. The man who opened the drawer was the professor.
_____ 8. The professor ran down the corridor.
_____ 9. The drawer was never actually opened.
_____10. Three persons are referred to in this report.

After you answer all ten questions, form small groups of five or six and discuss the answers. Look at each statement from each member's point of view. For each statement, ask yourself "How can you be absolutely certain that the statement is true or false?"

CORRECTING FACT-INFERENCE CONFUSION. Any inferential statements should be made tentatively. Recognize that they may prove to be wrong. Inferential statements should leave open the possibility of alternatives. If, for example, you treat the statement "Our biology teacher was fired for poor teaching" as factual, you eliminate any alternatives. When making inferential statements, be psychologically prepared to be proved wrong. If you are prepared to be wrong, you will be less hurt if you are shown to be wrong.

Be especially sensitive to this distinction when you are listening. Most talk is inferential. Beware of the speaker (whether in interpersonal, group, or public speaking) who presents everything as fact. Analyze closely and you'll uncover a world of inferences.

### Bypassing

*Bypassing* is a pattern of misevaluation in which people fail to communicate their intended meanings. William Haney (1973) defines it as "the miscommunication pattern which occurs when the *sender* (speaker, writer, and so on) and the *receiver* (listener, reader, and so forth) *miss each other with their meanings.*"

Bypassing can take either of two forms. In the first, two people use different words but give them the same meaning. On the surface there is disagreement but at the level of meaning there is agreement. Consider the following dialogue:

PAT: *I want a permanent relationship. I'm not interested in one-night stands.* [meaning: I want to date you exclusively and I want you to date me exclusively].

CHRIS: *I'm not ready for that* [thinking and meaning: marriage]. *Let's keep things the way they are* [meaning: let's continue dating only each other exclusively].

This is a not-uncommon situation in which two people agree but assume, because they use different words (some of which may never be verbalized), that they disagree.

The second type of bypassing is more common. It occurs when two people use the same words but give them different meanings. On the surface it appears that the two people agree (simply because they are using the same words), but a closer look shows that the apparent agreement masks real disagreement. Consider this brief dialogue:

**How is bypassing related to the principle that meanings are in people?**

*"It states quite clearly . . . 'evening dress.'"*

CARLOS: *I don't really believe in religion* [meaning: I don't really believe in God].

BRUNO: *Neither do I* [meaning: I don't really believe in organized religions].

Here Carlos and Bruno assume they agree, but actually disagree. At some later date, the implications of these differences may well become crucial.

There are numerous other examples. Couples who say they are "in love" may mean different things: one may mean "a permanent and exclusive commitment" while the other may mean "a sexual involvement." "Come home early" may mean one thing to an anxious parent and quite another to a teenager.

The underlying assumption in bypassing is that words have intrinsic meanings. We incorrectly assume that two people using the same word mean the same thing, and two people using different words mean different things. Remember, words do not have meaning; people give words meaning.

CORRECTING BYPASSING. One way to correct this misevaluation, as Haney (1981) points out, is to look for meaning in the person, not in the words. As we pointed out earlier, different people may assign a variety of meanings to words and use different words to communicate the same meaning. Pay special attention to possible cultural differences.

It also helps to use the active listening techniques discussed in Chapter 3. Paraphrase the speaker to check on whether there is agreement or disagreement, not in the words but in the people. By reflecting back the speaker's thoughts and feelings, you will be able to see whether you understand the speaker. You will also provide the speaker with an opportunity to clarify any misunderstanding or ambiguity. Ask questions to check on your own perception of the speaker's meanings. Keep in mind that asking questions may be considered impolite or invasive in some cultures.

## Static Evaluation

*Static evaluation* is the tendency to retain evaluations without change while the reality to which they refer is constantly changing. Often a verbal statement we make about an event or person remains static—unchanging—while the event or person may change enormously. Alfred Korzybski (1933) used an interesting illustration. In a tank we have a large fish and many small fish—the natural food for the large fish. Given freedom in the tank, the large fish will eat the small fish. If we partition the tank, separating the large fish from the small fish by a clear piece of glass, the large fish will continue to attempt to eat the small fish but will fail, knocking instead into the glass partition. Eventually, the large fish will "learn" the futility of attempting to eat the small fish. If we now remove the partition, the small fish will swim all around the big fish, but the big fish will not eat them. In fact, the large fish will die of starvation while its natural food swims all around. The large fish has learned a pattern of behavior, and even though the actual territory has changed, the map remains static.

Have you ever experienced either form of bypassing? Why did it occur?

Language is a city to the building of which every human being brought a stone.
—RALPH WALDO EMERSON

The only man who behaves sensibly is my tailor; he takes my measure anew each time he sees me, whilst all the rest go on with their old measurements and expect them to fit me.
—GEORGE BERNARD SHAW

A million dollars is not what it used to be.
—HOWARD HUGHES

While we would probably all agree that everything is in a constant state of flux, do we act as if we know this? Do we act in accordance with the notion of change or just accept it intellectually? Do we realize, for example, that because we have failed at something once, we need not fail again? Our evaluations of ourselves and of others must keep pace with the rapidly changing real world; otherwise our attitudes and beliefs will be about a world that no longer exists.

CORRECTING STATIC EVALUATION. To guard against static evaluation, date your statements and especially your evaluations. Remember that Pat Smith $_{1984}$ is not Pat Smith $_{1992}$; academic abilities $_{1992}$ are not academic abilities $_{1993}$. T. S. Eliot, in *The Cocktail Party*, said, "What we know of other people is only our memory of the moments during which we knew them. And they have changed since then . . . at every meeting we are meeting a stranger."

In listening, look carefully at messages that claim that what was true still is. It may or may not be. Look for change.

## Allness

We can never know all or say all about anything. The parable of the six blind men and the elephant is an excellent example of an "allness" orientation and its problems. You may recall the John Saxe poem that tells of six blind men of Indostan who examine an elephant, an animal they had only heard about. The first blind man touched the elephant's side and concluded the elephant was like a wall. The second felt the tusk and said the elephant must be like a spear. The third held the trunk and concluded the elephant was like a snake. The fourth touched the knee and knew the elephant was like a tree. The fifth felt the ear and said the elephant was like a fan. And the sixth grabbed the tail and said that the elephant was like a rope.

Each reached his own conclusion; each argued that he was correct and that the others were wrong. Each was correct; and at the same time, wrong.

We are all in the position of the six blind men. We never see all of anything. We never experience anything fully. We see a part, then conclude what the whole is like. We have to draw conclusions on the basis of insufficient evidence (we always have insufficient evidence). We must recognize that when we make judgments based only on a part, we are making inferences that can later prove wrong.

ALLNESS AND CONFLICT. In conflict situations, negative allness statements—especially those containing *always* and *never*—are particularly troublesome. Allness statements ("You *always* criticize me in front of your friends." "You *never* do what I want." "You're *always* nagging." "You *never* want to visit my family.") encourage defensiveness.

It would be just as easy and much more constructive to say, "At Rajiv's party, you talked about my being a terrible cook. I got really embarrassed and felt hurt. If you want to criticize something, please do it when we're alone." Expressed this way, there is no attack and no encouragement of

> The opinions we hold of one another, our relations with friends and kinfolk are in no sense permanent, save in appearance, but are as eternally fluid as the sea itself.
> —MARCEL PROUST

> To be conscious that you are ignorant is a great step toward knowledge.
> —BENJAMIN DISRAELI

> Do you ever commit the fallacy of allness? Do you, for example, group all teachers together? All gay people? All politicians? All born-again Christians? All atheists?

> The map does not represent all the territory.
> —ALFRED KORZYBSKI

defensiveness. Instead, there is a clear and descriptive statement of the problem and a proposed solution that can be discussed reasonably.

CORRECTING ALLNESS. A useful device to help remember the non-allness orientation is to end each statement, verbally or mentally, with *etc.*—a reminder that there is more to learn, more to know, and more to say—that every statement is inevitably incomplete.

Some people overuse the *etc.* They use it not as a mental reminder, but as a substitute for being specific.

### Indiscrimination

*Indiscrimination* refers to the failure to distinguish between similar but different people, objects or events. It occurs when we focus on classes and fail to see that each is unique and needs to be looked at individually. Everything is unique. Everything is unlike everything else.

Our language, however, provides us with common nouns, such as *teacher, student, friend, enemy, war, politician,* and *liberal.* These lead us to focus on similarities—to group together all teachers, all students, and all politicians. At the same time, the terms divert attention away from the uniqueness of each person, each object, and each event.

This misevaluation is at the heart of stereotyping on the basis of nationality, race, religion, sex, and affectional orientation. A *stereotype* (Chapter 3) is a fixed mental picture of a group that we apply to each individual in the group without regard to his or her unique qualities.

Most stereotypes are negative and denigrate the group to which they refer. Some, however, are positive. A particularly glaring example is the popular stereotype of Asian-American students. The stereotype is that of successful, intelligent, and hardworking.

Whether the stereotypes are positive or negative, they create the same problem. They provide us with shortcuts that are often inappropriate. For instance, when you meet a particular person, your first reaction may be to pigeonhole him or her into some category—perhaps religious, national, or academic. Then you assign to this person all the qualities that are part of your stereotype. Regardless of the category you use or the specific qualities you are ready to assign, you fail to give sufficient attention to the individual's unique characteristics. Two people may both be Christian, Asian, and lesbian, for example, but each will be different from the other. Indiscrimination is a denial of another's uniqueness.

CORRECTING INDISCRIMINATION. A useful antidote to indiscrimination is the *index.* This verbal or mental subscript identifies each individual as an individual even though both may be covered by the same label. Thus, politician $_1$ is not politician $_2$, teacher $_1$ is not teacher $_2$. The index helps us to discriminate *among* without discriminating *against.*

## Barriers in Talking with Others

We can gain additional insight into language and meaning by looking at some of the barriers created in talking with others: in-group talk, self and other talk, gossip, disconfirmation, racism, and sexism.

> As for me, all I know is that I know nothing.
> —SOCRATES

> Do others commit the fallacy of indiscrimination in dealing with you? What problems does this cause? How might you prevent this from happening in the future?

> How many examples of the barriers to language and verbal interaction (polarization, intensional orientation, fact-inference confusion, bypassing, allness, static evaluation, and indiscrimination) can you find in one evening of television?

## In-Group Talk

An annoying and destructive verbal habit is the use of *in-group talk* in the presence of an out-group member—someone who is not a member of this in-group. When doctors get together and discuss medicine, there is no problem. But when they are with someone who is not a doctor, they often fail to adjust. They simply continue discussing prescriptions, symptoms, medication, and other in-group talk that could interest only another doctor.

A variant of this habit occurs when people of the same nationality get together within a larger, more heterogeneous group and use the group's language—words, sentences, or even entire conversations. In public speaking we see this when speakers use jokes or references that only certain members of the audience understand. This is not merely a question of understandability. In many instances, the foreign term serves no purpose other than to mark the in-group members as united and the out-group members as outsiders.

If, on the other hand, such foreign terms are used to add color or a multi-cultural atmosphere to the conversation, then this is not in-group talk and poses no barrier to effective communication.

*While doctors are comfortable using technical jargon in their conversations, in what ways would the doctor-patient relationship change if technical jargon was totally eliminated?*

CORRECTING IN-GROUP TALK. Instead of excluding one or more members, consider the *principle of inclusion*. Regardless of the communication situation, we need to include everyone. Even when we have to "talk shop," we can include nonmembers. We can seek a nonmember's perspective, or perhaps draw an analogy with that person's field. With inclusion, everyone seems to gain a great deal more satisfaction from the interaction.

### Self-Talk and Other-Talk

Many people focus almost totally on themselves. They talk constantly about themselves—their jobs, accomplishments, families, love lives, problems, successes, and sometimes even failures. Rarely do they ask how you are, what you think (except perhaps about them), or what your plans are. A perfect example of this type of person is Blanche Devereau on *Golden Girls*.

There are other people who go to the opposite extreme and never talk about themselves. These are the underdisclosers, discussed in Chapter 3, who want to learn everything about you but are not willing to share themselves. They do not want to reveal anything that might make them vulnerable. As a result, we leave the interaction with the feeling that they did not like or trust us.

CORRECTING SELF-TALK AND OTHER-TALK. All our interactions need to be characterized by the *principle of balance*—some self-talk and some other-talk. Communication is a two-way process. Each person needs to function as source and as receiver and each needs a chance to function as subject. Balanced communication interactions are more satisfying and result in a great deal more interesting interactions (Hecht 1978a, 1978b). We all get bored with too much talk about the other person—and others get bored with too much about us. The principle of balance is a sorely needed guide.

### Gossip

According to the *Random House Dictionary*, gossip is "idle talk or rumor, esp. about the personal or private affairs of others." A gossiper, then, is a person who engages in this idle talk. There can be no doubt that we spend a great deal of time gossiping.

Gossip is an inevitable part of our daily interactions. Not gossiping would eliminate one of the most frequent and enjoyable forms of communication. Ogden Nash put it this way: "There are two kinds of people who blow through life like a breeze/And one kind is gossipers, and the other kind is gossipees."

SOME PROBLEMS OF GOSSIP. Nevertheless, gossip does create serious problems when it is not managed correctly or fairly. When you tell someone that you fear you are falling out of love with your fiancé, you expect the conversation to be held in confidence. If you wanted it relayed to a third party or to your fiancé, you probably would have done that yourself. When such a conversation is relayed without your knowledge or approval, you feel your confidence has been betrayed.

What is the single most popular topic for gossip among your peer group? What accounts for its popularity?

Keep some opinions to yourself. Say what you please to others, but never repeat what you hear said of them to themselves.
—WILLIAM HAZLITT

The following questions—or ones very similar—seem to cause difficulty for many people. What, if anything, should you do in each situation?
a. You see your best friend's spouse in a romantic liaison with another person.
b. You see two students cheating on an examination.
c. Your friend dresses so badly (though not for any financial reason) that everyone else laughs and pokes fun.

Quite often the person who repeats such remarks is seeking, perhaps subconsciously, to create friction. And this motivation is usually recognized, sooner or later, by all parties involved. To claim—as some do—that they didn't realize the information was confidential is absurd. It is usually obvious from the context what should and should not be held in confidence. You have little trouble in deciding when something is said in confidence, and it does not seem unreasonable to expect others to be equally discerning.

ETHICAL IMPLICATIONS. In some instances gossip is unethical. Sissela Bok, in *Secrets* (1983), identifies three kinds of gossip that she considers unethical. First, it is unethical to reveal information that you have promised to keep secret. When that is impossible (Bok offers the example of the teenager who confides a suicide plan), the information should be revealed only to those who must know it, not to the world at large.

Second, gossip is unethical when you know it to be false and nevertheless pass it on. Third, gossip is unethical when it is invasive—when it invades someone's privacy. More specifically, invasive gossip concerns matters that are properly considered private and can hurt the individual involved.

These three conditions provide excellent starting points for asking ourselves, "Is this talk about another person ethical?"

DEALING WITH GOSSIP. The *principle of confidentiality* presents a good guideline for dealing with gossip: Keep confidential all private conversations about third parties. Messages that begin with "He said. . . ." or "She thinks that you. . . ." should be automatically suspect as potential violators of the principle of confidentiality. Remember too the *principle of irreversibility*—once you say something, you cannot uncommunicate it.

## Disconfirmation

Pat arrives home late one night. Chris is angry and complains. Consider some responses Pat might make:

1. Stop screaming. I'm not interested in your babbling. I'll do what I want, when I want. I'm going to bed.
2. What are you so angry about? Didn't you get in three hours late last Thursday when you went to that office party? So, knock it off.
3. You have a right to be angry. I should have called when I was going to be late but I got involved in an argument at work and I couldn't leave until it was resolved.

No more fiendish punishment could be devised, even were such a thing physically possible, than that one should be turned loose in society and remain absolutely unnoticed by all the members thereof.
—WILLIAM JAMES

In (1) Pat dismisses Chris's anger and even indicates a dismissal of Chris as a person. In (2) Pat rejects the validity of Chris's reasons for being angry but does not dismiss Chris's feelings of anger or Chris as a person. In (3) Pat acknowledges Chris's anger and the reasons for it. In addition Pat provides an explanation that shows that Chris's feelings and Chris as a person are important and deserve to know what happened. The first response is an example of disconfirmation, the second of rejection, and the third of confirmation.

Can you recall a specific instance in which you were disconfirmed or in which you witnessed the disconfirmation of others? What were the effects of such disconfirmation? How might it have been avoided?

*Disconfirmation* is a communication pattern in which we ignore someone's presence as well as that person's communications. It is a clear violation of the quality of equality (see Chapter 6). We say, in effect, that this person and his or her contributions are so unimportant or insignificant that there is no reason to concern ourselves with them.

In *rejection* you disagree with the person, indicating your unwillingness to accept something the other person says or does. In disconfirming someone, however, you claim that what this person says or does simply does not count.

> The compulsive preoccupation with being seen, or simply with being visible suggests that we must be dealing with underlying fantasies of not being seen, of being invisible.
> —R. D. LAING

CONFIRMATION. *Confirmation* is the opposite communication pattern. In confirmation we not only acknowledge the presence of the other person but also our acceptance of this person, of this person's definition of self, and of our relationship as defined or viewed by this person.

DIFFERENCES BETWEEN DISCONFIRMATION AND CONFIRMATION. Disconfirmation and confirmation may be communicated in a wide variety of ways. Table 4.2 shows just a few. As you review this table, try to imagine a specific illustration for each (Pearson 1989; Galvin and Brommel 1991).

**Table 4.2** *Confirmation and Disconfirmation*

| Confirmation | Disconfirmation |
|---|---|
| 1. Acknowledge the presence of the other verbally or nonverbally; acknowledge the contributions of the other by either supporting or taking issue with them. | 1. Ignore the presence of the other and ignore what the other says; appear indifferent to the person and to what he or she says. |
| 2. Make nonverbal contact by maintaining direct eye contact, touching, hugging, kissing, and otherwise demonstrating acknowledgment of the other. | 2. Make no nonverbal contact; for example, avoid direct eye contact, avoid touching the other person, avoid showing acknowledgment of the other. |
| 3. Engage in dialogue—communication in which both persons are speakers and listeners, both are involved, and both are concerned with and have respect for each other. | 3. Engage in monologue—communication in which in which one person speaks and one person listens, and there is no real interaction, and no real concern or respect for the other. |
| 4. Reflect back the other person's feelings to demonstrate your understanding of them. | 4. Express one's own feelings; ignore feelings of the other; or give abstract intellectualized responses. |
| 5. Ask questions of the other concerning both thoughts and feelings. | 5. Make statements about oneself; ignore any lack of clarity in the other's remarks. |
| 6. Acknowledge the other's requests; answer the other's questions; return phone calls; and answer letters. | 6. Ignore the other's requests; fail to answer questions, return phone calls, and answer letters. |
| 7. Encourage the other to express thoughts and feelings. | 7. Interrupt or otherwise make it difficult for the other to express himself or herself. |
| 8. Respond directly and exclusively to what the other says. | 8. Respond tangentially by acknowledging the other's comment but then shift the focus of the message in another direction. |

## Racism

According to Andrea Rich (1974), "any language that, through a conscious or unconscious attempt by the user, places a particular racial or ethnic group in an inferior position is racist." Racist language expresses racist attitudes. It also contributes to the development of racist attitudes in those who use or hear the language.

Racist terms are used by members of one culture to disparage members of other cultures—their customs or accomplishments. Racist language emphasizes differences rather than similarities and separates rather than unites members of different cultures. Generally, racist language is used by the dominant group to establish and maintain power over other groups. The social consequences of racist language in terms of employment, education, housing opportunities, and general community acceptance are well known.

Many people feel that it is permissible for members of a culture to refer to themselves with the same racist terms. That is, gay men may use the negative terms referring to gay men, blacks may use the negative terms referring to blacks, and so on. The reasoning seems to be that groups should be able to laugh at themselves. One possible problem, though, is that these terms may reinforce the negative stereotypes that society has already assigned this group. By using these terms, members may come to accept these labels with their negative connotations and thus contribute to their own stereotyping.

It is interesting to note that terms denoting some of the major art movements, for example, *impressionism* and *cubism,* were originally applied negatively. The terms, after use by the artists, eventually became positive. A parallel can be seen in use of the word *queer* by some of the more militant lesbian and gay organizations. Their purpose is to make it lose its negative connotation.

It has often been pointed out (Davis, in DeVito 1973; Bosmajian 1974) that there are aspects of language that may be inherently racist. For example, one examination of English found 134 synonyms for *white*. Of these 44 had positive connotations (such as, "clean," "chaste," and "unblemished") and only 10 had negative connotations ("whitewash," "pale"). The remaining were relatively neutral. Of the 120 synonyms for *black* 60 had unfavorable connotations ("unclean," "foreboding," and "deadly") and none had positive connotations.

Consider the following phrases:

- the Korean doctor
- the Chicano prodigy
- the black mathematician
- the white nurse

In some cases, of course, the racial identifier may be relevant as in, say, "The Korean doctor argued for hours with the French [doctors] while the others tried to secure a compromise." Here the aim might be to identify the nationality of the doctor or the specific doctor (as you would if you forgot her or his name).

What examples of racist language do you hear most often? How do most of your peers respond to racist language?

The language of racism is not merely reflective of racist thought and attitude in the culture; its use also produces racist thought in those exposed to it and helps to shape certain forms of racist behavior.
—ANDREA L. RICH

For a black writer in this country to be born into the English language is to realize that the assumptions on which the language operates are his enemy. . . . I was forced to reconsider similes: as black as sin, as black as night, blackhearted.
—JAMES BALDWIN

In what cases do you think it would be appropriate to identify the race of someone you're talking about?

Often, however, such identifiers are used to emphasize that the combination of race and occupation (or talent or accomplishment) is rare and unexpected—that the racial member is an exception. It also implies that racial factors are important in the context. As noted, there are times when this may be true but most often race would be irrelevant.

## Sexism

Consider some of the language used to refer to women. A woman loses her last name when she marries and in certain instances loses her first name as well. She changes from "Ann Smith" to "Mrs. John Jones."

We hold these truths to be self-evident, that all men and women are created equal.
—ELIZABETH CADY STANTON

We say that a woman "marries into" a man's family and that a family "dies out" if there are no male children. We do not speak of a man marrying into a woman's family (unless the family is extremely prestigious, wealthy, or members of royalty), and a family can still "die out" even if there are ten female children. In the traditional marriage ceremony, we hear "I now pronounce you man and wife," not "man and woman" or "husband and wife." The man retains his status as man, but the woman changes hers from woman to wife. Barrie Thorne, Cheris Kramarae, and Nancy Henley, in their *Language, Gender and Society* (1983), summarize this line of research by noting that "women tend to be defined by their relation to men. . . . The available and 'approved' titles, pronouns, lexicons, and labels," they note, "reflect the fact that women (as well as other subordinates) have been named by others."

Julia Stanley researched terms indicating sexual promiscuity and found 220 terms referring to a sexually promiscuous woman but only 22 for a sexually promiscuous man (Thorne, Kramarae, and Henley 1983). Surely, there are as many promiscuous men as promiscuous women, yet our language fails to reflect this. If we assume that the number of terms indicates the importance of a concept to a culture, then we might argue that promiscuity among women *is* significant (that is, it is "abnormal" or "beyond the norm") and something to take special notice of, but that promiscuity among men *is not* significant (that is, it is "normal") and therefore no special notice need be taken. Since a volume could be written on the implications and consequences of such a double standard, you can draw your own conclusions.

Look through one of your textbooks. Can you find examples of sexist language? Can you find examples of sexist language in your own speech?

Judy Pearson (1985) has noted that another important instance of sexist language may be seen in the language of the deaf or Ameslan (American Sign Language). Pearson notes that masculine references are used to compliment women, as in "she thinks like a man" and "she acts like a man." Similarly, the sign for *secretary* is composed of the signs for *girl* and *writes* ("a girl who writes"), while the sign for *president* is composed of the signs for *man* and a *type of salute* to form "a respected man."

The National Council of Teachers of English (NCTE) has proposed guidelines for nonsexist (gender-free, gender-neutral, or sex-fair) language. These concern the use of generic "man," the use of generic "he" and "his," and sex role stereotyping (Penfield 1987).

GENERIC MAN. The word *man* refers most clearly to an adult male. To use the term to refer to both men and women emphasizes "maleness" at the expense of "femaleness." Similarly, the terms *mankind* or the *common man* or even *cavemen* imply a primary focus on adult males. Gender-neutral terms can easily be substituted; for *mankind*, say *humanity, people,* or *human beings*; for *the common man* say *the average person* or *ordinary people*; and instead of *cavemen*, say *prehistoric people* or *cave dwellers*.

Similarly, such terms as *policeman, fireman, salesman, chairman, mailman,* and others that presume maleness as the norm and femaleness as a deviation are clear and common examples of sexist language. Consider using nonsexist alternatives and make these alternatives (for example, *police officer* and *firefighter*) a part of your active vocabulary.

Can you think of other examples of "generic man" terms? What might be appropriate substitutes?

GENERIC HE AND HIS. Use of the masculine pronoun to refer to any individual regardless of sex further illustrates the extent of linguistic sexism. There seems to be no legitimate reason why the feminine pronoun could not alternate with the masculine pronoun in referring to hypothetical individuals, or why *he and she* or *her and him* could not be used instead of just *he* or *him*.

Alternatively, we can restructure sentences to eliminate any reference to gender. Here are a few examples from the NCTE Guidelines (Penfield 1987):

Some quotations in this text use *man* and *he* generically. How would you reword them?

| Sexist | Gender-Free |
| --- | --- |
| The average student is worried about his grades. | The average student is worried about grades. |
| Ask the student to hand in his work as soon as he is finished. | Ask students to hand in their work as soon as they are finished. |
| When a teacher asks his students for an evaluation, he is putting himself on the spot. | When you ask your students for an evaluation, you are putting yourself on the spot. |

SEX ROLE STEREOTYPING. The words we use often reflect a sex role bias—the assumption that certain roles or professions belong to men and others to women. To eliminate sex role stereotyping, avoid, for example, making the hypothetical elementary school teacher female and the college professor male; to doctors as male and nurses as female. Avoid noting the sex of a professional such as "female doctor" or "male nurse." When you are referring to a specific doctor or nurse, the person's sex will become clear when you use the appropriate pronoun: *Dr. Smith wrote the prescription for her new patient* or *The nurse recorded the patient's temperature himself.*

Do you hold any sex role stereotypes? How did you develop these stereotypes?

## Heterosexism

In what way is heterosexism a form of disconfirmation? Is the same true of racism and sexism?

The first need of a free people is to be able to define their own terms and have those terms recognized by their oppressors.
—STOKLEY CARMICHAEL

What are the most common examples of heterosexism that you observe? What do you consider an appropriate response to heterosexist language?

A close relative of sexism is heterosexism—a relatively new addition to our list of linguistic prejudices. As the term implies, heterosexism refers to language used to disparage gay men and lesbians. As with racist language, we see heterosexism in the derogatory terms used for lesbians and gay men. As with racist language, we hear these terms on the street. Unlike racist language, however, we also hear these terms in the media. The media's use of such terms is a clear example of the institutionalization of prejudice against a minority group.

As with sexism, however, we also see heterosexism in more subtle forms of language usage. For example, when we qualify a profession—as in "gay athlete" or "lesbian doctor" we are in effect stating that athletes and doctors are not normally gay or lesbian. Further, we are highlighting the affectional orientation of the athlete and the doctor in a context where it may have no relevance. This practice is the same as qualifying by race or gender.

Still another instance of heterosexism—perhaps the most difficult to deal with—is the presumption of heterosexuality. Usually, people assume the person they are talking to or about is heterosexual. They are usually correct since the majority of the population is heterosexual. At the same time, the presumption denies the lesbian and gay male their real identity. The practice is very similar to the presumption of whiteness and maleness that we have made significant inroads in eliminating.

# FEEDBACK

In this chapter we considered verbal messages. We looked at meaning and its implications for communication, the barriers in thinking and communicating, and the barriers in talking with other people.

**1. Meaning** is central to the process of communication. (1) Meanings may be denotative or connotative. (2) Meanings are in people. (3) Words make sense when they are anchored in some way to referents in the real world. (4) Disagreements frequently arise when we forget that the same word may have multiple meanings. (5) Words communicate only a small part of a person's total meaning.

**2. Polarization** occurs when we divide reality into two unrealistic extremes—such as black and white, good and bad.

**3. Intensional** orientation occurs when we respond to the way something is talked about or labeled rather than to the reality. **Extensional orientation** is the tendency to respond to things as they are, not how they are labeled or talked about.

**4. Fact-inference confusion** occurs when we treat inferences as if they were facts.

**5. Bypassing** occurs when speaker and listener miss each other with their meanings. It may occur when different words are given the same meaning or when the same word is given different meanings.

**6. Static evaluation** occurs when we ignore change and assume that reality is static.

**7. Allness** refers to the tendency to assume that one knows all there is to know, or that what has been said is all there is to say.

**8. Indiscrimination** occurs when we group unlike things together and assume that because they have the same label, they are all alike.

**9. In-group talk** occurs when members of a particular group discuss their concerns or use their group's language in the presence of outsiders.

**10. Self-talk and other-talk,** when extreme, create communication problems by distorting the normal give-and-take.

**11. Gossip,** although inevitable, creates problems when it betrays a confidence, is known to be false, or is used to hurt another person.

**12. Disconfirmation** refers to the process of ignoring the presence and the communications of others. **Confirmation** refers to accepting, supporting, and acknowledging the importance of the other person.

**13. Racist, sexist, and heterosexist language** puts down and negatively evaluates various cultural groups.

The study of meaning and the barriers in thinking, communicating, and in talking with others have important implications for developing the skills of effective communication. Check your ability to apply these skills. Use a rating scale such as: (1) = almost always, (2) = often, (3) = sometimes, (4) = rarely, (5) = hardly ever.

_____ 1. I take special care to **make spoken messages clear and unambiguous.**

_____ 2. **I ask questions** whenever meaning is in doubt.

_____ 3. I connect my words and meanings to the real world, to their **referents.**

_____ 4. I try to understand not only the objective, **denotative meanings** but also the subjective, **connotative meanings.**

_____ 5. I recognize **snarl and purr words** as describing the speaker's feelings and not objective reality.

_____ 6. I avoid **polarization** by using "middle ground" terms and qualifiers in describing the world and especially people.

_____ 7. I avoid **responding (intensionally)** to labels as if they are objects; instead, I respond extensionally and look first at the reality and only then at the words.

_____ 8. I **distinguish facts from inferences** and respond to inferences with tentativeness.

_____ 9. I avoid **bypassing** by not assuming that different words must have different meanings and that the same word must have the same meaning when used by different people.

_____ 10. I mentally date my statements and thus avoid **static evaluation.**

_____ 11. I **end my statements with an implicit** *etc.* in recognition that there is always more to be known or said.

_____ 12. I avoid using **negative allness statements** (particularly those using *always* and *never*) in conflict situations.

_____ 13. I avoid **indiscrimination** by treating each person and situation as unique.

_____ 14. I avoid **in-group talk** in the presence of nonmembers and instead seek to include all persons in the interaction (both verbally and nonverbally).

_____ 15. I avoid **gossip** when it betrays a confidence, is known to be false, or may hurt another person.

_____ 16. I avoid **disconfirmation** and instead use responses that confirm the other person.

_____ 17. I avoid **racist, sexist,** and **heterosexist language** and, in general, language that puts down other groups.

# SKILL DEVELOPMENT EXPERIENCES

## 4.1 SELF-SERVING LANGUAGE

The way we phrase something often influences the way it is perceived. This is especially true when talking about people. We do not talk about ourselves in the same way that we talk about the people we are with or about third parties.

Recognizing this simple language habit, British philosopher and mathematician, Bertrand Russell proposed a conjugation of "irregular" verbs. One example he used was:

I am firm.

You are obstinate.

He is a pig-headed fool.

The *New Statesman* and *The Nation* picked up on this and offered prizes for contributions in the style of these irregular verbs. One of the best was:

I am sparkling.

You are unusually talkative.

He is drunk.

Here are ten sentences phrased in the first person. Following Russell's lead, "conjugate" these irregular verbs.

1. I speak my mind.
2. I believe in what I say.
3. I take an occasional drink.
4. I smoke.
5. I like to talk with people about people.
6. I am frugal.
7. I am concerned with what other people do.
8. I have been known to get upset at times.
9. I am concerned with my appearance.
10. I will put off certain things for a few days.

## 4.2 CONFIRMATION, REJECTION, AND DISCONFIRMATION

Classify the following responses as confirmation, rejection, or disconfirmation:

*Enrique receives this semester's grades in the mail; they are a lot better than previous semesters' grades but are still not great. After opening the letter, Enrique says: "I really tried hard to get my grades up this semester." Enrique's parents respond:*

_____ Going out every night hardly seems like trying very hard.

_____ What should we have for dinner?

_____ Keep up the good work.

_____ I can't believe you've really tried your best; how can you study with the stereo blasting in your ears.

_____ I'm sure you've tried real hard.

_____ That's great.

_____ What a rotten day I had at the office.

_____ I can remember when I was in school; got all B's without ever opening a book.

*Pat, who has been out of work for the past several weeks, says: "I feel like such a failure; I just can't seem to find a job. I've been pounding the pavement for the last five weeks and still nothing." Pat's friend responds:*

_____ I know you've been trying real hard.

_____ You really should get more training so you'd be able to sell yourself more effectively.

_____ I told you a hundred times; you need that college degree.

___ I've got to go to the dentist on Friday. Boy, do I hate that.

___ The employment picture is real bleak this time of the year but your qualifications are really impressive. Something will come up soon.

___ You are not a failure. You just can't find a job.

___ What do you need a job for? Stay home and keep house. After all, Chris makes more than enough money to live in style.

___ What's five weeks?

___ Well, you'll just have to try harder.

For each of the following situations, write an example or provide an illustration of confirmatory, rejecting, and disconfirmatory responses.

SITUATION 1. Pat: *"I haven't had a date in the last four months. I'm getting really depressed over this." A friend responds:*

Confirmation:

Rejection:

Disconfirmation:

SITUATION 2. *Pat and Chris have just had another fight. Pat is telling a friend about what has been going on. "We just can't seem to get along anymore. Everyday is a hassle. Everyday, there's another conflict, another battle. I feel like walking away from the whole mess." The friend responds:*

Confirmation:

Rejection:

Disconfirmation:

## 4.3. PRACTICING INCLUSIVE LANGUAGE

"Inclusive language" includes all people rather than restricting reference to one particular group, for example, to men or to women only. The objectives of this brief exercise are (1) to sensitize you to some of the ways language is used to exclude others and (2) to provide some practice in rephrasing our thoughts into inclusive language. The examples that follow are all drawn from sexist language—language that discriminates against women.

Each of the following terms—although technically used to refer to all people, actually refer to only one sex while excluding the other. What alternatives can you offer for each of these terms? What advantages/disadvantages do the alternatives have to the terms given here.

| | |
|---|---|
| man | mankind |
| countryman | manmade |
| the common man | cave man |
| manpower | repairman |
| doorman | policeman |
| fireman | stewardess |
| waitress | salesman |
| mailman | actress |

Rewrite each of the following sentences—which purposely recall popular stereotypes—into more inclusive language that does not limit the referent to one sex and eliminates these limiting and discriminating stereotypes. In doing so, however, be sure to retain the intended meaning. What advantages or disadvantages do you see in the rewritten versions?

1. You really should get a second doctor's opinion. Just see what he says.
2. Johnny went to school today and met his kindergarten teacher. I wonder who she is.
3. Everyone needs to examine his own conscience.
4. No one can tell what his ultimate fortune will be.
5. The effective communicator is a selective self-discloser; he discloses to some people about some things some of the time.
6. I wonder who the new chairman will be.
7. The effective waitress knows when her customers need her.
8. Advertisers don't care what the intellectual thinks; they want to know what the man-in-the-street thinks.
9. What do you think the ideal communicator should be like? How should he talk? How should he gesture?
10. The history of man is largely one of technology replacing his manual labor.

# Nonverbal Messages

## Goals

*After completing this chapter, you should be able to*

1. *define the six ways in which verbal and nonverbal messages interact*
2. *define and provide examples of the five kinds of body movements*
3. *describe the types of information communicated by the face and the eyes*
4. *explain the four spatial distances and give examples of the kinds of communication that take place at each distance*
5. *define* territoriality *and* marker
6. *explain artifactual communication*
7. *explain the major meanings communicated by touch*
8. *define* paralanguage *and its role in making judgments about people, about conversational turns, and about believability*
9. *explain* cultural *and* psychological time

What one question about non-verbal communication would you most like to have answered in the following pages?

*How do you communicate without words?* ■ *Can you read a person's thoughts and feelings from the way the person stands, gestures, or speaks?* ■ *What meanings can you communicate with facial expressions?* ■ *With your eyes?* ■ *How does your personal space—your home furnishings and arrangement of your office, for example—communicate?* ■ *How do you know who to touch and how to touch them?* ■ *What kind of meanings do you communicate through touch?* ■ *Do men and women communicate nonverbally in the same way?* ■ *Can you tell if someone is lying? If so, how?* ■ *Do you judge others on the basis of their voices?* ■ *Do others judge you on your voice?* ■ *How accurate are these judgments?*

These and many similar questions focus on nonverbal communication—communication without words. In this chapter we look at the way verbal and nonverbal messages interact and the forms nonverbal messages may take: body, facial, eye, space, touch, vocal, and time communication.

Besides being the first form of communication in the history of the species and in the life span of the individual, nonverbal behavior has primacy in the opening minutes of interpersonal and mediated communication events. Before people even open their mouths, their nonverbal behaviors are supplying a wealth of information to onlookers.
—JUDEE BURGOON, DAVID BULLER, AND W. GILL WOODALL

## Thinking Critically About Nonverbal Communication

Before beginning this study, begin to think critically about nonverbal communication.

■ Analyze your own nonverbal communication patterns. If you are to use this material in any meaningful way, for example, to change some of your behaviors, then self-analysis is essential.

■ Observe. Observe. Observe. Observe the behaviors of those around you as well as your own. See in everyday behavior what you read about here and discuss in class.

■ Resist the temptation to draw conclusions from nonverbal behaviors. Instead, develop hypotheses (educated guesses) about what is going on and test the likelihood of their being correct on the basis of other evidence.

■ Connect and relate. Although the areas of nonverbal communication are presented separately in textbooks, in actual communication situations, they all work together.

Have you or anyone you know ever incorrectly judged the meaning of nonverbal movements? What contributed to the error in judgment?

## Nonverbal and Verbal Communication

Nonverbal communication interacts with verbal communication. We don't speak without facial expression, rather our verbal and nonverbal message system works together. We can identify six ways in which nonverbal and verbal messages interact (Knapp 1978; Ekman 1965).

TO ACCENT. We use nonverbal signals to highlight or emphasize some part of the verbal message. For example, we might smile to emphasize a word or phrase or bang our fist on a desk to stress a conclusion.

To COMPLEMENT. We also use nonverbal signals to reinforce our verbal message, as by laughing when telling a funny story or frowning when describing someone's deceit.

To CONTRADICT. We may contradict our verbal messages with nonverbal signals. For instance, we might cross our fingers or wink to show we are lying. Often, of course, we see nonverbal messages contradicting verbal messages unintentionally. We see this in the group member who professes commitment to the group but who always arrives late and leaves early. Or we see it in the public speaker who speaks of enthusiasm and dedication but does so without facial expression and vocal variation.

To REGULATE. Nonverbal movements may signal our desire to control the flow of verbal messages. Pursing our lips, leaning forward, or making hand movements to show that we want to say something are clear examples of the regulating function. We might also put up our hand or vocalize pauses (such as, "um") to show that we have not finished speaking.

To REPEAT. We can repeat or restate the meaning of the verbal message. We may, for example, follow our verbal "Is that all right?" with an "Okay?" sign made with our fingers. Or, we could motion with our head or hand to repeat our verbal "Let's go."

To SUBSTITUTE. Nonverbal communication may also take the place of verbal messages. We can, for example, say "okay" with our hand without any verbalization. We can nod our head to indicate "yes" or shake our head to indicate "no."

## Body Movements

Table 5.1 summarizes some of the ways in which we communicate with our bodies (Ekman and Friesen 1969). Examine this table and try to identify other meanings that these types of movements may communicate.

In reviewing this table also note that the meanings that you might assign to any given hand movement will not be the same as those a member of another culture would assign. Although some meanings seem universal, most vary widely from one culture to another (Axtell 1990). For example, in America you would wave hello or goodbye with your whole hand moving from side to side. In much of Europe this gesture would mean "no." Instead, you would wave hello or good-bye with the palm of your hand exposed and with your fingers going up and down. In Greece, however, this would be considered insulting to the person to whom you are waving.

## Facial Movements

Facial messages communicate types of emotion as well as selected qualities or intensities of emotion. Facial messages may communicate at least the following emotions: happiness, surprise, fear, anger, sadness, and disgust/contempt (Ekman, Friesen, and Ellsworth 1972). Nonverbal researcher Dale Leathers (1986) proposes that facial movements may also communicate bewilderment and determination.

> Good actors are good because of the things they can tell us without talking. When they are talking, they are the servants of the dramatist. It is what they can show the audience when they are not talking that reveals the fine actor.
> —CEDRIC HARDWICKE

> As the tongue speaketh to the ear, so the hand speaketh to the eye.
> —FRANCIS BACON

> Face—the mirror of the mind.
> —ST. JEROME

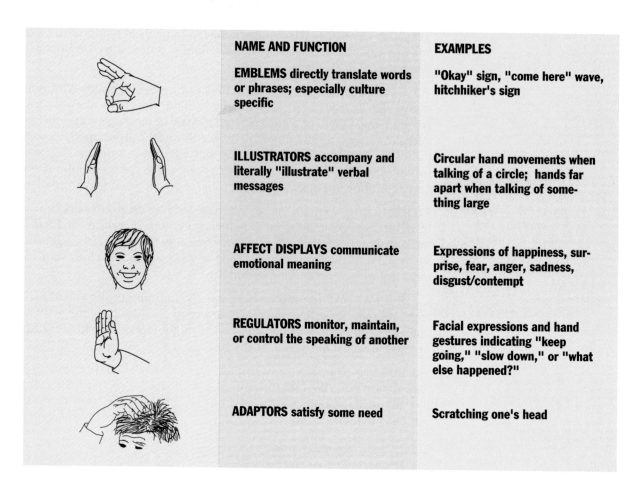

| | NAME AND FUNCTION | EXAMPLES |
|---|---|---|
| | **EMBLEMS** directly translate words or phrases; especially culture specific | "Okay" sign, "come here" wave, hitchhiker's sign |
| | **ILLUSTRATORS** accompany and literally "illustrate" verbal messages | Circular hand movements when talking of a circle; hands far apart when talking of something large |
| | **AFFECT DISPLAYS** communicate emotional meaning | Expressions of happiness, surprise, fear, anger, sadness, disgust/contempt |
| | **REGULATORS** monitor, maintain, or control the speaking of another | Facial expressions and hand gestures indicating "keep going," "slow down," or "what else happened?" |
| | **ADAPTORS** satisfy some need | Scratching one's head |

**Table 5.1**
*The Five Body Movements*

Research shows that women smile more than men when making negative comments or expressing negative feelings. What implications does this have for male-female communication? What implications might this have for child rearing? For teaching?

Without wearing any mask we are conscious of, we have a special face for each friend.
—OLIVER WENDELL HOLMES

The six emotions identified by Ekman and his colleagues are pure, single emotions. Other emotional states and other facial displays are combinations of these various pure emotions. Researchers have identified about 33 of these emotion combinations which we can recognize consistently.

You communicate these emotions with different parts of your face. Thus, you may experience both fear and disgust at the same time. Your eyes and eyelids may signal fear, while movements of your nose, cheek, and mouth area may signal disgust.

Do all people throughout the world communicate their emotions facially in the same way or do they each have their own unique style? That is, are these expressions universal or are they relative to the culture? How would you answer this question? Some researchers investigated children who were blind from birth and found that they communicated their emotions facially in the same way that sighted children did. The researchers thus concluded that these expressions are universal; they do not vary from one culture to another.

There are, however, cultural differences in the likelihood that some emotions will be expressed facially. For example, at the sight of unpleasant pictures, members of some cultures (American and European) will facially express disgust. Members of other cultures (Japanese, for example) will avoid facially expressing disgust (Ekman 1975).

## Eye Movements

From Ben Jonson's poetic observation "Drink to me only with thine eyes, and I will pledge with mine" to the scientific observations of contemporary researchers (Hess 1975; Marshall 1983), the eyes are regarded as the most important nonverbal message system.

The messages communicated by the eyes vary depending on the duration, direction, and quality of the eye behavior. For example, in every culture there are rather strict, though unstated, rules for the proper duration for eye contact. In our culture, the average length of gaze is 2.95 seconds. The average length of mutual gaze (two persons gazing at each other) is 1.18 seconds (Argyle and Ingham 1972; Argyle 1988). When eye contact falls short of this amount, you may think the person is uninterested, shy, or preoccupied. When the appropriate amount of time is exceeded, you might perceive the person as showing unusually high interest.

Although Americans consider direct eye contact an expression of honesty and forthrightness, the Japanese often view this as a lack of respect. The Japanese will glance at the other person's face rarely and then only for very short periods (Axtell 1990a).

The direction of the eye also communicates. According to our culture, you glance alternatively at the other person's face, then away, then again at the face, and so on. The rule for the public speaker is to scan the entire audience; not focusing for too long or ignoring any one area of the audience. When you break these directional rules, you communicate different meanings—abnormally high or low interest, self-consciousness, nervousness over the interaction, and so on. The quality—how wide or how narrow your eyes get during interaction—also communicates meaning, especially interest level and such emotions as surprise, fear, and disgust.

> **What nonverbal cues do you find generally reliable in showing that someone likes you? In showing that someone dislikes you?**

*What do the facial expressions in this photo communicate? On the basis of the expressions and other nonverbal cues, what might you assume is going on among the people?*

## The Functions of Eye Movements

With eye movements you can communicate a variety of messages. You can *seek feedback* with your eyes. In talking with someone, we look at her or him intently, as if to say, "Well, what do you think?" As you might predict, listeners gaze at speakers more than speakers gaze at listeners. In public speaking, we might scan hundreds of people to secure this feedback.

Women make eye contact more and maintain it longer (both in speaking and in listening) than do men. This holds true whether the woman is interacting with other women or with men. This difference in eye behavior may result from women's tendency to display their emotions more than men.

A second message you can communicate with your eyes is *to inform the other person that the channel of communication is open* and that he or she should now speak. We see this in the college classroom, when the instructor asks a question and then locks eyes with a student. Without saying anything, the instructor expects that student to answer the question.

Eye movements might *signal the nature of a relationship*, whether positive (an attentive glance) or negative (eye avoidance). You can also signal your power through "visual dominance behavior" (Exline, Ellyson, and Long 1975). The average speaker, for example, maintains a high level of eye contact while listening and a lower level while speaking. When people want to signal dominance, they may reverse this pattern—maintaining a high level of eye contact while talking but a much lower level while listening.

By making eye contact you psychologically *lessen the physical distance between yourself and another person.* When you catch someone's eye at a party, for example, you become psychologically close even though far apart.

> An eye can threaten like a loaded and leveled gun, or it can insult like hissing or kicking; or, in its altered mood, by beams of kindness, it can make the heart dance for joy.
> —RALPH WALDO EMERSON

### Eye Avoidance Functions

The eyes are "great intruders," observed sociologist Erving Goffman in *Interaction Ritual* (1967). When you avoid eye contact or avert your glance, you help others to maintain their privacy. You might do this when you see a couple arguing in public. You turn our eyes away (though your eyes may be wide open) as if to say, "I don't mean to intrude; I respect your privacy." Goffman refers to this behavior as *civil inattention*.

Eye avoidance can also signal lack of interest—in a person, a conversation, or some visual stimulus. At times, you might hide your eyes to block off unpleasant stimuli or close your eyes to block out visual stimuli and thus heighten other senses. For example, you might listen to music with your eyes closed. Lovers often close their eyes while kissing, and many prefer to make love in a dark or dimly lit room.

> Keep your eyes wide open before marriage, and half-shut afterwards.
> —BENJAMIN FRANKLIN

### Pupil Dilation

In the fifteenth and sixteenth centuries in Italy, women put drops of belladonna (which literally means "beautiful woman") into their eyes to dilate the pupils so they would look more attractive. Contemporary research supports the logic of these women; people judge dilated pupils as more attractive (Hess 1975).

Your pupils enlarge when you are interested in something or emotionally aroused. Perhaps you judge dilated pupils as more attractive because you judge an individual's dilated pupils to indicate interest in you. More generally, Ekhard Hess (1985) has claimed that pupils dilate in response to positively evaluated attitudes and objects, and constrict in response to negatively evaluated attitudes and objects.

## Space Communication

Your use of space speaks as surely and loudly as words and sentences. Speakers who stand close to their listener, with their hands on the listener's shoulders and their eyes focused directly on those of the listener, communicate something very different from speakers who stand in a corner with arms folded and eyes downcast. Similarly, the executive office suite on the top floor with huge windows, private bar, and plush carpeting communicates something totally different from the six-by-six-foot cubicle occupied by the rest of the workers.

Space communication (*proxemics*) refers to the messages that space and spaces communicate. Here we look at the four major spatial distances that people maintain when they communicate and some of the influences on these spatial distances.

### Spatial Distances

Edward Hall (1959, 1966) distinguishes four distances that define the type of relationship between people (see Figure 5.1).

In *intimate distance,* ranging from actual touching to 18 inches, the presence of the other individual is unmistakable. Each person experiences the sound, smell, and feel of the other's breath. You use intimate distance for lovemaking and wrestling, for comforting and protecting. This distance is so short that most people do not consider it proper in public.

Each of us, says Hall, carries around a protective "bubble" that defines our *personal distance,* ranging from 18 inches to 4 feet. This imaginary

Some nonverbal researchers (Burgoon and Hale 1988) have proposed that when people violate the expected distance in conversation, attention shifts from the topic to the person. Do you notice this? What else happens when expected distances are violated?

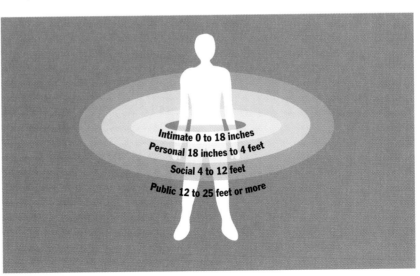

Intimate 0 to 18 inches
Personal 18 inches to 4 feet
Social 4 to 12 feet
Public 12 to 25 feet or more

**Figure 5.1** *Proxemic distances*

Why do you suppose people who are angry or tense need greater space around them? Do you find this true from your personal experience?

bubble keeps us protected and untouched by others. You can still hold or grasp another person at this distance but only by extending your arms; allowing you to take certain individuals such as loved ones into your protective bubble. At the outer limit of personal distance, you can touch another person only if *both* of you extend your arms.

At *social distance,* from 4 to 12 feet, you lose the visual detail you have at personal distance. You conduct impersonal business and interact at a social gathering at this social distance. The more distance you maintain in your interactions, the more formal they appear. In offices of high officials, the desks are positioned so the official is assured of at least this distance from clients.

In *public distance,* from 12 to more than 25 feet, you are protected by space. At this distance you could take defensive action if threatened. On a public bus or train, for example, you might keep at least this distance from a drunkard.

Although at this distance you lose fine details of the face and eyes, you are still close enough to see what is happening.

### Spatial Distances and Culture

These differences are greatly influenced by culture. For example, in the United States if you live next door to someone, you are almost automatically expected to be friendly and to interact with that person. It seems so natural that we probably don't even consider that this is a cultural expectation not shared by all cultures. In Japan, the fact that your house is next to another's does not imply that you should become close or visit each other.

Consider, therefore, the situation in which a Japanese buys a house next to an American. The Japanese may well see the American as overly familiar and as taking friendship for granted. The American may see the Japanese as distant, unfriendly, and unneighborly. Yet, each person is merely fulfilling the expectations of his or her own culture (Hall and Hall 1987).

*"Never let her catch you in her garden … Humans are very territorial."*

REPRINTED COURTESY OF BUNNY HOEST AND PARADE MAGAZINE

**Table 5.2**
*Factors Influencing Space
Communication*

| Status | People of equal status maintain shorter distances between themselves than do people of unequal status. When the status is unequal, the higher-status person may approach the lower-status person more closely than the lower-status person may approach the higher-status person. |
|---|---|
| Culture | Americans stand fairly far apart when conversing, compared with southern European and Middle Eastern cultures. Arabs, for example, stand much closer to each other than do Americans. Italians and Spaniards also maintain less distance in their interactions than many northern Europeans. |
| Context | The larger the physical space you are in, the smaller the interpersonal space. Thus, the space between two people will be smaller in a large room than in a small room. |
| Subject Matter | If you talk about personal matters or share secrets, you maintain a short distance. When you talk about impersonal, general matters, the space is larger. You probably also maintain less distance from someone who is praising you than from someone who is blaming you. |
| Sex and Age | Women stand closer to one another than do men. Opposite sex pairs stand the farthest apart. Children stand closer to each other than do adults, showing that the distances you maintain are learned behaviors. |
| Positive and Negative Evaluation | You stand farther from enemies than from friends, from authority figures and higher-status persons than from peers. You maintain more distance between yourself and people you may subconsciously evaluate negatively. |

**What other factors influence spatial distances?**

## Influences on Space Communication

Several factors influence the way we treat space in communication. Among the most important factors are status, culture, context, subject matter, sex and age, and the positive or negative evaluation we may be expressing. Table 5.2 summarizes these factors.

## Territoriality

**Nothing succeeds like address.**
**—FRAN LEBOWITZ**

*Territoriality*, a term that comes to us from ethology (the study of animals in their natural habitat), refers to the ownership-like reaction toward a particular space or object.

The size and location of human territory also say something about status (Sommer 1969; Mehrabian 1976). An apartment or office in midtown Manhattan or downtown Tokyo is extremely high-status territory since the cost restricts it to the wealthy.

**Have you seen any examples of territorial behavior today? Can you recall a situation in which your territory was violated? Invaded? Contaminated? How did you respond to such encroachments?**

Status is also indicated by the unwritten law granting the right of invasion. In some cultures and in some organizations, for example, higher-status individuals have more of a right to invade the territory of others than vice versa. The president of a large company can invade the territory of a junior executive by barging into her or his office, but the reverse would be unthinkable.

**Table 5.3**

*Three Types of Markers*

| Marker | Function | Examples |
|---|---|---|
| Central | To reserve a territory | A drink at the bar, books on your desk, and a sweater over the chair let others know that this territory belongs to you |
| Boundary | To set boundaries between your territory and that of others | The bar in the supermarket checkout line, the armrests separating your chair from those on either side |
| Ear | To identify your possessions | Trademarks, initials, nameplates, and initials on a shirt or attaché case |

Have you seen any examples of marking behavior today? Look around your home and at your belongings. Can you identify examples of *central*, *boundary*, and *ear* markers?

## Markers

Like animals, humans also mark their territory. We make use of three types of markers: central, boundary, and ear markers (Hickson and Stacks 1988). Table 5.3 identifies the function of these markers and gives some examples.

## Artifactual Communication

Artifactual messages are those made by human hands. Thus, color, clothing, jewelry, and the decoration of space would be considered artifactual. Let's look at each of these briefly.

### Color Communication

Henry Dreyfuss, in his *Symbol Sourcebook* (1971), points out some of the positive and negative meanings associated with various colors. Some of these are presented in Table 5.4. Dreyfuss also notes some cultural comparisons. For example, red in China is used for joyous and festive occasions, whereas in Japan it signifies anger and danger. Blue signifies defeat for the Cherokee Indian, but virtue and truth for the Egyptian. In the Japanese theater, blue is the color for villains. Yellow signifies happiness and prosperity in Egypt, but in tenth-century France yellow colored the doors of criminals. Green communicates femininity to certain American Indians, fertility and strength to Egyptians, and youth and energy to the Japanese. Purple signifies virtue and faith in Egypt, grace and nobility in Japan.

"Yes," I answered you last night; "No," this morning, sir, I say: Colors seen by candlelight Will not look the same by day.
—ELIZABETH BARRETT BROWNING

There is some evidence that colors affect us physiologically. For example, respiratory movements increase with red light and decrease with blue light. Similarly, eye blinks increase in frequency when eyes are exposed to red light and decrease when exposed to blue. This seems consistent with our intuitive feelings about blue being more soothing and red more arousing. After changing a school's walls from orange and white to blue, the blood pressure of the students decreased while their academic performance increased.

If you were the designer of this text, what colors would you have used? Why?

Colors surely influence our perceptions and our behaviors (Kanner 1989). People's acceptance of a product, for example, is largely determined by its package. The very same coffee taken from a yellow can was

Table 5.4
*Positive and Negative
Messages of Color*

| Color | Positive Messages | | Negative Messages | |
|-------|-------------------|--|-------------------|--|
| red | warmth<br>passion<br>life | liberty<br>patriotism | death<br>war<br>revolution | devil<br>danger |
| blue | religious feeling<br>devotion | truth<br>justice | doubt | discourage-<br>ments |
| yellow | intuition<br>wisdom | divinity | cowardice<br>malevolence | impure love |
| green | nature<br>hope | freshness<br>prosperity | envy<br>jealousy | opposition<br>disgrace |
| purple | power<br>royalty | love of truth<br>nostalgia | mourning<br>regret | penitence<br>resignation |

*Source: Adapted from Henry Dreyfuss,* Symbol Sourcebook *(New York; McGraw-Hill, 1971).*

described as weak, from a dark brown can too strong, from a red can rich, and from a blue can mild. Even our acceptance of a person may depend on the colors worn. Consider, for example, the comments of one color expert (Kanner 1989): "If you have to pick the wardrobe for your defense lawyer heading into court and choose anything but blue, you deserve to lose the case. . . . " Black is so powerful it could work against the lawyer with the jury. Brown lacks sufficient authority. Green would probably elicit a negative response.

### Clothing and Body Adornment

Clothing serves a variety of functions. It *protects* you from the weather and, in sports like football, from injury. It helps conceal parts of your body thus serving a *modesty* function. Clothing also serves as a *cultural display* (Morris 1977) communicating your cultural and subcultural affiliations. In the United States where there are so many different ethnic groups, we frequently see types of dress that indicate the country from which the people have come.

People make inferences about who you are—in part—by the way you dress. Whether these inferences are accurate or not, they will influence what people think of you and how they react to you. Your social class, your seriousness, your attitudes (for example, whether you are conservative or liberal), your concern for convention, your sense of style and perhaps even your creativity will all be judged—in part at least—by the way you dress. In fact, the very popular *Dress for Success* and *The Woman's Dress for Success Book* by John Molloy (1975, 1977) instructed men and women in how to dress to communicate the image they wanted: efficient, reliable, authoritative.

Similarly, college students will perceive an instructor dressed informally as friendly, fair, enthusiastic, and flexible and the same instructor dressed formally as prepared, knowledgeable, and organized (Malandro, Barker, and Barker 1989).

> Beware of all enterprises that require new clothes.
> —Henry David Thoreau

> Look carefully at the way you're dressed. What messages is your clothing (include your jewelry, hairstyle, make-up, and colors you're wearing) communicating? Is it communicating different messages to different (types of) people? Are these the messages you want to communicate?

> To choose clothes, either in a store or at home, is to define and describe ourselves.
> —Alison Lurie

*"I'm looking for a tie that says, 'Hey, I can handle the job, Mr. Harrison, if you'll just give me the chance.'"*

COURTESY OF THE WEST SIDE SPIRIT

Your jewelry also communicates messages about you. Wedding and engagement rings are obvious examples that communicate specific messages. College rings and political buttons likewise communicate specific messages. If you wear a Rolex watch or large precious stones, for example, others are likely to infer that you are rich. Men who wear earrings will be judged differently from men who don't.

The way you wear your hair communicates about who you are—from caring about being up-to-date to a desire to shock, to perhaps a lack of concern for appearances. Men with long hair will generally be judged as less conservative than those with shorter hair.

### Space Decoration

The way you decorate your private spaces also tells about you. The office with mahogany desk and bookcases and oriental rugs communicates your importance and status within the organization just as the metal desk and bare floors indicate a worker much further down in the hierarchy.

Do you form impressions of your teachers on the basis of how they decorated their offices? What things have the greatest impact on your perceptions?

Similarly, people will make inferences about you based on the way you decorate your home. The expensiveness of the furnishings may communicate your status and wealth; their coordination, your sense of style. The magazines may reflect your interests while the arrangement of chairs around a television set may reveal how important watching television is to you. And, bookcases lining the walls reveal the importance of reading. In fact, there is probably little in your home that would not send messages that others would not use in making inferences about you. Computers, wide screen televisions, well-equipped kitchens, and oil paintings of great grandparents, for example, all say something about the people who live in the home.

Similarly, the lack of certain items will communicate something about you. Consider what messages you would get from a home where there is no television, phone or books.

## TEST YOURSELF:

### *What's Wrong with the Gift?*

One aspect of nonverbal communication that is frequently overlooked is the giving of gifts, a practice in which rules and customs vary according to each culture. Here are a few situations where gift giving backfired and created barriers rather than bonds. These examples are designed to heighten your awareness of both the importance of gift giving and of recognizing intercultural differences. What might have gone wrong in each of these situations (Axtell 1990a)?

1. An American brings chrysanthemums to a Belgian colleague and a clock to a Chinese colleague. Both react negatively.
2. Upon meeting an Arab businessman for the first time—someone with whom you wish to do considerable business—you present him with a gift. He becomes disturbed.
3. When visiting an Arab family in Oman, you bring a bottle of your favorite brandy for after dinner. Your host seems annoyed.
4. Arriving for dinner at the home of a Kenya colleague, you present flowers as a dinner gift. Your host accepts them politely but looks puzzled.
5. In arriving for dinner at the home of a Swiss colleague, you bring 14 red roses. Your host accepts them politely but looks strangely at you.

Possible reasons:

1. Chrysanthemums in Belgium and clocks in China are both reminders of death.
2. Gifts given at the first meeting may be interpreted as a bribe; thus should be avoided.
3. Alcohol is prohibited by Islamic law, so should be avoided when selecting gifts for most Arabs.
4. In Kenya, flowers are only brought to express condolence.
5. In Switzerland red roses are a sign of romantic interest. Also, an even number of (or 13) flowers is generally considered bad luck, so should be avoided.

## *Touch Communication*

Touch communication (*haptics*) is perhaps the most primitive form of communication (Montagu 1971). Touch develops before the other senses; even in the womb the child is stimulated by touch. Soon after birth the child is fondled, caressed, patted, and stroked. In turn, the child explores its world through touch and quickly learns to communicate a variety of meanings through touch.

Who would touch whom—say, by putting an arm on the other person's shoulder or by putting a hand on the other person's back—in the following pairs: teacher and student, doctor and patient, manager and worker, minister and parishioner, police officer and accused, business executive and secretary?

The most humanizing, and in many respects the most crucial, of all of the senses is that of touch.
—ASHLEY MONTAGU AND FLOYD MATSON

When one person has access to another person's body, but the first person is not allowed the same privilege in return, touch becomes an indicator of status rather than of solidarity.
—JUDY CORNELIA PEARSON

Nancy Henley (1977) argues that touching demonstrates the assertion of male power over women. Men may, says Henley, touch women during their daily routine. In the restaurant, office, and school, for example, men touch women and thus indicate "superior status." When women touch men, on the other hand, the interpretation that it designates a female-dominant relationship is not acceptable (to men). So, men may explain and interpret this touching as a sexual invitation. What do you think of Henley's observations?

Touching varies greatly from one culture to another. For example, blacks touch each other more than do whites. Similarly, touching declines from kindergarten to the sixth grade for white but not for black children (Burgoon, Buller, and Woodall 1989). Similarly, Japanese touch each other much less than do Anglo-Saxons who in turn touch each other much less than do southern Europeans (Morris 1977; Burgoon, Buller, and Woodall 1989).

## The Meanings of Touch

Nonverbal researchers Stanley Jones and Elaine Yarbrough (1985) have identified the major meanings of touch. Here we consider five of the most important.

POSITIVE EMOTION. Touch may communicate positive feelings. This occurs mainly between intimates or others who have a close relationship. "Touch is such a powerful signalling system," notes Desmond Morris (1972), "and it's so closely related to emotional feelings we have for one another that in casual encounters it's kept to a minimum. When the relationship develops, the touching follows along with it." Among the most important positive emotions are support, appreciation, inclusion, sexual interest or intent, and affection.

PLAYFULNESS. Touch often communicates our intention to play, either affectionately or aggressively. The playful manner lessens the emotion and tells the other person not to take it seriously. Playful touches lighten an interaction.

CONTROL. Touch may also direct the behaviors, attitudes, or feelings of the other person. In compliance, you touch the other person to communicate "move over," "hurry," "stay here," and "do it." In attention-getting, you touch the person to gain his or her attention, as if to say "look at me" or "look over here."

Touching to control may also communicate dominance. For example, it is the higher-status person who is permitted to touch the lower-status person. In fact, it would be a breach of etiquette for the lower-status person to touch the person of higher status.

RITUAL. Ritualistic touching centers on greetings and departures. Shaking hands to say "hello" or "goodbye" is a clear example. Ritual touching also includes hugging, kissing, or putting your arm around another's shoulder when greeting or saying farewell.

TASK-RELATEDNESS. Task-related touching occurs while you are performing some function. This ranges from removing a speck of dust from another person's face to helping someone out of a car or checking someone's forehead for fever.

## Touch Avoidance

Much as we have a tendency to touch and be touched, we also have a tendency to avoid touch from certain people or in certain circumstances. Researchers in nonverbal communication have found some interesting relationships between touch avoidance and other significant communication variables (Andersen and Leibowitz 1978). For example, touch avoidance is positively related to communication apprehension; those who fear oral communication also score high on touch avoidance. Touch avoidance is also high with those who self-disclose little. Both touch and self-disclosure are intimate forms of communication; thus people who are reluctant to get close to another person by self-disclosing also seem reluctant to get close by touching.

Older people have higher touch-avoidance scores for opposite-sex persons than do younger people. As we get older we are touched less by members of the opposite sex. This decreased frequency may lead us to avoid touching.

Males score higher on same-sex touch avoidance than do females, which matches our stereotypes. Men avoid touching other men, but women may and do touch other women. On the other hand, women have higher touch-avoidance scores for opposite-sex touching than do men.

## Paralanguage

*Paralanguage* refers to the vocal (but nonverbal) dimension of speech. It refers to *how* you say something not *what* you say. An old exercise to increase a student's ability to express different emotions, feelings, and attitudes was to have the student say a sentence while accenting or stressing different words. One popular sentence was, "Is this the face that launched a thousand ships?" Significant differences in meaning are easily communicated depending on where the stress is placed. Consider the following variations:

1. *Is* this the face that launched a thousand ships?
2. Is *this* the face that launched a thousand ships?
3. Is this the *face* that launched a thousand ships?
4. Is this the face that *launched* a thousand ships?
5. Is this the face that launched a *thousand ships*?

Each sentence communicates something different, in fact, each asks a different question even though the words are the same. All that distinguishes the sentences is stress, one aspect of *paralanguage*.

In addition to stress or pitch, paralanguage includes such vocal characteristics as rate, volume, and rhythm. It also includes vocalizations you make in crying, whispering, moaning, belching, yawning, and yelling (Trager 1958, 1961; Argyle 1988). A variation in any of these features communicates. When you speak quickly, for example, you communicate something different from when you speak slowly. Even though the words might be the same, if the speed (or volume, rhythm, or pitch) differs, the meanings people receive will also differ.

### Judgments About People

We are quick to make judgments about another's personality based on paralinguistic cues. You may, for example, conclude that those who speak softly feel inferior, believing that no one wants to listen and nothing they say is significant. Similarly, you may assume that people who speak loudly have overinflated egos and think everyone in the world wants to hear them. Those who speak with no variation, in a complete monotone, seem uninterested in what they are saying and you might perceive them as having a lack of interest in life in general. All these conclusions are, at best, based on little evidence, yet we continue to make them.

People can accurately judge the status (whether high, middle, or low) of speakers from 60-second voice samples (Davitz 1964). Many listeners made their judgments in fewer than 15 seconds. Speakers judged to be of high status were also given higher credibility than speakers rated middle and low.

Listeners can also accurately judge the emotional states of speakers from vocal expression alone. In these studies, speakers recite the alphabet or numbers while expressing emotions. Some emotions are easier to identify than others; it is easy to distinguish between hate and sympathy but more difficult to distinguish between fear and anxiety. And, of course, listeners vary in their ability to decode, and speakers in their ability to encode emotions (Scherer 1986).

### Judgments About Conversational Turns

We also use paralinguistic cues to signal conversational turns—whose turn it is to speak (Knapp 1978; Malandro, Barker, and Barker 1988). The following description is based on research on English speakers. Those of other languages and from other cultures will indicate speaking turns somewhat differently.

TURN-MAINTAINING CUES. With paralinguistic cues you can communicate your desire to maintain your speaking position. Thus, during conversation you may pause while vocalizing "-em, -er," and the like. These pauses ensure that no one else will jump in and take over before you are finished.

TURN-YIELDING CUES. Paralinguistic cues also announce that you have finished speaking and it is now someone else's turn. For example, you may at the end of a statement add a paralinguistic cue such as "Eh?" which asks the others to speak now. Often, you indicate you have finished speaking by dropping your voice, by a prolonged silence, or by asking a general question.

TURN-REQUESTING CUES. As a listener you use paralinguistic cues to let the speaker know that you would like to say something. You may do this through a vocalized "-er" or "-um" that tells the speaker (at least the sensitive speaker) that you would now like to speak. You can also request a turn with facial and mouth gestures. You might open your eyes and mouth wide as if to say something and perhaps gesture with your hand.

TURN-DENYING CUES. You may show your reluctance to assume the role of speaker by intoning a slurred "I don't know." Or, you might give a brief grunt that signals you have nothing to say. You can also deny your turn by avoiding eye contact with the speaker who signals you to take on the role. Or, you might engage in some behavior that is incompatible with speaking—such as coughing or blowing your nose.

Do you make any judgments about people on the basis of their paralanguage? How accurate do these prove to be?

Never say more than is necessary.
—RICHARD BRINSLEY SHERIDAN

He knew the precise psychological moment when to say nothing.
—OSCAR WILDE

What other nonverbal cues accompany the paralanguage cues in signaling the four conversational turns?

In what ways are highway signs and signals similar to conversational turns? Can you provide examples of highway signs or signals that serve functions similar to each of the four types of conversational turns discussed in this chapter? What "turn function" does the sign in this photo serve?

Some people will believe anything if you whisper it to them.
—LOUIS B. NIZER

Does your own experience support or contradict the findings on the values of fast talking? In what situations would fast talking work against the speaker?

## Judgments About Communication Effectiveness

The rate or speed at which people speak is the aspect of paralanguage that has received the most attention (MacLachlan 1979). It is of interest to the advertiser, the politician, and, in fact, anyone who tries to convey information or influence others. It is especially important when time is limited or expensive.

In one-way communication (when one person is doing all or most of the speaking and the other person is doing all or most of the listening), those who talk fast (about 50 percent faster than normal) are more persuasive. People agree more with a fast speaker than with a slow speaker and find the fast speaker more intelligent and objective.

When we look at comprehension, rapid speech shows an interesting effect. When the speaking rate is increased by 50 percent, the comprehension level only drops by 5 percent. When the rate is doubled, the comprehension level drops only 10 percent. These 5 and 10 percent losses are more than offset by the increased speed; thus the faster rates are much more efficient in communicating information. If the speeds are more than twice normal speech, however, comprehension begins to fall dramatically.

Exercise caution in applying this research to all forms of communication (MacLachlan 1979). While the speaker is speaking, the listener is generating or framing a reply. If the speaker talks too rapidly, there may not be enough time to compose this reply and the listener may become resentful. Furthermore, the increased rate may seem so unnatural that the listener may focus on the speed rather than the thought.

## Time Communication

Temporal communication (*chronemics*) concerns the use of time—how you organize it, react to it, and the messages it communicates (Bruneau 1985, 1990). Cultural and psychological time are two aspects of particular interest in human communication.

## Cultural Time

Cultural time refers to the way a particular culture defines and talks about time. Two types of cultural time are especially important in non-verbal communication.

In our culture, *formal time* is divided into seconds, minutes, hours, days, weeks, months, and years. Other cultures may use phases of the moon or the seasons to delineate time periods.

We divide college courses into 50- or 75-minute periods that meet two or three times a week for 14-week periods called semesters. Eight semesters of 15 or 16 50-minute periods per week equal a college education. As these examples illustrate, formal time units are arbitrary. The culture establishes them for convenience.

*Informal time* refers to the use of general time terms—for example, "forever," "immediately," "soon," "right away," "as soon as possible." This area of time creates the most communication problems because the terms have different meanings for different people.

How might informal time terms create problems between a teenager and parents?

## Psychological Time

*Psychological time* refers to the importance we place on the past, present, and future. In a *past orientation*, we have particular reverence for the past. We relive old times and regard the old methods as the best. We see events as circular and recurring, so the wisdom of yesterday is applicable also to today and tomorrow. In a *present orientation*, we live in the present; for now, not tomorrow. In a *future orientation*, we look toward and live for the future. We save today, work hard in college, and deny ourselves luxuries because we are preparing for the future.

Attitudes toward time vary from one culture to another. In one study, for example, the accuracy of clocks was measured in six cultures—Japan, Indonesia, Italy, England, Taiwan, and the United States. Japan had the most accurate and Indonesia had the least accurate clocks. A measure of the speed at which people in these six cultures walked, found that the Japanese walked the fastest, the Indonesians the slowest (LeVine and Bartlett 1984).

Alexander Gonzalez and Philip Zimbardo (1985) have provided some interesting conclusions about ourselves based on the way we view time. Before reading these conclusions take the time test yourself.

> Know the true value of time; snatch, seize, and enjoy every moment of it. No idleness, no laziness, no procrastination; never put off till tomorrow what you can do today.
> —LORD CHESTERFIELD

> Gather ye rose-buds while ye may.
>     Old Time is still aflying,
> And this same flower that smiles today,
>     Tomorrow will be dying.
> —ROBERT HERRICK

## TEST YOURSELF:

### *What Time Do You Have?*

For each statement, indicate whether the statement is true (T) or untrue (F) of your general attitude and behavior.

_____ 1. Meeting tomorrow's deadlines and doing other necessary work comes before tonight's partying.

_____ 2. I meet my obligations to friends and authorities on time.

_____ 3. I complete projects on time by making steady progress.

_____ 4. I am able to resist temptations when I know there is work to be done.

_____ 5. I keep working at a difficult, uninteresting task if it will help me get ahead.

_____ 6. If things don't get done on time, I don't worry about it.

_____ 7. I think that it's useless to plan too far ahead because things hardly ever come out the way you planned anyway.
_____ 8. I try to live one day at a time.
_____ 9. I live to make better what *is* rather than to be concerned about what *will* be.
_____10. It seems to me that it doesn't make sense to worry about the future, since fate determines that whatever will be, will be.
_____11. I believe that getting together with friends to party is one of life's important pleasures.
_____12. I do things impulsively, making decisions on the spur of the moment.
_____13. I take risks to put excitement in my life.
_____14. I get drunk at parties.
_____15. It's fun to gamble.
_____16. Thinking about the future is pleasant to me.
_____17. When I want to achieve something, I set subgoals and consider specific means for reaching those goals.
_____18. It seems to me that my career path is pretty well laid out.
_____19. It upsets me to be late for appointments.
_____20. I meet my obligations to friends and authorities on time.
_____21. I get irritated at people who keep me waiting when we've agreed to meet at a given time.
_____22. It makes sense to invest a substantial part of my income in insurance premiums.
_____23. I believe that "A stitch in time saves nine."
_____24. I believe that "A bird in the hand is worth two in the bush."
_____25. I believe it is important to save for a rainy day.
_____26. I believe a person's day should be planned each morning.
_____27. I make lists of things I must do.
_____28. When I want to achieve something, I set subgoals and consider specific means for reaching those goals.
_____29. I believe that "A stitch in time saves nine."

This time test measures seven different factors. If you selected true (*T*) for all or most of the questions within any given factor, you are probably high on that factor. If you selected untrue (*F*) for all or most of the questions within any given factor, you are probably low on that factor.

The first factor, measured by questions 1-5, is a future, work motivation, perseverance orientation. These people have a strong work ethic and are committed to completing a task despite difficulties and temptations. The second factor (questions 6-10) is a present, fatalistic, worry-free orientation. High scorers on this factor live one day at a time, not necessarily to enjoy the day but to avoid planning for the next day or anxiety about the future.

The third factor (questions 11-15) is a present, pleasure-seeking, partying orientation. These people enjoy the present, take risks and engage in a variety of impulsive actions. The fourth factor (questions 16-18) is a future, goal-seeking and planning orientation. These people derive special pleasure from planning and achieving a variety of goals.

The fifth factor (questions 19-21) is a time-sensitivity orientation. People who score high are especially sensitive to time and its role in social obligations. The sixth factor (questions 22-25) is a future, practical action orientation. These people do what they have to do—take practical actions—to achieve the future they want.

*Continued*

Time is very important in television. We buy it, we fill it, we start on it, we finish on it. And appropriately enough, we occasionally kill it.
—ALFRED HITCHCOCK

Do not squander time for that is the stuff life is made of.
—BENJAMIN FRANKLIN

What is your own psychological time orientation? Will this help you achieve your goals? Are you generally satisfied with this orientation? Dissatisfied? If dissatisfied, what do you intend to do about it?

This time, like all times, is a very good one, if we but know what to do with it.
—RALPH WALDO EMERSON

Consider some of the findings on psychological time. Future income is positively related to future orientation; the more future oriented you are, the greater your income is likely to be. Present orientation is strongest among lowest income males.

The time orientation you develop depends on your socioeconomic class and your personal experiences. Gonzalez and Zimbardo (1985), who developed this scale and upon whose research these findings are based, observe: "A child with parents in unskilled and semiskilled occupations is usually socialized in a way that promotes a present-oriented fatalism and hedonism. A child of parents who are managers, teachers, or other professionals learns future-oriented values and strategies designed to promote achievement."

Different time perspectives also account for much intercultural misunderstanding since different cultures often teach their members drastically different time orientations. For example, members from some Latin cultures would rather be late for an appointment than end a conversation abruptly or before it has come to a natural end. So, the Latin sees this behavior as politeness. But, others may see this as impolite to the person with whom he or she had the appointment (Hall and Hall 1987).

What a wonderful life I've had! I only wish I'd realized it sooner.
—COLETTE

Similarly, the future-oriented person who works for tomorrow's goals will frequently look down on the present-oriented person as lazy and poorly motivated for enjoying today and not planning for tomorrow. In turn, the present-oriented person may see those with strong future orientations as obsessed with amassing wealth or rising in status.

## Time and Appropriateness

What one rule of nonverbal behavior would a Martian find helpful when interacting with Earthlings? How would that rule appear in a guide to intergalactic communication? Have you seen any examples of territorial behavior today?

Promptness or lateness in responding to letters, returning telephone calls, acknowledging gifts, and returning invitations all communicate significant messages. You can analyze these messages on such scales as interest-disinterest, organized-disorganized, considerate-inconsiderate, sociable-unsociable, and so on.

Also, there are appropriate and inappropriate times for certain activities. Thus, it is permissible to make a social phone call during the late morning, afternoon, and early evening. It would be inappropriate, however, to make the same call before 8:00 or 9:00 in the morning, during dinner time, or after 11:00 at night.

Similarly, in making dates, an appropriate amount of notice is customary. The invitation to a public speaker would be extended weeks or perhaps months in advance. When you give an acceptable amount of notice, you communicate a recognition of accepted standards and a respect for the individual. Violating any of these time conventions, however, would communicate other meanings.

# FEEDBACK

In this chapter we explored nonverbal communication—communication without words.

**1.** Nonverbal messages interact with verbal mes-sages in six major ways: to accent, to complement, to contradict, to regulate, to repeat, and to substitute.

**2.** The five body movements are **emblems** (nonverbal behaviors that rather directly translate words or phrases), **illustrators** (nonverbal behaviors that accompany and literally "illustrate" the verbal messages), **affect displays** (nonverbal movements that communicate emotional mean-ing), **regulators** (nonverbal movements that coordinate, monitor, maintain, or control the speaking of another individual), and **adaptors** (nonverbal behaviors that are emitted without conscious awareness and that usually serve some kind of need, as in scratching an itch).

**3.** **Facial movements** may communicate a wide variety of emotions. The most frequently studied are happiness, surprise, fear, anger, sadness, and disgust/contempt. Communications of these six emotions are **primary affect displays.**

**4.** **Eye movements** may seek feedback, inform others to speak, signal the nature of a relationship, and compensate for increased physical distance.

**5.** **Pupil size** shows one's interest and level of emotional arousal. Pupils enlarge when one is interested in something or is emotionally aroused in a positive way.

**6.** **Proxemics** refers to the communicative function of space and spatial relationships.

**7.** Four major proxemic distances are: (1) **intimate distance** ranging from actual touching to 18 inches; (2) **personal distance,** ranging from 18 inches to 4 feet; (3) **social distance**, ranging from 4 to 12 feet; and (4) **public distance,** ranging from 12 to more than 25 feet.

**8.** Our treatment of space is influenced by such factors as **status, culture, context, subject matter, sex, age,** and **positive** or **negative evaluation** of the other person.

**9.** **Territoriality** refers to one's possessive reaction to an area of space or to particular objects.

**10. Markers** are devices that identify a territory as ours; these include **central, boundary,** and **ear markers.**

**11. Artifactual communication** refers to messages that are human-made, for example, the use of color, clothing and body adornment, and space decoration.

**12. Touch communication** (or **haptics**) may communicate a variety of meanings, the most important being positive affect, playfulness, control, ritual, and task-relatedness.

**13. Touch avoidance** refers to our desire to avoid touching and being touched by others.

**14. Paralanguage** refers to the vocal but nonverbal dimension of speech. It includes rate, pitch, volume, resonance, and vocal quality as well as pauses and hesitations.

**15.** On the basis of paralanguage we make **judgments about people, conversational turns,** and **believability.**

**16. Time communication (chronemics)** refers to the messages communicated by our treatment of time.

**17. Cultural time** focuses on how our culture defines and teaches time, and with the difficulties created by the different meanings people have for informal time terms. **Psychological time** focuses on time orientations, whether past, present, or future.

Throughout our discussion we covered a wide variety of communication skills. Check your ability to apply these skills. Use the following rating scale: (1) = almost always, (2) = often, (3) = sometimes, (4) = rarely, (5) = hardly ever.

_____ 1. I recognize messages communicated by body gestures and facial and eye movements.

_____ 2. I recognize that what I perceive is only a part of the total nonverbal expression.

_____ 3. I use my eyes to seek feedback, to inform others to speak, to signal the nature of my relationship with others, and to compensate for increased physical distance.

_____ 4. I give others the space they need, for example, giving more space to those who are angry or disturbed.

_____ 5. I am sensitive to the markers (central, boundary, and ear) of others and use these markers to define my own territories.

_____ 6. I use artifacts to communicate the desired messages.

_____ 7. I am sensitive to the touching behaviors of others and distinguish among those touches that communicate positive emotion, playfulness, control, ritual, and task-relatedness.

_____ 8. I recognize and respect each person's touch-avoidance tendency. I am especially sensitive to cultural and gender differences in touching preferences and in touch-avoidance tendencies.

_____ 9. I vary paralinguistic features (rate, pausing, quality, tempo, and volume) to communicate my intended meanings.

_____ 10. I specify what I mean when I use informal time terms.

_____ 11. I interpret time cues from the cultural perspective of the person with whom I am interacting.

# SKILL DEVELOPMENT EXPERIENCES

## 5.1. YOUR PROBLEM NONVERBALS

Part of effective nonverbal communication involves eliminating problem behaviors—those that interfere with communication effectiveness.

Each class member should write down on an index card—no names, please—at least three specific nonverbal behaviors that she or he feels create problems. These cards should be collected and read aloud or recorded on the chalkboard. Class members should then consider the following issues:

1. Why do these nonverbals create problems? Why do these behaviors interfere with communication effectiveness?
2. Select any one nonverbal and indicate your impressions of the person who uses this nonverbal?
3. In what communication situations are these problem behaviors most likely to occur?
4. How can these nonverbals be eliminated?

## 5.2. PRAISING AND CRITICIZING

This exercise aims to show that the same verbal statement can communicate praise and criticism depending on the paralinguistic cues that accompany it. Read each of the ten statements, first to communicate praise and second, criticism. One procedure is to seat the class in a circle and begin with one student reading statement No. 1 with a praising meaning, and the next student reading the same statement with a criticizing meaning. Continue around the circle until all ten statements are read.

1. Now that looks good on you.
2. You lost weight.
3. You look younger than that.
4. You're gonna make it.
5. That was some meal.
6. You really know yourself.
7. You're an expert.
8. You're so sensitive. I'm amazed.
9. Your parents are really something.
10. Are you ready? Already?

After all the statements are read from both a praising and a criticizing perspective, consider these questions:

1. What paralinguistic cues communicate praise? Criticism?
2. What paralinguistic cue was most helpful in enabling the speaker to communicate praise or criticism?
3. Most people would claim it is easier to decode than to encode the praise or criticism. Was this true in this experience? Why or why not?
4. Although this exercise focused on paralanguage, the statements were probably read with different facial expressions, eye movements, and body postures. How would you describe these other nonverbals when communicating praise and criticism?

### 5.3. NONVERBAL DATING BEHAVIORS

Assume that a friend of yours (male or female) is having trouble dating. The general feeling is that your friend communicates a cold, unemotional, and unromantic image. What advice for nonverbal communication could you give your friend to make him or her a more attractive, more appealing dating partner? What common nonverbals would you tell your friend to avoid? Organize your advice around the areas of nonverbal communication as covered in this chapter. For each area include nonverbals to use as well as to avoid.

1. Body communication
2. Facial communication
3. Eye communication
4. Space communication
5. Artifactual communication
6. Touch communication
7. Paralanguage communication

# PART ONE
# CRITICAL THINKING
# PERSPECTIVES AND
# REVIEW

Of all the advantages humans have over animals, the most important is our ability to reason—to think. It has enabled us to find cures for hundreds of illnesses, to build faster, more efficient means of communication, and—unfortunately—to create the means of our own destruction.

We are time-binders; we have the ability to communicate to future generations all that we have learned—our successes and our failures—so they can start from where we left off (Korsybski 1933). Just as your generation did not have to reinvent radio, television, and air travel, so the next generation will not have to reinvent satellites, personal computers, and the polio vaccine.

But these abilities would count for little if we failed to find the relevant information, reason to logical conclusions, and communicate accurately and effectively. This is when critical thinking counts. As our world revolves more and more around information—already more than 50 percent of all workers in the United States are employed in processing or communicating information—it becomes increasingly important for us to sharpen our abilities to deal with information. We need to know the best ways to get information and evidence; to analyze and evaluate it; to apply it to new situations; to use it to solve problems; and to communicate it efficiently and effectively.

In a world in which information is generated so rapidly that much of what you learn in college will be dated in five, ten, or fifteen years, the learning of facts and figures is obviously not enough. [This is not to say that facts and figures are unimportant. They are essential to critical thinking; they are the building blocks that critical thinking skills can erect into a skyscraper.] Fortunately, we can learn to improve our thinking so we can update our knowledge and generate and evaluate brand new ideas.

This emphasis aims to make you a better thinker not only about communication, but in general as well.

## What Is Critical Thinking?

Here is how a few theorists have defined critical thinking:

*Critical thinking simply means a way of thinking intelligently, carefully, and with as much clarity as possible. It is the opposite of what we might call sloppy thinking* (McCarthy 1991).

*Critical thinking is reasonable reflective thinking that is focused on deciding what to believe or do* (Ennis 1987).

*Critical thinking involves the ability to raise powerful questions about what's being read, viewed or listened to* (Adams and Hamm 1990).

*[Critical thinking is] the process of examining ...information and reaching a judgment or decision* (Wade and Tarvis 1990).

Critical thinking takes us beyond information and knowledge so we can make more reasoned and more reasonable decisions. Critical thinking comprises a variety of skills, some of which, noted by leading critical thinking experts, are presented in Table I.1 As you have seen and will continue to see, many of these skills are integrated and illustrated throughout this text. You will also see that critical thinking is not new; you have been thinking critically all your life. Our aim is to provide additional tools and insights to improve your already well-developed critical-thinking capacity.

## TABLE 1.1 A SAMPLE OF CRITICAL THINKING SKILLS*

1. To ask and answer questions of clarification or challenge
2. To observe and judge observation reports
3. To draw and evaluate conclusions
4. To identify specific instances from a generalization
5. To make value judgments
6. To define terms and evaluate the validity of definitions
7. To identify assumptions
8. To interact with others logically and effectively
9. To use evidence skillfully and impartially
10. To organize your thoughts and speak or write them coherently
11. To distinguish between logical and illogical inferences
12. To suspend judgment in the absence of sufficient evidence
13. To use problem-solving techniques appropriately
14. To weigh the truth or falsity of arguments instead of just accepting them on faith
15. To make connections between new knowledge and what you already know
16. To obtain relevant and valid information
17. To organize and present information so that others can understand it
18. To evaluate the quality and reasonableness of ideas
19. To define a problem precisely
20. To explore and evaluate possible strategies for solving a problem

*Numbers 1-8 are from Ennis (1987), 9-13 are from Nickerson (1987), 14-15 are from McCarthy (1991), 16-18 are from Adams and Hamm (1991), and 19-20 are from Bransford, Sherwood, and Sturdevant (1987).

## Critical Thinking Attitudes

In addition to specific skills, the critical thinker must have an appropriate attitude—a willingness and readiness to use critical thinking skills and abilities. The critical-thinking attitude in human communication consists of at least the following.

**1. A willingness to analyze yourself** as a critical thinker and a communicator. Self-analysis is essential if you are to use this material in any meaningful sense, say, to change some of your own behaviors. Be open-minded to new ideas, even those that contradict your existing beliefs.

**2. A tendency to observe** the behaviors of those around you as well as your own is essential. You need to see in real life what you read about here if it is to have any application to your own day-to-day interactions.

**3. A willingness to delay conclusions** until you have collected sufficient information. While doing so, the critical thinker is not inactive. There comes a time to make decisions and to take action.

**4. A readiness to connect and relate** the material presented to your own everyday communications. Part of your task as a critical thinker is to connect and relate the varied communication principles to each other (to see, for example, the relationship between verbal and nonverbal messages and the usefulness of interpersonal communication principles in interviewing and small group communication).

**5. A determination to become well-informed** about communication. Communication is not something you will study and then forget once the course is over. Your ability to communicate effectively will determine much of your personal, social, and professional success. Therefore, make a commitment to learn more than what is offered in any single course or textbook.

**6. A readiness to analyze and evaluate ideas** instead of accepting them just because they appear in a textbook or are mentioned by a teacher.

**7. A willingness to change** your ways of communicating and even your ways of thinking. Carefully assess what you should and should not change, what you should strengthen or revise and what you should leave as is.

## Transferring Skills

In reading this section and all the critical thinking material throughout this text, you will find that skills learned here will transfer to other areas of your life if you do three things (Sternberg 1987).

- Think about the principles flexibly and recognize exceptions to the rule. Consider where the principles seem useful and where they need to be adjusted. Recognize especially that the principles discussed here are largely the result of research conducted in the United States. Ask yourself if they apply to other cultures.

- Seek analogies between current situations and those you experienced earlier. What are the similarities? What are the differences? For example, most people repeat relationship problems because they fail to see the similarities (and sometimes the differences) between the old and destructive relationship and the new and soon-to-be equality destructive relationship.

- Look for situations at home, work, and school where you could transfer the skills discussed here. For instance, how can active listening skills improve your family communication? How can brainstorming and problem-solving skills help you deal with work-related difficulties?

## Critical Thinking Skills (Communication-Specific)

Throughout these first five chapters of *Essentials of Human Communication*, we covered a variety of critical thinking skills. You exercised your critical thinking facilities in learning and applying the text material, in responding to the critical thinking questions and observations, and in completing the Skill Development Experiences. This end-of-the-part section summarizes and highlights only a few of the principles that are especially applicable to critical thinking. We've singled out ten in all, five for this Part I summary and five for the Part II summary.

### Think Critically about Communication

In thinking critically about communication, remember to analyze communication as a transactional process—one that involves the simultaneous sending and receiving of messages (Chapter 1, Skill Development Experience 1.5). Even when sending messages, you are receiving the reactions and responses of others.

Analyze communication for its punctuation, recalling that this is an arbitrary process. Effective interaction will depend to an extent on how ably you communicate your particular punctuation to the other person and perceive the other's punctuation (Chapter 1).

Remember that communication is a package of signals. As a result, conclusions drawn from isolated bits of verbal or nonverbal behaviors are

likely to be wrong. The most you can do is make guesses and then test them with further observation and analysis (Chapter 1).

Analyze communication for both content and relationship. Hear both sets of messages and respond to each as appropriate (Chapter 1, SDEx 1.2, 1.3).

### Critically Evaluate Your Perceptions

Common perceptual processes—such as implicit personality theory, the self-fulfilling prophecy, primacy-recency, and stereotyping—can influence what you think you see or hear (Chapter 3). Analyze your perceptions in light of these influences (SDEx 3.1).

In gathering information through interpersonal perception, use all three strategies: observe the person, actively seek information about the person, then interact with the person and observe the interaction (Chapter 3).

In forming conclusions about a person, gather information from a variety of cues and then formulate hypotheses (not conclusions). Be especially alert to contradictory cues—information that may prove your initial hypothesis incorrect. Recognize the diversity in people (especially cultural) and avoid assuming that others share your attitudes, beliefs, or values. Beware of your own biases. They can seriously distort our perceptions without our being aware we are not being objective (Chapter 3, SDEx 3.5).

### Listen Critically

Since so much information comes from listening, it is essential to process this information critically—to evaluate as well as understand what you hear (Chapter 3). You'll gain more if you avoid focusing on yourself or on issues outside the subject under discussion. Similarly, beware of the tendencies to sharpen, assimilate, and hear good things about friends and bad things about enemies, and to hear what you expect to hear.

Critical listening means keeping an open mind and delaying judgments until you fully understand the issue. The simple skill of paraphrasing can help a great deal. (SDEx 3.2). Avoid filtering out difficult or undesirable messages. Recognize that people (all of us) often listen through their own biases and prejudices.

## Critically Decode and Encode Verbal Messages

The verbal messages you send or are about to send as well as those you receive need to be evaluated and critically analyzed. One of the most important types of messages that need careful regulation are those of self-disclosure. Remember the benefits and the dangers and regulate your disclosures after critical analysis (Chapter 2).

A chief concern should be to recognize what critical thinking theorists call "conceptual distortions" and what we have called "barriers to verbal interaction." Avoid the barriers and substitute a more critical, more realistic analysis (Chapter 4, SDEx 4.1, 4.2). Be especially careful to avoid dividing an issue into two extremes and then assuming they represent all ways of looking at things (polarization); confusing the label with what it stands for (intentional orientation); confusing inferences with facts (fact-inference confusion); assuming disagreement where there is none or agreement where there is actually disagreement (bypassing); acting as if you know all about anything (allness); treating a person as unchanging (static evaluation); and assuming that all people are the same because they are covered by the same label, for example, "teachers," "Asians," or "homeless" (indiscrimination).

## Critically Decode and Encode Nonverbal Messages

Critically assess the nonverbal messages that you send or receive. Ask yourself what meanings you are sending as well as receiving from nonverbals (Chapter 5).

Pay attention to contradictory messages—those that communicate opposite meanings, most often seen when nonverbal and verbal messages contradict. Be sure to use both verbal and nonverbal messages to consistently express your ideas. When you receive contradictory messages, stop—call up your mindful state—and figure out what is going on and to which message(s) you should respond.

Avoid the tendency to draw firm conclusions from the nonverbal behaviors of others since only general guesses can be logically drawn.

Verbal and nonverbal messages do not occur in isolation. To understand the meaning of any given message, look at all the communication process elements: context, sources-receivers, verbal and nonverbal messages (including feedback and feedforward), channel, noise, effects, and ethics.

---

## Critical Thinking Experience

### Thinking Critically about the Fundamentals of Human Communication

The objectives of this exercise are (1) to provide practice in applying critical thinking skills to the basic concepts of human communication (through defining and providing examples and through asking questions) and (2) to provide a useful procedure for reviewing the important concepts covered in Chapters 1 through 5.

Presented below are 78 concepts covered in this first part of *Essentials of Human Communication*. Taking the concepts in turn, each member of the group or class (1) defines it and gives an example and (2) asks a question about it.

1. Take special care to distinguish between but include both definitions and examples. This will avoid the tendency to substitute examples for definitions. It will also underscore the importance of examples. If we cannot give an example of a concept, it is a pretty good indication that the concept is really not clear. Both definitions and examples are crucial for understanding these concepts.

2. Questions asked may be of any type. Here are a few that might prove useful.

   **Questions of clarification:** How are feedback and feedforward related? How does our tendency to stereotype hinder intercultural communication?

   **Questions of challenge:** Can we really improve our listening effectiveness? Can't slang be effective?

   **Questions of application:** How might the concept of symmetrical and complementary relationships apply to the workplace? What listening skills are most important in parent-child communication?

   **Questions of ethics:** Is stereotyping unethical? Is it unethical to use racist, sexist, or heterosexist language?

   **Questions of supposition (what if):** What would happen if we could read another person's facial expressions like we read a book? What would happen if no one gossiped ever again?

communication
context
culture
source-receiver
encoding-decoding
competence
message
channel
feedback
feedforward
noise
effects
ethics
package of signals
process of adjustment
content and relationship dimensions
symmetrical and complementary relationships
punctuation
transactional nature of communication
inevitability
communication purposes
irreversibility
self-awareness
open self
blind self
hidden self

unknown self
self-esteem
self-disclosure
perception
implicit personality theory
self-fulfilling prophecy
primacy-recency
stereotyping
attribution
self-attribution
self-serving bias
mind reading
overattribution
listening
active listening
meaning
connotation and denotation
snarl and purr words
meanings are in people
polarization
intensional orientation
extensional orientation
fact-inference confusion
bypassing
static evaluation
allness
indiscrimination

in-group talk
self-talk, other-talk
gossip
confirmation and disconfirmation
racist language
sexist language
heterosexist language
nonverbal communication
body communication (kinesics)
emblems
illustrators
affect displays
regulators
adaptors
facial communication
primary affect displays
eye size and movements
space communication (proxemics)
territoriality
markers
artifactual communication
touch (haptics)
paralanguage
conversational turns
time communication

*Raphael's famed "School of Athens" depicts the great minds of Ancient Greece in discussion and argument. It includes Plato (center, under arch) pointing to heaven as the source of all ideas; Aristotle (center, on Plato's left) holding the* Ethics; *and Socrates (upper tier, ninth figure from left) discussing philosophy with Athens' youth. If you were to paint a picture of the great minds of the twentieth century, who would you include? What great ideas would you include?*

# CONTEXTS OF HUMAN COMMUNICATION

*Your most important communication experiences will occur in three major contexts: interpersonal, small group, and public. In the **interpersonal context** you interact with colleagues at work and with friends, lovers, and family in social situations. You also exchange information with others in formal and informal interviews.*

*In the **small group context** you interact with others—sometimes as group member and sometimes as group leader—to learn, solve problems, generate ideas, and acquire valuable coping skills.*

*In the **public speaking context** you deliver a wide variety of formal and informal presentations—explaining information to colleagues at work or persuading others to accept your point of view or to change their behaviors. The public speaking techniques of organization, research, audience analysis, supporting a point of*

*view, and using language that is appropriate and effective are skills you will be able to apply in all your communications throughout your professional career.*

*We present the three contexts in a natural progression, beginning with the simplest and the one with which you have had the most experience—two-person or interpersonal communication. We follow with small group communication which is somewhat more complex, but with which you have had considerable experience. We then cover public speaking, the most difficult and the one with which you have probably had the least experience.*

*At the end of this part, we will again highlight and summarize the critical thinking principles covered.*

*This part answers a number of significant questions that will help you improve your communication skills. Here is a sampling:*

## 6. INTERPERSONAL COMMUNICATION

*How can I make conversation more interesting and enjoyable? Can I learn to fight so that my relationships improve rather than deteriorate?*

## 7. INTERPERSONAL RELATIONSHIPS

*How can I develop relationships more effectively? How can I improve or repair my current relationships and prevent them from deteriorating?*

## 8. INTERVIEWING

*How can I best secure information in an interview? How can I better present myself to get that job I want? How do I write a job resumé?*

## 9. SMALL GROUPS

*How can I communicate in groups to solve problems more effectively and to learn more efficiently? What types of groups can best help me achieve my purposes?*

## 10. MEMBERS AND LEADERS IN GROUP COMMUNICATION

*How can I become a more productive group member? How can I learn to become a group leader?*

## 11. PUBLIC SPEAKING

*Can I overcome my fear of public speaking? How should I prepare a public speech?*

## 12. INFORMATION AND PERSUASION

*How can I present information effectively and efficiently? How can I persuade others to do as I think best?*

## 13. STYLE, DELIVERY, AND CRITICISM

*How can I make my ideas easily understood? How can I become an effective and dynamic speaker?*

## CRITICAL THINKING PERSPECTIVES AND REVIEW

*How can I critically evaluate interpersonal communication strategies? How can I critically evaluate persuasive appeals?*

CHAPTER 6

## Interpersonal Communication

### Goals

*After completing this chapter, you should be able to*

1. *define* interpersonal communication
2. *identify and explain "skills about skills"*
3. *define the ten characteristics of interpersonal communication effectiveness*
4. *describe the eight unproductive methods of conflict resolution*
5. *explain the five guides to effective conflict management*

*■ How effective are you interpersonally? ■ Can you feel the emotions others are feeling? ■ Are you confident? ■ Are you open? ■ In what ways might you increase your effectiveness in one-on-one encounters? ■ Why do so many important conflicts center on trivial issues? ■ Why do so many conflicts create additional problems? ■ How can you engage in conflict with your partner without destroying your relationship? ■ Is it possible to fight with your partner and have your relationship strengthened instead of weakened?*

## Interpersonal Communication

Interpersonal communication is communication between two persons who have a clearly established relationship. Thus interpersonal communication would include what takes place between a waiter and a customer, a son and his father, two people in an interview, and so on. This definition makes it is almost impossible to have a two-person communication that is not interpersonal. Not surprisingly, it is also referred to as the *dyadic* definition. Almost inevitably, there is some relationship between two persons. Even the stranger in the city who asks directions from a resident has a clearly defined relationship as soon as the first message is sent. Sometimes this relational or dyadic definition is extended to include small groups of persons, such as family members or groups of three or four friends.

Interpersonal communication, like any form of behavior, varies from extremely effective to extremely ineffective; no interpersonal encounter is a total failure or a total success. Some, however, are more effective than others. In the first part of this unit we review the characteristics of effective interpersonal communication—those qualities that foster meaningful, honest, and satisfying interactions and relationships (Bochner and Kelly 1974). They are also the qualities that make you effective in presenting yourself and in achieving your goals (Wiemann 1977; Wiemann and Backlund 1980; Spitzberg and Hecht 1984; Spitzberg and Cupach 1984, 1989; Ruben 1988).

In the second part, we examine the qualities of effectiveness given their severest test: in interpersonal conflict.

> **What is the most important type of interpersonal communication that you engage in? What type do you find the most difficult?**

## Effectiveness in Interpersonal Communication

We need to look at interpersonal communication skills on two levels. On one level there are the skills of effectiveness that you apply directly in your own communications (for example, openness or expressiveness). On another level, however, there are the guidelines that help you decide how to apply the specific skills to the specific communication situation. We need to discuss these "skills about skills" first; then we can turn to the more specific skills.

> **What characteristics would you include in your personal definition of interpersonal communication effectiveness?**

## Skills about Skills

There are four important skills to help you decide if, how, and when to apply the skills of interpersonal communication: mindfulness, cultural awareness, flexibility, and metacommunicational skills. These skills about skills will prove useful for applying the ten skills of interpersonal communication discussed next as well as the skills for managing interpersonal conflict.

## Mindfulness

After learning a skill or rule, we often apply it without thinking or "mindlessly," without considering the novel aspects of the unique situation (Langer 1989). For example, after learning active listening skills, many will respond to all situations with active listening responses. Sometimes these responses will be appropriate but at other times they will prove inappropriate and ineffective. Before responding, call up your mindful state. Think about the unique communication situation and consider your alternatives. Be alert and responsive to small changes in the situation that may cue which behaviors will be effective and which not.

> Speaking without thinking is shooting without aiming.
> —W. G. BENJAMIN

## Cultural Sensitivity

In applying interpersonal effectiveness skills, be sensitive to the cultural differences among people. What may prove effective for upper income people working in the IBM subculture of Boston or New York, may prove ineffective for lower income people working as fruit pickers in Florida or California. What works in Japan may not work in Mexico. The direct eye contact that signals immediacy in most of the United States may be considered rude or too intrusive in other cultures. The specific skills that we discuss are considered to be generally effective among most people in the United States. But, do note that these skills and how we communicate them verbally or nonverbally are specific to general United States culture.

> A slip of the foot may be soon recovered; but that of the tongue perhaps never.
> —THOMAS FULLER

Effectiveness in intercultural communication requires that we be (Kim 1991):

- *open* to new ideas and to differences among people;
- *flexible* in ways of communicating and in adapting to the communications of the culturally different;
- *tolerant* of other attitudes, values, and ways of doing things; and
- *creative* in seeking varied ways to communicate.

> If we understand others' languages, but not their culture, we can make fluent fools of ourselves.
> —WILLIAM B. GUDYKUNST

These qualities—along with some knowledge of the other culture and the general effectiveness skills "should enable a person to approach each intercultural encounter with the psychological posture of an interested learner. . . and to strive for the communication outcomes that are as effective as possible under a given set of relational and situational constraints" (Kim 1991).

## Flexibility

All effectiveness qualities need to be used flexibly (Hart and Burks 1972; Hart, Carlson, and Eadie 1980). Although we provide general principles for effective interpersonal communication, when applying them, be flexible and sensitive to the unique factors present. Thus, you may be frank and spontaneous when talking with a close friend about your feelings but you may not want to be so open when talking with your grandparents about the dinner they prepared that you disliked.

## Metacommunicational Ability

Much of our talk concerns people, objects, and events in the world. But, we also talk about our talk. We metacommunicate; we communicate about our communication. Our interpersonal effectiveness often hinges on this ability. Let's say that someone says something positive but in a negative way, for example, "Yes, I think you did [long pause] a good job" but with no enthusiasm and an avoidance of eye contact. You are faced with several alternatives. You may respond to the message as positive or as negative.

A third alternative, however, is to talk about the message. You could say something like, "I'm not sure I understand if you're pleased or not with what I did. You said you were pleased but I seem to detect dissatisfaction in your voice. Am I wrong?" In this way, you may avoid many misunderstandings. When you do talk about your talk, do so only to gain an understanding of the other person's thoughts and feelings. Avoid substituting talk about talk for talk about a specific problem.

### TEST YOURSELF:

### How Effective Are You Interpersonally?

Test yourself on your interpersonal communication skills. Indicate the degree to which each of the following is true of your general interpersonal communications. Use the following scale:

1 = always or almost always true

2 = frequently true

3 = sometimes true

4 = rarely true

5 = never or almost never true

_____ 1. In my communications I am willing to reveal myself to others.

_____ 2. When communicating, I can feel what the other person is feeling.

_____ 3. In my interpersonal interactions I describe rather than evaluate and I state my views tentatively rather than with certainty.

_____ 4. I express positive attitudes, and compliment the person I communicate with.

_____ 5. I look upon the other person and myself as essentially equal partners in the communication act.

_____ 6. I am confident and communicate this confidence in my interpersonal interactions.

_____ 7. I communicate a sense of togetherness, of oneness, with my listener.

*Continued*

_____ 8. I manage the interpersonal communication situation to both my own and the other person's satisfaction.
_____ 9. I communicate my genuine involvement in the interpersonal interaction.
_____10. I adapt to the needs of the other person (rather than only considering my own needs) during the interpersonal interaction.

*Scoring:* This test was designed to introduce the concepts of interpersonal effectiveness to be discussed in this chapter and not to provide you with a specific score. The effectiveness concepts are discussed in the same order as the questions here: (1) openness, (2) empathy, (3) supportiveness, (4) positiveness, (5) equality, (6) confidence, (7) immediacy, (8) interaction management, (9) expressiveness, and (10) other-orientation.

As you read about these concepts, keep in mind that the most effective communicator is flexible and adapts to the individual situation. Although to be always open, empathic, or supportive will probably prove ineffective, these qualities are generally appropriate to most interpersonal interactions. So, perhaps responses of 2's and 3's would be most representative of effective communication. And, remember that the ability to control these qualities—rather than exhibit them reflexively—is the ultimate aim of a course in interpersonal communication.

> [Communication competence] is the yardstick for measuring the quality of our interpersonal relationships. Moreover, the acquisition of communication competence is necessary to fulfill the general need of all humans to control their environment.
> —BRIAN H. SPITZBERG AND WILLIAM R. CUPACH

> Have you ever been too open with someone? What happened?

> Patience is an important ingredient for open communication.
> —KEVIN J. MURPHY

> Beware of people who don't know how to say "I am sorry." They are weak and frightened, and will, sometimes at the slightest provocation, fight with the desperate ferocity of a frightened animal that feels cornered.
> —THOMAS SZASZ

## Openness

*Openness* refers to at least three aspects of interpersonal communication. First, effective interpersonal communication requires an appropriate degree of openness with others. This does not mean that you should immediately pour out your entire life history. Interesting as that may be, it is not usually helpful to the communication. Rather, there should be a willingness to self-disclose—to reveal information about yourself—provided such disclosures are appropriate (see Chapter 3).

A second aspect of openness refers to a communicator's willingness to react honestly to incoming messages. Silent, uncritical, and immovable people are generally boring conversationalists.

The third aspect of openness concerns the "owning" of feelings and thoughts (Bochner and Kelley 1974). To be open in this sense is to acknowledge that the feelings and thoughts you express are yours and that you bear the responsibility for them. The best way to express this responsibility is with "I" messages.

"I" messages show that you own your feelings and thoughts, unlike Flip in the cartoon. When you use "I" messages you say, in effect, "This is how *I* feel," "This is how *I* see the situation," "This is what *I* think." Instead of saying, "This conversation is useless," you would say, "*I'm* bored by this conversation," or any other statement that shows that *I* am making an evaluation and not describing objective reality.

## Empathy

Empathy is "the ability of one person to 'know' what another is experiencing at any given moment, from the latter's frame of reference, through the latter's eyes" (Backrack 1976). To sympathize, on the other

"I didn't track it in, it followed me in."

FLIP, REPRINTED BY PERMISSION OF JERRY MARCUS

In what types of situations are you most likely to talk like Flip and deny responsibility for your thoughts or actions?

hand, is to feel *for* the individual—to feel sorry for the person, for example. To empathize is to feel *as* the individual feels—to feel the same feelings in the same way.

Empathic people are able to understand other people's motivations and experiences, their present feelings and attitudes, and their hopes and expectations for the future. Such empathic understanding better enables you to adjust your communications. You might avoid certain topics or introduce others. You might remain silent or engage in self-disclosure. In fact, your ability to communicate this empathic feeling is part of your empathy. "Accurate empathy," writes C. Truax (1961), "involves both the sensitivity to current feelings and the verbal facility to communicate this understanding."

How empathic do you consider yourself to be? Who is the most empathic person you've ever met? How did this person communicate this empathic feeling?

The first step in achieving empathy is to resist the temptation to evaluate, judge, interpret, and criticize. It is not that these responses are "wrong," but that they often get in the way of understanding. Focus on understanding.

Second, learn as much as you can about the person—her or his desires, experiences, abilities, fears, and so on. The more you know, the more you will be able to see and feel what that person sees and feels. If you have difficulty understanding the other person's perspective, ask questions, seek clarification, and encourage the person to talk.

Third, try to experience what the other person is feeling from his or her point of view. Playing the other's role in your mind (or even aloud) can help you see the world a little more as the other person does.

How can you tell when another person feels empathy toward you?

You can communicate empathy both nonverbally and verbally. Nonverbally, you communicate empathy by (1) an active involvement with the other person through appropriate facial expressions and gestures, (2) a focused concentration including eye contact, attentive body posture, and physical closeness, and (3) appropriate touching.

Verbally you communicate empathy in several ways (Authier and Gustafson 1982).

- Reflect back to the speaker the feelings (and their intensity) that you think are being experienced. This helps to check the accuracy of your perceptions and to show you are trying to understand.

- Consider making tentative statements rather than asking questions. Thus, instead of saying, "Are you really angry with your father?" you might say, "I get the impression you're angry with your father" or "I hear anger in your voice."

- Question mixed messages in which the verbal and nonverbal components contradict each other: "You say everything is fine with you and Chris but you don't sound convincing. You seem down." This helps foster more open and honest communication.

- Self-disclose related incidents and feelings to communicate your appreciation and understanding of what the other is experiencing. This says to the other person: "I can feel what you are feeling."

**Has your empathy ever caused you any difficulties?**

### Supportiveness

An effective interpersonal relationship is supportive—a concept that owes much to the work of Jack Gibb (1961; Brougher 1982; Wells 1980). Open and empathic communication cannot survive in an unsupportive atmosphere. You demonstrate supportiveness by being (1) descriptive rather than evaluative, and (2) provisional rather than certain.

DESCRIPTIVENESS. A communication perceived as a request for information or a description of some event, is generally not perceived as threatening. You are not being challenged and have no need to defend yourself. On the other hand, a judgmental communication ("Why are you so hostile?") often leads us to become defensive—to respond with statements that protect and defend: "I am not hostile!"

> **We rarely confide in those who are better than we are.**
> **—ALBERT CAMUS**

This is not to imply that all evaluative communications elicit defensive responses. People often respond to positive evaluations without defensiveness. Even here, however, the very fact that someone has the power to evaluate you in any way (even if positively) may make you feel uneasy and perhaps defensive. You may anticipate that the next evaluation will not be so positive. Similarly, negative evaluations do not always elicit defensive responses. The aspiring actor who wants to improve and perfect technique often welcomes negative (but constructive) evaluations.

These three rules may help you to be more descriptive, less evaluative, and hence less encouraging of another's defensiveness (Brougher 1982).

- Describe what happened: "I lost the promotion."
- Describe how you feel: "I feel miserable and I feel I've failed."
- Describe how this relates to the other person: "Would you mind if we went to the city tonight? I need to forget the job and everything about it." Avoid accusations or blame. Avoid negative evaluative terms: "Didn't your sister look *horrible* in that red dress?" Avoid preaching: "Why don't you learn something about word processing before you open your mouth?"

PROVISIONALISM. Being provisional means having a tentative, open-minded attitude, a willingness to hear opposing views and to change your position if warranted. Such provisionalism, rather than unwavering certainty, helps create a supportive atmosphere.

We resist people who "know everything" and who always have a definite answer to any question. Such people are set in their ways and will tolerate no differences. They have arguments ready for any alternative attitude or belief. After a very short time, we become defensive with such people, and hold back our attitudes rather than subject them to attack. But we open up with people who take a more provisional position and are willing to change their minds. With such people we feel equal.

When we act certain and closed-minded, we encourage defensive behavior in the listener. When we act in a provisional manner—with an open mind, with full recognition that we might be wrong, and with a willingness to revise our attitudes and opinions—we encourage supportiveness.

### Positiveness

Positiveness refers to an optimistic, favorable, or complimentary point of view. We communicate positiveness interpersonally in at least two ways: (1) stating favorable attitudes and (2) complimenting or stroking the person with whom we interact.

ATTITUDES. A positive regard for yourself fosters interpersonal communication. If you feel negatively about yourself, you will invariably communicate these feelings to others. If you convey positive feelings about yourself to others, they are likely to reflect this positive regard.

A positive feeling for the general communication situation is also important for effective interaction. Nothing is more unpleasant than communicating with someone who does not enjoy the exchange or does not respond favorably to the situation or context. A negative response to the situation ("I can't wait to get out of this dump") makes you feel almost as if you are intruding, and communication seems sure to break down quickly.

STROKING. Stroking behavior contributes to positiveness by acknowledging the existence, and in fact the importance, of the other person; it is the antithesis of indifference. Stroking may be verbal ("I enjoy being with you" or "You're a pig") or nonverbal (a pat on the back or a punch in the mouth). As these examples illustrate, stroking may be positive or negative.

Positive stroking (similar to our concept of positiveness) generally takes the form of compliments or rewards, and consists of behaviors we would normally look forward to, enjoy, and take pride in. They bolster our self-image and make us feel better. Negative strokes, on the other hand, are punishing and aversive.

### Equality

In any situation, there is probably some inequality. One person will be smarter, richer, better looking, or more athletic than the other. Never are two people absolutely equal in all respects. Despite this inequality,

> Reading made Don Quixote a gentleman, but believing what he read made him mad.
> —GEORGE BERNARD SHAW

> I can live for two months on one good compliment.
> —MARK TWAIN

> How would you rate yourself on a positive (10) to negative (1) scale? Would others who know you well rate you in the same way?

> A plastic compliment is a compliment that starts out feeling good but ends up feeling bad. "You sound good for a kid who can't carry a tune," "That looks good considering you made it," or "I like you no matter what anybody says" are examples.
> —JEAN ILLSLEY CLARKE

interpersonal communication is more effective when the atmosphere is one of equality. That is, there should be a tacit recognition that both parties are valuable and worthwhile and that each has something important to contribute (also see discussion of disconfirmation in Chapter 4).

One of the most frequent ways we neglect equality is in the way we ask questions. Compare these examples:

1. "When will you learn to phone for reservations? Must I do everything?"
2. "One of us should phone for reservations. Do you want me to do it, or do you want to do it?"

In the first sentence, there is no equality. One person demands compliance from the other. Such questions encourage defensiveness, resentment, and hostility. They provoke arguments rather than solve problems. In the second sentence, there is equality—an explicitly stated desire to work together to address a specific problem. As a general rule, requests (especially courteous ones) communicate equality; demands (especially discourteous ones) communicate superiority.

In an interpersonal relationship characterized by equality, disagreement and conflict are seen as attempts to understand inevitable differences rather than as opportunities to put the other person down. Equality does not require that we accept or approve all the verbal and nonverbal behaviors of the other person.

> [Equality is] a condition we desire only with our superiors.
> —ANON

### Confidence

The effective communicator has social confidence; any anxiety is not readily perceived by others. The effective communicator feels comfortable with the other person and with the communication situation generally. This quality also enables the speaker to deal effectively with people who are anxious, shy, or apprehensive and to make them feel more comfortable.

The socially confident communicator is relaxed, rather than rigid; flexible in voice and body, rather than locked into one or two ranges of voice or body movement; and controlled, rather than shaky or awkward.

A relaxed posture, researchers find, communicates a sense of control, status, and power. Tenseness, rigidity, and discomfort, on the other hand, signal a lack of self-control, which in turn signals an inability to control your environment or fellow workers and an impression of being under the power and control of some outside force or person.

> As is our confidence, so is our capacity.
> —WILLIAM HAZLETT

> Only trust thyself, and another shall not betray thee.
> —WILLIAM PENN

## TEST YOURSELF:

### How Apprehensive Are You in Interpersonal Conversations?*

Although we often think of apprehension or fear of speaking in connection with public speaking, each of us has a certain degree of apprehension in all forms of communication. The following brief test is designed to measure your apprehension in interpersonal conversations.

This questionnaire consists of six statements concerning your feelings about interpersonal conversations. Indicate in the space provided the

*Continued*

degree to which each statement applies to you by marking whether you (1) Strongly Agree, (2) Agree, (3) Are Undecided, (4) Disagree, or (5) Strongly Disagree with each statement. There are no right or wrong answers. Do not be concerned that some of the statements are similar to others. Work quickly, just record your first impression.

_____ 1. While participating in a conversation with a new acquaintance, I feel very nervous.
_____ 2. I have no fear of speaking up in conversations.
_____ 3. Ordinarily I am very tense and nervous in conversations.
_____ 4. Ordinarily I am very calm and relaxed in conversations.
_____ 5. While conversing with a new acquaintance, I feel very relaxed.
_____ 6. I'm afraid to speak up in conversations.

*Scoring:* To obtain your apprehension score, use the following formula:

18 plus scores for items 2, 4, and 5;
minus scores for items 1, 3, and 6.

A score above 18 shows some degree of apprehension.

*From An Introduction to Rhetorical Communication*, 4th ed. by James C. McCroskey. Reprinted by permission of the author.

Why is apprehension so important in interpersonal communication? How might apprehension hinder effective interpersonal communication?

## Immediacy

*Immediacy* refers to the joining of the speaker and listener, the creation of a sense of togetherness, of oneness. The communicator who demonstrates immediacy conveys a sense of interest and attention, a liking for and an attraction to the other person. People respond more favorably to language that demonstrates immediacy than to language that demonstrates nonimmediacy. Immediacy joins speaker and listener; nonimmediacy separates them.

Nonverbally we communicate immediacy by maintaining appropriate eye contact, a physical closeness that echoes a psychological closeness, and a direct and open body posture. This involves arranging the body to keep others away from you, limiting looking and smiling at others, and similar behaviors.

Immediacy is communicated verbally in a variety of ways.

- Use the other person's name: "Joe, what do you think?" "I like that, Mary."

- Use pronouns that include both speaker and listener. For example, use *we, us,* and *our* instead of *you and I.* Say, "Why don't we go out tonight?" instead of "Why don't you and I go out tonight."

- Provide relevant feedback. For example, acknowledge and comment on what the other person has said. Use comments such as "That sounds right," "I understand what you mean," and "I think you're right."

- Show that you are focusing on the other person's remarks. For example, use questions that ask for clarification or elaboration, such as "Do you think the same thing is true of baseball?" Also, include references to the speaker's previous remarks, such as "Colorado does sound like a great vacation spot."

- Reinforce, reward, or compliment the other person: "I like your new outfit" or "Your comments were really to the point."
- Incorporate self-references into evaluative statements rather than depersonalizing them. Say, for example, "I think your report is great" rather than "Your report is great" or "Everyone likes your report."

## Interaction Management

The effective communicator controls the interaction to the satisfaction of both parties. In effective interaction management, neither person feels ignored or on stage. Each contributes to the total communication interchange.

What television character do you think best exemplifies the qualities of interpersonal effectiveness described here?

Maintaining your role as speaker or listener and passing back and forth—through appropriate eye movements, vocal expressions, and body and facial gestures—the opportunity to speak are interaction management skills. Similarly, keeping the conversation flowing and relatively fluent, without long and awkward pauses, are signs of effective interaction management.

The effective interaction manager presents consistent verbal and nonverbal messages that reinforce each other. As Jacqueline Shannon (1987) notes, women generally use more positive or pleasant nonverbal expressions than men. For example, women smile, nod in agreement, and openly verbalize positive feelings more. When expressing anger or power, however, many women continue to use these positive nonverbal signals, which dilute the verbally expressed anger or power. The net result is that such women appear uncomfortable with strong negative emotions and expressions of power, and other people are therefore less likely to believe or feel threatened by them.

Do you agree with Shannon's observation? If so, what advice would you give women? What advice would you give men?

SELF-MONITORING. Integrally related to interpersonal interaction management is *self-monitoring*. Before reading further, take the self-monitoring test.

### TEST YOURSELF:

### *Are You a High Self-Monitor?*

These statements concern personal reactions to a number of different situations. No two statements are exactly alike, so before answering, carefully consider each statement as it applies to you. If a statement is true or mostly true, write *T*. If a statement is false or not usually true, write *F*.

_____ 1. I find it hard to imitate the behavior of other people.
_____ 2. I guess I do put on a show to impress or entertain people.
_____ 3. I would probably make a good actor.
_____ 4. I sometimes appear to others to be experiencing deeper emotions than I actually am.
_____ 5. In a group of people, I am rarely the center of attention.
_____ 6. In different situations and with different people, I often act like very different persons.
_____ 7. I can argue only for ideas I already believe.

*Continued*

_____ 8. In order to get along and be liked, I tend to be what people expect me to be rather than who I really am.

_____ 9. I may deceive people by being friendly when I really dislike them.

_____10. I am always the person I appear to be.

*Scoring.* Give yourself one point for each of questions 1, 5, and 7 that you answered *F*. Give yourself one point for each of the remaining questions that you answered *T*. Add up your points. If you are a good judge of yourself and scored 7 or above, you are probably a high self-monitoring individual; 3 or below, you are probably a low self-monitoring individual.

SOURCE: THIS TEST APPEARED IN MARK SNYDER, "THE MANY ME'S OF THE SELF-MONITOR," *PSYCHOLOGY TODAY* 13 (MARCH 1980), P. 34, AND IS REPRINTED HERE BY PERMISSION OF MARK SNYDER.

Self-monitoring refers to the manipulation of the image that we present to others (Snyder 1986). High self-monitors carefully adjust their behaviors on the basis of feedback from others, to produce the most desirable effect. Low self-monitors, on the other hand, are not concerned with the image they present. Rather, their interactions are characterized by an openness in which they communicate their thoughts and feelings with no attempt to manipulate the impressions they create.

Although these seem to be two relatively clear-cut types, we all engage in selective monitoring, depending on the situation. You are more likely to monitor your behavior at a job interview, for example, than when interacting with a group of friends.

### Expressiveness

**In what situations would increased self-monitoring increase your interpersonal effectiveness? Is there an ethical dimension to self-monitoring?**

*Expressiveness* refers to the skill in communicating genuine involvement in the conversation. It is similar to openness in its emphasis on involvement, and includes, for example, expressing responsibility for ("owning") your thoughts and feelings, encouraging expressiveness or openness in others, and providing feedback that is relevant and appropriate. This quality also includes taking responsibility for both talking and listening and in this way is similar to equality.

**How expressive are you? Ask a close friend to comment on your expressiveness. Do your opinions match?**

You can demonstrate expressiveness by using appropriate variations in vocal rate, pitch, volume, and rhythm to convey involvement and interest and by allowing your facial muscles to reflect and echo your inner involvement. Similarly, the use of gestures (appropriate in style and frequency) communicates involvement. Using too few gestures signals lack of interest; too many may communicate discomfort, uneasiness, and awkwardness.

The motionless speaker who talks about sex, winning the lottery, and fatal illnesses all in the same monotone, with a static posture and an expressionless face, is the stereotype of the nonexpressive speaker.

### Other-Orientation

**All the thoughts of a turtle are turtle.**
—RALPH WALDO EMERSON

Other-orientation is the opposite of self-orientation. It refers to your ability to adapt to the other person during the interpersonal encounter. It involves communicating attentiveness and interest in what the other

*What quality of interpersonal communication effectiveness most closely draws you to others? What quality is the most difficult for you to incorporate into your own interpersonal behaviors? Why?*

**Never speak of yourself to others; make them talk about themselves instead: therein lies the whole art of pleasing.**
**—J. AND E. DE GONCOURT**

**How would you describe the self-oriented speaker? The self-oriented listener?**

**What characteristic of interpersonal effectiveness do you think is the most important? For each quality can you identify a situation in which it should *not* be applied?**

person is saying. As an other-oriented communicator you see the situation and the interaction from the viewpoint of the other person and appreciate the different ways in which this other person punctuates the sequence of events.

You communicate your orientation toward another person nonverbally through focused eye contact, smiles, head nods, leaning toward the other person, and displaying feelings and emotions through appropriate facial expression. Verbally you show interest through such comments as "I see" and "Really," through requests for further information ("What else did you do in Vegas?"), and through expressions of empathy ("I can understand what you're going through; my parents divorced recently, too").

## *Effectiveness in Interpersonal Conflict*

The principles of interpersonal effectiveness receive their toughest test in interpersonal conflict. During such a conflict you are least likely to be mindful, sensitive to cultural differences, flexible, or to want to talk about your talk. Let's look first at the nature of interpersonal conflict and then examine the various strategies we use when we fight.

## What Is Interpersonal Conflict?

From a communication perspective, *conflict is an expressed struggle between at least two interdependent parties who perceive incompatible goals, scarce rewards, and interference from the other party in achieving their goals.*
—JOYCE HOCKER AND
  WILLIAM WILMOT

Tom wants to go to the movies and Sara wants to stay home. Tom's insisting on going to the movies interferes with Sara's staying home and Sara's determination to stay home interferes with Tom's going to the movies. Randy and Grace have been dating. Randy wants to get married; Grace wants to continue dating. Opposing goals interfere with each attaining his or her goals.

As experience teaches us, conflicts can be of various types:

- goals to be pursued ("We want you to go to college and become a teacher or a doctor, not a disco dancer");

- allocation of resources such as money or time ("I want to spend the tax refund on a car, not on new furniture");

- decisions to be made ("I refuse to have the Jeffersons over for dinner");

- behaviors considered appropriate or desirable by one person and inappropriate or undesirable by the other ("I hate it when you get drunk, pinch me, ridicule me in front of others, flirt with others, dress provocatively....").

How would you describe your own interpersonal conflicts? Do the types identified here cover most interpersonal conflicts? What other types would you identify?

### Content and Relationship Conflicts

Using concepts developed earlier (Chapter 1), we may distinguish between content conflict and relationship conflict. *Content conflict* centers on objects, events, and persons that are usually, but not always or entirely, external to the parties involved in the conflict. These include the millions of issues that we argue and fight about every day—the value of a particular movie, what to watch on television, the fairness of the last examination or job promotion, and the way to spend our savings.

*Relationship conflicts* are equally numerous and include such conflict situations as a younger brother who disobeys his older brother, two partners who want an equal say in making vacation plans, and the mother and daughter who each want to have the final word concerning the daughter's life-style. Here the conflicts do not concern some external object as much as relationships between the individuals—issues such as who is in charge, the equality of a primary relationship, and who has the right to set down rules of behavior.

Which type of conflict is easier to resolve? Why? Which type is potentially the most destructive of interpersonal relationships?

It is easier to separate content and relationship conflicts in a textbook than in real life, where many contain both elements. But if we can recognize which issues pertain to content and which to relationship, we can understand the conflict well enough to manage it effectively and productively.

### Myths about Interpersonal Conflict

One of the problems in studying and dealing with interpersonal conflict is that we may have false assumptions about what conflict is and what it means. For example, do you think the following are true or false?

- If two people in a relationship fight, it means their relationship is a bad one.

- Fighting hurts an interpersonal relationship.

What beliefs do you have about interpersonal conflict? How do these beliefs influence the way you engage in interpersonal conflict?

- Fighting is bad because it reveals our negative selves, for example, our pettiness, our need to be in control, our unreasonable expectations.

As with many things, the easy answer is not always correct. The three assumptions above may all be true or false. It depends. In and of itself, conflict is neither good nor bad. Conflict is a part of every interpersonal relationship, between parents and children, brothers and sisters, friends, lovers, co-workers. If it isn't, then the relationship is probably dull, irrelevant, or insignificant. Conflict is inevitable in any meaningful relationship.

It is not so much the conflict that creates the problem as the way in which the individuals approach and deal with it. Some approaches can resolve difficulties and improve the relationship while others can do damage—destroy self-esteem, create bitterness, and foster suspicion. Our task is not to create conflict-free relationships but to learn appropriate and productive ways to manage with conflict.

Similarly, it is not the conflict that will reveal our negative side but our fight strategies. We reveal our negative side when we personally attack the other person, use force, or personal rejection or manipulation. But, we can also reveal our positive selves—our willingness to listen to opposing points of view, to change unpleasant behaviors, and to accept imperfection in others.

When we attempt to resolve conflict within an interpersonal relationship, we are saying in effect that the relationship is worth the effort; otherwise we would walk away. Although there may be exceptions—as when we confront to save face or to gratify some ego need—usually confronting a conflict indicates concern, commitment, and a desire to preserve the relationship.

We need to learn not to avoid conflict but to engage in it with effective and productive strategies that will address our problem and improve our relationship. As a preface to this discussion take the "How Do You Fight?" test.

> Never go to bed mad. Stay up and fight.
> —PHYLLIS DILLER

> Where there is no difference, there is only indifference.
> —LOUIS NIZER

> In one sentence, how would you describe your style of conflict?

## TEST YOURSELF:

### *How Do You Fight?*

*Instructions:* The following statements refer to ways in which you may communicate in an interpersonal conflict situation—one involving a disagreement between yourself and some other individual with whom you have an interpersonal relationship, such as a friend, lover, or family member. For each of the following statements indicate *T* (true) if the statement is a generally accurate description of your conflict behavior, and *F* (false) if the statement is a generally inaccurate description of your conflict behavior.

_____ 1. I avoid conflict situations by physically leaving the situation.
_____ 2. I state my feelings and thoughts openly, directly, and honestly without any attempt to disguise the real object of my disagreement.
_____ 3. I try to force the other person to accept my way of thinking by physically overpowering the individual or by threatening to use physical force.
_____ 4. I take responsibility for my thoughts and feelings. I say "I feel hurt. . . ." rather than "You hurt me. . . ."

*Continued*

Never argue at the dinner table, for the one who is not hungry always gets the best of the argument.
—Richard Whately

_____ 5. I use humor (especially sarcasm or ridicule) to minimize the conflict.

_____ 6. I try to feel what the other person is feeling and see the situation as the other person does.

_____ 7. I try to establish blame before attempting to resolve the conflict.

_____ 8. I validate the other person's feelings. I let the other person know that I think his or her feelings are legitimate and appropriate.

_____ 9. I cry and sometimes pretend to be extremely emotional in order to get my way or win the argument.

_____10. I concentrate on describing the behaviors with which I have difficulty rather than evaluating them.

_____11. I remember and store up grievances (for example, past indiscretions and mistakes) and bring them up when a conflict arises.

_____12. I state my position tentatively—provisionally—rather than as the final word. Further, I demonstrate flexibility and a willingness to change my opinion or position should appropriate reasons be given.

_____13. In an interpersonal conflict situation, I bring up the strongest arguments I can find, even if they are ones the other person cannot deal with effectively or they may hurt the other person's ego or self-esteem.

_____14. I emphasize areas of agreement before approaching the disagreements.

_____15. I attempt to manipulate the other person by being especially charming (even disarming) and getting the other into a receptive and non-combative frame of mind.

_____16. I express positive feelings for the other person and for the relationship between us even during the actual conflict exchange.

_____17. I withhold love and affection and attempt to win the argument by getting the other person to break down under this withdrawal.

_____18. I treat my combatant as an equal.

_____19. I sometimes refuse to discuss the conflict or disagreement and even to listen to the other person's argument or point of view.

_____20. I engage in conflict actively rather than passively as both speaker and listener.

_Scoring:_ This conflict scale was developed to sensitize you to some of the conflict strategies to be discussed in this chapter rather than to provide you with a specific score. Generally, however, you would be following recommended conflict resolution procedures if you responded _T_ to the even-numbered statements and _F_ to the odd-numbered statements.

Some of the statements refer to general principles of effective interpersonal communication that we've covered. These are statements (2) openness, (4) openness, (6) empathy, (8) empathy, (10) supportiveness, (12) supportiveness, (14) positiveness, (18) equality, and (20) equality. The other statements refer to strategies and techniques covered in this chapter. These are statements (1) avoidance, (3) force, (5) using humor to ridicule, (7) blame, (9) silencers, (11) gunnysacking, (13) beltlining, (15) manipulation, (17) personal rejection, and (19) nonnegotiation.

Actually, conflict can be either good or bad. To a large degree it depends on what we make of it. The desired goal of a dispute should not be victory but peace. Each conflict can be the beginning of the solution to painful problems.
—John W. Vale and Robert B. Hughes

## Unproductive Conflict Management

The major value in examining ineffective methods is to help us identify them in the behaviors of others and ultimately in our own behaviors. Once we can identify them, we can try to reduce them in our own communications.

*"We only learned to talk yesterday, and now we're not speaking."*

AVOIDANCE. *Avoidance* is well illustrated in the cartoon of the cave-dwellers. Often this takes the form of actual physical flight. The person may leave the scene of the conflict, fall asleep, or blast the stereo.

At times the conflict is defined out of existence, as when someone says, "It was not a date—it was a business trip that we had to take together." At other times, the conflict may be redefined so that it becomes a totally different issue, as when someone says, "Your jealousy is getting out of hand. You really had better see a therapist about it."

Notice that with these types of behavior, the conflict source is never confronted. It is just pushed aside. You can be almost certain, however, that it will surface again.

FORCE. When confronted with conflict, many people prefer not to deal with the issues but rather to physically force their position on the other person. At times, the force used is more emotional than physical. In either case, however, the issues are avoided and the person who "wins" is the one who exerts the most force. This is the technique of warring nations, children, and even some normally sensible and mature adults.

More than 50 percent of couples, both single and married, reported that they had experienced physical violence in their relationship. If we add symbolic violence (for example, threatening to hit the other person or throwing something), the percentages are above 60 percent for singles and above 70 percent for marrieds (Marshall and Rose 1987). In another study, 47 percent of a sample of 410 college students reported some experience with violence in a dating relationship. In most cases the violence was reciprocal—each person in the relationship used violence.

One of the most puzzling findings is that many victims of violence interpret it as a sign of love. For some reason, they see being beaten, verbally abused, or raped as a sign that their partner is fully in love with them. Many victims, in fact, accept the blame for contributing to the violence instead of blaming their partners (Gelles and Cornell 1985).

MINIMIZATION. Sometimes we deal with conflict by making light of it. We say and perhaps believe that the conflict, its causes, and its consequences

---

Every difficulty slurred over will be a ghost to disturb your repose later on.
—CHOPIN

---

The aim of an argument or discussion should not be victory, but progress.
—JOSEPH JOURBERT

---

What part has force played in your own interpersonal relationships?

---

*"You know what your problem is? You don't know what your problem is … That's what your problem is!!"*

CARTOON BY RICK STROMOSKI

are really not important. We use minimization when we make light of the other person's feelings: "What are you so angry about? I'm only forty minutes late." When you do this, you are in effect telling the other person that his or her feelings are not legitimate. Rather than minimize the other person's feelings, try to validate and acknowledge their legitimacy: "You have a right to be angry. I should have called when I knew I'd be late."

BLAME. Most often conflict is caused by such a wide variety of factors that any attempt to single out one or two is doomed to failure. And yet, a frequently employed fight strategy is to avoid dealing with the conflict by blaming someone else. In some instances we blame ourselves, but more often, we blame the other person. For example, a couple has a conflict over a child's getting into trouble with the police. Instead of dealing with the conflict itself, the parents blame each other for the child's troubles. Such blaming does nothing to resolve the conflict or to help the child.

SILENCERS. *Silencers* include a wide array of fight techniques that literally silence the other individual. One frequently used silencer is crying. When unable to deal with a conflict or when winning seems unlikely, an individual may silence the other person by crying. Another silencer is to feign extreme emotionalism—to yell and scream and pretend to lose control. Still another is to develop some "physical" reaction—headaches and shortness of breath are probably the most popular.

One of the major problems with silencers is that you can never be certain if they are strategies to win the argument or real physical reactions that need attention. Regardless of what you do, the conflict remains unexamined and unresolved.

GUNNYSACKING. A gunnysack is a large bag, usually made of burlap. As a conflict strategy, *gunnysacking* refers to the practice of storing up grievances and then unloading them during a fight. The immediate occasion may be relatively simple (or so it might seem at first), such as coming home late without calling. Instead of arguing about this, the gunnysacker unloads all past grievances: the birthday you forgot, the time two months ago when you arrived late for an important dinner, the time last year when you delayed making hotel reservations until the

**What are some other consequences of blaming?**

**Silence—the most perfect expression of scorn.**
—GEORGE BERNARD SHAW

**What effects does gunnysacking have on future attempts to discuss and resolve conflicts?**

rooms were all taken, and on and on. As can be expected, the original problem frequently does not get addressed. Instead, resentment and hostility escalate. The true gunnysacker, even after unloading these grievances, will put them right back in the sack to be dumped out at some later date.

MANIPULATION. In *manipulation*, there is avoidance of open conflict. The individual tries to divert the conflict by being especially charming (disarming, actually). The objective is to get the other person into a receptive and noncombative frame of mind before disagreeing. By so handling the conflict situation and the other person, the manipulating individual may eventually win the argument or disagreement.

PERSONAL REJECTION. In *personal rejection*, the individual withholds love and affection, seeking to win the argument by getting the other person to break down under this withdrawal. The individual acts cold and uncaring, trying to demoralize the other person. In withdrawing affection, the individual hopes to make the other person question his or her self-worth. Once the other is demoralized and feels unworthy, it is relatively easy to get one's own way. The person simply makes the restitution of love and affection contingent upon resolving the conflict in his or her favor.

## Productive Conflict Management

We approach effective conflict management by examining some of the insights provided by George Bach and Peter Wyden in their influential *Intimate Enemy*. Their simple but powerful guides to fair fighting will go a long way toward making our interpersonal conflicts more productive.

FIGHT ABOVE THE BELT. Restrict your blows (in topic and in intensity) to what the other person can absorb without severe emotional injury. Don't hit Jessica with her inability to have children or Michael with his failure to secure a permanent job. These attacks may easily prevent continued communication and may encourage resentment and perhaps retaliation.

FIGHT ACTIVELY. Play an active role in your interpersonal conflicts. Don't close your ears (or mind), blast the television, or walk out of the house during an argument. This is not to say that a cooling-off period is not at times desirable. It is to say that if you are to resolve conflicts, you need to confront them actively.

TAKE RESPONSIBILITY FOR YOUR THOUGHTS AND FEELINGS. When you disagree with your partner or find fault with her or his behavior, take responsibility for these feelings. Say, for example, "I disagree with. . . ." or "I don't like it when you. . . ." Don't avoid responsibility by saying, for example, "Everybody thinks you're wrong about. . . ." or "Chris thinks you shouldn't. . . ." Own your own thoughts and feelings and make this ownership explicit with "I" messages.

BE DIRECT AND SPECIFIC. Focus on the here-and-now rather than on issues that occurred two months ago (as in gunnysacking). Similarly, focus on the person with whom you are fighting, not on the person's mother, boss, child, or friends.

What unproductive conflict strategies do you use? Have they proved effective in the short run? In the long run?

One of the greatest gifts you can give the people you love is to hear their anger and frustration without judging or contradicting them.
—HAROLD H. BLOOMFIELD

Make the most of the best and the least of the worst.
—ROBERT LOUIS STEVENSON

Why do statements such as "You make me so angry," "You make me feel stupid," and "You never want to have any fun" cause interpersonal difficulties?

*Which strategies (unproductive as well as productive) do you use in your own interpersonal conflicts? Which do you most resent others using on you? Why? Will this discussion influence you to change the way you engage in interpersonal conflict?*

**Can you indicate a situation in which each of these unproductive strategies might actually prove helpful?**

**Which of these conflict strategies have you used in the past two weeks? Which have others used in conflicts with you? Describe the effects of these strategies? Does your analysis support or refute the discussion presented in the text?**

**The only way to speak the truth is to speak lovingly.**
**—HENRY DAVID THOREAU**

Focus your conflict on observable behaviors—on what the other person did that bothers you. Avoid *mind reading:* don't try to attribute motives to the person without first describing and understanding the behavior. Thus, if the person forgot your birthday and this disturbs you, fight about the forgetting of the birthday (the actual behavior). Try not to presuppose motives: "Well, it's obvious you just don't care about me. All you really care about is yourself! If you really cared, you could never have forgotten my birthday!"

USE HUMOR FOR RELIEF, NEVER FOR RIDICULE. In almost any conflict situation, humor will be used. Unfortunately, most often it is used sarcastically to ridicule or embarrass the other person—a use that aggravates and intensifies the conflict. Use humor to provide a momentary break in the tension. Avoid using it as a strategy to win the battle or put down the other person.

### A Note on Cultural Differences

It needs to be emphasized that members of different cultures will view conflict management techniques differently. For example, one study (Collier 1991) found that African-American men preferred clear argument and a focus on problem-solving while African-American women preferred assertiveness and respect. Mexican-American men emphasized mutual understanding through discussing the reasons for the conflict while women focused on support for the relationship. Anglo-American men preferred direct and rational argument while women preferred flexibility. These examples underlie the important principle that different cultures will view interpersonal conflict techniques differently.

# FEEDBACK

In this chapter we looked at the nature of interpersonal communication, especially the qualities that make for effectiveness in interpersonal communication (in general) and in interpersonal conflict.

**1.** Interpersonal communication and conflict skills need to be applied **mindfully,** with **cultural awareness, flexibly,** and **metacommunication.**

**2.** The qualities of interpersonal communication effectiveness are **openness, empathy, supportiveness** (descriptiveness and provisionalism), **positiveness, equality, confidence, immediacy, interaction management, expressiveness,** and **other-orientation.**

**3.** Eight **unproductive conflict strategies** are **avoidance, force, minimization, blame, silencers, gunnysacking, manipulation,** and **personal rejection.**

**4.** Useful **guides to fair fighting** are: **fight above the belt, fight actively, take responsibility for your thoughts and feelings, be direct and specific,** and **use humor for relief but never for ridicule.**

The skills covered in this chapter are vital to effective interpersonal interactions and relationships. Check your ability to use these skills. Use the following rating scale: (1) = almost always, (2) = often, (3) = sometimes, (4) = rarely, (5) = hardly ever.

_____ 1. I approach communication situations with an appropriate degree of mindfulness.

_____ 2. I engage in communication with cultural awareness.

_____ 3. I am flexible in the way I communicate and adjust my communications on the basis of the unique situation.

_____ 4. I use metacommunication to clarify ambiguous meanings.

_____ 5. I practice an appropriate degree of openness.

_____ 6. I communicate empathy to others.

_____ 7. I express supportiveness.

_____ 8. I communicate positiveness in attitudes and through stroking others.

_____ 9. I express equality in my interpersonal interactions.

_____ 10. I communicate confidence in voice and bodily actions.

_____ 11. I express immediacy both verbally and nonverbally.

_____ 12. I manage interpersonal interactions to the satisfaction of both parties.

_____ 13. I self-monitor my verbal and nonverbal behaviors in order to communicate the desired impression.

_____ 14. I communicate expressiveness verbally and nonverbally.

_____ 15. I communicate other-orientation in my interactions.

_____ 16. I avoid using unproductive methods of conflict resolution.

_____ 17. I make active use of fair fighting guides.

# SKILL DEVELOPMENT EXPERIENCES

## 6.1 GIVING COMPLIMENTS

One of the most difficult forms of interpersonal communication is giving compliments gracefully and comfortably. This exercise is designed to help you gain some experience in phrasing these seemingly simple sentences. Presented below are several situations that might normally call for giving the other person a compliment. For each situation, write at least two compliments that are appropriate to the situation.

1. Your friend has just received an "A" in the history final.

**Sample Response:** *That's just great. You're going to have a great index this semester.*

2. Your mother has just prepared an exceptional dinner.

3. Your kid brother tells you he hit a home run in the Little League game.

4. Your teacher gave an exceptionally interesting lecture.

5. Your classmate has just received a scholarship to graduate school.

6. Your friend comes to class in a new outfit that looks particularly good.

7. A stranger on a train moves over so that you can sit down.
8. A friend offers to lend you the money you need to buy that new pair of jeans.
9. A waiter has given your table particularly good service.
10. A colleague from work not only remembers your birthday but gives you a really great gift.

## 6.2 RECEIVING COMPLIMENTS

Perhaps even more difficult than giving compliments is receiving them without awkwardness and uneasiness. Too often people respond to compliments in inappropriate ways that make it even more difficult for the person offering the compliment. Respond to the following compliments by (a) acknowledging the compliment and your pleasure in receiving it, and (b) thanking the person for the compliment.

1. That was a really persuasive argument you made. You really are so articulate.

    **Sample Response:** *Thanks. I appreciate that. I worked all last night on that seemingly off-the-cuff speech.*

2. Wow! You look great.
3. You should have no trouble getting that job. You have everything they're asking for—intelligence, communication ability, and dedication.
4. Your hair looks really great. How did you do it?
5. You really are great at the computer.
6. I really appreciate your helping me with this term paper. You're a good friend.
7. That dinner was just great.
8. Your latest book was the best I've read all year. You have a great writing style—so smooth and easy.
9. You really deserved that scholarship.
10. I really enjoyed this class. It was the best class I had all semester.

## 6.3 POSITIVELY SPEAKING

This exercise is performed by the entire class. One person is "it" and takes a seat in the front of the room or in the center of the circle. (It is possible, though not desirable, for the person to stay where she or he normally sits.) Going around the circle or from left to right, each person says something positive about the person who is "it."

For this exercise, only volunteers should be chosen. Students should be encouraged but not forced to participate. It is best done when the students know each other fairly well.

Persons must tell the truth; that is, they are not allowed to say anything about a person that they do not believe. At the same time, however, all statements must be positive. Persons may, however, "pass" and say nothing. No one may ask why something was said or not said. The positive words may refer to the person's looks, behavior, intelligence, clothes, mannerisms, and so on. One may also say, "I don't know you very well, but you seem friendly," or "You seem honest," or whatever. These statements, too, must be believed to be true.

After everyone has said something, another person becomes "it." After all volunteers have been "it," consider the following questions individually.

1. Describe your feelings when thinking about becoming "it."
2. How did you feel while people were saying positive words?
3. What comments were the most significant to you?
4. Were you "it"? If so, would you be willing to be "it" again? If not, why not?
5. How do you feel now that the exercise is over? Did it make you feel better? Why do you suppose it had the effect it did?
6. What implications may be drawn from this exercise for application to everyday living?
7. Will this exercise change your behavior in any way?

After you have completed these questions, share whatever comments you would like with the class.

## 6.4 PAT AND CHRIS: A CASE IN INTERPERSONAL CONFLICT

The following brief dialogue was written to illustrate the eight unproductive conflict strategies we have discussed (avoidance or redefinition; force; minimization; blame; silencers; gunnysacking; manipulation; and personal rejection) and to provide a stimulus for considering other, more productive methods of conflict management.

Locate examples of each of the unproductive strategies as well as examples that violate such productive conflict management principles as fighting above the belt and being direct. Write or discuss alternative responses that are more effective.

You may also analyze this dialogue in terms of the following four principles of interpersonal communication. Try to locate examples of the failure to recognize and act on: (1) the irreversibility of communication; (2) the distinction between content and relationship messages, particularly the failure to hear and respond to relational messages; (3) the punctuation of communication events, especially the failure to see the events punctuated in any other way but one's own; and (4) the owning of one's own thoughts and feelings. Explain how these combatants might have taken these principles into consideration.

PAT: It's me. Just came in to get my papers for the meeting tonight.

CHRIS: You're not going to another meeting tonight, are you?

PAT: I told you last month that I had to give this lecture to the new managers—on how to use some new research methods. What do you think I've been working on for the past two weeks? If you cared about what I do, you'd know that I was working on this lecture and it's especially important that it go well.

CHRIS: What about shopping? We always do the shopping on Friday night.

PAT: The shopping will have to wait; this lecture is important.

CHRIS: Shopping is important, too, and so are the children and so is my job and so is the leak in the basement that's been driving me crazy for the past week and that I've asked you to look at every day since then.

PAT: Get off it. We can do the shopping any time. Your job is fine and the children are fine and we'll get a plumber just as soon as I get his name from the Johnsons.

CHRIS: You always do that. You always think only you count, only you matter. Even when we were in school, your classes were the important ones, your papers, your tests. Remember when I had that chemistry final and you had to have your history paper typed? We stayed up all night typing your paper. I failed chemistry, remember? That's not so good when you're pre-med! I suppose I should thank you for my not becoming a doctor? But you got your A in history. It's always been that way. You never give a damn about what's important in my life.

PAT: I really don't want to talk about it. I'll only get upset and bomb out with the lecture. Forget it. I don't want to hear any more. So just shut up before

I do something I should do more often.

CHRIS: You hit me and I'll call the cops. I'm not putting up with another black eye or another fat lip—never, never again.

PAT: Well, then, just shut up. I just don't want to talk about it anymore. Forget it. I have to give the lecture and that's that.

CHRIS: The children were looking forward to going shopping. Johnny wanted to get a new record, and Jennifer needed to get a book for school. You promised them.

PAT: I didn't promise anyone anything. You promised them and now you want me to take the blame. You know, you promise too much. You should only promise what you can deliver—like fidelity. Remember you promised to be faithful? Or did you forget that promise? Why don't you tell the kids that? Or do they already know? Were they here when you had your sordid affair? Did they see their loving parent loving some stranger?

CHRIS: I thought we agreed not to talk about that. You know how bad I feel about what happened. And anyway, that was six months ago. What has that to do with tonight?

PAT: You're the one who brought up promises, not me. You're always bringing up the past. You live in the past.

CHRIS: Well, at least the kids would have seen me enjoying myself—one enjoyable experience in eight years isn't too much, is it?

PAT: I'm leaving. Don't wait up.

## 6.5 HEARING CONFLICT STRATEGIES
Watch an evening of television, concentrating on situation comedies. Listen for the unproductive and the productive conflict strategies. Identify as many specific strategies as you can. On the basis of your analysis, respond to the following questions:

1. What types of conflicts occur most often?
2. What conflict strategies are used most often?
3. What effects did each of the conflict strategies have?
4. How did the conflicts eventually get resolved?
5. Were unproductive conflict strategies used in the beginning of the show and productive conflict strategies used at the end?

Share these insights in small groups or with the class as a whole. Do the findings of the class support the recommendations made in this chapter?

# CHAPTER 7

# Interpersonal Relationships

## HOW RELATIONSHIPS WORK

## RELATIONSHIP DEVELOPMENT
- *Interpersonal Attraction*
- *Rewards and Costs*

## RELATIONSHIP MAINTENANCE
- *Need Satisfaction*
- *Maintenance Behaviors*

## RELATIONSHIP DETERIORATION
- *Some Causes of Relationship Deterioration*
- *Communication in Relationship Deterioration*
- *The Strategies of Disengagement*

## RELATIONSHIP REPAIR
- *Reversing Negative Communication Patterns*
- *Cherishing Behaviors*
- *Adopting a Positive Action Program*

## IF THE RELATIONSHIP ENDS

## FEEDBACK

## SKILL DEVELOPMENT EXPERIENCES

## *Goals*

*After completing this chapter, you should be able to*

1. *explain the five-stage model of interpersonal relationships*
2. *describe relationship development, maintenance, deterioration, and repair*
3. *define* interpersonal attraction *and explain the five factors that account for our attraction to others*
4. *define* social exchange *and* equity *theories*

*How do your relationships develop?* ■ *How do they deteriorate?* ■ *Why?* ■ *What attracts you to certain people and not to others?* ■ *Why are you in the relationships you are in now?* ■ *What rewards do these relationships provide?* ■ *What are the costs or difficulties?* ■ *How can you repair an ailing relationship?* ■ *What should a person do when an important relationship ends?*

## How Relationships Work

Most relationships, possibly all, pass through stages (Knapp 1984; Wood 1982). We do not become intimate friends or lifetime lovers immediately. Rather, we grow into an intimate relationship gradually, through a series of steps or stages.

The five-stage model presented in Figure 7.1 describes the significant stages in developing relationships. For each specific relationship, you might wish to modify and revise the basic model. As a general description of relationship development, however, the stages are fairly standard. The five stages are *contact, involvement, intimacy, deterioration,* and *dissolution.* These stages describe relationships as they are, not as they should be.

CONTACT. At the first stage, we make *contact.* There is some kind of sense perception; you see, hear, and smell the person. According to some researchers (Zunin 1972), it is during this stage—within the first four minutes of interaction—that you decide whether or not to pursue the

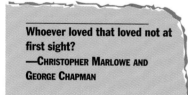

How long does it take you to decide whether to pursue a relationship with someone you have just met? Is four minutes too short a time? Unnecessarily long?

**Figure 7.1** *The Five Stage Model of Relationships*

Whoever loved that loved not at first sight?
—CHRISTOPHER MARLOWE AND GEORGE CHAPMAN

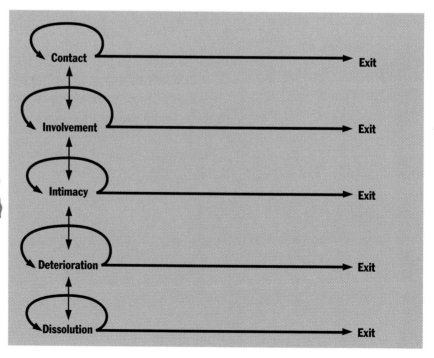

relationship. Also at this stage physical appearance is important because physical dimensions are open to easy inspection. Yet, qualities such as friendliness, warmth, openness, and dynamism are also revealed at this stage. If you like the individual and want to pursue the relationship, you proceed to the second stage.

## TEST YOURSELF:

### What Should You Do?

Initial relationships are always more difficult because we don't know each other. We therefore don't know what will be responded to positively or negatively. This is especially true in intercultural situations as these examples make clear (Axtell 1990a, 1990b). In each situation, what should you do?

1. You are introduced to the president of a large company in Singapore. You know his name is Lo Win Hao. Do you say "Hello Lo?" "Hello Win?" "Hello Hao?" "Hello Mr. Lo?" "Hello Mr. Win?" Hello Mr. Hao?"

2. You are to meet the Latin-American professor Dr. Juan Gonzalez-Gomez. Do you address him "Dr. Juan?" "Mr. Juan?" "Dr. Gonzalez-Gomez?" "Dr. Gonzalez?" "Dr. Gomez?" "Mr. Gomez?"

3. You are having dinner at the home of a Chinese colleague in China. The dinner is elaborate and you are really full. Before dessert is served, however, your host serves you a dish of boiled rice. What should you do? Refuse it? Eat as little as possible? Eat it all?

4. You are at a meeting with an Arab businessman. During the meeting, the Arab conducts a variety of other business. Sometimes these interruptions take 20 to 30 minutes. What should you do? Voice your disturbance and assert yourself, saying that your business was scheduled for this time and you resent the interruptions? Do not say anything but show your disturbance nonverbally, lest he think you are too unimportant to object to his treatment? Say nothing and show no disturbance nonverbally?

5. You want to give flowers to a German colleague and a fountain pen to a Japanese colleague. What should you do about the wrapping? Wrap both? Wrap neither? Wrap one and not the other?

### Appropriate Responses

1. "Hello Mr. Lo" is the appropriate response. In Chinese the surname comes first. "Hello Mr. Hao" would be equivalent to "Hello Mr. Joe."

2. In most Spanish speaking countries the last name is a combination of the father's and mother's last names (with the father's name coming first). The person is addressed with the father's last name. Also, when the person has a title, it is polite to use it. Thus, "Dr. Gonzalez" would be the preferred mode of address.

3. Refuse it. By eating the boiled rice you are in effect saying that the dinner was insufficient which would insult your host.

4. Do nothing, say nothing. This is the normal way in which Arabs conduct business. Rather than handle one thing at a time, as Americans are used to, they do several things during the same period.

5. Wrap the fountain pen since the Japanese prefer to open their gifts privately. Do not wrap the flowers.

COPYRIGHT 1990, LOS ANGELES TIMES SYNDICATE.
REPRINTED WITH PERMISSION.

What dating strategies have you
used? What dating strategies
have been used on you? Were
they effective?

INVOLVEMENT. The *involvement* stage occurs when you commit your-self to getting to know the other person better and also to revealing your-self. If this is to be a romantic relationship, then you might date at this stage. If it is to be a friendship, you might share your mutual interests— go to the movies or to a sporting event. Throughout the relationship pro-cess, but especially during the involvement and early stages of intimacy, we test our partner; we try to find out how our partner feels about the relationship. Among strategies we use are (Bell and Buerkel-Rothfuss 1990; Baxter and Wilmot 1984):

- *Directness:* we ask our partner directly how he or she feels or we self-disclose, assuming that our partner will also self-disclose

- *Endurance:* we subject our partner to various negative behaviors, assuming that if our partner endures them, he or she is really serious about the relationship. Examples include behaving badly toward the partner or making requests that are inconvenient

- *Indirect suggestion:* we might joke about a shared future together, touch more intimately, or hint that we are serious about the relation-ship; we assume that similar responses from our partner mean that he or she wishes increased intimacy

- *Public presentation:* for example, we might introduce our partner as our "boyfriend" or "girlfriend" and see how our partner responds

- Separation: separating ourselves physically to see how the other person responds; if our partner calls, then we know that he or she is interested in the relationship
- *Third party:* we might question mutual friends as to our partner's feelings and intentions

INTIMACY.  At the *intimacy* stage, you further commit yourself to the other person. You may establish a primary relationship in which this individual becomes your best or closest friend or lover. This commitment may take many forms: marriage, helping the person, or revealing your deepest secrets. This stage is reserved for a few people—from just one to two, three, or perhaps four. Rarely do people have more than four intimates, except in a family situation.

When the intimacy stage involves marriage, people face three main premarital anxieties (Zimmer 1986):

- Security anxiety: Will my mate leave me for someone else? Will my mate be sexually unfaithful?
- Fulfillment anxiety: Will we be able to achieve a close, warm, and special rapport? Will we be able to have an equal relationship?
- Excitement anxiety: Will boredom and routine set in? Will I lose my freedom and become trapped?

*The intimacy stage is often symbolized by marriage. In what other ways might a couple publicly symbolize their commitment to a permanent relationship?*

> True intimacy is a positive force only if it is a combining of strengths and energies with other mature persons for the continued growth of each.
> —LEO F. BUSCAGLIA

> A happy marriage is a long conversation that always seems too short.
> —ANDRÉ MAUROIS

Love is like war: easy to begin
but very hard to stop.
—H.L. MENCKEN

Of course, not everyone strives for intimacy (Bartholomew 1990). Some may consciously desire intimacy, but so fear its consequences that they avoid it. Others dismiss intimacy, defensively denying their need for more and deeper interpersonal contact. To some people relational intimacy is extremely risky. To others, it involves only low risk. For example, how true of your attitudes are the following statements.

- It is dangerous to get really close to people.
- I'm afraid to get really close to someone because I might get hurt.
- I find it difficult to trust other people.
- The most important thing to consider in a relationship is whether I might get hurt.

People who agree with these statements (and other similar statements), which come from recent research on risk in intimacy (Pilkington and Richardson 1988), perceive intimacy to involve great risk. Such people, it has been found, have fewer close friends, are less likely to be involved in a romantic relationship, have less trust in others, have a low level of dating assertiveness, and are generally less sociable than those who see intimacy as involving little risk.

How would you describe the relationship between yourself and your best friend, using the concepts of breadth and depth?

As we move from contact through involvement to intimacy, we increase the number of topics we talk about (*breadth*) and the degree of "personalness" or intimacy to which we pursue these topics (*depth*) (Altman and Taylor 1973; Taylor and Altman 1987).

DETERIORATION. This stage and the next represent the other side of the progression, where bonds between the parties weaken. At the *deterioration* stage you begin to feel that the relationship may not be as important as you had once thought. You grow further and further apart. You share less of your free time. When you are together there are awkward silences, fewer self-disclosures, and a self-consciousness in your exchanges. If this awkward in-between stage—the deterioration stage—continues, you enter the stage of dissolution.

DISSOLUTION. The *dissolution* stage is cutting the bonds that tie you together, such as establishing separate lives or perhaps divorcing. Sometimes there is relief and relaxation. At other times there is anxiety and frustration—recriminations, hostility, and resentment over time ill-spent and now lost.

Can you describe one of your own relationships—a friendship or a love relationship—in terms of the five stage model? What stage provided the greatest satisfaction?

Table 7.1 provides examples of the kinds of statements we might make at each of these five stages. These statements should further clarify the five stages.

MOVEMENT AMONG THE STAGES. Figure 7.1 contains three types of arrows. The Exit arrows show that each stage offers the opportunity to exit the relationship. After saying "hello," you can say "goodbye" and exit. The vertical or "movement" arrows between the stages represent your ability to move to another stage. You can move to a stage that is more intense (say from involvement to intimacy) or less intense (from intimacy to deterioration). You can also go back to a former stage. For example, you may have established an intimate relationship but no longer want to maintain it at that level. At the same time, you are relatively pleased with the relationship, so it is not really deteriorating. You

The first part of our marriage was very happy. But then, on the way back from the ceremony...
—HENNY YOUNGMAN

**Table 7.1** *Stage Talk*

| Stage/Sample Statement | Meaning |
|---|---|
| **Contact** | |
| *Hello; Hi* | Surface-level messages that we say to just about everyone as acknowledgment |
| *How are you?* | Another way of saying hello |
| *Didn't I see you here last week?* | Phatic communion; an indirect attempt to make contact |
| *May I join you for coffee?* | A direct statement expressing the desire to make contact |
| **Involvement** | |
| *I like to cook too.* | Establishing and talking about common interests |
| *How are you?* | A request for some (mostly positive) information |
| *I want to succeed at my job so badly that sometimes I get frightened. What if I fail?* | Sharing feelings of some importance |
| *I'd like to take you to dinner; I'd like to get to know you.* | Direct statements expressing the desire for involvement |
| **Intimacy** | |
| *Let's go dancing.* | Expression of togetherness |
| *How are you?* | A request for significant information about health or feelings, especially if there's reason to believe there's been a recent change; a way of saying "I care" |
| *I'm really depressed.* | Significant self-disclosure |
| *I love you.* | A direct expression of intimacy |
| *I want to marry you.* | A direct request for committed intimacy |
| **Deterioration** | |
| *I need some space.* | Self concerns surface; a desire to spend less time together |
| *I can't stand ____.* | Negative evaluations increase |
| *I'd like to start seeing others.* | Direct statement expressing desire to reduce the present level of commitment |
| *Why don't you go to Kate and Allie's by yourself?* | Expression of desire to separate in the eyes of others |
| *You never listen to my needs; It was all your fault.* | Fault-finding, criticism, and blaming |
| **Dissolution** | |
| *I want a divorce.* | A direct request to dissolve the relationship |
| *This is Sandy, whom I'm seeing now.* | A clear statement expressing intent to dissolve the relationship |
| *I tried but I guess it wasn't enough.* | Attempt to gain "social credit," approval from others |
| *Goodbye.* | The ultimate expression of dissolution |

just want it to be less intense. So, you might go back to the involvement stage and reestablish the relationship at that more comfortable level.

The "self-reflexive" arrows return to the beginning of the same level or stage. These signify that any relationship may become stabilized at any point. You may, for example, maintain a relationship at the intimate level without the relationship deteriorating or reverting to the less intense stage of involvement. Or you might remain at the "Hello, how are you?" stage—the contact stage—without further involvement.

With this basic overview, we can now look more closely at relationship development, maintenance, deterioration, and repair.

## Relationship Development

Why do we develop the relationships we do? We can look at this question in two ways. At the most obvious level, we develop relationships with people to whom we are attracted. At a less obvious level, we develop relationships that will provide us with more rewards than costs. Let's look at interpersonal attraction first.

What is the best opening line you have ever heard? What is the worst? What makes one great and another terrible?

### Interpersonal Attraction

Why are we attracted to some people but not to others? Research in interpersonal attraction finds five major factors: attractiveness (physical and personality), proximity, reinforcement, similarity, and complementarity.

We are attracted to people who are physically *attractive* and have a pleasing personality. Further, we attribute positive qualities to attractive people and negative qualities to unattractive people.

What comes to your mind when you see couples who differ greatly in physical attractiveness? Do you think that there must be "compensating factors"—for example, that the less attractive person is rich or has prestige or power?

What factors of attraction are most important to you? Which played the most important role in establishing your previous and current relationships?

"Kevin's sort of a negative person, while I tend to be positive, so we have an electrical connection."

DRAWING BY WEBER; © 1991 THE NEW YORKER MAGAZINE, INC.

> Of all the girls that are so smart
> There's none like pretty Sally:
> She is the darling of my heart,
> And lives in our alley.
> —HENRY CAREY

> What constitutes a pleasing personality to you? Can you identify five or six specific qualities?

> Does the matching hypothesis accurately describe the relationships of your friends? That is, are your friends in relationships with people who are about as attractive as they are? Does the matching hypothesis describe your own relationships?

> What is sauce for the goose may be sauce for the gander but it is not necessarily sauce for the chicken, the duck, the turkey, or the guinea hen.
> —ALICE B. TOKLAS

> What are five major rewards you derive from any one of your close relationships? What are five major costs of this same relationship? Do the rewards exceed the costs?

We are attracted to people who are physically *close* to us. For example, we become friends with and form romantic relationships with those we come into contact most often. Physical closeness (proximity) is most important in the early stages of interaction. But if your initial interaction with a person is unpleasant, repeated exposure will not increase attraction. Proximity works when the initial interaction is favorable or neutral.

We are attracted to people who *reward* or reinforce us (socially as with compliments or praise or materially as with gifts or a promotion). We also become attracted to those we reward; we come to like people for whom we do favors. Perhaps we need to justify going out of our way and so need to convince ourselves that the person is likable and worth the effort.

We are attracted to people who are *similar* to us, to people who look, act, and think much like ourselves. We are particularly attracted to people who have attitudes and preferences similar to our own. The more significant the attitude, the more important the similarity. Attitudinal similarity, in fact, is even more important than cultural similarity (Kim 1991). We also like people who are similar to us in nationality, race, ability, physical characteristics, and intelligence. The *matching hypothesis* predicts that we date and mate those who are similar to us in physical attractiveness.

We are attracted to those who *complement* or complete us. For example, we might be attracted to those we actually envy for characteristics we do not have. The introvert who is displeased with being shy might be attracted to an extrovert.

### Rewards and Costs

According to *social exchange theory*, we develop relationships that we think will provide more rewards than costs (Thibaut and Kelley 1959; Kelley and Thibaut 1978). While providing an insightful way of looking at relationships, this theory may be resisted because it seems quite mechanical. The general assumption is that you develop (and will maintain) relationships in which your rewards are greater than your costs. Rewards are those things that fulfill your needs for security: sex, social approval, financial gain, status, and so on. But rewards also involve some cost or "payback." In order to acquire the reward of financial gain, for example, you must take a job and thus give up some freedom (a cost).

Using this basic model, the theory puts into perspective our tendency to seek gain or reward while incurring the least cost (punishment or loss).

*Equity theory* builds on social exchange theory. It claims that not only do we seek to establish relationships in which rewards exceed costs, but that we experience relationship satisfaction when there is equity in the distribution of rewards and costs between the two persons in the relationship (Berscheid and Walster 1978; Hatfield and Traupman 1981). That is, not only do we want our rewards to be greater than our costs, we also want our rewards and our partner's rewards to be proportional to the costs we each pay. Thus, if you pay the larger share of the costs, you expect to receive the larger share of the rewards. In this situation you would be relatively happy. On the other hand, you would be unhappy if you paid the larger share of the costs and your partner derived the larger share of the rewards.

# Relationship Maintenance

Before looking into relationship maintenance, take the accompanying test that will help you examine your relationship communication.

## TEST YOURSELF:

### *How Effective Is Your Relational Communication?*

This questionnaire is designed to stimulate partners to discuss their relational communication patterns with each other.

### *My Relational Communications*

Partners should respond to these 12 statements with reference to their own communication patterns when communicating with their partner.

Use the following scale:

1 = always or almost always true

2 = somewhat true

3 = neither true nor false

4 = somewhat false

5 = always or almost always false

_____ 1. I tell my partner what I am feeling.

_____ 2. I can feel what my partner is feeling.

_____ 3. I communicate my similarity of feeling to my partner.

_____ 4. I avoid evaluating my partner's feelings.

_____ 5. I communicate a positive attitude toward myself when communicating with my partner.

_____ 6. I communicate a positive attitude toward my partner (for example, compliment or "stroke" my partner) in my verbal and nonverbal behaviors.

_____ 7. I communicate with my partner as an equal.

_____ 8. I communicate with my partner with confidence in myself and in what I am saying.

_____ 9. I communicate a liking and an attraction for my partner in my verbal and nonverbal behaviors.

_____10. I try to make sure our communication is satisfying to both of us.

_____11. In our mutual interactions, I communicate a genuine involvement in my partner as a person and in what my partner says.

_____12. I communicate a sense of interest and attention in what my partner says.

*Scoring:* Although all communication situations are different, calling for different strategies, the ones noted here are generally considered helpful to improving relational communication. Since the statements are all phrased positively (so that each describes effective relationship communication), a low score represents effective communication and a high score represents ineffective communication.

The statements refer to the qualities of effective interpersonal communication discussed in Chapter 6 as follows: Statement 1 = openness; 2 and 3 = empathy; 4 = supportiveness; 5 and 6 = positiveness; 7 = equality; 8 = confidence; 9 = immediacy; 10 = interaction management; 11 = expressiveness; and 12 = other-orientation.

---

How equitable are your relationships? Do you give more than you get? Do you get more than you give? If there is inequity, how does it affect the relationship?

---

Communication is to a relationship what breathing is to maintaining life.
—VIRGINIA SATIR

---

Since there is rarely any lasting advantage of ignorance about compatibility, open communication is essential to developing healthy relationships.
—MICHAEL J. BEATTY

Now that both partners have completed the scales for themselves and for their partners as they perceive them to be, consider the following questions:

- How different are your communications from those of your partner (as least as you perceive your partner's)?
- How different are the scores? Do you and your partner follow essentially the same patterns of communication? Do you see yourself following more acceptable patterns than your partner? Your partner following more acceptable patterns than you?
- What are the two most important communication skills that your partner should work on? What are the two that your partner thinks you should work on?

Relationships are maintained because they satisfy our needs and because we do certain things to keep them together. Let's look at need satisfaction first.

## Need Satisfaction

Although each of us looks to relationships to satisfy different needs, some generalizations seem useful. Contact with another human being helps *alleviate loneliness*. We want to feel that someone cares, likes us, will protect us, and ultimately will love us. Close relationships assure us that someone does care, and will be there when we need human contact.

We need contact with other human beings for *self-knowledge*; it is largely through our relationships that we learn about ourselves. How we perceive ourselves depends greatly on what we think others think of us. If our friends see us as warm and generous, we probably will, too. We also evaluate and assess ourselves—our attitudes, talents, values, accomplishments, abilities—primarily by comparing ourselves with others. These comparisons are, in large part, accomplished through our interpersonal relationships.

Our relationships also *enhance our self-esteem and self-worth*. Just having a relational partner makes us feel worthy of love and desirable. When we are fortunate enough to have a supportive partner, the relationship can enhance self-esteem even more.

The most general function served by our interpersonal relationships, and one that could encompass all the others, is that of *maximizing our pleasures and minimizing our pains*. We have a need to share our good fortune with other people—perhaps to earn their praise or so they can participate with us in new-found pleasures. We also have a need to seek out others when we are in emotional or physical pain. Friends, it seems, lessen our pain.

Of course, some relationships are maintained for less noble reasons. For example, many people maintain their relationships because they fear being alone or they fear criticism from others for "relational failure." Some stay together because it is more convenient—perhaps they are partners in a business, have children, or simply need a second income for financial security.

> Finding someone to love is not the solution to loneliness. The solution is learning to love yourself. Once you love and appreciate yourself, you'll discover that other people will love you too, and your loneliness will only be a memory.
> —DAVID D. BURNS

> Exclusively depending upon one other individual for our sense of self-esteem and personhood, we become an emotional hostage to that person.
> —JOHN AMODEO AND KRIS AMODEO

> What needs motivate your current relationships?

> People are more frightened of being lonely than of being hungry, or being deprived of sleep, or of having their sexual needs unfulfilled.
> —FRIEDA FROMM REICHMAN

In one survey, 40,000 respondents selected from a wide number of activities the ones they had engaged in with friends over the past month. Table 7.2 presents the ten most frequently noted activities. As the list indicates, friendship seems to serve the same needs that all relationships serve (for example, alleviating loneliness and encouraging self-knowledge).

### Maintenance Behaviors

Another reason relationships last is that people in them try to make them work. Couples use a variety of strategies to maintain their relationships. Here are the four most common (Dindia and Baxter 1987):

*Prosocial* behaviors include being courteous and polite, cheerful and friendly, avoiding criticism, and compromising even when it involves self-sacrifice. Prosocial behaviors also include talking about a shared future, for example, buying a house.

*Ceremonial* behaviors include celebrating birthdays and anniversaries, discussing past pleasurable times, and eating at a favorite restaurant.

*Communication* behaviors include calling just to say "How are you?" talking about the honesty and openness in the relationship, and talking about shared feelings.

*Togetherness* behaviors include visiting mutual friends, doing things as a couple, and sometimes just spending time together with no concern for what is done.

## Relationship Deterioration

*Relational deterioration* refers to the weakening of bonds that hold people together. The process may be sudden or gradual. Sometimes a relationship rule (say, the rule of fidelity) is broken and the relationship ends almost immediately. At other times, displeasures grow over time and the relationship dies gradually.

1. Had an intimate talk

2. Had a friend ask you to do something for him or her

3. Went to dinner in a restaurant

4. Asked your friend to do something for you

5. Had a meal together at home or at your friend's home

6. Went to a movie, play, or concert

7. Went drinking together

8. Went shopping

9. Participated in sports

10. Watched a sporting event

Source: Based on Mary Brown Parlee and the Editors of Psychology Today, "The Friendship Bond," Psychology Today 13 (October 1979): 43-54, 113.

**Table 7.2**
*Ten Common Activities Shared with Friends*

*What specific maintenance behaviors do you use in your friendship relationships? In your romantic relationships? Are maintenance behaviors also used in family relationships? If so, in what ways?*

**Have you ever had a relationship where the depth or breadth *increased* after the break up?**

**The way to love anything is to realize that it might be lost.**
**—GILBERT K. CHESTERTON**

**How thorough an explanation of relational dissolution do these five stages provide?**

When a relationship begins to deteriorate, the breadth and depth often reverse themselves—a process of *depenetration* (Taylor and Altman 1987; Baxter 1983). For example, while ending a relationship, you might eliminate certain topics from your conversations and discuss the remaining topics in less depth. You also would probably reduce the level of your self-disclosures and reveal less of your innermost feelings.

Interpersonal researcher Steve Duck (1986) proposes that we can best understand the process of deterioration by identifying the phases that one goes through in passing from deterioration to dissolution. The first phase is the *breakdown phase* during which the individuals experience dissatisfaction with the relationship and with each other.

During the second phase, the *intrapsychic phase,* the individuals brood privately about their dissatisfaction with the relationship and with each other. Eventually we may share our feelings, initially with relative strangers, and then gradually with close friends.

The third or *dyadic phase* involves discussing the problems with one's partner and attempting to remedy or correct the difficulties.

If the problems cannot be worked out and one decides to exit the relationship, he or she enters the *social phase.* At this time the individual shares with others the dissatisfaction and the decision to exit the relationship. The individual attempts to enlist the support of others, seeking understanding, supportiveness, empathy, and, in general, the social support needed to get through the breakup.

Fifth and final is the *grave dressing phase* during which we develop a kind of history of the relationship—its beginnings, its development, and its eventual dissolution. Our intention is to distance ourselves from the relationship at least a bit so that others will look upon us favorably or at least not too negatively.

## Some Causes of Relationship Deterioration

The causes of relationship deterioration are as numerous as the individuals involved. We can, however, examine some of the major causes; all of which may also be seen as effects of relational deterioration. For example, when the relationship starts to deteriorate, the individuals may remove themselves physically from one another. This physical separation may cause further deterioration by driving the individuals farther apart emotionally and psychologically.

REASONS FOR ESTABLISHING THE RELATIONSHIP HAVE DIMINISHED. When the reasons we developed the relationship change drastically, the relationship may deteriorate. For instance, when loneliness is no longer lessened, the relationship may suffer. When stimulation is weak, one or both may begin to look elsewhere. When self-knowledge and self-growth are insufficient, you may become dissatisfied with yourself, your partner, and the relationship. When attractiveness fades, an important reason for establishing the relationship in the first place is lost. We know, for example, that when relationships break up, it is the more attractive partner who leaves (Blumstein and Schwartz 1983).

CHANGES. Changes in one or both parties may encourage relational deterioration. Psychological changes such as the development of different intellectual interests or incompatible attitudes may create problems as may behavioral changes such as preoccupation with business or schooling.

SEX. Few sexual relationships are free of problems. In fact, sexual problems rank among the top three problems in most studies of newlyweds (Blumstein and Schwartz 1983). In one survey, for example, 80 percent of the respondents described their marriages as either "very happy" or "happy." But some 90 percent of these said that they had sexual problems (Freedman 1977).

Research clearly shows that it is the quality, not the quantity of a sexual relationship that is crucial. When the quality is poor, partners may seek sexual affairs outside the primary relationship. And research on the effects of this is again clear: Extrarelational affairs contribute significantly to breakups for all couples, whether married or cohabiting, heterosexual or homosexual. Even "open relationships"—ones based on sexual freedom outside the primary relationship—experience these problems and are more likely to break up than the traditional "closed" relationship (Blumstein and Schwartz 1983).

WORK. Unhappiness with work often leads to difficulties with relationships and is often associated with relationship breakup. People cannot separate work problems from their relationships (Blumstein and Schwartz 1983). This is true for all types of couples. With heterosexual couples, if the man is disturbed over the woman's job—for example, if she earns much more than he does or devotes much time to the job—the relationship could be in for trouble. Often the man expects the woman to work but does not reduce his expectations concerning her household responsibilities. The man becomes resentful if the woman does not fulfill these expectations, and the woman becomes resentful if she takes on both outside work and full household duties.

---

In every marriage more than two weeks old, there are grounds for divorce. The trick is to find and continue to find, grounds for marriage.
—ROBERT ANDERSON

If you have ever loved, been loved, or wanted to be in love, you have had to face a frustrating fact: different people can mean different things by that simple phrase 'I love you.'
—JOHN ALAN LEE

Marriage makes you legally half a person, and what man wants to live with half a person?
—GLORIA STEINEM

Sexual intimacy without interpersonal intimacy is like a diploma without an education.
—THOMAS ODEN

I do not like work even when someone else does it.
—MARK TWAIN

**FINANCIAL DIFFICULTIES.** In surveys of problems among couples, financial difficulties loom large. Money is important in relationships largely because of its close connection with power. Money brings power which can quickly generalize to nonfinancial issues as well.

Money also creates problems because men and women view it differently. To men, money is power. To women, it is security and independence. Conflicts over how to spend the money can easily result from such different perceptions.

The most general statement we can make is that dissatisfaction with money will mean dissatisfaction with the relationship (Blumstein and Schwartz 1983). Research finds that this is true for married and cohabiting heterosexual couples and gay male couples. It is not true for lesbian couples, who seem to care a great deal less about financial matters. This difference has led some researchers to speculate that concern over money and its equation with power and relational satisfaction are largely male attitudes.

**REWARDS AND COSTS.** Generally, we stay in relationships that are rewarding, and leave those that are punishing. Further, we expect and desire equity in our relationships. When partners see their relationship as equitable, they will continue together. When the relationship is seen as not equitable, it may deteriorate.

**COMMITMENT.** When relationships show signs of deterioration and yet there is still a strong commitment—a strong desire to keep the relationship together—the individuals may well surmount the obstacles and reverse the deterioration. When their commitment is weak and the individuals see no good reasons for staying together, relational deterioration comes faster and stronger.

### Communication in Relationship Deterioration

Relational deterioration involves unique, specialized communication. Look at these communication patterns in two ways. First, as responses to the deterioration: You communicate as you do because you sense your relationship is deteriorating. Second, recognize that these patterns may also contribute to the deterioration.

*Withdrawal* is probably the easiest pattern to observe. When people are close emotionally, they can occupy close physical quarters, but when they are growing apart, they need wider spaces. They literally move away from each other. Other nonverbal signs include the failure to engage in eye contact, to look at each other generally, and to touch each other (Miller and Parks 1982). Verbally, withdrawal in less talking and especially less listening. It is also seen in the decline of self-disclosing communications.

*Deception* increases as relationships break down. Sometimes this involves direct and clear-cut lies; at other times the lies are more like exaggeration or omission.

Relational deterioration often brings an increase in negative *evaluations* and a decrease in positive evaluations. Where once you praised the other's behaviors, talents, or ideas, you now criticize them. Often the behaviors have not changed significantly. What has changed is your way of looking at them.

---

> When money speaks the truth is silent.
> —RUSSIAN PROVERB

---

> How important is money in your relationships? Would money influence—in any way—with whom you develop a relationship?

---

> Which of the factors influencing relationship deterioration do you find most important in your own relationships? Why?

---

> Why do you think self-disclosure declines during relationship deterioration?

---

> Lying in an intimate relationship undermines the relationship. Even if your partner doesn't know about the lie and never finds out, the relationship will probably still be damaged. You have devaluated your partner and will therefore have less respect for her/him and for yourself.
> —ALLEN FAY

During relational deterioration there is a marked change in our *request behaviors* (Lederer 1984). When a relationship is deteriorating, requests decrease for pleasurable behaviors ("Will you fix me my favorite dessert?" or "Hug me real tight."). At the same time, requests to stop unpleasant or negative behaviors increase ("Will you stop monopolizing the phone every evening?").

Another symptom is the decrease in social niceties that accompany requests. There is a progression from, say, "Would you please make me a cup of coffee, honey?" to "Get me some coffee, will you?" to "Where's my coffee?"

In relational deterioration there is little *favor exchange.* Compliments, once given frequently and sincerely, are now rare. Positive stroking is minimal. Nonverbally, we avoid looking directly at the other and seldom smile. We touch, caress, and hold each other infrequently, if at all.

What other communication patterns do you see in relationship deterioration?

## The Strategies of Disengagement

When we wish to exit a relationship, we need some way to explain this to ourselves as well as to our partner. That is, we must develop a strategy for getting out of a relationship that is no longer satisfying or profitable. Michael Cody (1982) has identified five major disengagement strategies (see Table 7.3).

What disengagement strategies have you heard or used? Can you fit them into one of the categories identified here?

**Table 7.3** *Five Disengagement Strategies*

| Strategy | Function | Examples |
|---|---|---|
| Positive tone | To maintain a positive relationship<br><br>To express positive feelings for the other person | *I really care for you a great deal but I'm just not ready for such an intense relationship.* |
| Negative identity management | To blame the other person for the breakup<br><br>To absolve oneself of the blame for the breakup | *I can't stand your jealousy, your constant suspicions, your checking up on me. I need my freedom and my privacy.* |
| Justification | To give reasons for the breakup | *I'm going away to college for four years; there's no point in continuing to date each other exclusively.* |
| Behavioral deescalation | To reduce the intensity of the relationship | Avoidance; cut down on phone calls; reduce time spent together, especially time spent alone with partner. |
| Deescalation | To reduce the exclusivity and hence the intensity of the relationship | *I'm just not ready for so exclusive a relationship. I think we should each see other people.* |

*Source: Based on* "A Typology of Disengagement Strategies and an Examination of the Role Intimacy Reactions to Inequity and Relational Problems in Strategy Selections" *by Michael J. Cody,* Communication Monographs 49, 1982. *Reprinted by permission of the author and the Speech Communication Association.*

# Relationship Repair

If we wish to salvage a relationship, we may attempt to change our communication patterns, in effect, putting into practice the insights and skills learned in this course. We briefly note some of the more significant areas for relationship repair.

## Reversing Negative Communication Patterns

If the relationship is to be repaired and again become rewarding, then withdrawal and deception must give way to open and honest communication. As with alcohol or drug addiction, before we can work on a cure, we have to admit we have a problem. And we have to be honest about what the problem is.

Supportiveness and positive evaluations need to be increased. For example, in their review of research on happily married couples, Kathryn Dindia and Mary Anne Fitzpatrick (1985) report that happily married couples engage in greater positive behavior exchange; they communicate more agreement, approval, and positive affect than do unhappily married couples. Clearly, these behaviors result from the positive feelings these spouses have for each other. But, it can also be argued that these

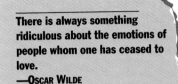

There is always something ridiculous about the emotions of people whom one has ceased to love.
—OSCAR WILDE

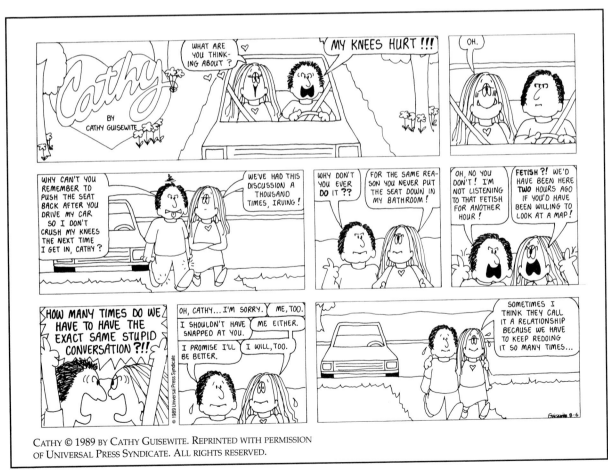

CATHY © 1989 BY CATHY GUISEWITE. REPRINTED WITH PERMISSION OF UNIVERSAL PRESS SYNDICATE. ALL RIGHTS RESERVED.

expressions help to increase the positive regard that each has for his or her partner. Needed also is an exchange of favors; compliments, positive stroking, and all the nonverbals that say "I care" become especially important when we wish to reverse negative communication patterns.

### Cherishing Behaviors

One way to reverse increasingly negative evaluations is to incorporate a specific kind of favor exchange, namely, cherishing behaviors (Lederer 1984). They are those small gestures that we enjoy receiving from our relational partner (a smile, a wink, a squeeze, a kiss). Cherishing behaviors should be (1) specific and positive, (2) focused on the present and future rather than past issues about which the partners have argued, (3) capable of being performed daily, and (4) easily executed.

Both can make lists of cherishing behaviors they wish to receive and then exchange the lists. Each then performs the cherishing behaviors desired by the partner. While at first these behaviors may seem self-conscious and awkward, in time they will become a normal part of interaction.

### Adopting a Positive Action Program

You now have a great deal of insight into communication in general and interpersonal communication in particular and numerous suggestions for relationship improvement. Although each person should develop a program tailored to his or her specific relationship, these three general principles should prove useful.

#### Identify the Problems

Specify what is wrong with your present relationship and what changes are needed to make it better (both in concrete terms). Without this first step there is little hope for improving any interpersonal relationship. Create a picture of your relationship as you want it to be and compare that picture to the way it is. Specify changes necessary to replace the present picture with the idealized one.

#### Apply the Skills

Apply your newly acquired skills and insights to relationship improvement. This course has covered a wide variety of suggestions for improving interpersonal communication and relationships; put them into practice; make them a normal part of your interactions. The following suggestions are designed to refresh your memory.

- Look closely for relational messages that will help clarify motivations and needs; respond to these as well as to the content messages.
- Exchange perspectives with your relational partner and see the sequence of events as punctuated by each other.
- Exchange favors and cherishing behaviors, especially when "costs" are running high.
- Practice empathic and supportive responses even in conflict situations.

> Some people pay a compliment as if they expected a receipt.
> —KIM HUBBARD

> Approach each new problem not with a view of finding what you hope will be there, but to get the truth, the realities that must be grappled with.
> —BERNARD M. BARUCH

> Action to be effective must be directed to clearly conceived ends.
> —JAWAHARLAL NEHRU

Using any of the insights presented in this section, how would you describe the interpersonal communication and the interpersonal relationships of one couple in a television situation comedy or drama?

- Eliminate unfair fighting habits and substitute productive conflict strategies.

- Be descriptive when discussing grievances, being especially careful to avoid troublesome terms such as *always* and *never*.

- Listen to your partner actively, empathically, and with an open mind.

- Own your feelings and thoughts; use "I" messages and take responsibility for your feelings.

- Remember the principle of irreversibility; think carefully before saying things you may regret later.

- Keep the channels of communication open; be available to discuss problems, to negotiate solutions, and to practice new and more meaningful interaction patterns.

- Bear your share of the costs; when costs weigh unfairly on your partner, share them to make the relationship more equitable.

- Intensify the exchange of rewards in times of rising costs; when costs begin to exceed rewards, increase their exchange.

### Take Risks

Take risks in attempting to improve any relationship. Risk giving favors without any certainty of reciprocity. Risk rejection; make the first move to make up or say you are sorry. Be willing to change, to adapt, to take on new tasks and responsibilities.

A coward is incapable of exhibiting love; it is the prerogative of the brave.
—MAHATMA GANDHI

## If the Relationship Ends

Of course, some relationships end. Sometimes there are problems that cannot be resolved. Sometimes the costs are too high and the rewards too few or the relationship is recognized as destructive and escape seems the only alternative. Given the inevitability that some relationships will end, here are some suggestions to ease the difficulty of a breakup. They can apply to the termination of any type of relationship, between friends or lovers, through death, separation, or breakup. The language of romantic breakups is used because these are the ones we deal with most frequently.

—Are you in trouble?—Do you need advice?—Write-to-Miss-Lonelyhearts-and-she-will-help-you. . . . The Miss Lonelyhearts are the priests of twentieth-century America.
—NATHANAEL WEST

### Break the Loneliness-Depression Cycle

Loneliness and depression—the two feelings most experienced after a relationship ends—should be treated with seriousness. Recognize that depression often leads to serious illness. Ulcers, high blood pressure, insomnia, stomach pains, and sexual difficulties frequently accompany or are seriously aggravated by depression. In most cases loneliness and depression are temporary. Our task then is to eliminate or lessen these uncomfortable and potentially dangerous feelings by changing the situation. When depression does last or proves particularly upsetting, it is time for professional help.

## Take Time Out

Be neither a "leaper" nor an "abstainer." Resist the temptation to jump into a new relationship while the old relationship is still warm or before a new one can be assessed with some degree of objectivity. Also resist swearing off all relationships. Neither extreme works well.

Take time out for yourself. Renew your relationship with yourself. If you were in a long-term relationship, you probably saw yourself as part of a team, as one of a pair. Now get to know yourself as a unique individual, standing alone now but fully capable of entering a meaningful relationship in the near future.

## Bolster Self-Esteem

When relationships fail, self-esteem often declines. We may feel guilty for having been the cause of the breakup, inadequate for not holding on or unwanted and unloved. All these feelings lower self-esteem. Our task is to regain a positive self-image so we may function effectively as individuals and as members of another interpersonal relationship.

Take positive action to increase your self-esteem. Oddly enough, helping others is one of the best ways to do this. When we do things for others, either informally for people we know or by volunteer work in some community agency, we get the positive stroking from others that helps us to feel better about ourselves. Positive and successful experiences help build self-esteem, so engage in activities that you enjoy, do well, and that are likely to result in success.

## Seek Support

Although many people believe they should bear their burdens alone (men, in particular, have been taught this is the "manly" way to handle things), seeking the support of others is one of the best antidotes to the unhappiness caused when a relationship ends. Avail yourself of your friends and family for support. Tell your friends of your situation—in general terms, if you prefer—and make it clear that you need support right now. Seek out people who are positive and nurturing. Avoid negative individuals who will paint the world in even darker tones. Make the distinction between seeking support and seeking advice. If you feel you need advice, seek out a professional. For support, friends are best.

## Avoid Repeating Negative Patterns

We seem to enter second and third relationships with the same blinders, faulty preconceptions, and unrealistic expectations with which we entered earlier relationships. We need to learn from failed relationships and not repeat the same patterns. We need to ask ourselves at the start of a new relationship if it is modeled on the previous one. If the answer is yes, we must guard against repeating the same mistakers.

At the same time, do not become a prophet of doom. Do not see vestiges of the old in every new relationship. Do not jump at the first conflict and say, "Here we go again." Treat the new relationship as the unique relationship it is. Do not evaluate it through past experiences. Past relationships and experiences should be guides, not filters.

> No one can make you feel inferior without your consent.
> —ELEANOR ROOSEVELT

> Friendship is always a sweet responsibility, never an opportunity.
> —KAHIL GIBRAN

> Though we travel the world over to find the beautiful, we must carry it with us or we find it not.
> —RALPH WALDO EMERSON

> What other suggestions would you offer to someone who has just broken up a serious relationship?

# FEEDBACK

In this chapter we explored interpersonal relationships—their nature, development, maintenance, deterioration, and repair.

**1. Relationships are established in stages.** At least the following five stages should be recognized: **contact, involvement, intimacy, deterioration,** and **dissolution.**

**2. Relationships vary in breadth** (the number of topics talked about) and **depth** (the degree of "personalness" or intimacy to which the topics are pursued).

**3. Social penetration theory** holds that as relationships develop, the breadth and depth increase. When a relationship deteriorates, the breadth and depth will often (but not always) decrease, a process referred to as **depenetration.**

**4.** Relationships may be considered in terms of exchanging **rewards** and **costs.** Rewards are things we enjoy and want. Costs are unpleasant things we try to avoid.

**5. Relationships develop for a variety of reasons.** Some of the most important are **to lessen loneliness, to acquire self-knowledge,** and **to maximize pleasures** and **minimize pain.**

**6. Interpersonal attraction** depends on at least five factors: **attractiveness (physical** and **personality); proximity; reinforcement; similarity;** and **complementarity.**

**7.** Relationships are **maintained** because they satisfy our needs and because we engage in specific behaviors to keep the relationship intact.

**8. Relationship deterioration**—the weakening of bonds that hold people together—may be gradual or sudden.

**9.** Among the causes for relationship deterioration are diminution of the reasons for establishing the relationship, **changes, sex, work, financial difficulties, the undesirable distribution of rewards and costs,** and **a decrease in commitment.**

**10.** Among the **communication changes** that take place during relationship deterioration are **general withdrawal, an increase in deception, a decrease in positive** and **an increase in negative evaluative responses, a decrease in requests for pleasurable behaviors** and **an increase in requests to cease negative ones,** and **a decrease in the exchange of favors.**

Check your competence in using these skills for effective relationship development. Use the following rating scale: (1) = almost always, (2) = often, (3) = sometimes, (4) = rarely, (5) = hardly ever.

_____ 1. I adjust my communication patterns on the basis of the relationship's intimacy.

_____ 2. I gradually increase the breadth and depth of a relationship.

_____ 3. I can identify the rewards and costs of my relationships.

_____ 4. I can effectively manage physical proximity, reinforcement, and emphasizing similarities as ways to increase interpersonal attractiveness.

_____ 5. I can identify changes in communication patterns that may signal relationship deterioration.

_____ 6. I can use the accepted repair strategies to heal an ailing relationship, for example, reversing negative communication patterns, using cherishing behaviors, and adopting a positive action program.

_____ 7. I can apply to my own relationships such communication skills as identifying relational messages, exchanging perspectives due to differences in punctuation, empathic and supportive understanding, and eliminating unfair fight strategies.

# SKILL DEVELOPMENT EXPERIENCES

## 7.1 CHERISHING BEHAVIORS

William Lederer (1984) suggests that partners make lists of cherishing behaviors (see earlier discussion) they each wish to receive and then exchange the lists. Each person then performs the cherishing behaviors desired by the partner. At first these behaviors may seem self-conscious and awkward. In time, however, they will become a normal part of interaction and will help offset the inevitable costs in any relationship.

Compile a list of cherishing behaviors you would like to receive. Have your friend or partner do likewise. Exchange the lists. Agree to exchange a fixed number of cherishing behaviors per day. Continue the exchange for at least five days. Report on your experiences.

## 7.2 SEEKING AFFINITY

Here are ten affinity-seeking strategies—the techniques we use to get others to like us (Bell and Daly 1984). Select one of the following situations and indicate—with reference to specific communication behaviors—how you might use any three of the strategies to achieve your goal. In the definitions, the term *"Other"* is used as shorthand for "other person or persons."

Situations

1. You're at an employment interview and want the interviewer to like you.

2. You are introduced to Chris and would like to get to know Chris better and perhaps go on a date .

3. You are on a new job and want your co-workers to like you.

4. You just opened a small business in a new neighborhood. You want the people in the area to like you and buy in your store.

Affinity-Seeking Strategies

*Elicit Other's disclosures.* Stimulate and encourage Other to talk about himself or herself; reinforce disclosures and contributions of Other.
*Facilitate enjoyment.* Ensure that activities with Other are enjoyable and positive.
*Inclusion of Other.* Include Other in your social activities and groupings.

*Nonverbal immediacy.* Communicate interest in Other.
*Openness.* Engage in self-disclosure with Other.
*Present interesting self.* Appear to Other as an interesting person to get to know.
*Reward association.* Appear as one who is able to administer rewards to Other for associating with you.
*Self-concept confirmation.* Show respect for Other and help Other to feel positively about himself or herself.
*Similarity.* Demonstrate that you share significant attitudes and values with Other.
*Supportiveness.* Communicate supportiveness in Other's interpersonal interactions.

## 7.3 THE GREETING CARD AND THE POPULAR SONG

This exercise aims (1) to familiarize you with some of the popular conceptions and sentiments concerning interpersonal relationships, and (2) to introduce a wide variety of concepts important in the study of interpersonal relationships.

Methods and Procedures

1. Bring to class a greeting card or song that expresses a sentiment that is significant for any of the following reasons. This list is not exhaustive and items are not mutually exclusive.

   - It expresses a popular sentiment that is correct or true, or incorrect or false.

   - It expresses a sentiment that incorporates a concept or theory that can assist us in understanding interpersonal relationships.

   - It illustrates a popular problem in interpersonal relationships.

   - It illustrates a useful strategy for relationship development, maintenance, repair, or dissolution.

   - It illustrates a significant concept or theory in interpersonal relationships.

   - It suggests a useful question (or hypothesis for scientific study) that should be asked in the study of interpersonal relationships.

   - It supports or contradicts some currently accepted theory in interpersonal relationships.

2. Be prepared to explain the greeting card or song sentiment in a brief discussion (three to five minutes) as it relates to the study of interpersonal relationships.
3. Identify one principle of interpersonal communication that your card or song suggests.

*Remember:* Sentiments in greeting cards and songs are communicated through a number of different channels. Therefore, consider the sentiments communicated through the verbal message but also through the illustrations, the colors, the card's physical form, the type of print, the song's tempo, the music's volume, and so on.

## 7.4 MALE AND FEMALE
This exercise is designed to increase your awareness of matters that may prevent meaningful interpersonal communication between the sexes. It is also designed to encourage meaningful dialogue among class members.

The women and men are separated with one group going into another classroom. Each group's task is to write on the blackboard all the things that they dislike having the other sex think, believe, do, or say about them in general—and that prevent meaningful interpersonal communication from taking place.

After this is done, the groups should change rooms so the men can discuss what the women have written and the women discuss what the men have written. After satisfactory discussion, the groups should get together in the original room. Discussion might center on the following questions.

1. Were there any surprises?
2. Were there any disagreements? That is, did members of one sex write anything that members of the other sex argued they do not believe, think, do, or say?
3. How do you suppose the ideas about the other sex got started?
4. Is there any reliable evidence in support of the beliefs of the men about the women or the women about the men?
5. What is the basis for the dislikes? Or, why was each statement written on the blackboard?
6. What kind of education or training program (if any) do you feel is needed to eliminate these problems?

7. In what specific ways do these beliefs, thoughts, actions, and statements prevent meaningful interpersonal communication?
8. How do you feel now that these matters have been discussed?

## 7.5 ANALYZING A RELATIONSHIP
The dialogue that follows is an abbreviated account of a relationship's development and dissolution. Consequently, the five stages are easy to see and clearly differentiated. In reality and in longer dialogues, these divisions would not be so obvious. The main purpose is to provide a focus to discuss interpersonal relationships. Examine the dialogue, taking into consideration some or all of the following questions:

1. *Reasons for relational development.* What reasons seem to account for the development of relationships among most college students?

2. *Stages in interpersonal relations.* Identify the stages in the dialogue. What specific phrases in the dialogue cue you to the stages of the relationship? What conversational cues signal movement from one stage to another?

3. *Developing relationships.* Illustrate (by actual or hypothetical examples) how the steps for initiating relationships might have been followed. Identify specific verbal messages (and hypothetical nonverbal messages) that might have influenced the development of this initial relationship.

4. *Breadth and depth of relationships.* What would you expect the breadth and depth of the relationship to be at each of the five stages? At what stage is there greatest breadth? Least? At what stage is there greatest depth? Least?

5. *Rewards and costs.* What are the possible rewards and costs in this relationship?

6. *Relationship Maintenance.* What seems to be keeping this relationship together?

7. *Relational deterioration and dissolution.* Why might this relationship have deteriorated?

8. *Communication in relational deterioration.* How would you compare the communication at the deterioration stage with the communication at the contact, involvement, and intimacy stages?

## THE SAGA OF CHRIS AND PAT

PAT: Hi. Didn't I see you in English last semester?

CHRIS: Yeah. I'm surprised you noticed me. I cut that class more than I attended. I really hated it.

PAT: So did I. Higgins never did seem to care much about whether you learned anything or not.

CHRIS: That's why I think I cut so much. Your name's Pat, isn't it?

PAT: Yes. And you're Chris. Right?

CHRIS: Right. What are you doing in Interpersonal Communication?

PAT: I'm majoring in communication. I want to go into advertising or public relations or something like that. I'm not really sure. What about you?

CHRIS: It's required for engineering. I guess they figure engineers should learn to communicate.

PAT: You gonna have lunch after this class?

CHRIS: Yeah. You?

PAT: Yeah. How about going over to the Union for a burger?

[At the Union Cafeteria]

CHRIS: I'm not only surprised you noticed me in English, I'm really flattered. Everyone in the class seemed to be interested in you.

PAT: Well, I doubt that, but it's nice to hear.

CHRIS: No, I mean it. Come on. You know you're popular.

PAT: Well, maybe . . . but it always seems to be with the wrong people. Today's the exception, of course.

CHRIS: You sure know the right things to say.

PAT: Okay, then let me try another. What are you doing tonight? Want to go to a movie? I know it's late and all, but I thought just in case you had nothing to do.

CHRIS: I'd love to. Even if I had something else planned, I'd break it.

PAT: That makes me feel good.

CHRIS: That makes me feel good, too.

[Six months later]

PAT: I hope this doesn't cause problems, but I got you something.

CHRIS: What is it?

PAT: Take a look. I hope you like it.

CHRIS: [opens the package and finds a ring] I love it. I can't believe it! You know, a few weeks ago when we had to write up a recent fantasy for class, I wrote one I didn't turn in. And this was it. My very own fantasy coming true. I love you.

PAT: I love you ... very much.

[Chris and Pat have now been living together for about two years]

PAT: It's me. I'm home.

CHRIS: So am I.

PAT: That's not hamburgers I smell, is it?

CHRIS: Yes, it is. I like hamburgers. We can afford hamburgers. And I know how to cook hamburgers. Make something else if you don't want to eat them.

PAT: Thanks. It's nice to know that you go to such trouble making something I like. I hate these damn hamburgers. And I especially hate them four times a week.

CHRIS: Eat out.

PAT: You know I have work to do tonight. I can't go out.

CHRIS: So shut up and eat the burgers. I love them.

PAT: That's good. It's you for you. Whatever happened to us and we?

CHRIS: It died when I found out about your little side trips upstate.

PAT: But I told you I was sorry about that. That was six months ago anyway. I got involved, I know, but I'm sorry. What do you want to do, punish me for the rest of my life? I'm sorry, damn it. I'm sorry!

CHRIS: So am I. But I'm the one who was left at home alone while you were out fooling around.

PAT: Is that why you don't want to make love? You always have some kind of excuse.

CHRIS: It's not an excuse. It's a reason. And the reason is that I've been lied to and cheated on. How can I make love to someone who treats me like dirt?

PAT: But I don't. I love you.

CHRIS: But I don't love you. Maybe I never have.

PAT: I will *eat out*.

[Two weeks later]

PAT: Did you mean what you said when you said you didn't love me?

CHRIS: I think I did. I've just lost my feelings. I can't explain it. When I learned about your upstate trips, I just couldn't deal with it. I guess I tried to protect myself and, in the process, lost my feelings for you.

PAT: Then why do you stay with me? Why don't you leave?

CHRIS: I don't know. Maybe I'm afraid to be alone. I'm not sure I can do it alone.

PAT: So you're going to stay with me because you're afraid to be alone? That's crazy. Crazy. I'd rather see us break up than live like this—a loveless relationship where you go out on Tuesdays and I go out on Wednesdays. What kind of life is that?

CHRIS: Not much.

PAT: Then let's separate. I can't live with someone who stays with me out of fear of being alone, who doesn't want to be touched, who doesn't want to love me. Let's try to live apart and see what happens. Maybe we need some distance. Maybe you'll want to try again.

CHRIS: I won't, but I guess separation is the best thing.

PAT: Why don't you stay here and I'll go to my brother's tonight. I'll pick up my things tomorrow when you're at work. I don't think I can bear to do it when you're here.

CHRIS: Goodbye.

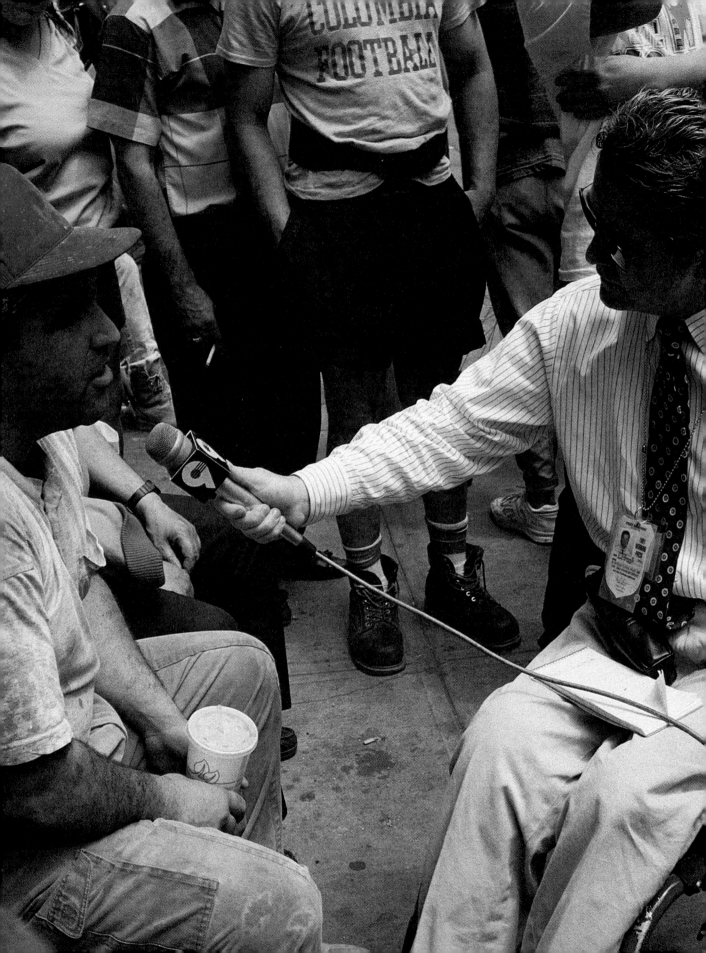

CHAPTER 8

## Interviewing

INTERVIEWING DEFINED

KINDS OF INTERVIEWS
- *The Persuasion Interview*
- *The Appraisal Interview*
- *The Exit Interview*
- *The Counseling Interview*
- *The Information Interview*
- *The Employment Interview*

QUESTIONS AND ANSWERS
- *Openness*
- *Neutrality*

LAWFUL AND UNLAWFUL QUESTIONS
- *Possible Strategies*

FEEDBACK

SKILL DEVELOPMENT EXPERIENCES

## Goals

*After completing this chapter, you should be able to*

1. *define* interviewing
2. *explain the characteristics of six major types of interviews*
3. *describe the sequence of steps you should follow in conducting an information interview*
4. *explain the principles you should follow before, during, and after the employment interview*
5. *explain how questions differ in terms of openness and neutrality*
6. *identify at least three types of questions that are unlawful to ask and explain how you would deal with them*

*■ Have you ever been interviewed for a job? ■ For a promotion? ■ How can you most effectively present your best side? ■ How can you make sure an interviewer gets the impression you want? ■ How can you best present your competencies and abilities? ■ In what ways is a date like an interview? ■ Have you ever interviewed someone to gain information? ■ How can you best ask questions to get the information you want? ■ What should you do when you are asked unfair or illegal questions?*

Interviewing includes a range of communication situations. Here are some examples:

- A salesperson tries to sell a client a new car.
- A teacher talks with a student about the reasons the student failed the course.
- A counselor talks with a family about their communication problems.
- A recent graduate applies to IBM for a job in the product development division.
- A building owner talks with a potential apartment renter.
- A priest talks with a parishioner about marital problems.
- A lawyer examines a witness during a trial.
- A theatrical agent talks with a potential client.
- A client discusses with a dating service employee some of the qualities desired in a potential mate.
- A boss talks with an employee about some of the reasons for terminating a contract.

## Interviewing Defined

**How will interviewing fit into your professional life?**

[An interview is] a communication transaction involving two people, one of whom has a definite purpose, and both of whom speak and listen from time to time.
—JOSEPH P. ZIMA

*Interviewing* is a particular form of interpersonal communication in which two persons interact, largely through a question-and-answer format, to achieve specific goals. While interviews *usually* involve two people, some, however, involve more. At job fairs, for example, where many people apply for the few available jobs, interviewers may talk with several persons at once. Similarly, therapy frequently involves entire families, groups of co-workers, or other related individuals. Nevertheless, the two-person interview is certainly the most common and the one we will be referring to throughout this unit.

The interview is different from other forms of communication because it proceeds through questions and answers. Both parties in the interview can ask and answer questions, but most often the interviewer asks and the interviewee answers.

The interview has specific goals that guide and structure its content and format. In an employment interview, for example, the interviewer's

The first key to wisdom is this—
constant and frequent question-
ing . . . for by doubting we are
led to question and by question-
ing we arrive at the truth.
—PETER ABELARD

goal is to find an applicant who can fulfill the tasks of the position. The interviewee's goal is to get the job, if it seems desirable. These goals guide the behaviors of both parties, are relatively specific, and are usually clear to both parties.

We can gain added insight into the nature of interviews by looking at their general structures. Interviews vary from relatively informal talks that resemble everyday conversations to those with rigidly prescribed questions in a set order. Table 8.1 presents the major types of general interview structures (Patton 1980; Hambrick 1991). You would select the interview structure that best fits your specific purpose, or combine the various types and create an interview structure that will best suit your needs.

## Kinds of Interviews

In what ways is a date like an
interview? In what ways is an
engagement like an interview?

We can distinguish between the different types of interviews by the goals of interviewer and interviewee. Some of the most important interviews are: persuasion, appraisal, exit, counseling, information, and employment (Stewart and Cash 1988; Zima 1983). The information and employment interviews are probably the most important for most college students, so these are covered in considerable length. In the information interview we concentrate on the role of the interviewer and in the employment interview, on the role of the interviewee. Of course, the principles for effective information and employment interviews will also prove useful for other types.

**Table 8.1** *General Interview Structures*

| Interview Structure | Characteristics and Uses |
|---|---|
| Informal Interview | Resembles conversation; general theme is chosen in advance but specific questions arise from the context; useful for obtaining information informally |
| Guided Interview | topics are chosen in advance but specific questions and wordings are guided by the ongoing interaction; useful in assuring maximum flexibility and responsiveness to the dynamics of the situation |
| Standard Open Interview | open-ended questions and their order are selected in advance; useful when standardization is needed, for example, when interviewing several candidates for the same job |
| Quantitative Interview | questions and their order are selected in advance as are the possible response categories, for example, A,B,C,D; agree-disagree; check from 1 to 10; useful when large amounts of information (which can be logically categorized) are to be collected and statistically analyzed |

What general interview structure would be most appropriate
for surveying students' opinions
on curriculum revision? Interviewing successful couples on
"Donahue"? Interviewing abused
children? Interviewing potential
"Jeopardy" contestants?

## The Persuasion Interview

The persuasive interview has a unique advantage over the public speaker and the mass persuader (radio, television, newspaper). The interviewer can tailor a persuasive effort to fit a particular person, at a particular time, in a particular place.
—CHARLES J. STEWART AND WILLIAM B. CASH, JR.

In the persuasion interview, the goal is to change an individual's attitudes, beliefs, or behaviors. The interviewer may either ask questions that will lead the interviewee to the desired conclusion or answer questions in a persuasive way. For example, if you go into a showroom to buy a new car, you interview the salesperson. The salesperson's goal is to get you to buy a particular car. He or she attempts to accomplish this by answering your questions persuasively. You ask about mileage, safety features, and finance terms. The salesperson discourses eloquently on the superiority of this car above all others.

All interviews contain elements of both information and persuasion. When, for example, a guest appears on "The Tonight Show" and talks about a new movie, information is communicated. But, there is also persuasion. The performer is trying to persuade the audience to see the movie.

*What kinds of persuasion interviews have you engaged in recently? How would you describe one such interview? Was it successful from the interviewer's point of view? The interviewee's? What kinds of persuasion interviews have you seen in the media? How would you describe them?*

### The Appraisal Interview

In the appraisal, or evaluation interview, the interviewee's performance is assessed by management, or more experienced colleagues. The general aim is to discover what the interviewee is doing well (and to praise this), and not doing well and why (to correct this). These interviews are important because they help new members of an organization see how their performances match the expectations of those making promotion and firing decisions.

### The Exit Interview

The exit interview is used widely by organizations in the United States and throughout the world. When an employee leaves a company voluntarily, it is important to know why. All organizations compete for superior workers; if an organization is losing its workers, it must discover why, to prevent others from leaving. This type of interview also provides a method for making the departure as pleasant and efficient as possible for both employee and employer.

### The Counseling Interview

Counseling interviews provide guidance. The goal is to help the person more effectively deal with problems—work, friends or lovers, or day-to-day living. For the interview to be of any value, the interviewer

"When you have a spare minute, Benson, crawl into my office."

CARTOON BY BOB ZAHN

Have you ever participated in a counseling interview? What specific skills does a counselor need to be effective?

must learn a considerable amount about the person's habits, problems, self-perceptions, goals, and so on. With this information, the counselor tries to persuade the person to alter certain aspects of his or her thinking or behaving. The counselor may try to persuade you, for example, to listen more attentively when your spouse argues or to devote more time to your classwork.

## The Information Interview

In the information interview, the interviewer tries to learn something about the interviewee, usually a person of some reputation and accomplishment. The interviewer asks the interviewee a series of questions designed to elicit his or her views, beliefs, insights, perspectives, predictions, life history, and so on. Examples of the information interview are those published in popular magazines. The television interviews conducted by Johnny Carson, Ted Koppel, and Barbara Walters as well as those conducted by a lawyer during a trial are all information interviews. Each aims to elicit specific information from someone who supposedly knows something others do not.

If you could interview any person in the world, who would it be? What three questions would you like to ask?

Let's say that your interview is designed to get information about a particular field—say, the available job opportunities, and the preparation you would need to get into desktop publishing. Here are a few guidelines for conducting such an information-gathering interview.

### Select the Person(s) You Wish to Interview

You might, for example, look through your college catalog for a desktop publishing course and interview the instructor. Or you might call a local publishing company and ask for the person in charge of desktop publishing. You have now taken your first step; you've selected a person you hope to interview. But, don't stop there. Before you pursue the interview, try to learn something about the person. For example, has the instructor written a book or articles about the field? Look at the book catalog and at indexes to periodicals.

To question a wise person is the beginning of wisdom.
—GERMAN PROVERB

### Secure an Appointment

Phone the person or send a letter requesting an interview. In your call or letter, identify the purpose of your request and that the interview can be brief. For example, you might say: "I'm preparing for a career in desktop publishing and I would appreciate an interview with you to learn more about the subject. The interview would take about 15 minutes." [This helps since the person now knows it will not take overly long and is more likely to agree to being interviewed.] Generally, it is best to be available at the interviewee's convenience. So, indicate flexibility on your part, for example, "I can interview you any day after 12 P.M."

You may find it necessary to conduct the interview by phone. In this case, call to set up a time for a future call. For example, you might say: "I'm interested in a career in desktop publishing and I would like to interview you about job opportunities. If you agree, I can call you back at a time that's convenient for you." In this way, you don't run the risk of asking the person to hold still for an interview while eating lunch, talking with colleagues, or running to class.

### Prepare Your Questions

The 'silly question' is the first intimation of some totally new development.
—ALFRED NORTH WHITEHEAD

This will ensure using the time available to your best advantage. Of course, as the interview progresses, other questions will come to mind and should be asked. But, a prepared list of questions (to be altered or even eliminated as the interview progresses) will help you obtain the information you need most easily.

### Establish Rapport with the Interviewer

In what other ways might you seek to establish rapport with an interviewer?

Open the interview by thanking the person for making the time available and again state your purpose. Many people receive numerous requests and it helps to remind the person of your specific purpose. You might say something like: "I really appreciate your making time for this interview. As I mentioned, I'm interesting in learning about job opportunities in desktop publishing and your expertise and experience in this area will help a great deal."

### Ask Permission to Tape the Interview

Generally, it is a good idea to tape the interview. But, ask permission first. Some people prefer not to have informal interviews taped. Even if the interview is being conducted by phone, ask permission if you intend to tape the conversation.

### Ask Open-ended Questions

A prudent question is one-half of wisdom.
—FRANCIS BACON

Use questions that provide the interviewee with room to discuss the issues you want to raise. Thus, instead of asking "Do you have formal training in desktop publishing?" (a question which requires a simple "yes" or "no" and will not be informative), you might ask, "Can you tell me about your background in this field?" (a question which is open-ended and allows the person greater freedom).

### Close the Interview with an Expression of Appreciation

Thank the person for making the time available, for being informative, cooperative, helpful, or whatever. On the more practical side, this could make it easier to secure a second interview.

### Follow-up the Interview

Follow-up the interview with a brief note of thanks. You might express your appreciation for the person's time, your enjoyment in speaking with the person, and your accomplishing your goal of getting the information you needed. A sample letter might look like this:

555 Anystreet
Anytown, Anystate 10000
December 14, 1993

Ms. Anita Brice
Brice Publishers, Inc.
17 Michigan Avenue
Chicago, Illinois 60600

Dear Ms. Brice:

It was a pleasure meeting you on Tuesday. I greatly appreciate your giving me so much of your time and for sharing your insights into desktop publishing

I now understand the field a lot better and have a clear idea of the kinds of skills I'll need to succeed.

Again, thank you for your time and your willingness to share your expertise.

Sincerely,

*Carlos Villas*

Carlos Villas

## The Employment Interview

Perhaps of most concern to college students is the employment, or selection, interview. In such an interview, a great deal of information and persuasion will be exchanged. The interviewer will learn about you, your interests, your talents—and, if clever enough, some of your weaknesses and liabilities. You will be informed about the nature of the company, its benefits, its advantages—and, if you are clever enough, some of its disadvantages and problems.

The interview sequence might, for convenience, be divided into three main periods: a preparatory period, in which you prepare for the interview; the interview proper; and the postinterview period, in which you reflect on and follow up the interview. The major goal of this discussion is to provide specific suggestions to make the interview work more effectively for you. Although these principles will prove useful for all interviews, we use the employment interview with you as the interviewee for illustration.

### Before the Interview

The preinterview period has no clear beginning. Let's say you are to be interviewed for an accounting job. Your preparation might logically be said to have begun when you enrolled as an accounting major or when you entered college. For our purposes, however, the preinterview period starts at the time you begin specific preparation for the interview. In this period, you should do three things. First, prepare yourself intellectually and physically. Second, establish your goals. Third, prepare answers to predicted questions.

PREPARE YOURSELF. This is perhaps the most difficult aspect of the entire interview process. It is also the step that is most often overlooked.

*Prepare yourself intellectually.* Educate yourself as much as possible about relevant topics. Learn something about the company and its specific product or products. Call and ask the company to send you any company brochures, newsletters, or perhaps a quarterly report. If it's a publishing company, familiarize yourself with their books. If it's an advertising agency, familiarize yourself with their major clients and major advertising campaigns.

If you are applying for a job, both you and the company want something. You want a job that will meet your needs. The company wants an employee who will meet its needs. In short, you each want something that the other has. View the interview as an opportunity to engage in a joint effort to each gain something beneficial. If you approach the interview in this cooperative frame of mind, you are much less likely to become defensive, which, in turn, will make you a more appealing potential colleague.

A great number of jobs are won or lost solely on physical appearance, so also give attention to *physical preparation.* Dress in a manner that shows you care enough about the interview to make a good impression. At the same time, dress comfortably. Perhaps the most specific advice we can give is to avoid extremes. If in doubt, it is probably best to err on the side of formality: Wear the tie, high heels, or dress.

Bring with you the appropriate materials, whatever they may be. At the very least, bring a pen and paper, an extra copy or two of your resumé

> When your credentials are similar to other candidates', thorough information about the company will set you apart.
> —SAM DEEP AND LYLE SUSSMAN

> If you want to succeed, you'd better look as if you mean business.
> —JEANNE HOLM

*What are your most important assets as a job candidate? How might you bring these out in an interview?*

*"I want a really easy, high-paying job like yours."*

CARTOON BY MARTIN J. BUCELLA

Examine the resumé on page 192. How might you tailor it to your own needs? What other general categories might be useful for your resumé?

and, if appropriate, a business card. If you are applying for a job in which you have experience, you might bring samples of your previous work.

The importance of your resumé cannot be stressed too much. The resumé is a summary of essential information about your experience, goals, and abilities. Often, a job applicant first submits a resumé. If the employer thinks it is interesting, the candidate is asked in for an interview. Because of the importance of the resumé and its close association with the interview, a sample resumé and some guidelines to assist you in preparing your own are provided on pages 192-193.

ESTABLISH GOALS.   All interviews have specific objectives. As part of your preparation, fix these goals firmly in mind. Use them to guide the remainder of your preparation and your behavior during and even after the interview.

After establishing your objectives clearly in your own mind, relate your preparation to these goals. For example, ask yourself how your goals might help you answer questions such as how to dress, what to learn about the specific company, and what questions to ask during the interview.

PREPARE ANSWERS AND QUESTIONS.   If the interview is at all important to you, you will probably think about it for some time. Use this time productively by rehearsing the interview's predicted course. Try also to predict the questions that you will be asked.

Think about these questions and consider how you will answer them. Table 8.2 presents a list of questions commonly asked in employment interviews. You may find it helpful to rehearse with these before going into the interview. Although not all of these questions would be asked in any one interview, be prepared to answer all.

Even though the interviewer will ask most of the questions, you also will want to ask questions. In addition to rehearsing some answers to predicted questions, fix firmly in mind the questions you want to ask.

When they ask about hobbies, you must tell them the only hobbies you enjoy are active ones. You're a doer. You don't read books, go to the opera, or watch television. You participate in sports, particularly status sports such as golf or tennis. You're not an observer, you're an active participant.
—JOHN T. MOLLOY

**Table 8.2**
*Common Interview Questions*

How would you answer each of
these questions?

What are your three greatest
strengths as a prospective
employee?

## Education

Why did you choose your particular field of study?
How did you choose your major?
What courses did you like best? Why?
What courses did you like least? Why?
Do you feel you have done the best scholastic work of which you are capable?
If you could start over in school, what would you do differently?
Do you plan to continue your education? When? In what areas?

## Work Experience

What jobs have you held? How were they obtained?
Why did you leave your last position?
What portion of your college expenses did you earn?
What features of your previous jobs have you disliked?
Can you describe a few situations in which your work was critical?

## Professional Expectations

What are your long-range goals?
Specifically, what position are you interested in?
Why are you interested in our organization?
What do you know about our organization?
What are your short-range objectives?
What are you looking for in a job?
What is your philosophy of management?
Why do you want to work for us?
How long do you plan to stay with our organization?

## Qualifications

What qualifications do you possess for success in your field?
What are your major strengths?
What are your major weaknesses?
What can you do for us that someone else cannot do?
Why should we hire you?
Can you work under pressure, deadlines, etc.?
Are you creative? Give an example.
Are you analytical? Give an example.
Are you a good manager? Give an example.
Are you a leader or follower? Explain.

## Personal Interests

Tell me about yourself.
What are your three biggest accomplishments?
Do you generally speak to people before they speak to you?
How have your goals or objectives changed in the last five years?
How would you describe the essence of success?
What was the last book you read?
What was the last movie you saw?
What was the last sporting event you attended?
List your extracurricular activities?
What offices have you held?

*Source: From Eric William Skopec,* Situational Interviewing *(Copyright © 1986) reissued 1988 by
Waveland Press, Inc., Prospect Heights, Illinois. Reprinted with permission from the publisher.*

**❶** Chris Williams
166 Josen Road
Accord, New York 12404
(914) 555-1221

**❷ Objective**
To secure a position with a college textbook publisher as a sales representative

**❸ Education**
A.A., Bronx Community College, 1984
B.A., Hunter College, 1993 [expected]
*Major:* Communications, with emphasis in interpersonal and public communication
*Minor:* Psychology
*Courses included:* Interpersonal Communication, Public Speaking, Small Group Communication, Interviewing, Organizational Communication, Public Relations, Persuasion: Theory and Practice, Psychology of Attitude Change
*Extracurricular activities:* Debate team (2 years), reporter on student newspaper (1 year)

**❹ Work Experience**
Two years, sales clerk in college bookstore (part-time)
Six years in retail sales at Macy's; managed luggage department for last three years

**❺ Special Competencies**
Working knowledge of major word processing and spreadsheet programs
Basic knowledge of college bookstore operation
Speaking and writing knowledge of Spanish

**❻ Personal**
Enjoy working with computers and people; willing to relocate and travel

**❼ References**
References from the following people are on file in the office of Student Personnel, Hunter College (695 Park Avenue, New York, NY 10021):
Dr. Martha Hubbard (Hunter College), major advisor and instructor for three courses
Mr. Jack Sprat (Hunter College, Bookstore), manager
Professor Mary Contrari (Hunter College), debate coach
Dr. Robert Hood (Bronx Community College), communication
**❽** instructor

1. Your name, address, and phone number are generally centered at the top of the resumé.

2. For some people, employment objectives may be more general than indicated here, for example, "to secure a management trainee position with a transportation company." If you do have more specific goals, put them down. In stating your objectives, do not imply that you will take just anything. At the other extreme, do not appear too specific or demanding.

3. It will be helpful to potential employers if you provide more information than simply your educational degree. Even the major department in which you earned your degree might be too vague, so clarify when necessary. If relevant (as it is in theis example), specify some of the most relevant courses you have taken. List honors or awards if they are relevant to your educational or job experience. Note, for example, that you were on the Dean's List, received departmental honors, or won awards for work in your field. If the awards are primarily educational (for example, Dean's List), list them under the *Education* heading; if job-related, list them under the *Work Experience* heading.

4. List work experience in chronological order, beginning with your latest position and working back. Depending on your work experience, you may have to pare down what you write; or, you may have little or nothing to write, so will have to search through your history for some relevant experience. Often the dates of the various positions are included.

5. The section on special competencies is often overlooked, but one where college students and recent graduates actually have a great deal to say. Do you have some foreign language ability? Do you know how to perform statistical analyses? Do you know how to write a computer program? Do you know how to keep profit-and-loss statements? If you do, put it down. Such competencies are relevant to many jobs.

6. You may also include relevant personal information. Since a sales position often involves travel and even relocation, it is especially important to indicate this willingness here.

7. References may be handled in a number of ways. Here, the specific names of people the potential employer may write to are listed. Sometimes phone numbers are included. If your school maintains personnel files for its students, you may simply note that references may be obtained by writing to the relevant office or department (as is done here). Otherwise, include addresses so that the employer may write to these people. Be sure you keep your file up to date. Three or four references are generally enough. Note that the people listed should have special knowledge about you that is relevant to the job.

8. Give special care to the form of your resumé. Typographical errors, incorrect spelling, poorly spaced headings and entries, and generally sloppy work will not produce the effect you want. Make sure your resumé gives the impression you want to give. It is the first sample of your work the employer sees.

| Characteristic | Behaviors |
|---|---|
| Openness | Answer questions fully. Avoid one-word answers that may signal a lack of interest or knowledge. |
| Empathy | See the questions from the asker's point of view. Focus your eye contact and orient your body toward the interviewer. Lean forward as appropriate. |
| Supportiveness | Be supportive of the interviewer. Avoid defensiveness. View questions not as personal attacks but as legitimate inquiries into your abilities and attitudes. |
| Positiveness | Emphasize your positive qualities. Express positive interest in the position. Avoid statements critical of yourself and others. |
| Equality | Avoid appearing too much of a subordinate by, for example, using overly polite forms of expressions or apologizing too much. |
| Confidence | Display confidence at every turn. Present a relaxed posture and general appearance. Be flexible in voice and body. Avoid disclaimers (Chapter 3) that may signal a lack of conviction or expertise. Avoid adaptors (Chapter 5) that may convey nervousness or discomfort. |
| Immediacy | Connect yourself with the interviewer throughout the interview by, for example, using the interviewer's name, focusing clearly on the interviewer's remarks, and expressing responsibility for your thoughts and feelings. |
| Interaction management | Ensure the interviewer's satisfaction by being positive, complimentary, and generally cooperative. |
| Expressiveness | Let your nonverbal behaviors (especially facial expression and vocal variety) reflect your verbal messages and your general enthusiasm. |
| Other Orientation | Focus on the interviewer and on the company. Express agreement and ask for clarification as appropriate. |

**Table 8.3** *Effective Interpersonal Behavior in an Interview Situation*

> What is your greatest strength as a job applicant going through an employment interview? How might you demonstrate this strength during an actual interview?

> I met Curzon in Downing Street from whom I got the sort of greeting a corpse would give to an undertaker.
> —STANLEY BALDWIN

## During the Interview

After the preparations, you are ready for the interview proper. Several suggestions may guide you through this sometimes difficult procedure.

MAKE AN EFFECTIVE PRESENTATION OF SELF. This is probably the most important part of the entire procedure. If you make a bad initial impression, it will be difficult to salvage the rest of the interview.

Devote special care to the way you present yourself. Arrive on time—in interview situations, this means five to ten minutes early. This will allow you time to relax, get accustomed to the general surroundings, and perhaps fill out any required forms. And it gives you a cushion should something delay you on the way.

Be sure you know the name of the company, the job title, and the interviewer's name. Although you will have much on your mind, the interviewer's name is not one of the things you can afford to forget (or mispronounce).

In presenting yourself, try not to be too casual or too formal. When there is doubt, choose increased formality. Slouching back in the chair, smoking, and chewing gum or candy are obvious behaviors to avoid when you are trying to impress an interviewer.

DEMONSTRATE EFFECTIVE INTERPERSONAL COMMUNICATION. Throughout the interview, be certain you demonstrate the interpersonal communication skills spelled out in this book. The interview is the ideal place to put into practice all the skills you have learned. Table 8.3 shows ten characteristics of interpersonal effectiveness (from Chapter 6) with special reference to the interview situation.

In addition to demonstrating these qualities of effectiveness, avoid those behaviors that create negative impressions during employment interviews (Table 8.4).

**What would you identify as your weakest qualities when being interviewed for a job? How might you correct this weakness?**

As an interviewee you are primarily a salesman. The product you are selling is yourself, and the assets of the product consist of your experience, skills, and personality. You communicate your experience and skills in your resume. Your personality comes across in the interview.
—H. ANTHONY MEDLY

**What other behaviors would you add to this list?**

Poor communication skills, inability to express oneself clearly, weak voice; errors in grammar or diction

Poor personal appearance, inappropriate attire, poor grooming

Lack of interest or enthusiasm, apathy, failure to try to sell oneself

Lack of confidence or poise, tendency to fidget or play with notes, resumé, and so on

Lack of courtesy, poor manners, lack of concern for the interviewer

Failure to maintain eye contact with the interviewer

Weak, limp, or fishy handshake

Inattention to details in application, resumé, portfolio, or other supporting materials

Indefinite responses to questions, avoidance of explicit responses or details, evasiveness, tendency to ramble without coming to the point

Lack of initiative, failure to take control of the interview when given the opportunity, inability to sustain conversation

Evidence of poor preparation, appearance of being caught off guard by commonplace questions and topics, lack of familiarity with the company and its activities

*Source: From Eric William Skopec,* Situational Interviewing *(Copyright © 1986) reissued 1988 by Waveland Press, Inc., Prospect Heights, Illinois. Reprinted with permission from the publisher.*

**Table 8.4**
*Behaviors Creating Negative Impressions*

*After the Interview*

Even after the interview, you still have work to do.

MENTALLY REVIEW THE INTERVIEW. This review will fix it firmly in your mind. What questions were asked? How did you answer them? Recall and write down any important information the interviewer gave. Ask yourself what you could have done more effectively. Consider effective behavior that you can repeat in other interviews. Ask yourself how you might correct your weaknesses and capitalize on your strengths.

FOLLOW UP. In most cases, follow up an interview with a thank-you note to the interviewer. In this brief, professional letter, thank the interviewer for his or her time and consideration. Reiterate your interest in the company and perhaps add that you hope to hear from him or her soon. Even if you did not get the job, you might ask to be kept in mind for future openings.

This letter provides you with an opportunity to resell yourself—to mention qualities you possess and wish to emphasize, but may have been too modest to discuss at the time. It will help you stand out in the mind of the interviewer, since not many interviewees write letters of thanks. It will also remind the interviewer of your interview and tell her or him you are interested in the position. It's a kind of pat on the back to the interviewer and says, in effect, that the interview was an effective one.

## Questions and Answers

> He had a way of meeting a simple question with a compound answer—you could take the part you wanted, and leave the rest.
> —EVA LATHBURY

The interviewer's principal tool is the question. Understanding the different types of questions may help you to respond to questions more effectively—as in an employment interview—and to ask questions more effectively—as in an information gathering interview.

Questions may be approached in at least the following two dimensions: open-closed and neutral-biased.

### Openness

> The scientist is not a person who gives the right answers, he's one who asks the right questions.
> —CLAUDE LEVI-STRAUSS

"Openness" refers to the degree of freedom the interviewee has to respond, both in content and format. At times there is almost unlimited latitude in what may constitute an answer. At the opposite extreme are questions that require only a "yes" or "no." Between these extremes are short-answer questions; those that are relatively closed and to which the responder has only limited freedom in responding. Representative questions varying in terms of openness-closedness arranged on a scale are provided in Figure 8.1. Note that the first of the five questions allows the interviewee the greatest freedom and the last allows the least. The questions in between allow more freedom than a simple "yes" or "no," but less freedom that the most open question.

Part of the art of successful interviewing is to respond with answers that are appropriate to the question's level of openness. Thus, if you are asked a question like No. 1 in Figure 8.1, you are expected to speak at some length. If you are asked a question like No. 5, then a simple sentence or two should suffice.

| | |
|---|---|
| 1. | **What are some of the problems you see in your family?** |
| 2. | **What are some of the communication problems you see in your family?** |
| 3. | **What communication problems do you see between your children?** |
| 4. | **What do you think can be done to make Pat more communicative?** |
| 5. | **Do you enjoy spending the weekend with the family?** |

CLOSED

**Figure 8.1** *Examples of Questions Varying in Openness*

> Can you develop examples of increasingly *open* questions beginning with "Do you dislike your current job?" Can you develop increasingly *closed* questions beginning with "What can you do for our company?"

## Neutrality

"Neutrality" and its opposite, "bias," refers to the extent to which the question provides the answer the interviewer wants from the interviewee. Some questions are neutral and do not specify any answer as more appropriate than any other. At the other extreme are questions that are biased, or loaded. These indicate quite clearly the particular answer the interviewer expects or wants. Compare the following questions:

> Can any question be totally neutral?

- How did you feel about managing your own desktop publishing company?
- You must really enjoy managing your own desktop publishing company, don't you?

The first question is neutral and allows the listener to respond in any way; it asks for no particular answer. The second question is biased; it specifies that the interviewer expects a "yes." Between the neutrality of "How did you feel about your previous job?" and the bias of "You must have loved your previous job, didn't you?" there are questions that specify with varying degrees of strength the answer the interviewer expects or prefers. For example:

- Did you like your previous job?
- Did you dislike your previous job very much?
- It seems like it would be an interesting job, no?

> Occasionally, it [a biased or leading question] is used to test whether the interviewee has the courage to disagree, and how the interviewee handles pressure.
> —SAM DEEP AND LYLE SUSSMAN

An interviewer who asks too many biased questions will not learn about the interviewee's talents or experiences, but only about the interviewee's ability to give the desired answer. As an interviewee, pay special attention to the biased type of question. Do not give the responses your interviewer expects if they are not what you believe to be correct or know to be the truth. This would be unethical. However, when your responses are not what the interviewer expects, consider explaining why you are responding as you are. For example, to the biased question, "It seems like it would be an interesting job, no?" you might respond: "It was interesting most of the time, but it didn't allow for enough creativity."

## Lawful and Unlawful Questions

Through the Equal Employment Opportunity Commission, the federal government has determined that questions concerning race, religion, and national origin—except under rare circumstances—are irrelevant to a candidate's ability to function effectively on the job. Hence, interview questions focusing on these areas serve no useful or ethical function.

The various state laws are more explicit on questions that may or may not be asked during employment interviews. H. Anthony Medley, in his *Sweaty Palms: The Neglected Art of Being Interviewed*, discusses some of these areas and provides helpful illustrations. His insights are followed here. To obtain additional guidance for a particular state, contact your state office of employment or the Equal Employment Opportunity Commission.

Some important areas in which unlawful questions are frequently asked concern age, marital status, race, religion, nationality, citizenship, and physical condition. For example, in California and New York, it is legal to ask applicants whether they can provide proof that they meet the job's legal age requirements. But it is unlawful to ask their exact age. In

"Have you had any leadership experience
other than having a dog?"

CARTOON BY GEORGE B. ABBOTT

both California and New York, it is unlawful to ask about a person's marital status. An interviewer may ask you, however, to provide the name of a close relative or guardian if you are a minor, or any relative who currently works for the company.

Questions concerning your race, religion, and national origin are unlawful in many states, as are questions that obliquely seek this same information. Thus, the interviewer may ask you what languages you are fluent in but may not ask what your native language is, what language you speak at home, or what language your parents speak. The interviewer may not ask you whether you or your parents are citizens. But he or she may ask if you are in this country legally. The interviewer may inquire into your physical condition insofar as the job is concerned. For example, the interviewer may ask, "Do you have any physical problems that might prevent you from fulfilling your responsibilities at this job?" But the interviewer may not ask if you have any physical disabilities.

These are merely examples of some of the legal and illegal questions you may be asked during an interview. Since the regulations vary from state to state, you should investigate those governing your particular state (Zincoff and Goyer 1984). Once you discover what questions are unlawful, consider how to deal with them during an interview.

Do you agree that certain questions should be considered illegal in a job interview? What types of questions do you think should be considered illegal?

The things most people want to know are usually none of their business.
—GEORGE BERNARD SHAW

### Possible Strategies

Your first strategy should be to answer the part of the question you do not object to and omit any information you do not want to disclose. For example, if you are asked the unlawful question concerning what language is spoken at home, you may respond with a statement such as "I have some language facility in German and Italian," without directly answering the question. If you are asked to list all the organizations of which you are a member (an unlawful question in many states, since it often indicates political affiliation, religion, or nationality), you might respond, "The only organizations I belong to that are relevant to this job are the International Communication Association and the Speech Communication Association."

This type of response is preferable to immediately telling the interviewer he or she is asking an unlawful question. In many cases, the interviewer may not be aware of a question's legality and may not be trying to get information you are not obliged to give. It is easy to conceive of situations in which the interviewer, for example, recognizes the nationality of your last name and wants to mention that he or she is of the same nationality. If you immediately take issue with the question, you will be creating problems where none exist.

On the other hand, recognize that in many employment interviews, the unwritten intention is to keep certain people out, whether it is people who are older or those of a particular marital status, sexual orientation, nationality, religion, and so on. If you are confronted by unlawful questions that you do not want to answer, and if the gentle method does not work and your interviewer persists—saying, for example, "Is German the language spoken at home?" or "What other organizations

Questions are never indiscreet. Answers sometimes are.
—OSCAR WILDE

have you belonged to?"—you might counter by saying that such information is irrelevant to the interview and to the position you are seeking. Again, be courteous but firm. Say something like "This position does not call for any particular language skill so it does not matter what language is spoken in my home." Or you might say, "The organizations I mentioned are the only relevant ones; whatever other organizations I belong to will certainly not interfere with my ability to perform at this job."

If the interviewer still persists—and I doubt that many would after these rather clear and direct responses—you might note that these questions are unlawful and you are not going to answer them.

> Don't fight a battle if you don't gain anything by winning.
> —GEN. GEORGE PATTON

# FEEDBACK

**1. Interviewing** is a form of interpersonal communication in which two persons interact largely through a question-and-answer format to achieve specific goals.

**2.** Six types of interviewing are the **persuasive interview,** the **appraisal interview,** the **exit interview,** the **counseling interview,** the **information interview,** and the **employment interview.**

**3.** In the **information interview** the following guides should prove useful: select the person you wish to interview, secure an appointment, prepare your questions, establish rapport with the interviewer, ask permission to tape the interview, ask open-ended questions, and follow-up the interview.

**4. Before the employment interview,** prepare yourself intellectually and physically for the interview; establish your objectives; and prepare answers to predicted questions.

**5. During the interview,** make an effective presentation of yourself and demonstrate effective interpersonal communication skills.

6. **After the interview,** mentally review the interview and follow it up with a brief letter.

**7. Questions** may be indexed in terms of **open-closed** and **neutral-biased.** The type of question asked will influence the usefulness of the information obtained.

8. Interviewees should familiarize themselves with possible **unlawful questions** and develop strategies to deal with them.

Throughout this chapter, we stressed the skills of interviewing. Check your ability to apply these skills. Use the following scale: (1) = almost always, (2) = often, (3) = sometimes, (4) = rarely, (5) = hardly ever.

_____ 1. I follow the basic guidelines in conducting informative interviews.

_____ 2. Before the interview, I prepare myself intellectually and physically; establish my objectives as clearly as I can; and prepare answers to predicted questions.

_____ 3. During the interview, I make an effective presentation of myself and demonstrate effective interpersonal communication skills.

_____ 4. After the interview, I mentally review the interview and follow it up with a letter.

_____ 5. I can frame questions varying in terms of openness-closedness and neutral-biased depending on my purpose.

_____ 6. I can effectively deal with unlawful questions.

# SKILL DEVELOPMENT EXPERIENCES

## 8.1 THE CONFIDENT (?) INTERVIEWEE

Here are some suggestions for communicating confidence. How many of these suggestions does the interviewee in the dialogue violate? How might the interviewee's comments be rephrased to communicate greater confidence?

1. Control your emotions, especially in conflict situations or when you are in strong disagreement with others. Once your emotions get the best of you, you will have lost your power and influence and will appear to lack the confidence necessary to deal with the relevant issues.

2. Admit your mistakes. Attempting to cover up obvious mistakes communicates a lack of confidence. Only a confident person can openly admit one's mistakes and not worry about what others will think.

3. Take the initiative in introducing yourself to others and in initiating specific topics of conversation. Don't wait for others and then simply react to what they say. That is the easy way out and communicates a lack of confidence and ability to control the social situation.

4. Don't ask for agreement from others by using tag questions, for example, _"That was appropriate, don't you think?"_ Don't turn normally declarative sentences into questions by a rising intonation, for example, _"I'll arrive at nine?"_ By asking for agreement we communicate a lack of confidence in making decisions and in expressing opinions.

5. Use open-ended questions to involve the other person in the interaction and follow these up with appropriate comments and/or questions.
6. Use "you" statements to signal your personal attention to the other person. This one feature, incidentally, has been shown to increase men's attractiveness to women.

Confidence, as are all qualities of interpersonal effectiveness, is communicated nonverbally. Here are a few suggestions:

a. Avoid excessive movements, especially self-touching. Tapping a pencil, crossing and uncrossing one's legs in rapid succession, or touching the face or hair all communicate uneasiness, a lack of social confidence.
b. Maintain eye contact. People who avoid eye contact are often judged to be ill-at-ease—afraid to engage in meaningful interaction.
c. Allow your facial expressions to reflect your feelings. Smile, for example, to signal positive reactions.
d. Avoid vocalized pauses—the *ers* and *ahs*—that frequently punctuate our conversations when we are not quite sure of what to say next or while we attempt to maintain our turn as speaker.
e. Maintain reasonably close distances between yourself and those with whom you interact.

The following brief dialogue might take place during an initial job interview. Read through the transcript and identify the elements that demonstrate a lack of confidence. Indicate how the applicant might have better represented himself as a more confident, more in-control type of individual.

MR. ROSS: And you are?

PHIL SNAP: Me? Oh, I'm Phil. Mr. Snap. Phil Snap.

MR. ROSS: So, Mr. Snap, what can I do for you?

PHIL SNAP: I'm here for, I mean I'm applying for that job.

MR. ROSS: So, you'd like a job with DATACOMM. Is that right?

PHIL SNAP: Well, er, yes. Don't you think that's a good idea? I mean it's a good company, no?

MR. ROSS: Tell me what you know about communications.

PHIL SNAP: Well, I guess, I mean I took lots of courses in college. Here's my transcript.

MR. ROSS: I can read your transcript. But, I want to hear from you, exactly what you know about communications.

PHIL SNAP: Well, I took courses in interpersonal communication, television production, organizational communication, nonverbal communication.

MR. ROSS: Don't tell me your courses. Tell me what you know.

PHIL SNAP: Excuse me. I guess I'm a little nervous. This is my first interview and I really don't know what to say.

MR. ROSS: (Smiling) Are you sure you were a communications major?

PHIL SNAP: Oh, yes, I was. See, it's on the transcript.

MR. ROSS: Yes, I know. Let me put it this way: do you think you can do anything for DATACOMM?

PHIL SNAP: Oh. Yes. Yes.

MR. ROSS: Okay, Mr. Snap, now exactly what can you do for DATACOMM that the next applicant can't do better?

PHIL SNAP: Oh, well, I really don't know much about DATACOMM. I mean, I may be wrong about this but I thought I would assist someone and learn the job that way.

MR. ROSS: Right. What skills can you bring to DATACOMM? Why would you make such a good learner?

PHIL SNAP: Damn, this isn't as easy as I thought it would be. Well, I'm not very good at giving speeches. But, I guess that's not too important anyway, right?

MR. ROSS: Everything is important, Mr. Snap. But, tell me what you are especially good at.

PHIL SNAP: Well, I guess I'm kind of good at group stuff—you know, working with people in groups.

MR. ROSS: No, I'm not sure I know what that means. Tell me.

PHIL SNAP: Like, I mean I'm pretty good at just working with people. People think I'm kind of a neat guy.

MR. ROSS: I don't doubt that Mr. Snap but do you have any other talents—other than being a neat guy?

PHIL SNAP: I can operate a Showpro system. Is that important?

MR. ROSS: Mr. Snap, I told you that everything is important.

PHIL SNAP: Is there anything else?

MR. ROSS: *I don't know, Mr. Snap, is there anything else?*

PHIL SNAP: *I don't know.*

MR. ROSS: *I want to thank you for your time, Mr. Snap. We'll be in touch with you.*

PHIL SNAP: *Oh, I got the job?*

MR. ROSS: *Not exactly. If we decide on you, we will call you.*

PHIL SNAP: *Okay.*

## 8.2 RESPONDING TO UNLAWFUL QUESTIONS

The following questions are often unlawful, and an interviewee is not required to answer them as a condition of employment. The interviewee, of course, must avoid answering the questions without antagonizing the interviewer and thus losing the job.

This exercise is designed to raise some of the unlawful questions that you don't have to answer, and provide you with some practice in developing responses that protect your privacy while maintaining a positive relationship with the interviewer.

Indicate how you would deal with each question. Write your responses and then compare them with those of other students, either in groups or with the class as a whole. Or form two-person groups and role-play the interviewer-interviewee situation. To make this realistic, the person playing the interviewer should press for an answer, while the interviewee should continue to avoid answering, yet respond positively and cordially. You will discover this is not always easy; tempers often flare in this type of interaction.

1. I see that you've been married for two years. Any plans to have children?
2. I notice a gap in your employment record from 1978 to 1982. Did you by any chance serve time in prison?
3. "Jones?" Is that a family name or did you change it?
4. I see you've written two articles on lesbian feminism. Do you personally identify with this philosophy? Would you define yourself as a lesbian feminist?
5. You've been working in the field—I see from your resumé—for 23 years. That must put you pretty close to retirement age, no?
6. Are you married?
7. I notice that you were exempt from physical education class in college. Do you have any physical disabilities?
8. You seem to be in your middle to late thirties and yet I don't notice any reference to marital status. Have you ever been married?
9. It's most helpful that you have fluency in Korean and Spanish. Which was your native language?
10. When I called the other day to arrange this interview, a man answered the phone. Do you live with a man?

## 8.3 INTERVIEWS: EXPERIENCING AND ANALYZING

Form three-person groups, preferably among persons who do not know each other well or who have had relatively little interaction. One person should be designated the interviewer, another the interviewee, and the third the interview analyst. The interview analyst should choose one of the following situations:

1. An interview for the position of camp counselor for retarded children
2. An interview for a part in a new Broadway musical
3. A therapy interview to focus on communication problems in relating to superiors
4. A teacher-student interview in which the teacher is trying to discover why the course taught last semester was such a dismal failure
5. An interview between the Chair of the Communication Department and a candidate for the position of instructor of Human Communication.

After the situation is chosen, the interviewer should interview the interviewee for approximately ten minutes. The analyst should observe but not interfere in any way. After the interview is over, the analyst should offer a detailed analysis, considering each of the following:

1. What happened during the interview (essentially a description of the interaction)?
2. What was well handled?
3. What went wrong? What aspects of the interview were not handled as effectively as they might have been?
4. What could have been done to make the interview more effective?

The analysts for each interview may then report their major findings to the class as a whole. A list of "common faults" or "suggestions for improving interviews" may then be developed by the instructor or group leader.

# CHAPTER 9

## Small Groups

## Goals

After completing this chapter, you should be able to

1. *define* small group communication
2. *identify* the steps that should be followed in problem-solving discussions
3. *explain* the six-hats critical thinking technique
4. *explain* the four principles of brainstorming
5. *describe* the personal growth group and explain one set of procedures that may be followed in consciousness-raising groups
6. *describe* the educational or learning group
7. *define* the panel or round table, the colloquy, the symposium, and the symposium-forum

*■ What can you use groups for? ■ How can you make your groups more effective? ■ In what ways can you make groups more enjoyable? ■ How can you increase your ability to solve problems? ■ How can groups help in generating ideas? ■ In what ways are groups suitable for dealing with personal issues and difficulties? ■ How can you share information more efficiently?*

How many groups are you a member of? Why do you belong to these groups? What needs do these groups serve?

We are all members of small groups. The family is the most obvious example, but we are also members of a team, a class, a collection of friends, and so on. Some of our most important and satisfying communications take place in small groups.

In this chapter we first look at the small group's nature and characteristics. With this foundation, we examine four types of small groups and the procedures for participating in them. Last, we examine four popular small group formats.

## The Small Group

A *small group* is a relatively small number of individuals who are related to each other by some common purpose and share some degree of organization.

A small group is, first, a collection of individuals, few enough in number that all may communicate with relative ease as both senders and receivers. Generally, a small group consists of approximately 5 to 12 people. The important point is that each member should be able to function as both source and receiver with relative ease. If the group is much larger than 12 this becomes difficult.

Society in its full sense . . . is never an entity separable from the individuals who compose it.
—Ruth Benedict

Second, group members must be connected to one another in some way. People in a movie theater would not constitute a group, since there is no relationship between them. In a small group, one member's behavior is significant for all members.

What group to which you belong is the most satisfying? Why?

Third, there must be some common purpose among the group's members. This does not mean that all members must have exactly the same purpose. But there must be some similarity in their reasons for interacting.

A group is best defined as a dynamic whole based on interdependence rather than on similarity.
—KURT LEWIN

Fourth, the people must be connected by some structure of organizing rules. Sometimes the structure is rigid—as in groups operating under parliamentary procedure, where comments must follow prescribed rules. At other times, the structure is loose, as in a social gathering. Yet both groups have some organization and structure: Two people do not speak at the same time, a member's comments or questions are responded to, not ignored, and so on.

### Small Group Norms

Most groups develop *norms* or rules for appropriate behavior. Sometimes these rules are explicitly stated as in a company contract or

*"Yes, Ted, on this team we take off our jackets,
but we don't loosen our ties."*

> **What norms govern your class in human communication? What norms govern your family? Do you have any difficulty with these norms?**

> **Can you identify any other cultural differences in small group communication?**

> *Group norms define the limits within which behavior is deemed acceptable or appropriate. They establish the group basis for controlling behavior, and set the standards by which individual behavior is judged.*
> —CHARLES S. PALAZZOLO

policy: all members must attend department meetings. Sometimes the rules are implicit: members should be well-groomed. Regardless of whether norms are spelled out or not, they are powerful regulators of members' behaviors.

Norms may apply to individual members as well as to the group as a whole and, of course, will differ from one group to another. For example, one family's norm might be to never discuss financial matters outside the immediate family. A college faculty's norm might allow members to dress as they like during normal teaching days, but more formally when meeting with the president. In Japan it is customary to begin meetings with what Americans would think is unnecessary socializing. While Americans prefer to get right down to business; the Japanese prefer rather elaborate socializing before getting to the business at hand (Axtell 1990a).

Norms that regulate a particular member's behavior are called *role expectations*: the new person in an organization is expected to play the role of secretary; Mary, who knows a lot about photography, is expected to play the role of photographer at the company parties; Tom, whose family owns a bakery, is expected to bring rolls and coffee to early morning group meetings.

Some norms govern the behavior of the group as a whole: all family members must help a family member in trouble; the group only parties after it gets its work done.

## Test Yourself:

### How Apprehensive Are You in Group Discussions and Meetings?*

How do your apprehension scores for group discussions and meetings compare with your score for interpersonal conversations (see pages 139–140)? How do you account for the differences?

Just as we are apprehensive in interpersonal conversations (see Chapter 6) and public speaking (see Chapter 11), each of us is apprehensive to some degree in group discussions and meetings. This brief test is designed to measure your apprehension in these small group communication situations.

This questionnaire consists of 12 statements concerning your feelings about communication in group discussions and meetings. Indicate the degree to which each statement applies to you by marking whether you (1) Strongly Agree, (2) Agree, (3) Are Undecided, (4) Disagree, or (5) Strongly Disagree with each statement. There are no right or wrong answers. Do not be concerned that some of the statements are similar. Work quickly; just record your first impression.

_____ 1. I dislike participating in group discussions.
_____ 2. Generally, I am comfortable while participating in group discussions.
_____ 3. I am tense and nervous while participating in group discussions.
_____ 4. I like to get involved in group discussions.
_____ 5. Engaging in a group discussion with new people makes me tense and nervous.
_____ 6. I am calm and relaxed while participating in group discussions.
_____ 7. Generally, I am nervous when I have to participate in a meeting.
_____ 8. Usually, I am calm and relaxed while participating in meetings.
_____ 9. I am very calm and relaxed when I am called upon to express an opinion at a meeting.
_____10. I am afraid to express myself at meetings.
_____11. Communicating at meetings usually makes me uncomfortable.
_____12. I am very relaxed when answering questions at a meeting.

*Scoring:* This test will enable you to obtain two subscores, one for group discussions and one for meetings. To obtain your scores use the following formulas:

FOR GROUP DISCUSSIONS:

> 18 plus scores for items 2, 4, and 6
> minus scores for items 1, 3, and 5

FOR MEETINGS:

> 18 plus scores for items 8, 9, and 12
> minus scores for items 7, 10, and 11

Scores above 18 show some degree of apprehension.

*From *An Introduction to Rhetorical Communication*, 4th ed. by James C. McCroskey. Reprinted by permission of the author.

> ...high communication apprehensives typically attempt to avoid small group communication or to sit rather quietly in a group if they must be present.
> —Virginia P. Richmond and James C. McCroskey

## The Problem-Solving Group

A problem-solving group meets to solve a particular problem or to reach a decision on some issue. In one sense, this is the most demanding kind of group. It requires not only a knowledge of small group communication techniques, but a thorough knowledge of the particular problem. And, it usually demands faithful adherence to a set of procedural rules.

The problem-solving approach, which owes its formulation to the philosopher John Dewey's steps in reflective thinking, identifies six steps (see Figure 9.1). These steps are designed to make problem solving more efficient and effective.

### Define and Analyze the Problem

In many instances the nature of the problem is clearly specified. For example, a group of designers might discuss how to package a new soap. In other instances, the problem may be vague, and it is up to the group to define it. Thus, for example, the general problem may be poor campus communications. But such a vague and general topic is difficult to tackle in a problem-solving discussion, so it is helpful to be more specific. So, for purposes of discussion, a group might specify the problem as "How can we improve the student newspaper?"

Generally, it is best to define the problem as an open-ended question ("How can we improve the student newspaper?") rather than as a statement ("The student newspaper needs to be improved") or a yes/no question ("Does the student newspaper need improvement?"). The open-ended question allows greater freedom of exploration.

> Part of the problem today is that we have a surplus of simple answers and a shortage of simple problems.
> —SYRACUSE HERALD

> Is this problem-solving sequence also appropriate for resolving interpersonal conflicts? Can you trace an example through this sequence?

**Figure 9.1** *The Problem-Solving Sequence*

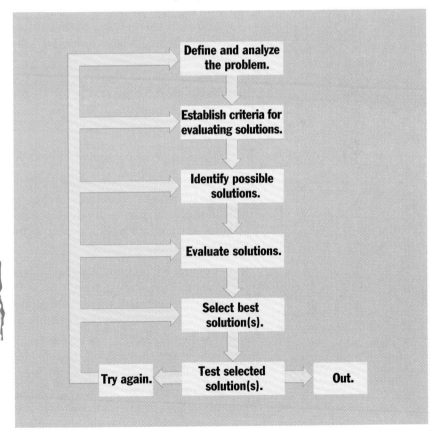

The problem should also be limited to a manageable area for discussion. A question such as "How can we improve the university?" is too broad and general. It would be more effective to limit the problem by focusing on one subdivision of the university. For example, you might select one of the following categories for discussion: the student newspaper, student-faculty relationships, registration, examination scheduling, or student advisory services.

In defining the problem, the group must analyze it—identify its dimensions. Although there are no prescribed questions that apply to all problems, appropriate questions (for most problems) seem to revolve around the following issues.

- *Duration:* How long has the problem existed? Is it likely to continue? What is its predicted course? For example, will it grow or lessen in influence?
- *Causes:* What are the problem's major causes? How certain are we that these are the actual causes?
- *Effects:* What are the problem's effects? How significant are they? Who does the problem affect? How significantly? Is this problem causing other problems? How important are these?

Applied to our newspaper example, the specific questions we ask in our analysis might look like this:

- *Duration:* How long has there been a problem with securing advertising? Does it look as though it will grow or lessen in importance?
- *Causes:* What seems to be the causing the newspaper problem? Are there specific policies (editorial, advertising, or design) that might be the cause?
- *Effects:* What effects is this problem producing? How significant are these effects? Who is affected: students? alumni? faculty? people in the community?

### The Six Critical Thinking Hats Technique

Critical thinking pioneer Edward deBono (1987) suggests we use six "thinking" hats to define and analyze problems. With each hat we look at the problem from a different perspective. The technique provides a convenient and interesting way to explore a problem from a variety of different angles.

- The **fact hat** focuses on the data—the facts and figures that bear on the problem. For example, *What are the relevant data on the newspaper? How can I get more information on the paper's history? How much does it cost to print? How much advertising revenue can we get?*
- The **feeling hat** focuses on our feelings, emotions, and intuitions concerning the problem. *How do I (we) feel about the newspaper and about making major changes?*
- The **negative argument hat** asks that we become the devil's advocate. *Why might this proposal fail? What are the problems with publishing reviews of courses? What is the worst-case scenario?*

Why is this six-hats technique useful in critical thinking? In what specific situations can this technique have practical value?

■ The **positive benefits hat** asks that we look at the upside. *What are the opportunities that this new format will open up? What benefits will reviewing courses provide for the students? What would be the best thing that could happen?*

■ The **creative new idea hat** focuses on new ways of looking at the problem and can be easily combined with brainstorming techniques discussed later in this chapter. *What other ways can we look at this problem? What other functions can a student newspaper serve? Can the student paper serve the non-academic community as well?*

■ The **control of thinking hat** helps us to analyze what we have done and are doing. It asks that we reflect on our own thinking processes and synthesize the results. *Have we adequately defined the problem? Are we focusing too much on insignificant issues? Have we given enough attention to the possible negative effects?*

### Establish Criteria for Evaluating Solutions

Before proposing any solutions, you need to decide how you will evaluate the solutions. At this stage, then, you identify standards or criteria that you will use in evaluating the solutions or in selecting one solution over another. Generally, two types of criteria need to be considered.

*In what types of problem solving discussions do you regularly engage? Will they be a part of your professional life? Your relationship life? In what way?*

First, there are the *practical criteria.* For example, you might decide that the solutions must not increase the budget. Or you might decide that the solution must lead to a greater number of advertisers, must increase the readership by at least 10 percent, and so on.

Second, there are the *value criteria.* These are more difficult to identify. They might include, for example, that the newspaper must be a learning experience for all who work on it or that it must reflect the attitudes of the board of trustees, the faculty, or the students.

After you identify the solutions, make certain they meet the criteria you have set.

What type of criteria would an advertising agency use in evaluating a campaign to sell soap? A university in evaluating a new multicultural curriculum? Parents in evaluating a preschool for their children?

## Identify Possible Solutions

At this stage identify as many solutions as possible. Focus on quantity rather than quality. Brainstorming may be particularly useful at this point (see discussion of idea-generation groups). Solutions to the student newspaper problem might include incorporating reviews of faculty publications, student evaluations of specific courses, reviews of restaurants in the campus area, outlines for new courses, and employment information.

Free and full discussion is an important right. It enables participants to see the various options available to them, whether as decision makers themselves or as a part of a decision-making body.
—James A. Jaksa and Michael S. Pritchard

## Evaluate Solutions

After all solutions have been proposed, group members evaluate each according to the established criteria. For example, does incorporating reviews of area restaurants meet the criteria? Would it increase the budget? Would it lead to an increase in advertising revenue? Each potential solution should be matched against the evaluating criteria.

## Select the Best Solution(s)

At this stage the best solution or solutions are selected and put into operation. Let's assume that reviews of faculty publications and outlines for new courses best meet the criteria for evaluating solutions. The group might then incorporate these two new items in the newspaper's next issue.

The great end of life is not knowledge but action.
—Thomas Huxley

## Methods for Decision-Making

Groups use different decision-making methods in deciding, for example, which solution to accept. In **authority** the members voice their feelings and opinions but the leader, boss, or chief executive makes the final decision. Under **majority rule** the group agrees to abide by the majority decision and may vote on various issues as the group searches to solve its problem. In **consensus** the group reaches a decision only when all group members agree as in the criminal jury system. The method to be used should naturally be stated at the outset of the group discussion.

What decision-making method is used in your family? Are you satisfied with this? What decision-making method is used in most of your college classes? Are you satisfied with this?

*"Now, that's a welcome sight! I was just beginning to miss decision-making."*

> Far from being necessarily dysfunctional, a certain degree of conflict is an essential element in group formation and the persistence of group life.
> —LEWIS A. COSER

### Test Selected Solution(s)

After putting the solution(s) into operation, test their effectiveness. The group might, for example, poll the students about the new newspaper or check the number of copies purchased. Or the group might analyze the advertising revenue or determine whether the readership did increase 10 percent.

If these solutions prove ineffective, the group returns to a previous stage and repeats part of the process. Often this is selecting other solutions to test. But, it may also involve going further back, for example, to a reanalysis of the problem, an identification of other solutions, or a restatement of criteria.

## The Idea-Generation Group

Many small groups exist solely to generate ideas. The process used is called *brainstorming* (Osborn 1957; Beebe and Masterson 1990). *Brainstorming,* a technique for analyzing a problem with as many ideas as possible, occurs in two phases. The first is the brainstorming period proper; the second is the evaluation period.

The procedures are simple. A problem is selected that is amenable to many possible solutions or ideas. Before the actual session, group members are informed of the problem so they can think about the topic. When the group meets, each person contributes as many ideas as he or she can think of. If ideas are to be recorded, a reporter is appointed or a tape recorder is set up and tested at the beginning of the session. During this idea-generating session, members follow four rules.

NO EVALUATION IS PERMITTED. All ideas are recorded. They are not evaluated or even discussed. Any evaluation—whether verbal or nonverbal—is criticized by the leader or members. By prohibiting evaluation, group members will more likely participate freely and without any concern for defending their ideas.

QUANTITY IS DESIRED. The more ideas the better. Somewhere in an accumulation of ideas will be one or two good ones. The more ideas generated, the more likely there will be a winner.

COMBINATIONS AND EXTENSIONS ARE DESIRED. While members may not criticize a particular idea, they may extend or combine it. The value of a particular idea may well be in the way it stimulates another member.

FREEWHEELING IS DESIRED. The wilder the idea, the better. It is easier to tone down an idea than to spice it up. A wild idea can be tempered easily, but it is not so easy to elaborate on a simple or conservative idea.

At times, the brainstorming session may break down with members failing to contribute new ideas. At this point, the moderator may prod members with statements such as:

- Let's try to get a few more ideas before we close this session.
- Can we piggyback any other ideas or extensions on the suggestion to . . . .
- Here's what we have so far. As I read the list of contributed suggestions, additional ideas may come to mind.
- Here's an aspect we haven't focused on . . . . Does this stimulate any ideas?

After all the ideas are generated—a period lasting no longer than 15 or 20 minutes—the entire list is evaluated. Unworkable ones are thrown out; those showing promise are retained and evaluated. During this phase, negative criticism is allowed.

Brainstorming is an effective idea-generating, problem-solving technique because it

- lessens the inhibition of members and encourages them to exercise their creativity;
- illustrates the effectiveness of cooperative team work; members soon learn that their own ideas and creativity are sparked by the contributions of others; and
- builds member pride in the final solution since all will have contributed to it.

> The best way to have a good idea is to have a lot of ideas.
> —LINUS PAULING

> Never, never rest contented with any circle of ideas, but always be certain that a wider one is still possible.
> —RICHARD JEFFERIES

> Of what value might brainstorming be to you in your academic life? In your personal and professional life?

> Your behavior influences others through a ripple effect. A ripple effect works because everyone influences everyone else.
> —JOHN HEIDER

# The Personal Growth Group

The wisest mind has something yet to learn.
—GEORGE SANTAYANA

Some personal growth groups aim to help members cope with particular problems, such as alcoholism, having an alcoholic parent, being an ex-convict, having an overactive child or an abusive spouse. Other groups are more clearly therapeutic and are designed to change significant aspects of one's personality or behavior.

## Some Popular Personal Growth Groups

The *encounter group* tries to facilitate personal growth and the ability to deal effectively with other people (Rogers 1970). One of its assumptions is that members will be more effective psychologically and socially if they get to know and like themselves better. Consequently, the atmosphere of the encounter group is one of acceptance and support. Freedom to express your inner thoughts, fears, and doubts is stressed.

The *assertiveness training group* aims to increase the willingness of its members to stand up for their rights and to act more assertively in a variety of situations (Adler 1977).

Are you or have you been a member of a personal growth group? Was it effective in achieving its aim?

The *consciousness-raising group* helps people cope with society's problems. Members all have one characteristic in common (for instance, they are all women, all unwed mothers, all new fathers, or all ex-priests). It is this commonality that leads members to join together and assist one another. In the consciousness-raising group, the assumption is that similar people are best equipped to assist each other's personal growth. Structurally, the group is leaderless. All members (usually 6 to 12 people) are equal in their control of the group and in their presumed knowledge.

## A Sample Consciousness-Raising Group

We all need encouragement and support in the human growth process.
—DONALD SIMMERMACHER

Here is the way in which one consciousness-raising group operates. While in this group, the procedures are rather rigidly formulated and enforced, others operate with more flexible rules. A topic, which may be drawn from a prepared list or suggested by one of the members, is selected by majority vote. Regardless of the topic, it is always discussed from the point of view of the larger topic that brings these particular people together—let's say, women's liberation. Whether the topic is "education," "employment," or "family," it is pursued in light of the issues and problems of the liberation of women.

After a topic is chosen, a member is selected (through some random procedure) to start. This member speaks for approximately 10 minutes about his or her feelings, experiences, and thoughts. The focus is always on oneself. No interruptions are allowed. After the member has finished, other group members may ask questions for clarification. The feedback from other members is to be totally supportive.

If you participated in a personal growth group, how did it work? Was its structure less prescribed than that outlined here?

After the questions have been answered, the next member speaks. The same procedure is followed until all members have spoken. Following the last member, there is a general discussion. During this time members may connect their own experience to the experiences of others. Or they may tell the group how they feel about some of the issues raised.

*Have you ever participated in a personal growth group? How did it compare with the one described here? What was its major purpose? Its general structure? Its major outcomes? What types of growth groups would you enjoy and profit from?*

Members raise their consciousness by formulating and verbalizing thoughts on a particular topic, hearing how others feel and think about the same topic, and formulating and answering questions.

## The Educational or Learning Group

The purpose of *educational* or *learning groups* is to acquire new information or skill through a sharing of knowledge. In most small group learning situations, all members have something to teach and something to learn. Members pool their knowledge to benefit all.

Members may follow a variety of discussion patterns (Christensen 1983). For example, a historical topic might be developed chronologically, with the discussion progressing from the past into the present and perhaps predicting the future. Issues in developmental psychology such as a child's language development or physical maturity, might also be discussed chronologically. Other topics lend themselves to spatial development. For example, the development of the United States might take a spatial pattern—from east to west—or a chronological pattern—from 1776 to the present. Other suitable patterns, depending on the topic and the group's needs, might be causes and effects, problems and solutions, or structures and functions.

**Would you define your human communication class as an educational or learning group? In what ways is it the same as the group described here? In what ways is it different?**

Have you ever participated in an educational or learning group? Was it effective? How might it have been more effective?

**Figure 9.2**
*Small Group Formats*

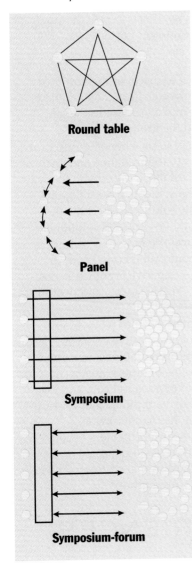

**Round table**

**Panel**

**Symposium**

**Symposium-forum**

Perhaps the most popular is the topical pattern. A group might discuss the legal profession by itemizing and discussing each of its major functions. A corporation's structure might also be considered in terms of its major divisions. As can be appreciated, each of these topics may be further systematized by, say, listing the legal profession's functions in terms of importance or complexity and ordering the corporation's major structures in terms of decision-making power.

## Small Group Formats

Small groups serve their functions in a variety of formats. Among the most popular are the round table, panel, symposium, and symposium-forum (Figure 9.2).

THE ROUND TABLE. In the round-table format, group members arrange themselves in a circular or semicircular pattern. They share information or solve the problem without any set pattern of who speaks when. Group interaction is informal and members contribute as they see fit. A leader or moderator may be present who may, for example, try to keep the discussion on the topic or encourage more reticent members to speak up.

THE PANEL. In the panel, group members are "experts" and participate in a round-table format. Here, too, their remarks are informal and there is no set pattern for speakers. The difference is that there is an audience whose members may interject comments or ask questions. Many talk shows, such as "Donahue" and "The Oprah Winfrey Show," use this format.

A variation is the two-panel format, with an expert panel and a lay panel. The lay panel discusses the topic but when in need of technical information, additional data, or direction, they may turn to the expert panel.

THE SYMPOSIUM. The symposium consists of a series of prepared presentations much like public speeches. All speeches are addressed to different aspects of a single topic. The leader of a symposium introduces the speakers, provides transitions from one speaker to another, and may provide periodic summaries.

THE SYMPOSIUM-FORUM. The symposium-forum consists of two parts: a symposium with prepared speeches; and a forum, a general discussion largely of questions and comments from the audience. The leader introduces the speakers and moderates the question-and-answer session.

# FEEDBACK

In this chapter we provided an overview of the small group's nature and the ways in which some major groups work.

**1.** A **small group** is a collection of individuals, few enough for all members to communicate with relative ease as both senders and receivers. The members are related by some common purpose and have some degree of organization or structure. Most small groups develop norms or rules identifying appropriate behavior for its members.

**2.** The **problem-solving group** attempts to solve a particular problem or at least reach a decision that may be a preface to solving the problem.

**3.** The six steps in the **problem-solving approach** are: define and analyze the problem, establish criteria for evaluating solutions, identify possible solutions, evaluate solutions, select best solution(s), and test solution(s).

**4.** A useful technique in analyzing problems is the **critical thinking hats** technique in which you approach a problem in terms of facts, feelings, negative arguments, positive benefits, creative ideas, and overall analysis.

**5.** The **idea-generation** or **brainstorming group** attempts to generate as many ideas as possible.

**6.** The **personal growth group** helps members to deal with personal problems and to function more effectively. Popular personal growth groups are the encounter group, the assertiveness training group, and the consciousness-raising group.

**7.** The **educational** or **learning group** attempts to acquire new information or skill through a mutual sharing of knowledge or insight.

**8.** Small groups make use of four major formats: the **round table, panel, symposium,** and **symposium-forum.**

The skills covered in this chapter focus on our ability to effectively use the various types of small groups. Check your ability to apply these skills. Use the following scale: (1) = almost always, (2) = often, (3) = sometimes, (4) = rarely, (5) = hardly ever.

_____ 1. I actively seek to discover the norms of the groups in which I function and take these norms into consideration when interacting in the group.

_____ 2. I follow the six steps when in group problem-solving situations: define and analyze the problem, establish the criteria for evaluating solutions, identify possible solutions, evaluate solutions, select the best solution(s), and test selected solution(s).

_____ 3. I use the critical thinking hats technique and think about problems in terms of facts, feelings, negative arguments, positive benefits, creative ideas, and overall analysis.

_____ 4. I follow the general rules when brainstorming: I avoid negative criticism, strive for quantity, combine and extend the contributions of others, and contribute as wild an idea as I can.

_____ 5. I appropriately re-stimulate a brainstorming group that has lost its steam.

_____ 6. I respond with supportiveness in consciousness-raising experiences.

_____ 7. I employ organizational structure in educational or learning groups.

# SKILL DEVELOPMENT EXPERIENCES

### 9.1 THE PROBLEM-SOLVING GROUP

Together with four, five, or six others, form a problem-solving group and discuss one of the following questions:

- What should we do about the homeless?

- What should we do to improve student morale?

- What should we do to better prepare ourselves for the job market?

- What should we do to improve student-faculty communication?

- What should be the college's responsibility concerning AIDS?

Before beginning the discussion, each member should prepare a discussion outline, answering the following questions:

What is the problem? How long has it existed? What caused it? What are the effects of the problem?

What criteria should be used to evaluate possible solutions?

What are some possible solutions?

What are the advantages and disadvantages of each of these possible solutions?

What solution seems best (in light of the advantages and disadvantages)?

How might we put this solution to a test?

## 9.2 BRAINSTORMING

Together with a small group or with the class as a whole, sit in a circle and brainstorm one of the topics identified in Skill Development Experience 9.1: The Problem-Solving Group. Be sure to appoint someone to write down all the contributions or use a tape recorder.

After this brainstorming session, consider these questions:

1. Did any members give negative criticism (even nonverbally)?
2. Did any members hesitate to contribute really wild ideas? Why?
3. Was it necessary to re-stimulate the group members at any point? Did this help?
4. Did possible solutions emerge in the brainstorming session that were not considered by members of the problem-solving group?

CHAPTER 10

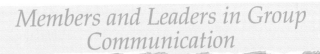

# Members and Leaders in Group Communication

## MEMBERS IN SMALL GROUP COMMUNICATION
- *Member Roles*
- *Interaction Process Analysis*
- *Member Participation*
- *Groupthink*

## LEADERS IN SMALL GROUP COMMUNICATION
- *Situational Leadership: The Concern for Task and People*
- *Leadership Styles*
- *Leader's Functions: Task and People*
- *Factors that Work Against Small Group Effectiveness*

## FEEDBACK

## SKILL DEVELOPMENT EXPERIENCES

## Goals
*After completing this chapter, you should be able to*

1. *identify the three major types of member roles and give three specific examples of each.*
2. *define* groupthink *and identify its major symptoms*
3. *explain the situational theory of leadership*
4. *describe the three leadership styles and when each of these would be most appropriate*
5. *explain at least four functions of leaders in small group communication*

*What kind of group member are you?* ■ *Are you effective in getting a task done?* ■ *Are you effective in getting the group members to enjoy themselves?* ■ *Do you use the group to serve your own interests?* ■ *How can you become a more valued and contributing group member?* ■ *Do you become the leader of groups to which you belong?* ■ *What kind of leader are you?* ■ *How can you become a more effective leader?*

In this chapter we consider membership and leadership in small groups. By gaining insight into the various roles of both members and leaders, you will be better able to analyze your own small group behavior and to change it if you wish.

## Members in Small Group Communication

Each of us serves in many roles. Javier, for example, is a part-time college student, father, bookkeeper, bowling team captain, and sometime poet. These roles represent Javier's customary and expected patterns of behavior. That is, he acts as a student—attends class, reads textbooks, takes exams, and does the things we expect of college students. Similarly, he performs those behaviors we associate with fathers, bookkeepers, and so on. In a similar way, people develop ways of behaving when participating in small groups. What are your major roles in small groups? How can you become a more effective participant?

> In what roles do you serve? In which do you serve most effectively? Least effectively?

### Member Roles

Kenneth Benne and Paul Sheats (1948) proposed a classification of members' roles in small group communication that is still the best overview of this important topic. They divide members' roles into three general classes: group task roles, group building and maintenance roles, and individual roles. Each of these is served by different, specific behaviors. These roles are, of course, frequently performed by leaders as well.

> I will pay more for the ability to deal with people than for any other ability under the sun.
> —JOHN D. ROCKEFELLER

### Group Task Roles

Group task roles help the group to focus more specifically on achieving its goals. In performing any of these roles, you do not act as an isolated individual, but rather as a part of the larger whole. The group's needs and goals dictate the roles you would fill. As an effective group member you serve in several roles, although some people do lock into a few specific roles. Thus, for example, one person may almost always seek the opinions of others while another may concentrate on elaborating details. Usually, this single focus is counterproductive—it is better for the roles to be spread more evenly among the members.

Twelve specific group task roles are described in Table 10.1.

Table 10.1
*Group Task Roles*

| Initiator-contributor | presents new ideas or new perspectives on old ideas, suggests new goals, or new procedures or organizational strategies |
| --- | --- |
| Information seeker | asks for facts and opinions, seeks clarification of issues being discussed |
| Opinion seeker | tries to discover the values underlying the group's task |
| Information giver | presents facts and opinions to group members |
| Opinion giver | presents values and opinions and tries to spell out what the group's values should be |
| Elaborator | gives examples and tries to work out possible solutions, trying to build on what others have said |
| Coordinator | spells out relationships among ideas and suggested solutions, coordinates the activities of the different members |
| Orienter | summarizes what has been said and addresses the direction the group is taking |
| Evaluator-critic | evaluates the group's decisions, questions the logic or practicality of the suggestions and thus provides the group with both positive and negative feedback |
| Energizer | stimulates the group to greater activity |
| Procedural technician | takes care of the various mechanical duties such as distributing group materials and arranging the seating |
| Recorder | writes down the group's activities, suggestions, and decisions; serves as the group's memory |

In which group task roles have you served? In which have you never served? In what type of role do those who emerge as leaders most frequently serve?

What other task roles can you identify?

What are some possible dangers of too great an emphasis on group building and maintenance?

## Group Building and Maintenance Roles

No individual or group can be task-oriented at all times. The group is a unit whose members have varied interpersonal relationships and these need to be nourished if the group is to function effectively. Group members need to be satisfied if they are to be productive. When they are not, they may become irritable when the group process gets bogged down, engage in frequent conflicts, or find the small group communication process unsatisfying.

There are seven specific group building and maintenance roles (Table 10.2).

## Individual Roles.

Group task roles and group building and maintenance roles are productive. They help the group achieve its goal, and are group-oriented.

Table 10.2
*Group Building and
Maintenance Roles*

| Encourager | provides members with positive reinforcement through social approval or praise for their ideas |
| Harmonizer | mediates the various differences between group members |
| Compromiser | tries to resolve conflict between his or her ideas and those of others; offers compromises |
| Gatekeeper-expediter | keeps open the communication channels by reinforcing the efforts of others |
| Standard setter | proposes standards for the group's functioning or for its solutions |
| Group observer and commentator | keeps a record of the proceedings and uses this in the group's evaluation of itself |
| Follower | goes along with members, passively accepts the ideas of others, and functions more as an audience than as an active member |

What group maintenance roles would you be most likely to fill if a small group was formed from members of this class?

Individual roles, on the other hand, are counterproductive. They hinder the group from achieving its goal and are individual rather than group-oriented. Such roles, often termed *dysfunctional,* hinder the group's effectiveness in both productivity and personal satisfaction. Eight specific types are identified (Table 10.3).

### Interaction Process Analysis

Another way to look at contributions that group members make is through interaction process analysis (Bales 1950; Schultz 1989). In this system you analyze members' contributions in four general categories. The *social-emotional positive contributions* category consists of such behaviors as showing solidarity, tension release, and agreement with other group members. The *social-emotional negative contributions* category includes displaying disagreement, tension, and antagonism. The *attempted answers* category includes giving suggestions, opinions, and information. The *questions* category includes asking for suggestions, opinions, and information. An analysis form for identifying these various behaviors is presented in Skill Development Experience 10.1 at the end of this chapter. Note that the categories under social-emotional positive are the opposites of those under social-emotional negative, and those under attempted answers are the opposites of those under questions.

Of the four major categories identified by Bales, in which have you served most often in the last week or two of small group interaction?

Both the Benne and Sheats's classification of members' roles and Bales's interaction process analysis categories are useful in viewing the contributions that members make in small group situations. You can see, for example, if one member is locked into a particular role or if the group process breaks down because too many people are serving individual rather than group goals. These systems are designed to help us see more clearly what is going on in a group and what specific contributions may mean to the entire group process.

Table 10.3
*Individual Roles*

| | |
|---|---|
| **Aggressor** | expresses negative evaluation of members' actions or feelings, attacks the group or the problem being considered |
| **Blocker** | provides negative feedback, is disagreeable, and opposes other members or their suggestions regardless of their merit |
| **Recognition seeker** | tries to focus attention on oneself, boasts about self-accomplishments rather than the task at hand |
| **Self-confessor** | expresses his or her own feelings and personal perspectives rather than focusing on the group |
| **Playboy/playgirl** | jokes around without any regard for the group process |
| **Dominator** | tries to run the group or members, by pulling rank, flattering members, or acting the role of boss |
| **Help seeker** | expresses insecurity or confusion or deprecates oneself and thus tries to gain sympathy from other members |
| **Special-interest pleader** | disregards the group's goals and pleads the case of some special group |

> Wear your learning like your watch, in a private pocket, and do not pull it out and strike it merely to show that you have one.
> —LORD CHESTERFIELD

> Do you ever serve in any of these individual roles? With what effects?

## Member Participation

Here are several guidelines to help make your participation in small group communication more effective and enjoyable. They are an elaboration and extension of the basic characteristics of effective interpersonal communication described in Chapter 6.

BE GROUP-ORIENTED. In the small group you are a member of a team—of some larger whole. Your participation is of value to the extent that it advances the group's goals and promotes member satisfaction. Pool your talents, knowledge, and insight so that the group arrives at a better solution than any one person could have developed. Solo performances hinder the group.

This call for group orientation is not to suggest that you abandon your individuality or give up your personal values or beliefs for the group's sake. What is advocated is individuality with a group orientation.

> Are there situations when you should abandon group-orientation?

CENTER CONFLICT ON ISSUES. Conflict in small group situations is inevitable; it is a natural part of the exchange of ideas. Don't fear or ignore it. Recognize conflict as a natural part of the small group process, but center it on issues rather than on personalities.

When you disagree, make it clear that your disagreement is with the solution suggested or the ideas expressed, and not with the person who expressed them. Similarly, when someone disagrees with you, do not take it as a personal attack. Rather, view it as an opportunity to discuss issues from an alternative point of view.

> What happens to a small group when members center conflict on personalities rather than on issues?

*Review the list of member roles. What general types of roles do you most often play in small groups (task, building and maintenance, or individual roles)? Within this general category, what more specific roles do you regularly play? What specific behaviors do you display that correspond to these roles?*

When conflict does center on personalities, you have a responsibility to redirect that conflict to the significant issues. For example, right before Chris and Pat come to blows, you might say: "Then, Chris, you disagree with Pat's proposal mainly because it ignores the needs of the handicapped, right?" You might go on to suggest that the group focus on how to alter the proposal to deal with the needs of the handicapped. When a more direct approach is necessary, you might say, for example: "Let's stick to the issue," "Can we get back to the proposal?" or perhaps, "Let's hear a third point of view."

BE CRITICALLY OPEN-MINDED. When members join a group with their minds already made up, the small group process degenerates into a series of debates in which each person argues for his or her position. Instead, come to the group with information that will be useful to the discussion. Do not decide on a solution or conclusion before discussing it with the group. Advance proposed solutions or conclusions tentatively rather than with certainty. Be willing to revise your suggestions in light of the discussion. Be willing to subject all suggestions—even your own— to the various critical thinking tests discussed throughout this text.

Listen openly but critically to comments of all members. Do not accept or reject any member's suggestions without critically evaluating them. Be *judiciously* open-minded. Be *judiciously* critical of your own contributions as well as those of others.

> **Honest criticism is hard to take, particularly from a relative, a friend, an acquaintance or a stranger.**
> —FRANKLIN P. JONES

ENSURE UNDERSTANDING. Make sure all participants understand your ideas and information. If something is worth saying, it is worth making it clear. When in doubt, ask: "Is that clear?" "Did I explain that clearly?"

Make sure too that you fully understand other members' contributions, especially before you take issue with them. In fact, it is often wise to preface disagreement with some kind of paraphrase (see Chapter 3). For example, you might say "As I understand you, you want to exclude freshmen from playing on the football team. Is that correct?" Then you would state your thoughts. In this way you give the other person the opportunity to clarify, deny, or otherwise alter what was said.

### Groupthink

*Groupthink,* according to Irving Janis (1983), is "the mode of thinking that persons engage in when *concurrence seeking* becomes so dominant in a cohesive in-group that it tends to override realistic appraisal of alternative courses of action." Janis also says the term itself is meant to signal a "deterioration in mental efficiency, reality testing, and moral judgments as a result of group pressures."

DRAWING BY ZIEGLER; © 1986 THE NEW YORKER MAGAZINE, INC.

Many specific behaviors of group members can lead to groupthink. One of the most significant occurs when the group limits its discussion to only a few alternative solutions. Another occurs when the group does not reexamine its decisions despite indications of possible dangers. Another is when the group spends little time discussing why certain initial alternatives were rejected. For example, if the group rejected a certain alternative because it was too costly, members will devote little time, if any, to ways to reduce the cost.

In groupthink, members are extremely selective in the information they consider seriously. While facts and opinions contrary to the group's position are generally ignored, those that support the group's position are readily and uncritically accepted.

The following symptoms should help you recognize groupthink in groups you observe or participate in.

- Group members think the group and its members are invulnerable.
- Members create rationalizations to avoid dealing with warnings or threats.
- Members believe their group is moral.
- Those opposed to the group are perceived in simplistic, stereotyped ways.
- Group pressure is applied to any member who expresses doubts or questions the group's arguments or proposals.
- Members censor their own doubts.
- Group members believe all are in unanimous agreement, whether this is stated or not.
- Group members emerge whose function it is to guard the information that gets to other members, especially when it may create diversity of opinion.

### Evaluating Group Membership

Figure 10.1 presents an evaluation form used in my small group communication course. It summarizes member's responsibilities and also contains some general effectiveness principles covered in interpersonal effectiveness (Chapter 6).

This form may be used to evaluate a small group interaction and provide the basis for a discussion of effective group membership.

## Leaders In Small Group Communication

In many small groups, one person serves as leader. In others, leadership is shared by several persons. In some groups, the leader is appointed. In others, the leader may simply emerge as a group progresses. In considering leaders and leadership, we focus on (1) situational leadership, (2) leadership styles, and (3) the major functions the leader should serve. Before reading further, analyze your own views on and style of leadership by taking the Leadership Test.

> Have you ever witnessed "groupthink?" What were the consequences?

> The more amiability and esprit de corps among the members of a policy-making in-group, the greater is the danger that independent critical thinking will be replaced by groupthink, which is likely to result in irrational and dehumanizing actions directed against out-groups.
> —IRVING JANIS

> Leadership is action, not position.
> —DONALD H. McGANNON

**Figure 10.1** *Group Member Evaluation Form*

## Group Membership Evaluation Form

**ROLES SERVED**

*Circle those roles played by the group member* and *indicate the specific behaviors that led to these judgments.*

*Group task roles:* initiator-contributor, information seeker, opinion seeker, information giver, opinion giver, elaborator, coordinator, orienter, evaluator-critic, energizer, procedural technician, recorder

*Group building and maintenance roles:* encourager, harmonizer, compromiser, gatekeeper-expediter, standard setter or ego ideal, group observer and commentator, follower

*Individual roles:* aggressor, blocker, recognition seeker, self-confessor, playboy-playgirl, dominator, help seeker, special-interest pleader

*Interaction process analysis:* shows solidarity, shows tension release, shows agreement, shows disagreement, shows tension, shows antagonism, gives suggestions, gives opinions, gives information, asks for suggestions, asks for opinions, asks for information

**SMALL GROUP PARTICIPATION**

| | | | | | | | |
|---|---|---|---|---|---|---|---|
| Is group-oriented | YES! | YES | yes | ? | no | NO | NO! |
| Centers conflict on issues | YES! | YES | yes | ? | no | NO | NO! |
| Is critically open-minded | YES! | YES | yes | ? | no | NO | NO! |
| Ensures understanding | YES! | YES | yes | ? | no | NO | NO! |
| Listens attentively | YES! | YES | yes | ? | no | NO | NO! |
| Is well-prepared | YES! | YES | yes | ? | no | NO | NO! |

**IMPROVEMENT SUGGESTIONS**

TEST YOURSELF:

## What Kind of Leader Are You?

Respond by indicating YES if the statement is a generally accurate description of your leadership style and NO if it is not.

_____ 1. I would speak as a representative of the group.
_____ 2. I would settle conflicts when they occur in the group.
_____ 3. I would be reluctant to allow the others freedom of action.
_____ 4. I would decide what should be done and how it should be done.
_____ 5. I would refuse to explain my actions when questioned.
_____ 6. I would allow members complete freedom in their work.
_____ 7. I would permit the others to use their own judgment in solving problems.
_____ 8. I would let the others do their work as they think best.
_____ 9. I would allow the others a high degree of initiative.
_____10. I would permit the group to set its own pace.

*Scoring:* These questions come from an extensive leadership test and should help you focus on some ways a leader can accomplish a task *and* ensure member satisfaction. Questions 1-5 are phrased so a leader concerned with completing the group's task would answer YES. Questions 6-10 are phrased so a leader concerned with ensuring that the group members are satisfied would answer YES.

"T-P LEADERSHIP QUESTIONNAIRE: AN ASSESSMENT OF STYLE" FROM J.W. PFEIFFER AND J.E. JONES, Structured Experiences FOR Human Relations Training. COPYRIGHT BY THE AMERICAN EDUCATIONAL RESEARCH ASSOCIATION. REPRINTED BY PERMISSION OF THE PUBLISHER.

> **When you work in small groups, are you more concerned with getting the task accomplished or with making sure everyone enjoys the experience?**

> **Learn to lead in a nourishing manner.**
> **Learn to lead without being possessive.**
> **Learn to be helpful without taking the credit.**
> **Learn to lead without coercion.**
> **—JOHN HEIDER**

> **What kind of leader are you? What situations seem to bring out the leader in you? What situations seem to inhibit your emergence as a leader?**

## Situational Leadership: The Concern for Task and People

Leaders must be concerned with getting the task accomplished *and* ensuring that members are satisfied. Groups don't work well when the leader focuses on one and neglects the other. A combined concern for both task and people satisfaction seems to work best.

The general idea of situational leadership is that although both task and people are significant concerns, each situation will call for a different combination. Some situations will call for high concentration on task issues but will need little people encouragement. For example, a group of scientists working on AIDS research would probably need a leader who provides them with information needed to accomplish their task. They would be self-motivating and probably would need little social encouragement. On the other hand, a group of recovering alcoholics might require leadership that stresses the members' emotional needs.

Therefore, leadership effectiveness depends on combining task and people concerns according to the situation—hence, the "situational theory of leadership." The most successful leader is flexible and can adapt his or her leadership style to the situation's unique demands.

### Leadership Styles

In addition to looking at leadership's major concerns, we can also look at leadership's three major styles: laissez-faire, democratic, and authoritarian (Shaw 1981; Bennis and Nanus 1985).

## Laissez-Faire Leader

*Laissez-faire* comes from the French and means literally "allow to do." The term is often applied to a government characterized by non-interference. Applied to group communication, it refers to a leadership style in which the leader takes no initiative in directing or suggesting alternative courses of action. Rather, the leader allows the group to develop and progress on its own, even allowing it to make its own mistakes. This leader gives up or denies any real authority. The laissez-faire leader answers questions or provides relevant information, but only when asked, and gives little if any reinforcement to group members. At the same time, this leader does not punish members, so is nonthreatening.

## Democratic Leader

The democratic leader provides direction, but allows the group to develop and progress the way members wish. The leader encourages members to determine goals and procedures and stimulates members' self-direction and self-actualization. Unlike the laissez-faire leader, the democratic leader reinforces members and contributes suggestions for alternatives. Always, however, this leader allows the group to make its own decisions.

## Authoritarian Leader

The authoritarian leader is the opposite of the laissez-faire leader. This leader determines the group's policies or makes decisions without consulting or securing agreement from members. This leader is impersonal. Communication goes to and from the leader, but rarely from member to member. This leader tries to minimize intragroup communication.

The authoritarian leader assumes the greatest responsibility for the group's progress and wants no interference from members. Concerned with getting the group to accept his or her decisions, this leader often satisfies the group's psychological needs. He or she rewards and punishes the group much as a parent does.

## Effectiveness and Leadership Styles

The laissez-faire group is generally inefficient for getting work done but is often preferred for social functions. In the democratic group, members are cohesive and satisfied. However, at least in some instances, the quality of the democratic group's work was not as high as that produced by the authoritarian-led group. Morale and satisfaction, however, are generally low in the authoritarian-led group (White and Lippitt 1960). When the authoritarian leader is especially knowledgeable, the group is likely to make fewer errors and accomplish its task in less time than the democratic group (Shaw 1955).

Cecil Gibb (1969), in summarizing the results of a series of studies on democratic as opposed to authoritarian leadership, notes that the authoritarian group produced "(1) a greater quantity of work, but (2)

> I must follow the people. Am I not their leader?
> —Benjamin Disraeli

> A group leader soliciting ideas from group members, a teacher asking students to suggest the due date for an assignment, and a district manager asking a salesperson for recommendations regarding the display of a new product are examples of democratic communicative behavior.
> —Michael Z. Hackman and Craig E. Johnson

> What kind of leadership style do you respond to best?

> Charlatanism of some degree is indispensable to effective leadership.
> —Eric Hoffer

less work motivation and (3) less originality in work; (4) a greater amount of aggressiveness expressed both toward the leader and other group members; (5) more suppressed discontent; (6) more dependent and submissive behavior; (7) less friendliness in the group; and (8) less 'group mindedness.'"

Each leadership style has its place, and we should not consider one style superior to the others. Each is appropriate for a different purpose or situation. In a social group at a friend's house, any leadership other than laissez-faire would be difficult to tolerate. But as Gibb notes, when speed and efficiency are paramount, authoritarian leadership may be the most effective. Authoritarian leadership is also appropriate when group members continue to lack motivation despite repeated democratic efforts. When all members are about equal in their knowledge of the topic or when the members are very concerned with their individual rights, the democratic leader seems the most appropriate.

### Leader's Functions: Task and People

With the situational view of leadership and the three general styles in mind, we can look at some of the major functions leaders serve. These functions are not exclusively the leader's. Nevertheless, when there is a specific leader, he or she is expected to perform them. Leadership functions are best performed unobtrusively—in a natural manner. Leaders carry out both task and people functions.

START GROUP INTERACTION. Many groups need some prodding and stimulation to interact. Perhaps the group is newly formed and members feel uneasy. Here the leader serves an important function by stimulating the members to interact. This function is also needed when members are acting as individuals rather than as a group and the leader must make members recognize they are part of a group.

MAINTAIN EFFECTIVE INTERACTION. Even after the group is interacting, the leader should see that members maintain the effective interaction. When the discussion begins to drag, the leader should prod the group: "Do we have any additional comments on the proposal to eliminate required courses?" "What do you members of the college curriculum committee think about the proposal?" The leader needs to ensure that all members have an opportunity to express themselves.

KEEP MEMBERS ON TRACK. It is the leader's task to keep all members reasonably on track. This may be accomplished by asking relevant questions, by interjecting internal summaries, or by providing transitions to make clear the relationship of an issue just discussed to one about to be considered. In some problem-solving and educational groups, a formal agenda may be used.

ENSURE MEMBER SATISFACTION. Members have different psychological needs and wants, and many people enter groups because of them. Even though a group may, for example, deal with political issues, members may have come together more for psychological than for political reasons. If a group is to be effective, it must meet not only the group's

---

Be willing to make decisions. That's the most important quality in a good leader. Don't fall victim to what I call the 'ready-aim-aim-aim-aim syndrome.' You must be willing to fire.
—T. BOONE PICKENS

---

The question, 'Who ought to be boss?' is like asking 'Who ought to be the tenor in the quartet?' Obviously, the man who can sing tenor.
—HENRY FORD

---

... the leader works in any setting without complaint, with any person or issue that comes on the floor; the leader acts so that all will benefit and serves well regardless of the rate of pay; the leader speaks simply and honestly and intervenes in order to shed light and create harmony.
—JOHN HEIDER

---

Leadership appears to be the art of getting others to want to do something you are convinced should be done.
—VANCE PACKARD

surface purposes (in this case, political), but also the underlying, or psychological, purposes that motivated many of the members to come together. One way to meet these needs is for the leader to allow digressions and personal comments, assuming they are not too frequent or overly long.

ENCOURAGE ONGOING EVALUATION AND IMPROVEMENT. All groups encounter obstacles as they try to solve a problem, reach a decision, or generate ideas. No group is totally effective. All groups have room for improvement. To improve, the group must focus on itself. Along with trying to solve some external problem, it must try to solve its own internal problems, for example, personal conflicts, failure of members to meet on time, or members who come unprepared.

PREPARE MEMBERS FOR THE DISCUSSION. Groups form gradually and need to be eased into meaningful discussion. The leader needs to prepare members for the small group interaction as well as for the discussion of a specific issue or problem.

*How would you characterize your leadership style? For example, are you usually more concerned with people or with task? Are you more likely to be a laissez-faire, democratic, or authoritarian leader? What major leadership roles are you most likely to fill? Are there any that you are likely to neglect?*

**Table 10.4**
*Qualities of the Effective Leader*

| An effective leader | |
|---|---|
| Values people | acknowledges the importance of and the contributions of others |
| Listens actively | works hard at understanding the wants and concerns of others |
| Is tactful | criticizes sparingly, constructively, and courteously |
| Gives credit | praises others and their contributions publicly |
| Is consistent | controls personal moods; treats others similarly; does not have favorites |
| Admits mistakes | willingly admits errors |
| Has a sense of humor | maintains a pleasant disposition and an approachable manner |
| Sets a good example | does what others are expected to do |

> Reason and judgment are the qualities of a leader.
> —TACITUS

Of the effective leader qualities listed in Table 10.4, which do you possess? Which do you need to cultivate?

Don't expect diverse members to discuss a problem without becoming familiar with each other. Similarly, if members are to discuss a specific problem, a proper briefing is necessary. Perhaps materials need to be distributed before the actual discussion. Or perhaps members need to read certain materials or view a particular film or television show. Whatever the preparations, the leader should organize and coordinate them.

In addition to these six functions—a mixture of task and people functions—the effective leader relates to group members in ways that encourage effective interaction. Nido Qubein (1986) provides a useful analysis of the general qualities of the effective leader (Table 10.4). These qualities, together with the six functions, should round out what makes an effective leader.

### Evaluating Leadership

What other factors would you include in your leadership evaluation form?

Figure 10.2 presents a form used in my small group communication courses to evaluate the group leader's effectiveness. As with the group member evaluation form, this leadership form summarizes the wide variety of functions a group leader is expected to perform.

### Factors that Work Against Small Group Effectiveness

While we need to actively use effective membership and leadership, we also need to avoid behaviors that work against small group effectiveness. Small group communication researchers have identified several important factors that limit the small group's effectiveness (Patton, Giffin, and Patton 1989).

**Figure 10.2** *Leadership Evaluation Form*

## Group Leadership Evaluation Form

**INTRODUCTORY REMARKS**

| | YES! | YES | yes | ? | no | NO | NO! |
|---|---|---|---|---|---|---|---|
| Opens discussion | YES! | YES | yes | ? | no | NO | NO! |
| Explains procedures | YES! | YES | yes | ? | no | NO | NO! |
| Gets group going | YES! | YES | yes | ? | no | NO | NO! |

**MAINTENANCE OF INTERACTION**

| | | | | | | | |
|---|---|---|---|---|---|---|---|
| Keeps members on schedule | YES! | YES | yes | ? | no | NO | NO! |
| Keeps to agenda | YES! | YES | yes | ? | no | NO | NO! |

**COMMUNICATION GUIDANCE**

| | | | | | | | |
|---|---|---|---|---|---|---|---|
| Encourages conflict resolution | YES! | YES | yes | ? | no | NO | NO! |
| Ensures members understanding | YES! | YES | yes | ? | no | NO | NO! |
| Involves all members | YES! | YES | yes | ? | no | NO | NO! |
| Encourages expression of differences | YES! | YES | yes | ? | no | NO | NO! |
| Uses transitions | YES! | YES | yes | ? | no | NO | NO! |

**DEVELOPMENT OF EFFECTIVE INTERPERSONAL CLIMATE**

| | | | | | | | |
|---|---|---|---|---|---|---|---|
| Works for member satisfaction | YES! | YES | yes | ? | no | NO | NO! |
| Builds open atmosphere | YES! | YES | yes | ? | no | NO | NO! |
| Encourages supportiveness | YES! | YES | yes | ? | no | NO | NO! |

**ONGOING EVALUATION AND IMPROVEMENT**

| | | | | | | | |
|---|---|---|---|---|---|---|---|
| Encourages process suggestions | YES! | YES | yes | ? | no | NO | NO! |
| Accepts disagreements | YES! | YES | yes | ? | no | NO | NO! |
| Directs group self-evaluation | YES! | YES | yes | ? | no | NO | NO! |
| Encourages improvement | YES! | YES | yes | ? | no | NO | NO! |

**CONCLUDING REMARKS**

| | | | | | | | |
|---|---|---|---|---|---|---|---|
| Summarizes | YES! | YES | yes | ? | no | NO | NO! |
| [Involves audience] | YES! | YES | yes | ? | no | NO | NO! |
| Closes discussion | YES! | YES | yes | ? | no | NO | NO! |

**IMPROVEMENT SUGGESTIONS**

Using the language introduced in these chapters on small group communication, how would you describe the communication that goes on in your human communication course?

*Procedural problems* center on role conflicts (members compete for leadership positions or are unclear as to their functions), faulty problem analysis (members shortcircuit the process of analyzing the problem), and faulty evaluation of proposals (members fail to agree on the criteria for judging proposals and solutions).

*Process problems* center on too little cohesion (members lack affiliation and may therefore leave the group) or too much cohesion (members may ignore problems to maintain harmony). Another process problem is the pressure to conform; members may be pleasant to each other and not, therefore, voice legitimate disagreements. Still another process problem occurs when members misunderstand the nature of the problem and reject accurate information.

*Personality problems* may occur when members are reticent to express themselves or when they take disagreements personally.

# FEEDBACK

In this chapter we looked at membership and leadership in the small group. We examined the roles of members—some productive and some counter-productive—groupthink, and leadership.

**1.** A popular classification of small group **member roles** is Kenneth Benne's and Paul Sheats's three-part system: **group task roles, group building** and **maintenance roles,** and **individual roles.**

**2.** Twelve **group task roles** are: initiator-contributor, information seeker, opinion seeker, information giver, opinion giver, elaborator, coordinator, orienter, evaluator-critic, energizer, procedural technician, and recorder.

**3.** Seven **group building** and **maintenance roles** are: encourager, harmonizer, compromiser, gate-keeper-expediter, standard setter or ego ideal, group observer and commentator, and follower.

**4.** Eight **individual roles** are: aggressor, blocker, recognition seeker, self-confessor, playboy or play-girl, dominator, help seeker, and special-interest pleader.

**5. Interaction process analysis** categorizes contributions into four areas: social-emotional positive, social-emotional negative, attempted answers, and questions.

**6. Member participation** should be group-oriented, should center conflict on issues, should be critically open-minded, and should ensure understanding.

**7. Groupthink** is defined by Irving Janis as "the mode of thinking that persons engage in when *concurrence seeking* becomes so dominant in a cohesive ingroup that it tends to override realistic appraisal of alternative courses of action."

**8.** In the **situational theory of leadership,** we view leadership as both accomplishing the task and serving the member's social and emotional needs. The degree to which either is emphasized should depend on the specific group, the unique situation.

**9.** Three major **leadership styles** are: **laissez-faire, democratic,** and **authoritarian.**

**10.** Among the **leader's task functions** are: to start the group interaction, maintain effective interaction, keep members on track, ensure member satisfaction, encourage ongoing evaluation and improvement, and prepare members for the discussion.

**11. The effective leader:** values people, listens actively, is tactful, gives credit, is consistent, admits mistakes, has a sense of humor, and sets a good example.

The skills identified in this discussion center on increasing your ability to function more effectively as small group member and leader. Check your ability to use these skills. Use the following rating scale:

(1) = almost always
(2) = often
(3) = sometimes
(4) = rarely
(5) = hardly ever.

_____ 1. I avoid playing the popular but dysfunctional individual roles in a small group: aggressor, blocker, recognition seeker, self-confessor, playboy-playgirl, dominator, help seeker, or special interest pleader.

_____ 2. In participating in a small group, I am group—rather than individual—oriented, center the conflict on issues rather than on personalities, am critically open-minded, and make sure that my meanings and the meanings of others are clearly understood.

_____ 3. I adjust my leadership style to the task at hand and on the needs of group members.

_____ 4. As a small group leader, I start group interaction, maintain effective interaction throughout the discussion, keep members on track, ensure member satisfaction, encourage ongoing evaluation and improvement, and prepare members for the discussion as necessary.

_____ 5. As a leader, I show that I value people, listen actively, am tactful, give credit to others, am consistent, admit mistakes, have a sense of humor, and set a good example.

# SKILL DEVELOPMENT EXPERIENCES

## 10.1 USING INTERACTION PROCESS ANALYSIS (IPA)

The aim of this experience is to gain some practice in using Bales's system of interaction process analysis. Five or six students should engage in a problem-solving discussion. The rest of the class should carefully observe the group interaction and, using the form on page 239, record the types of contributions each person makes. In the column under each participant's name, place a slash mark in one of the 12 categories for each contribution. An alternative procedure is to have the entire class watch a film such as "Twelve Angry Men" or "The Breakfast Club" and classify the characters' contributions. A general discussion should center on:

1. Does IPA enable you to identify the different types of contributions that individual members make during a discussion?

2. Can you offer suggestions for individual members based on this interaction process analysis?

3. Are members of the discussion group surprised at the types of contributions they made?

## 10.2 LOST ON THE MOON

This exercise is often used to illustrate the differences between individual and group decision making, almost always demonstrating that group decisions are much more effective and efficient than individual decisions. Of course, this is something that most people know intellectually, but this exercise dramatizes it for students in an interesting and provocative way.

The class is given the list of 15 items noted below. Each person is to visualize himself or herself as a member of a space crew stranded on the moon. Their ship is damaged and they must travel 200 miles to return to the mother ship. The 15 items have been salvaged from the crashed ship and their task is to rank the items in terms of their value in assisting them to return to the mother ship. Use number 1 for the most important item, number 2 for the next most important, and so on to 15 for the least important item.

After completing the rankings, form groups of five or six and construct a group ranking. After this is complete, correct answers and reasons should be give to students. They should then compute their individual error scores and the error score of the group decisions. The computations are made as follows: For each incorrect item, the student subtracts his or her score from the correct score, regardless of sign. This is the error score for that item. He or she does this for all 15 items and totals the error points. This is the total error score. The same procedure is followed for computing the group error score. A high error score (say, between 56 and 112) means that the student's or group's decisions were not very good ones; a low error score (say, between 0 and 45) means that the decisions were good ones or, more correctly, were similar to those responses supplied by NASA. Almost without exception the group score will be better than the individual scores.

box of matches

food concentrate

50 feet of nylon rope

parachute silk

solar-powered portable heating unit

2 .45-caliber pistols

1 case dehydrated milk

2 100-pound tanks of oxygen

stellar map (of moon's constellation)

self-inflating life raft

magnetic compass

5 gallons of water

signal flares

first-aid kit containing injection needles

solar-powered FM receiver-transmitter

*Source: From "Decisions, Decisions, Decisions," by Jay Hall. Reprinted with permission from* Psychology Today *Magazine. Copyright © 1971 (Sussex Publishers, Inc.)*

## Interaction Process Analysis Form

| | | | | | |
|---|---|---|---|---|---|
| **SOCIAL-EMOTIONAL POSITIVE** | | | | | |
| shows solidarity | | | | | |
| shows tension release | | | | | |
| shows agreement | | | | | |
| **SOCIAL-EMOTIONAL NEGATIVE** | | | | | |
| shows disagreement | | | | | |
| shows tension | | | | | |
| shows antagonism | | | | | |
| **ATTEMPTED ANSWERS** | | | | | |
| gives suggestions | | | | | |
| gives opinions | | | | | |
| gives information | | | | | |
| **QUESTIONS** | | | | | |
| asks for suggestions | | | | | |
| asks for opinions | | | | | |
| asks for information | | | | | |

# CHAPTER 11

## Public Speaking

### PREPARING THE PUBLIC SPEECH: A CAPSULE SUMMARY
- *Select the Subject and Purpose*
- *Analyze Your Audience*
- *Research the Topic*
- *Formulate Your Thesis and Identify the Major Propositions*
- *Support the Major Propositions*
- *Organize the Speech Materials*
- *Word the Speech*
- *Construct the Conclusion and the Introduction*

### SPEAKER APPREHENSION
- *Dealing with Speaker Apprehension*

### FEEDBACK

### SKILL DEVELOPMENT EXPERIENCES

### Goals

*After completing this chapter, you should be able to*

1. *define* public speaking
2. *identify the factors you should consider in audience analysis*
3. *define* thesis *and explain its function in the public speech*
4. *identify three organizational patterns and give examples of the kinds of speeches appropriate to each*
5. *identify at least three qualities that should characterize the style of a public speech*
6. *identify the functions of the conclusion and the introduction*
7. *define and explain how you can control* speaker apprehension

*■ How can you prepare an effective public speech? ■ How can you most effectively introduce a speech? ■ Conclude a speech? ■ What behaviors should you avoid in introducing and concluding a speech? ■ Are you frightened of speaking in public? ■ How might you reduce this fear and even come to enjoy public speaking?*

*Public speaking* is a form of communication in which a speaker addresses a relatively large audience with a relatively continuous discourse, usually face-to-face. A student delivering a report to a political science class, a teacher lecturing on the structure of DNA, a minister preaching a sermon, and a politician delivering a campaign speech are all examples of public speaking.

## Preparing The Public Speech: A Capsule Summary

Eight steps are necessary to prepare an effective public speech (Figure 11.1). You will probably not progress simply from step to step. For example, after selecting your subject and purpose (step 1), you may progress to step 2 and analyze your audience. On the basis of this analysis, however, you may go back and modify your subject, your purpose, or both. Similarly, after you research the topic (step 3), you may find you need additional information on your audience and go back to step 2.

How do you feel about approaching your study of public speaking?

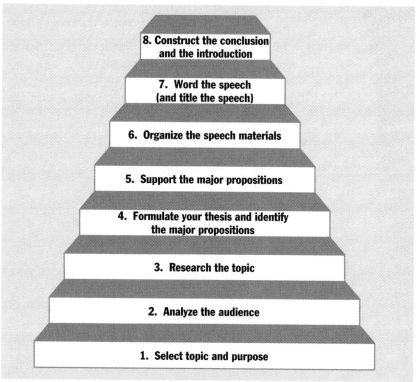

8. Construct the conclusion and the introduction

7. Word the speech (and title the speech)

6. Organize the speech materials

5. Support the major propositions

4. Formulate your thesis and identify the major propositions

3. Research the topic

2. Analyze the audience

1. Select topic and purpose

**Figure 11.1**
*The Steps in Preparing a Speech*

## Select the Subject and Purpose

The first step is to select the subject on which you will speak and the general and specific purposes you hope to achieve.

### The Subject

Select a worthwhile topic that will prove interesting to the audience. If your first speech is to be persuasive, select a topic about which you and the audience agree. Your aim would be to strengthen rather than change their attitudes. Or you might select a topic about which the audience is fairly neutral. Your aim would be to persuade them to feel either positively or negatively, as you think best. (See Table 11.1 for topic suggestions.)

FINDING TOPICS. Table 11.1 offers a variety of suggestions suitable for public speaking topics. In addition, you might find topics by examining surveys or news items or by brainstorming.

**Table 11.1**
*Suggestions for Speech Topics*

### Art/Music/Theater Topics

| | |
|---|---|
| *Abstract art:* | meaning of; and emotion; leading artists; Kandisky; Léger; Mondrian; Picasso; Pollock; contributions of movement; values of |
| *Entertainment:* | industry; benefits; abuses; tax; functions of; and communication |
| *Movies:* | censorship; famous; making; producing; directing; acting in; history in; economics of; career training; and communication |
| *Music:* | festivals; forms; instruments; composition; styles; drama; opera; rock; punk; disco; country-western; popular; symphonic; new wave |
| *Theater:* | Greek, Roman; commedia dell'arte; American; British; Eastern; Italian; French; performers; styles of; and television; and film; Broadway; and critics |

### Biological-Physiological Topics

| | |
|---|---|
| *Anesthesia:* | nature of; types of; uses of; development of; dangers of |
| *Biological:* | clock; control; warfare; rhythm; sciences |
| *Biorhythm:* | nature of; predictions from; life cycles; charting |
| *Brain:* | -washing; damage; genius; intelligence; aphasia |
| *Diseases:* | major diseases of college students; prevention; detection; treatment |
| *Food:* | health; preservatives; additives; red dye; and allergies; preparation |
| *Medicine:* | preventive; forensic; and health insurance; hisotry of; and poisoning |
| *Nutrition:* | nature of; functions of food; essential requirements; animal; human; and starvation; and diet; vitamins |
| *Transplants:* | nature of; rejection; donor selection; legal aspects; ethical aspects; religious aspects; future of; advances in |

### Communication Topics

| | |
|---|---|
| *Advertising:* | techniques; expenditures; ethical; unethical; subliminal; leading agencies |
| *Freedom of Speech:* | laws protecting; and Constitution; significance of; abuses of; and censorship; and economics |
| *Languages:* | artificial; sign; natural; learning of; loss of; pathologies of; sociology of; psychology of; international |
| *Media:* | forms of; contributions of; abuses; regulation of; popularity of; influences of; and violence; and censorship; Nielsen ratings |
| *Television:* | development of; history of; workings of; satellite; cable; commercials; propaganda; and leisure time; programming; economics |
| *Translation:* | computer; missionary impetus; problems in; history of |
| *Writing:* | styles; forms of; calligraphy; graphology; development of; and speech |

*Continued*

## Economic Topics

| | |
|---|---|
| *Business:* | cycles; associations; law; in performing arts; finance |
| *Capitalism:* | nature of; economics of; development of; depression and inflation |
| *Corporation:* | law; business; nature of; history; growth of the |
| *Inflation:* | and deflation; causes of; effects of; types of |
| *Investment:* | stocks; gold; real estate; art; restrictions on; bank; allowance |
| *Taxation:* | alcohol; cigarette; history of; purposes of; historical methods of; types of |
| *Treasury Department:* | monetary system; origin; functions of; and counterfeiting |
| *Wealth:* | economic; distribution of; primitive economic systems; contemporary view |

## Philosophical Topics

| | |
|---|---|
| *Empiricism:* | radical; nature of; doctrines; opposition to |
| *Existentialism:* | meaning of; and choice; history of; leaders in; movement |
| *Occultism:* | theories of; practices; rituals; astrology; theosophy; witchcraft; divination |
| *Phenomenology:* | characteristics of; principles of; growth of; development of |
| *Relativism:* | philosophy; ethical; meaning of; leaders of; influence |
| *Religion:* | different religions; leaders in; influence of; beliefs and agnosticism |
| *Witchcraft:* | meaning of; white and black; and magic; structure of; functions of; theories of; in primitive societies; in contemporary societies |
| *Zen:* | meaning of; principles of; historical development of; contemporary interest in; teachings of; influence of |

## Political Topics

| | |
|---|---|
| *Amnesty:* | in draft evasion; in criminal law; and pardons; in Vietnam War |
| *Communism:* | development of; theories of; religion and; ideologies |
| *Government:* | federal; state; city; powers of; abuses of; types of; democracy; socialism; communism |
| *Imperialism:* | nature of; economics of; problems with; practices; history |
| *Nationalism:* | nature of; history of; philosophy of; chauvinism; self-determination |
| *Supreme Court:* | judicial review; decisions; makeup of; chief justices; jurisdiction |
| *United Nations (UN):* | development of; functions of; agencies; and League of Nations; structure of; veto powers; Security Council |
| *War:* | conduct of; financing; destruction by: causes of; debts; games; casualties |

## Psychological Topics

| | |
|---|---|
| *Aggression:* | aggressive behavior in animals; in human beings; as innate; as learned |
| *Alcohol:* | alcoholism; nature of; Alcoholics Anonymous; Al Anon; physical effects of; among the young; treatment of alcoholism |
| *Autism:* | nature of; treatment for; symptoms; causes |
| *Depression:* | nature of; and suicide; among college students; dealing with |
| *Guilt:* | causes of; symptoms of; dealing with; effects of; and suicide; and religion |
| *Intelligence:* | quotient; tests; theories of; cultural differences; measuring |
| *Love:* | nature of; theories of; romantic; family; and hate; and interpersonal relationships; of self; and materialism |
| *Personality:* | development of; measurement of; theories of; disorders |

## Sociological Topics

| | |
|---|---|
| *Cities:* | problems of; population patterns; and crime; movement into and out of |
| *Crime:* | prevention; types of; and law; and punishment |
| *Divorce:* | rate; throughout world; causes of; advantages of; disadvantages of; proceedings; traumas associated with |
| *Ethnicity:* | meaning of; and prejudice; theories of; and culture |
| *Feminism:* | meaning of; implication of; changing concepts of; and chauvinism |
| *Gay:* | rights, life-style; laws against; prejudice against; and religion; and lesbian; statistics; relationships |
| *Prison:* | reform; systems; security; routine; effect on crime; personality; behavior |
| *Racism:* | nature of; self-hatred; genetic theory; human rights; education; religious |
| *Suicide:* | causes; among college students; laws regulating; methods; aiding the suicide of another; philosophical implications; and religion |

What topics would you like to hear other students speak on? What topics do you hope will be avoided? Why?

**Surveys.**   One excellent guideline to determine what is worthwhile, from your audience's point of view, is to look at some of the national and regional polls concerning what people think is important—the significant issues, the urgent problems. For example, a survey conducted by the Roper organization for H. & R. Block in *The American Public and the Income Tax System,* found that the most significant issues for Americans were: lowering the crime rate, making the tax system fair, improving the educational system, improving the nation's defense capabilities, setting up a national health  insurance program, decreasing unemployment, improving and protecting the environment, lowering Social Security taxes, and improving public transportation.

In a survey conducted by Public Research, the following issues were among the major problems confronting our country that the respondents themselves worried about: crime and lawlessness, the working American's tax burden, the rising costs of hospital and health care, unemployment, energy, the condition of older people, the declining quality of education, air and water pollution, and the condition of society's minority members.

How would you design a survey to discover the ten most important issues to college students?

A survey conducted for *Psychology Today* investigated the personal hopes and fears of Americans. Named as hopes were: a better or decent standard of living, good health for self, economic stability in general (no inflation), a happy family life, peace of mind, emotional maturity, to own a house or live in a better one, world peace, aspirations for children, a good job (congenial work), wealth, employment, good health for family, and to be a normal, decent person. The greatest personal fears were: lowered standard of living, ill health for self, war, economic instability in general, inflation, unemployment, ill health of family, and crime.

Naturally, all audiences are different. Yet, such surveys are useful starting points to give you some insight into what others think is important and, hence, interested in listening to.

**News Items.**   Another useful starting point is a good daily newspaper. Here you will find the important international and domestic issues, the financial issues, and the social issues all conveniently in one place. The editorial page and letters to the editor are also useful in learning what concerns people.

Newspapers are the world's mirrors.
—James Ellis

News magazines like *Time, Newsweek,* and such financial magazines as *Forbes, Money, Fortune* will provide a wealth of suggestions.

News shows like *20/20* and *60 Minutes* and the popular talk shows such as *Donahue* and *The Oprah Winfrey Show* often discuss the very issues that people are concerned with and hold different views on.

**Brainstorming.**   Another useful method is to brainstorm (Osborn 1957; Beebe and Masterson 1990), a procedure explained in detail in Chapter 9. You begin with your "problem" which in this case is "What will I talk about?" Then record any idea that occurs to you. Be sure to follow the four rules: avoid evaluation, strive for quantity, combine and extend ideas, and develop ideas as wild as possible. After you generate a sizable list—it should not take more than about 15 minutes—review the list and evaluate the suggestions.

What other suggestions can you offer for finding appropriate speech topics?

**LIMIT YOUR TOPIC.** Be certain to limit your topic to manageable proportions. It is better to cover a limited topic in depth than to cover a broad topic superficially. The limiting process is simple—repeatedly divide the topic into its significant parts. For example, divide your general topic into its component parts, then divide one of these parts into its component parts. Continue until the topic seems manageable, one that you can reasonably cover in some depth in the allotted time.

For example, take *television programs* as the first general topic area. You might divide this into such subtopics as *comedy, children's programs, educational programs, news, movies, soap operas, quiz programs,* and *sports.* You might then take one of these topics, say comedy, and divide it into subtopics. You might consider it on a time basis and divide television comedy into its significant time periods: pre-1960, 1961-1979, 1980 to the present. Or, you might focus on situation comedies. Here you might examine a topic such as "Women in Television Comedy," "Race Relations in Situation Comedy," or "Families in Television Comedies." The resultant topic is beginning to look manageable. *Television programs,* without some limitation, would take a lifetime to cover adequately.

Constructing a tree diagram might clarify the process of narrowing a topic. Let's say, for example, that you want to do a speech on literature. You might develop a tree diagram with branches for the division that interests you most, as shown in Figure 11.2. Thus you can divide *literature* into *fiction* and *nonfiction.* If *fiction* interests you most, then develop branches from *fiction. Novel, drama, poetry,* and *short story* would be appropriate. Now, let's say it is the *novel* that most interests you; you would create branches from *novel,* and so on. Keep dividing the topic until you get something that is significant, appropriate to you and your audience, and manageable in the allotted time. "The Contributions of Truman Capote to Fiction" or "Gore Vidal's Novels in Film" might be possible topics. Even though these topics are still broad, they illustrate what we mean by manageability and procedures you would use in narrowing a topic.

## The General Purpose

Speeches serve two general purposes: to inform and to persuade. The informative speech creates understanding; it clarifies, enlightens, corrects misunderstandings, demonstrates how something works, or explains how something is structured. In this type of speech, you rely most heavily on materials that amplify—examples, illustrations, definitions, testimony, visual aids, and the like.

The persuasion speech, on the other hand, influences attitudes or behaviors. It may strengthen existing attitudes or change the beliefs of the audience. Or, it may get the audience to do something. In the persuasion speech you rely heavily on materials that offer proof—evidence, argument, and psychological appeals, for example. Of course, the persuasion speech also contains materials that amplify, illustrate, and otherwise inform the audience. In strengthening or changing attitudes and behaviors, however, it must go beyond amplification to evidence, argument, and motivational appeals.

**Figure 11. 2**
*Narrowing a Topic*

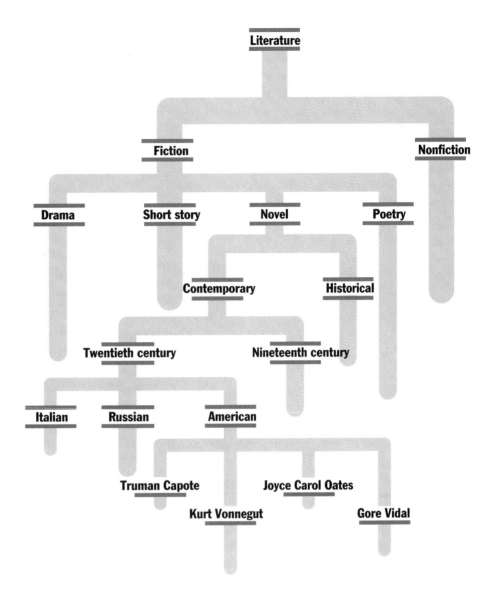

Literature

Fiction — Nonfiction

Drama — Short story — Novel — Poetry

Contemporary — Historical

Twentieth century — Nineteenth century

Italian — Russian — American

Truman Capote — Joyce Carol Oates

Kurt Vonnegut — Gore Vidal

How would you draw a similar tree diagram beginning with "entertainment"? "Sports"? "Politics"? "Education"?

How would you make these examples of specific purposes even more specific?

## The Specific Purpose

The specific purpose of your speech identifies the information you intend to communicate (if an informative speech) or the attitude or behavior you wish to change (if a persuasion speech). For example, your specific purpose in an informative speech might be:

   to inform my audience of the parts of a computer

   to inform my audience of the new grading procedures

   to inform my audience of the stages a child goes through in learning language

Your specific purpose in a persuasion speech might be:

   to persuade my audience that cigarette advertising should be abolished to persuade my audience that the college should establish courses in AIDS prevention

to persuade my audience to contribute time to serving disabled students

Whether you intend to inform or persuade, be sure your specific purpose is narrow enough so you will be able to go into some depth. Your audience will benefit more from a speech that covers a small area in some depth than from one that covers only the surface of a broad topic.

Select a few main issues and illustrate, explain, describe, and support them in a variety of ways. Thus, for example, do not try to inform the audience about the nature of drugs. This is too broad. Instead, select one drug and explain, perhaps, its structure and effects.

Avoid the common pitfall of trying to accomplish too much in too short a time. For example, "to inform my audience about the development of AIDS and the recent testing procedures for HIV infection" is actually two specific purposes. Select either one and build your speech around it. Thus, "to inform my audience about the development of AIDS" or "to inform my audience of the recent testing procedures for HIV infection" would be more appropriate.

Follow the same principle in developing your specific purpose for your persuasion speeches. Thus, for example, "to persuade my audience of the prevalence of AIDS in our community and that they should contribute money for AIDS services" contains two specific purposes. Select either "to persuade my audience of the prevalence of AIDS in our community" or "to persuade my audience to contribute money to services for persons with AIDS."

## Analyze Your Audience

If you are to inform or persuade an audience, you must know who they are. What do they already know? What would they want to know more about? What are their opinions, attitudes, and beliefs? Where do they stand on the issues you wish to address? Specifically, you might wish to focus on some of the following factors.

AGE. What is the general age of the audience? How wide is the range? Does it include different age groups that you will want to address differently? Does the age of the audience impose any limitations on the topic, the language, or the examples and illustrations you will select?

SEX. Is the audience predominantly of one sex? Do men and women view the topic differently? If so, how? Do men and women have different backgrounds, experiences, and knowledge about the topic? How will this influence the way you develop the topic?

CULTURAL FACTORS. What is the audience's ethnic and racial background? How might this affect how you develop your topic? Will your audience identify with you or see you as an outsider—as one outside their own cultural group? What are the implications of this?

OCCUPATION, INCOME, AND STATUS. What are the main occupations of the audience? How might this influence your speech? Does the

There is too much speaking in the world and almost all of it is too long. The Lord's Prayer, the Twenty third Psalm, Lincoln's Gettysburg Address are three great literature treasures that will last forever, no one of them is as long as 300 words. With such striking illustrations of the power of brevity it is amazing that speakers never learn to be brief.
—BRUCE BARTON

How would a speech on "the importance of hobbies" differ for an audience of elementary school children from one for senior citizens?

How might a speech on "the importance of establishing good credit" differ for an audience of all women from one for all men, or one that was equally mixed?

How might cultural factors influence the way you develop a speech on "the need to change immigration laws?"

*How would you describe your human communication class as an audience for an information speech on "How to Get the Job You Want"? For a persuasive speech on "The Need to Build Homeless Shelters in this Community"?*

income of the audience have any implications for your subject or the way you will develop it? What about the general status of audience members? Might this influence the speech in any way?

RELIGION AND RELIGIOUSNESS. What is the dominant religious affiliation of the audience? What are the implications of this for the speech? What is the strength of their belief? How might this relate to the topic?

CONTEXT. Will the context influence what you discuss or the way you will present your speech? Are there facilities for showing slides? Is there a chalkboard? Is there adequate light? Are there enough seats? Is there a podium? Is a microphone necessary?

OTHER FACTORS. What other factors will influence the way you prepare and present your speech? Is marital status relevant? Does the audience have special interests you might note in your speech?

### Research the Topic

If the speech is to be worthwhile and if you and the audience are to profit from it, you must research the topic. First read some general source—an article in an encyclopedia or a journal or magazine. You might pursue some of the references in the article or seek books on the topic in the library card catalog. You might also consult one or more of the guides to periodical literature for recent articles in journals, magazines, and newspapers. For some topics, you might want to consult individuals. Professors, politicians, physicians, or others with specialized information might prove useful.

Today, more and more research is being conducted via computer. Data bases, containing vast amounts of information on just about any topic, can be easily and efficiently accessed in many college libraries. What data bases will prove most useful in preparing your next speech? For what personal or professional interest might you access a computer data base? Which one(s) would you access?

## Computer Searches

Many college libraries now provide access to computer searches, such as those on CD ROM (Compact Disk Read Only Memory), which make research both enjoyable and efficient. These systems enable you to access a wide variety of specialized data bases. For example, the ABI/INFORM data base covers more than 500 periodicals in business; ERIC indexes more than 775 major journals as well as convention papers, dissertations, and curriculum materials in education; and PERIODICAL ABSTRACTS indexes more than 250 journals covered by *Reader's Guide to Periodical Literature*. With such systems you can access an annotated bibliography built around just about any topic.

One of the great advantages is that you can request references that deal with specific topics, for example, teenage drug abuse in schools, integrating multiculturalism into the college curriculum, or AIDS prevention programs in elementary schools. No longer do you have to look up, for example, drug abuse and then search each article to see if it deals with teenagers in school. The computer program will search the articles for you and indicate which of the articles deals with both drug abuse and teenagers in a school setting (as major topics). That is, the program will not—unless you direct it to do so—access articles that merely contain the words "drug abuse" or "teenagers in school." Most systems allow you to print out the bibliography or download it to your own computer disk.

Since these information retrieval systems vary so much from one school to another and since they are changing and expanding so rapidly, it is best to investigate the specific resources of your college or local library. Table 11.2 presents some helpful research sources.

**Table 11.2** *Some Research Sources*

## The Card/On-Line Catalog

| | |
|---|---|
| *Card Catalog* | Has given way to the computer catalog in many libraries. Contains "cards" of three types: title, subject, and author. The cards give the following information about each book: number of pages; whether there are illustrations, bibliographies, or index; date of publication; publisher; and identifying number, which tells where the book can be found in your library. |

## Encyclopedias

| | |
|---|---|
| *Encyclopaedia Britannica* | The most comprehensive and authoritative; 33 volumes |
| *Collier's Encyclopedia* | Distinguished by its illustrations and clarity of style; 24 volumes |
| *Encyclopedia Americana* | Especially useful for American topics; 30 volumes |
| *Columbia Encyclopedia, Random House Encyclopedia* | Useful one-volume encyclopedias |
| *The New Catholic Encyclopedia, Encyclopaedia Judaica, Encyclopedia of Islam, Encyclopedia of Buddhism, McGraw-Hill Encyclopedia of Science and Technology, International Encyclopedia of the Social Sciences* | More specialized works representing the wide variety of available encyclopedias [Some encyclopedias are available on CD ROM and computer disks.] |

## Biographical Material

| | |
|---|---|
| *Biography Index* | An index to biographies appearing in various sources |
| *Dictionary of National Biography (DNB)* | Articles on famous dead British men and women |
| *Concise Dictionary of National Biography* | Short edition of DNB |
| *Dictionary of American Biography (DAB)* | Articles on famous dead Americans |
| *The Concise Dictionary of American Biography* | Short edition of DAB |
| *Dictionary of Canadian Biography (DCB)* | Articles on those who have contributed significantly to Canada |
| *Current Biography* | A periodical containing articles, most with photographs, on living individuals |
| *Directory of American Scholars, International Who's Who, Who's Who in America, Who's Who, Dictionary of Scientific Biography, American Men and Women of Science* | Representative of the specialized biographical sources available |

## Newspaper, Magazine, and Journal Indexes

| | |
|---|---|
| *The New York Times Index* | Published since 1913, indexes all sorts of its articles |
| *Reader's Guide to Periodical Literature* | Published from 1900, indexes more than 100 popular magazines |
| *Education Index* | Articles from journals and magazines relevant to education |
| *The Catholic Periodical and Literature Index, The Social Science and Humanities Index, Business Periodicals Index, Art Index, Applied Science and Technology Index* | Specialized indexes |

*Continued*

| | |
|---|---|
| *Psychological Abstracts, Sociological Abstracts, Language and Language Behavior Abstracts, Communication Abstracts* | Brief summaries of articles in these areas of study [Many such indexes and abstracts are available on CD ROMs.] |

**Almanacs**

| | |
|---|---|
| *The World Almanac & Book of Facts* | Published since 1868, the most popular and probably the best almanac, containing information on just about every subject including the arts, science, governments, population, geography, religion, and just about every conceivable topic |
| *Information Please Almanac, Reader's Digest Almanac and Yearbook, The New York Times Encyclopedia Almanac, Universal Almanac* | Similar in style and purpose |
| *Whitaker's Almanac* | Focuses on Great Britain |
| *Canadian Almanac and Directory* | Focuses on Canada |
| *Statistical Abstracts of the United States* | Summarizes all types of facts and figures |

## Formulate Your Thesis and Identify the Major Propositions

The thesis of your speech is your main assertion—the essence of what you want your audience to get from your speech. From your thesis you will be able to develop your major propositions, the subtopics (D'Angelo 1980; Bradley 1988).

### The Thesis

The thesis is the main idea that you want to convey to the audience. The thesis of Lincoln's Second Inaugural Address was that Northerners and Southerners should work together for the good of the entire country. The thesis of the "Rocky" movies was that the underdog can win.

Let's say, for example, you are planning to deliver a persuasive speech in favor of Senator Winters. Your thesis statement might be: "Winters is the best candidate." This is what you want your audience to believe; what you want your audience to remember even if they forget everything else.

In an informative speech, on the other hand, the thesis statement focuses on what you want your audience to learn. For example, for a speech on jealousy, a suitable thesis might be: "There are two main theories of jealousy."

Limit the thesis statement to one central idea, focus, or purpose. Statements such as "We should support Winters and the entire Democratic party" contain not one but two basic ideas.

### Using Thesis Statements to Generate Main Ideas

Use your thesis statement to generate your main ideas. Once you phrase the thesis statement, the main divisions of your speech will suggest themselves. Let's say you are giving a speech to a group of high school students on the values of a college education. Your thesis is *A college education is valuable.* You then ask yourself, "Why is it valuable?" From these answers

> All my books literally come to me in the form of a sentence, an original sentence which contains the entire book.
> —RAYMOND FEDERMAN

> If you don't know where you are going, you will probably wind up somewhere else.
> —LAURENCE J. PETER

> What was the thesis of the last film you saw? The last novel, play, or short story?

> Develop the hunter's attitude, the outlook that wherever you go, there are ideas waiting to be discovered.
> —ROGER VON OECH

What main ideas might you generate from these theses: (1) College athletics should be expanded, (2) Students need to be educated about AIDS, and (3) The personal computer is a useful household product?

you generate your major propositions. You might first brainstorm the question and identify as many answers as you can. Don't evaluate them, just generate as many as possible. A college education is valuable because:

1. It helps you get a job.
2. It increases your potential to earn a good salary.
3. It gives you greater job mobility.
4. It helps you secure more creative work.
5. It helps you appreciate the arts more fully.
6. It helps you understand an extremely complex world.
7. It helps you understand different cultures.
8. It helps you avoid taking a regular job for a few years.
9. It helps you meet lots of people and make friends.
10. It helps you increase personal effectiveness.

For purposes of illustration, let's stop at this point. You have ten possible main points—too many to cover in a short speech. Further, not all are equally valuable or relevant to your audience. Look over the list to make it shorter and more meaningful. Here are some suggestions:

ELIMINATE POINTS THAT SEEM LEAST IMPORTANT TO YOUR THESIS. You might want to eliminate, say, number 8, since it's inconsistent with the positive values of college.

COMBINE POINTS THAT HAVE A COMMON FOCUS. Notice, for example, that the first four points center on jobs. You might, therefore, consider grouping them under a general heading:

A college education will help you secure a better job.

This might be one of your major propositions which you can develop by defining what you mean by "better job." You might also use some of the ideas you generated in your brainstorming session. This main point and its elaboration might look like this:

    I. A college education will help you secure a better job.

        A. College graduates earn higher salaries.

        B. College graduates have more creative jobs.

        C. College graduates have greater job mobility.

Note that A, B, and C are all aspects or subdivisions of "a better job."

SELECT POINTS THAT ARE MOST RELEVANT TO YOUR AUDIENCE. Ask yourself what will interest the audience most. On this basis, you might drop numbers 5 and 7 on the assumption that your audience, high school students, will not consider learning about the arts or different cultures to be particularly exciting. Further, you might conclude that high school students care most about increasing personal abilities. So you might include this point as your second major proposition:

    II. A college education will help you increase your personal effectiveness.

Much as you developed the subordinate points in your first proposition by defining what you meant by a "good job," you would define what you mean by "personal effectiveness":

How teach a barren world to dance? It is a contradiction that divides the world.
—ALICE WALKER

II. A college education will help you increase your personal effectiveness.

    A. A college education will help you increase your ability to communicate.

    B. A college education will help you acquire learning skills.

    C. A college education will help you acquire coping skills.

You then follow the same procedure used to generate these subordinate points (A, B, and C) to develop the subheadings. For example, you might divide A into two major subheads:

    A. A college education will improve your ability to communicate.

       1. A college education teaches writing skills.

       2. A college education teaches speech skills.

Here are a few additional guidelines for identifying and developing your main points.

How might you divide B and C into their subheadings as was done here for A?

**Use Two, Three, or Four Main Points at Most.** Remember, your aim is not to cover every aspect of a topic but to emphasize selected parts. Further, you want to have enough time to amplify and support the points you present. With too many propositions this becomes impossible. Also, you don't want to present too much information.

> What too many orators want in depth, they give you in length.
> —MONTESQUIEU

**Phrase Your Propositions in Parallel Style.** Use similar wording in your major propositions.

NOT THIS:

**Mass Media Functions**

    I. The media entertain.

    II. The media function to inform their audiences.

    III. Creating ties of union is a major media function.

    IV. The conferral of status is a function of all media.

THIS:

**Mass Media Functions**

    I. The media entertain.

    II. The media inform.

    III. The media create ties of union.

    IV. The media confer status.

In what other ways might you phrase these four propositions, again in parallel style?

**Develop Your Main Points So They Are Separate and Distinct.** Do not overlap your main points.

NOT THIS:

    I. Color and style are important in clothing selection.

THIS:

    I. Color is important in clothing selection.

    II. Style is important in clothing selection.

## Support the Major Propositions

Now that you have identified your thesis and your major propositions, you must support each. Tell the audience what it needs to know about color and style in clothing selection. Or, in the persuasive speech example, convince them that a college education does help you get a better job.

In the informative speech, your support primarily amplifies—describes, illustrates, defines, exemplifies—the concepts you discuss. You want the "color in clothing" to come alive to the audience. Amplification accomplishes this. Specifically, you might use examples, illustrations, and the testimony of various authorities. Definitions especially help to breathe life into abstract or vague concepts. Statistics (summary figures) that explain various trends are essential for certain topics. Audiovisual aids—charts, maps, objects, slides, films, tapes, records, and so on—help clarify vague concepts.

In a persuasive speech your support is proof—material that offers evidence, argument, and motivational appeal and that establishes your credibility and reputation. To persuade your audience to buy Brand X, in

> Of the modes of persuasion furnished by the spoken word there are three kinds. The first kind depends on the personal character of the speaker; the second on putting the audience into a certain frame of mind; the third on the proof, or apparent proof, provided by the words of the speech itself.
> —ARISTOTLE

*"And now I'd like to introduce our county's new tax collector."*

CARTOON BY EARL W. ENGLEMAN

part by demonstrating that it is cheaper, you must give proof that this is true. You might compare the price of Brand X to other brands. Or you might demonstrate that the same amount of Brand X will do twice the work of other brands selling at the same price.

You support your propositions with reasoning from specific instances, from general principles, from analogy, and from causes and effects. These may be thought of as logical support. Also, you support your position with motivational appeals. For example, you might appeal to the audience's desire for status, financial gain, or increased self-esteem: "No one wants to be at the low end of the hierarchy. Our new Management Seminar will help you climb that corporate ladder faster and easier than you ever thought possible." You also add persuasive force through your personal reputation or credibility. If audience members see you as competent, highly moral, and charismatic, they are more likely to believe you.

### Organize the Speech Materials

You must organize your material if the audience is to understand and remember it (Whitman and Timmis 1975). Here are six patterns you might use to organize the body of a speech.

TIME PATTERN. Organizing major issues on the basis of some temporal relationship is a popular pattern for informative speeches. Generally, when this pattern is used, the speech is organized into two or three major parts. You might begin with the past and work up to the present or future, or begin with the present or future and work back to the past. You might organize a speech on a child's development of speech and language in a time or temporal pattern. Major propositions might look like this:

    I. Babbling is the first stage.

    II. Lallation is the second stage.

    III. Echolalia is the third stage.

    IV. Communication is the fourth stage.

Most historical topics lend themselves to organization by a time pattern. Events leading to the Civil War, steps toward a college education, and the history of writing will all yield to temporal patterning.

PROBLEM-SOLUTION PATTERN. A popular pattern for organizing the persuasive speech is to present the main ideas in terms of problem and solution. The speech is divided into two parts. One part deals with the problem and the other with the solution. Let's say you are trying to persuade an audience that elementary school teachers should be given higher salaries and increased benefits. Here a problem-solution pattern might be appropriate. In the first part of the speech, you might discuss some of the problems confronting contemporary education: industry luring away the most qualified graduates of the leading universities, many teachers leaving the field after two or three years, and the low-status of the occupation in many undergraduates' minds. In the second part, you would consider the possible solutions: making teachers'

> Truth is worth more than victory.
> —JOHN GENUNG

> What practical advantages does an organized speech have over an unorganized speech?

> I have yet to see any problem, however complicated, which, when you looked at it in the right way, did not become still more complicated.
> —PAUL ANDERSON

salaries competitive with those in private industry, making benefits as attractive as those offered by industry, and raising the status of the teaching profession.

The speech, in outline form, would look like this:

I. There are three major problems confronting elementary education.
   A. Industry lures away the most qualified graduates.
   B. Numerous excellent teachers leave the field after two or three years.
   C. Teaching is currently a low-status occupation.
II. There are three major solutions to these problems.
   A. Increase salaries for teachers.
   B. Make benefits for teachers more attractive.
   C. Raise the status of the teaching profession.

TOPICAL PATTERN. Perhaps the most popular pattern of organization is the topical pattern, which divides the speech into major topics. This pattern is an obvious one for organizing a speech on the branches of government. Here the divisions are clear:

I. The legislative branch is controlled by Congress.
II. The executive branch is controlled by the President.
III. The judicial branch is controlled by the courts.

Speeches on problems facing the college graduate, great works of literature, and the world's major religions all lend themselves to a topical organizational pattern.

SPATIAL PATTERN. Similar to temporal patterning is patterning the main points of a speech on the basis of space. Both temporal and spatial patterns are especially appropriate for informative speeches. Most physical objects fit well into spatial patterns. For example, in a speech on places to visit in southern Europe, you might go from west to east, considering the countries to visit and, within these countries, the cities:

I. Your first stop is Portugal.
II. Your second stop is Spain.
III. Your third stop is Italy.
IV. Your fourth stop is Greece.

Similarly, the structure of a hospital, school, skyscraper, or even a dinosaur might be appropriately described using a spatial pattern.

CAUSE-EFFECT/EFFECT-CAUSE PATTERN. Similar to the problem-solution pattern of organization is the cause-effect or effect-cause pattern. Both are especially appropriate for persuasive speeches. Here you divide the speech into two major sections—causes and effects. For example, a speech on the reasons for highway accidents might fit into a cause-effect pattern. In such a speech you would first consider the causes of highway accidents and then some of the effects—the number of deaths, the number of accidents, and so on.

> The outline is the framework of the speech. It bears the same relationship to the finished talk that steel girders and uprights bear to the finished office building.
> —CHARLES HENRY WOOLBERT

> What topics would lend themselves to spatial organization?

A speech on high blood pressure, to spell out some of the causes and effects, might look like this:

I. There are three main causes of high blood pressure.

    A. High salt intake increases blood pressure.

    B. Excess weight increases blood pressure.

    C. Anxiety increases blood pressure.

II. There are three major effects of high blood pressure.

    A. Nervousness increases.

    B. Heart rate increases.

    C. Shortness of breath increases.

For what other topics would a cause-effect pattern be appropriate?

THE MOTIVATED SEQUENCE. The *motivated sequence* is a pattern of arranging your information to motivate your audience to respond positively to your purpose (Gronbeck, McKerrow, Ehninger, and Monroe 1990). In the motivated sequence there are five steps: (1) attention, (2) need, (3) satisfaction, (4) visualization, and (5) action. This pattern is appropriate for both informative and persuasive speeches.

(1) **Attention.** Make the audience give you their undivided attention. If you execute this step effectively, your audience should be anxious to hear what you have to say. You can gain audience attention through a variety of means (see p. 262).

For example, let's say you were giving an informative speech about the workings of home computers. In this attention step you might say: "By the time you graduate, there will be more home computers than automobiles." You might then explain the phenomenal growth of computers in education until you have the complete attention of your audience.

(2) **Need.** Here you would prove that a need exists. The audience should feel that they need to learn or do something because of this need. You can establish need by:

1. stating the need or problem as it exists or will exist;
2. illustrating the need with specific examples, illustrations, statistics, testimony, and other forms of support; and
3. pointing to how this need affects your specific listeners—for example, their financial status, career goals, or individual happiness.

In a speech on home computers, you might say in this step: "Much as it is now impossible to get around without a car, it will be impossible to get around the enormous amount of information without a home computer." You might then explain how knowledge is expanding so rapidly that without computer technology, it will be impossible to keep up with any field.

(3) **Satisfaction.** Here you would present the "solution" to satisfying the need that you demonstrated in step 2. The audience should believe that what you are informing them about or persuading them to do will satisfy the need. Here you would answer the question "How will the need be satisfied by what I am asking the audience to learn, believe, or do?" This step usually contains two types of information:

1. a clear statement (with examples and illustrations if necessary) of what you want the audience to learn, believe, or do; and
2. a statement of how or why what you are asking them to learn, believe, or do will lead to satisfying the need identified in step 2.

> The status quo protects itself by punishing all challengers.
> —GLORIA STEINEM

> When people change what they value so they have goals that are both important and achievable, they can be satisfied.
> —JUDITH M. BARDWICK

For example, you might say: "Learning a few basic principles of home computers will enable you to process your work more efficiently, in less time, and more enjoyably." You might then explain the various steps your listeners could take to satisfy the needs you have identified.

(4) **Visualization.** Visualization intensifies the audience's feelings or beliefs. It takes the audience beyond the present place and time and helps them imagine the situation as it would be if the need were satisfied as suggested in step 3. You can accomplish this by (1) demonstrating the positive benefits to be derived if this advocated proposal is put into operation or (2) by demonstrating the negative consequences that will occur if your plan is not put into operation.

Of course, you could combine the two methods and demonstrate both the positive benefits of your plan and the negative effects of the existing plan or of some competing proposal.

For example, you might say: "With these basic principles firmly in mind (and a home computer), you'll be able to stay at home and do the library research for your next speech by just punching in the correct code." You might then demonstrate the speech research process so your listeners will visualize exactly the advantages of computer research.

(5) **Action.** Here you would tell the audience what they should do to satisfy the need. You want to move the audience in a particular direction. For example, you might want them to speak for Farrington or against Williamson, to attend the next student government meeting, or to work for a specific political candidate. Here are a few ways to accomplish this step.

1. State exactly what audience members should do.
2. Appeal to your listeners' emotions.
3. Give the audience guidelines for future action.

For example, you might say: "Supplement these few principles by further study. Probably the best way is to enroll in a computer course. Also, read the brief paperback, *The Home Computer for the College Student.*" You might then identify the computer courses that would be appropriate for a beginning student. Further, you might identify a few other books or distribute a brief list of books suitable for your listeners.

Notice that an informative speech could have stopped after the satisfaction step. You accomplish the goal of informing the audience about some principles of home computers with the satisfaction step. In some cases, though, you may feel it helpful to complete the steps to emphasize your point.

In a persuasive speech, on the other hand, you must go at least as far as visualization (if you limit your purpose to strengthening or changing attitudes or beliefs) or to the action step (if you aim to get your listeners to behave in a certain way).

## Word the Speech

In wording the speech, put your main ideas and supporting materials into language your audience will easily understand. The audience will hear your speech only once, so make what you say *instantly intelligible.* Do not speak down to your audience, but make your ideas—even complex ones—easy to understand.

> People see only what they are prepared to see.
> —RALPH WALDO EMERSON

> Can you use the motivated sequence to analyze an advertisement appearing in newspapers or on television?

> I have a dream.
> —MARTIN LUTHER KING, JR.

> Are you impressed by those who use unfamiliar or complex words? Why?

Use words that are simple, not complex; concrete, not abstract. Use personal and informal rather than impersonal and formal language. Use simple and active rather than complex and passive sentences.

Be careful not to offend members of your audience. Remember that not all doctors are men and not all secretaries are women. Not all persons are married or want to be. Not all people love parents, dogs, and children. The hypothetical person does not have to be white, heterosexual, or male.

## Construct the Conclusion and the Introduction

Your conclusion and introduction need special care because they will determine, in large part, the effectiveness of your speech.

### The Conclusion

Devote special care to this brief but crucial part of your speech. In your conclusion summarize and close.

SUMMARIZE. You may summarize your speech in a variety of ways.

**Restate Your Thesis.** Restate the essential thrust of your speech—your thesis or perhaps the purpose you hoped to achieve.

**Restate Its Importance.** Tell the audience again why your topic or thesis is so important. Here is how one speaker used this type of conclusion (Light 1984):

> If we do not move to restore our universities and improve the educational infrastructure in Canada, we will be unilaterally withdrawing from the future. We will be condemning ourselves to the economic vassaldom of those who do perceive education and brains as the only real resource and, in fact, the ultimate resource of any nation.

**Restate Your Major Propositions.** Simply reiterate your two, three, or four major propositions.

PROVIDE CLOSURE. The conclusion's second function is to provide closure—to give the speech a crisp and definite end. Don't leave your audience wondering whether you have finished. You can achieve closure in several ways.

**Use a Quotation.** One that summarizes your thesis or provides an interesting perspective on your point of view often provides effective closure.

**Refer to Future Events.** In a speech on higher education, one speaker used this type of conclusion most effectively (Silber 1985):

> Each of these three issues has relevance not only for Americans but for any country seriously concerned about higher education and its relation to democracy. They are not the only issues of importance I have raised today, but they form a basis for further discussion. I am looking forward to a fruitful exchange of ideas in the panels that will follow.

**Pose a Challenge or Question.** You may wish to end your speech with a provocative question or challenge. Here, for example, a speaker concludes his speech by posing a question and answering it (Styles 1985):

What does that mean for Canada? Weighed in the global balance, as well as our trade balance, we have a working partnership with what is still the most powerful nation on earth. It's imperative that we maintain it and (with our, at times, somewhat different points of view) vital that we continue to work hard at explaining our interests, so that for both of us the best possible results are achieved.

**Refer Back to the Introduction.** Sometimes this is possible. For example, in a commencement address, the speaker noted in his introduction that he could not remember what the commencement speaker said at his own graduation. He then concluded his speech as follows (Borden 1985):

> People are always watching you, learning from you, and looking to you for inspiration. In other words, it is important how you play the game of life. If, sometime in the future, someone asks you to remember what was significant about your commencement speech, I hope that you will tell them you remember that. It is important how you play the game of life.

## The Introduction

The introduction, although delivered first, should be constructed last. You will see the entire speech and will be better able to figure out which elements should go into introducing it. Try to accomplish two goals in your introduction: gain attention and orient the audience as to what you will talk about. Let's look at ways to do this.

What are some disadvantages of composing your introduction first?

THE FAR SIDE © 1984 CHRONICLE FEATURES. REPRINTED WITH PERMISSION OF UNIVERSAL PRESS SYNDICATE. ALL RIGHTS RESERVED.

GAIN ATTENTION. The introduction must focus the audience's attention on your topic. Of course, you must maintain that attention, so what is said here also applies to other parts of the speech.

**Ask a Question.** Questions are effective because they represent a change from normal statements and also involve the audience. They tell the audience that you are talking directly to them and care about their responses.

**Refer to Specific Audience Members.** Involving members directly makes them perk up and pay attention.

**Refer to Recent Happenings.** Being familiar with such events, the audience will pay attention to your approach.

**Use an Illustration or Dramatic or Humorous Story.** We are all drawn to illustrations and stories about people—they make your speech vivid and concrete. Use them to secure audience attention in the introduction and to maintain it throughout.

**Use Audiovisual Aids.** These will engage attention because they are new and different. In Chapter 12 we provide specific examples of appropriate audiovisual aids.

ORIENT THE AUDIENCE. The introduction, or preview, should orient the audience; help them follow your thoughts more closely. You can orient the audience in several ways.

**Give the Audience a General Idea of Your Subject.** Here are some statements that provide a general preview of the speech:

> Tonight I want to discuss the proposed tax revision.

> I'm going to focus on gender differences in communication.

> I will cover the pros and cons of the Brommel proposal for dealing with atomic waste.

**Give a Detailed Preview of Your Main Propositions.** Identify the propositions you will discuss.

> In this brief talk I will cover four major attractions of New York City: the night life, theater, restaurants, and museums.

**Identify the Goal You Hope to Achieve.** A librarian addressing my public speaking class oriented the audience by stating goals in this way:

> Pay attention for the next few minutes and you'll be able to locate anything we have in the library by using the new touch-screen computer access system.

*Some Common Faults with Conclusions and Introductions*

Avoid these common faults made by many beginners:

DON'T APOLOGIZE. A common fault is to apologize for something in your speech. Don't. Your inadequacies—whatever they are—will be clear

The true art of memory is the art of attention.
—SAMUEL JOHNSON

What gains your attention most effectively? How might you adapt this attention-getting device to a public speech?

Do your college lecturers orient their audience? How?

**Apology is only egotism wrong side out.**
—OLIVER WENDELL HOLMES

enough to any discerning listener. Do not point them out. Avoid such expressions as:

I am not an expert on this topic.

I wanted to illustrate these ideas with a video tape but I couldn't get my hands on a VCR.

I didn't do as much reading on this topic as I should have.

And *never* start a speech with "I'm not very good at giving public speeches."

**Can you think of any other common faults with introductions? With conclusions?**

DON'T PREFACE YOUR INTRODUCTION. Don't begin with such common but ineffective statements as:

I'm really nervous, but here goes.

Before I begin my talk, I want to say. . . .

I hope I can remember everything I want to say.

**Begin low, speak low;
Take fire, rise higher;
When most impressed
Be self-possessed;
At the end wax warm,
And sit down in a storm.**
—JOHN LEIFCHILD

DON'T INTRODUCE NEW MATERIAL IN YOUR CONCLUSION. Instead, reinforce what you have already said, summarize your essential points, or give new expression to ideas already covered .

DON'T DRAG OUT THE CONCLUSION. End crisply and just once. Don't preface each sentence of the conclusion with terms that indicate the end. "In summary" or "in conclusion" and similar expressions will lead the audience to expect an ending. When you are ready to end, end.

### Before the Introduction and After the Conclusion

Think of your speech as beginning as soon as the audience focuses on you. Similarly, think of it ending not after you have spoken the last sentence but only after the audience directs its focus away from you. Here are a few suggestions.

Display enthusiasm when you get up from your seat and walk to your speaking position. Don't display signs of discomfort or displeasure. No one wants to listen to a speaker who is obviously miserable. Stand in front of the audience with a sense of control.

**What before and after behaviors work against the speaker achieving her or his purpose?**

Don't start your speech as soon as you get up from your seat or even as soon as you get to the front. Survey your audience; make eye contact and engage their attention. Pause briefly, then begin.

If a question period follows your speech and you are in charge of this, pause after completing your conclusion. Ask audience members if they have any questions. If there is a chairperson who will ask for questions, pause after your conclusion, and then nonverbally signal to the chairperson that you are ready.

If there are to be no questions, pause after your last statement. Maintain eye contact with the audience for a second or two and then walk (do not run) to your seat. Once you sit down, show no signs of relief. Do not sigh or otherwise indicate you are relieved the speech is over. Focus your attention on whatever activity is taking place.

## Speaker Apprehension

Of all public speaking issues, speaker apprehension (or "stage fright") is probably your most important concern. In fact, "communication apprehension is probably the most common handicap that is suffered by people in contemporary American society" (McCroskey and Wheeless 1976). Approximately 20 percent of the general population suffers from communication apprehension (Richmond and McCroskey 1989). Take the accompanying apprehension test to measure your own fear of speaking.

### TEST YOURSELF:

### *How Apprehensive Are You of Public Speaking?\**

This questionnaire consists of six statements concerning your feelings about public speaking. Indicate the degree to which each statement applies to you by marking whether you (1) Strongly Agree, (2) Agree, (3) Are Undecided, (4) Disagree, or (5) Strongly Disagree with each statement. There are no right or wrong answers. Do not be concerned that some of the statements are similar to others. Work quickly, just record your first impression.

_____ 1. I have no fear of giving a speech.
_____ 2. Certain parts of my body feel very tense and rigid while giving a speech.
_____ 3. I feel relaxed while giving a speech.
_____ 4. My thoughts become confused and jumbled when I am giving a speech.
_____ 5. I face the prospect of giving a speech with confidence.
_____ 6. While giving a speech, I get so nervous that I forget facts I really know.

*Scoring:* To obtain your public speaking apprehension score, use the following formula:

18   plus scores for items 1, 3, and 5;
       minus scores for items 2, 4, and 6.

A score above 18 shows some degree of apprehension. Most people score above 18, so if you scored relatively high, you are among the vast majority of people.

*\*From An Introduction to Rhetorical Communication, 4th ed. by James C. McCroskey. Reprinted by permission of the author.*

### *Dealing with Speaker Apprehension*

Five factors especially influence students' public speaking anxiety (Beatty 1988). Understanding these factors will help you control them and your fear of speaking.
1. *Perceived novelty.* New and different situations make us anxious. Therefore, gaining as much experience in public speaking as you can will lessen your anxiety.
2. *Subordinate status.* When you feel that others are better speakers or that they know more than you do, your anxiety increases. Thinking positively about yourself and being thorough in your preparation reduces this particular cause of anxiety.

How do the five factors that influence apprehension in public speaking apply to you speaking in this class? Which factor do you think is the most important to most speakers? Which is the most important to you?

3. *Conspicuousness.* When you are the center of attention, as you normally are in public speaking, your anxiety increases. Therefore, try thinking of public speaking as a type of conversation. If you are comfortable talking in small groups, then visualize your audience as an enlarged small group.

4. *Dissimilarity.* When you feel you have little in common with your listeners, you feel anxious. Try emphasizing your similarity with your listeners as you plan your speeches as well as during the actual presentation.

5. *Prior history.* When you have a prior history of apprehension, you are more likely to become anxious. Positive public speaking experiences will help reduce this cause of anxiety.

Here are a few additional suggestions to deal with and control speaker apprehension (Beatty 1988; Richmond and McCroskey 1992; Watson and Dodd 1984).

PREPARE AND PRACTICE THOROUGHLY. Inadequate preparation—not having rehearsed the speech enough, for example—is reasonable cause for anxiety. Much of your fear is a fear of failure. Preparation will lessen the possibility of failure and the accompanying apprehension.

Familiarize yourself with the public speaking context. Try, for example, to rehearse in the room in which you will give your speech. Or, stand in the front of the room before the actual presentation, as if you were giving your speech.

The skill to do comes from doing.
—CICERO

GAIN EXPERIENCE. Experience will help speakers who suffer moderate degrees of apprehension. It will show you that a public speech can be effective despite your fears and anxieties; give you feelings of accomplishment; and convince you that public speaking can be intellectually rewarding as well as enjoyable. The situation is similar to learning to drive a car or ski down a mountain. With experience, initial fears and anxieties give way to feelings of control, comfort, and pleasure.

PUT APPREHENSION IN PERSPECTIVE. Maintain realistic expectations for yourself and your audience. You do not have to be the best in the class or even as good as the person sitting next to you. Be the best you can—whatever that is. Compete with yourself. Your second speech does not have to be better than that of the previous speaker, but it should be better than your own first one.

Why do you suppose so many students have difficulty keeping speaker apprehension in perspective? What might you tell a fearful speaker to help him or her keep speaker apprehension in perspective?

Your audience does not expect perfection, either. Your classmates are not there to cut you down but to help you become a more effective public speaker, just as you are there to help them. Fear increases when you feel that the audience's expectations are very high. It decreases when you perceive their expectations to be lower (Ayres 1986).

USE PHYSICAL ACTIVITY AND DEEP BREATHING. Anxiety is generally lessened by physical activity—gross bodily movements and small movements of the hands, face, and head. If you are anxious, try including some chalkboard writing or a demonstration that requires movement.

What other suggestions might you offer the fearful speaker? How do you deal with your own apprehension?

Deep breathing relaxes the body. By breathing deeply a few times before getting up to speak, you will feel your body relax. This may help you overcome your initial fear of getting up and walking to the front of the room. If you find yourself getting nervous during your actual speech, again try deep breathing.

# FEEDBACK

In this chapter we outlined the steps to preparing a public speech and discussed the problem of speaker apprehension.

**1.** The preparation of a public speech involves eight steps: (1) **select the subject and purpose,** (2) **analyze the audience,** (3) **research the topic,** (4) **formulate the thesis and identify the major propositions,** (5) **support the major propositions,** (6) **organize the speech materials,** (7) **word the speech,** (8) **construct the conclusion and the introduction.**

**2. Speech topics** should deal with significant issues that interest the audience. Subjects and purposes should be limited in scope.

**3.** In **analyzing the audience,** consider age; sex; cultural factors; occupation, income, and status; and religion and religiousness; the occasion; and the specific context.

**4. Research the topic,** beginning with general sources and gradually exploring more specific and specialized sources.

**5.** Formulate the **thesis** of the speech. Develop your major propositions by asking relevant questions about this thesis.

**6.** Support the **major propositions** with a variety of materials that amplify and provide evidence.

**7. Organize** the speech materials into a clear, easily identifiable thought pattern, for example, temporal, problem-solution, or topical.

**8. Word the speech** using language that is simple to understand, personal, and informal.

**9.** Construct the **conclusion** to summarize your main ideas and to provide closure. Construct the **introduction** to gain the audience's attention and to orient them as to what will follow.

**10. Speaker apprehension** refers to one's fear of communication. To deal with it, prepare and practice thoroughly, gain experience, put apprehension in perspective, and use physical activity and deep breathing to help relax the body.

In this discussion we covered a variety of specific skills. Check your ability to use these skills.

Use the following rating scale:

(1) = almost always,

(2) = often,

(3) = sometimes,

(4) = rarely,

(5) = hardly ever.

_____ 1. In preparing a public speech, I follow the eight steps outlined here.

_____ 2. After selecting my thesis (the main assertion), I expand it by asking strategic questions to develop my main ideas or propositions.

_____ 3. After generating my possible major propositions, I eliminate those points that seem least important to my thesis, combine those that have a common focus, and select those most relevant to my audience.

_____ 4. I use transitions to connect the major parts of the speech and to provide the audience with guideposts that will help them follow my thoughts and arguments.

_____ 5. In organizing the speech's main points, I select a thought pattern appropriate to the subject matter.

_____ 6. I construct conclusions that summarize my speech and provide closure.

_____ 7. I avoid the common problems with conclusions: I don't apologize, introduce new material, or drag out the ending.

_____ 8. I construct an introduction that gains attention and orients the audience as to what is to follow.

_____ 9. I avoid the common faults with introductions: I don't apologize, make hollow promises, rely on gimmicks, or preface my introduction.

_____ 10. In dealing with my own speaker apprehension I prepare and practice thoroughly, gain as much experience as possible, put apprehension in perspective, and use physical activity and deep breathing to relax.

# SKILL DEVELOPMENT EXPERIENCES

## 11.1 LIMITING YOUR SPEECH TOPIC

For one of the following, narrow the topic sufficiently for a five-minute informative or persuasive speech. Once you have selected a suitably limited subject, formulate a specific purpose.

1. History
2. Emotions
3. Family
4. Communication problems
5. Psychology
6. Education
7. Mass media
8. Nonverbal communications
9. Politics
10. Religion
11. The United States
12. War
13. Sex
14. Philosophy
15. Language
16. Film
17. Energy
18. Television
19. Health
20. Work
21. Play
22. Economics
23. Conflict
24. Love

## 11.2 THESIS IDENTIFICATION

Every communication has a thesis. Select at least three different communication forms, for example, a soap opera, a situation comedy, a play, a film, a novel, a short story, or a public speech and identify their theses. Share these in small groups or with the whole class. From this brief experience, the following should be clear:

1. The thesis is the central idea—the main assertion—of the communication.
2. Although people will state the thesis differently, there should be a fair degree of agreement.
3. Identifying the thesis makes the work as a whole more understandable and meaningful.
4. Any communication work revolves around a central thesis; the examples, illustrations, behaviors of the characters, and even the music, support or elaborate the thesis.

## 11.3 CONSTRUCTING CONCLUSIONS

Prepare a conclusion to a hypothetical speech on one of the topics listed, making sure that you (1) review the speech's main points, (2) motivate the audience, and (3) provide closure. Be prepared to explain the methods you used to accomplish each of these functions.

1. Undergraduate degree programs should be five-year programs.
2. Proficiency in a foreign language should be required of all college graduates.
3. Children should be raised and educated by the state.
4. All wild-animal killing should be declared illegal.
5. Properties owned by churches and charitable institutions should be taxed in the same way as other properties are taxed.
6. History is bunk.
7. Suicide and its assistance by others should be legalized.
8. Teachers—at all levels—should be prevented from going on strike.
9. Gambling should be legalized by all states.
10. College athletics should be abolished.

## 11.4 CONSTRUCTING INTRODUCTIONS

Prepare an introduction to one of the topics listed, making sure that you (1) secure audience's attention and interest, (2) establish a connection between speaker, audience, and topic, and (3) orient the audience as to what is to follow. Be prepared to explain the methods you used to accomplish each of these aims.

1. College is not for everyone.
2. It is better never to love than to love and lose.
3. Tenure should be abolished.
4. Maximum sentences should be imposed even for first offenders of the drug laws.
5. All alcoholic beverages should be banned from campus.
6. Abortion should be declared illegal.
7. Psychotherapy is a waste of time and money.
8. Television should be censored for violence and sex.
9. Euthanasia should be legalized by the federal government.
10. Religion is the hope (opium) of the people.

## 11.5 BEGINNING INFORMATIVE SPEECHES: SOME TOPICS

Here are a few suggestions for topics built around the three types of informative speaking discussed: definition, description, and demonstration. As you read through the list, others will surely come to mind.

## Topics for Speeches of Definition

artificial intelligence

assault and battery

sexual harassment

felony and misde-
meanor

censorship

free speech

mysticism

id, ego, superego

ESP

ethics

friendship

love

infallibility

truth

propaganda

feminism

counterfeiting

cartel

violence

etiquette

prejudice

culture

primitivism

a specific type of
music

a particular sport's
rules

art and science

happiness

Freudian theory

cognitive therapy

Marxism

discrimination

religion

atheist

alcoholism

co-dependency

drug abuse

sexual ethics

neurosis and
psychosis

creative thinking

libel and slander

love and sex

## Topics for Speeches of Description

the computer
department of an ad
agency

a courtroom

the college hierarchy

a television station
(studio)

a photography
darkroom

the types of painting
brushes

a shopping center

the operation of the
heart

how cholesterol
works in the body

weight control
techniques

exercise guidelines

a bee colony

a computer

the skeletal struc-
ture of the body

a lie detector

a weather bureau

nuclear power plant

a specific country's
government

monetary systems

academic garb

time management
techniques

Fort Knox

a stock exchange

a publishing

company

a college newspaper
office

the structure of an
airplane, boat, car

a houseboat

a rental lease

an insurance policy

the library

## Topics for Speeches of Demonstration

how magazines (television) are censored

how advertising influences the media

how graduate and professional schools select
students

how a magazine or newspaper is put together

how to conduct an interview

how to form a campus organization or club

how to complain

how advertisers choose where to place ads

how to lessen guilt

how the brain works

how radar works

how to organize your time

how nicotine affects the body

how steroids works

how sound is produced

how clothing communicates status

how to buy insurance

how to save for retirement

how to apply for student loans, social security,
graduate school, life experience credits

how a jury is selected

how to write a will

how to adopt a child

how a bill becomes a law

how political candidates raise money

how to organize a protest

how power works in an organization

how to publicize your ideas

how an experiment is conducted

how IQ is measured

how dreams reveal the subconscious

how satellite television works

## 11.6 BEGINNING PERSUASIVE SPEECHES: SOME TOPICS

Prepare a persuasive speech of approximately four to seven minutes in length in which you attempt to (1) strengthen an existing attitude, (2) change an attitude from positive to negative or from negative to positive, (3) get the audience to behave in a certain way.

The following topics suggest issues that may prove suitable for such speeches. Naturally, you will have to phrase your own specific purpose. The 25 topics listed here are merely general suggestions.

1. Vote in the next election (college, city, state, national).
2. Support college athletics.
3. Support the college theater program.
4. Sex education in elementary schools should be expanded (eliminated).
5. Contribute time (or money) to a specific cause.
6. Teachers, police, and firefighters should (not) be permitted to strike.
7. Read a specific book, see a specific film, or watch a specific television show.
8. Buy (don't buy) a particular product or service.
9. Military recruitment should (not) be allowed on college campuses.
10. Alcohol should be prohibited (permitted) on college campuses.
11. Marriage licenses should be denied to any couple who have not known each other for at least one year.
12. Nuclear plants should be abolished (expanded).
13. The government should (not) support the expansion of solar energy utilization.
14. Required college subjects should (not) be abolished.
15. College athletics should (not) be abolished.
16. Gay men and lesbians should (not) be permitted to teach in elementary school, high school, or college.
17. Cheating on an examination should (not) result in automatic dismissal from college.
18. This country should (not) establish comprehensive health insurance for all citizens.
19. This country should (not) establish a system of free legal services for all its citizens.
20. Church property should (not) be taxed.
21. Personal firearms should be prohibited (permitted).
22. Devote time to read for the blind.
23. Join the Peace Corps.
24. Gay men and lesbians should (not) be permitted to adopt children.
25. Capital punishment should be abolished (extended).

CHAPTER 12

# Information and Persuasion

## Goals

*After completing this chapter, you should be able to:*

1. *explain the principles for informative and persuasive speaking*
2. *discuss the speech of* description, definition, *and* demonstration *and the strategies to use in each*
3. *explain the ways in which you can amplify your speech*
4. *describe the two types of persuasive speeches and the strategies to use in each*
5. *define the major types of reasoning and common fallacies to avoid*
6. *discuss the role of psychological appeals in motivating behavior*
7. *explain* speaker credibility

*■ How can you communicate information more effectively and efficiently? ■ In what ways can you persuade others to think or do as you want them to? ■ How can you develop and present logical arguments to convince others of your position? ■ In what ways can you arouse emotions? ■ How can you make yourself a more credible or believable person?*

In whatever occupation you find yourself, you will be asked to communicate information to others: to describe the new pension system, to demonstrate the new computer program, or to define your company goals. You will also find yourself persuading others: to accept or reject the union proposal, to change over to a new bookkeeping system, or to donate blood or money or time. The higher up you go in your organization's hierarchy, the more often you will be informing and persuading others.

In this chapter we cover speeches of information (in which you tell your listeners something they didn't know before) and speeches of persuasion (in which you change your listeners' attitudes or beliefs or get them to do something). Let's start with the easier one, the informative speech, and the principles you should follow in developing this type of speech.

> If all my possessions were taken from me with one exception, I would choose to keep the power of speech, for by it I would soon regain all the rest.
> —DANIEL WEBSTER

> Information is defined as any input that the person attends to for the purposes of reducing uncertainty or confirming prior knowledge.
> —BLAINE GOSS

> Blessed are they who have nothing to say, and who cannot be persuaded to say it.
> —JAMES RUSSELL LOWELL

> All we do is done with an eye to something else.
> —ARISTOTLE

## Guidelines For Informative Speaking

When you communicate information, you tell your listeners something they did not know before. Regardless of the type of information, the following guidelines should help.

### Limit the Amount of Information

Don't overload your listeners with information; limit the amount you communicate. It is better to present two new items of information with examples, illustrations, and descriptions than to present five without amplification.

### Stress Usefulness

Listeners will best remember information they see as useful to their own needs or goals. If you want the audience to listen, relate your speech to their needs, wants, or goals. For example, you might say:

> We all want financial security. We all want to be able to buy those luxuries we read so much about in magazines and see every evening on television. Wouldn't it be nice to be able to buy a car without worrying about where to get the down payment or how to make the monthly payments? Actually, that is not an unrealistic goal as I'll demonstrate in this speech. In fact, I will show you three ways you can invest your money to increase your income by at least 20 percent.

There should be little doubt that this speaker will have a most attentive and willing audience.

## Relate New Information to Old

Listeners will learn information more easily and retain it longer when you relate it to what they already know. To describe what something new looks or tastes like, compare it to something familiar: "The *jicama* is a Mexican potato. It looks like a brown-skinned turnip. It has a white inside and tastes something like crispy water chestnuts." Relate the new to the old, the unfamiliar to the familiar, the unseen to the seen, the untasted to the tasted.

## Present Information through Several Senses

Listeners best remember information they receive through several senses—hearing, seeing, smelling, tasting, feeling. Use as many senses as you can. If you are describing a football field's layout (presenting information through hearing), also show a picture of the field (presenting information through seeing as well). If you are giving a speech on stress and you are talking about muscular tension, make the audience feel their own muscle tension by asking them to tighten their leg or stomach muscles.

## Types of Informative Speeches

In informative speeches, you will focus on describing, demonstrating, and defining terms and processes. You might do all three in one speech or you might devote your entire speech to just one. Let's look at each type.

### The Speech of Description

In a description speech, you explain an object or person, an event, or process. Here are a few examples:

**Describing an Object or Person**

The structure of the brain

The inventions of Thomas Edison

The parts of a telephone

The layout of Philadelphia

**Describing an Event or Process**

Hugo: the hurricane of the eighties

The events leading to World War II

Organizing a body-building contest

Putting together the Columbus Day parade

### Strategies for Describing

Here are some suggestions for describing objects and people, events and processes.

1. Consider using a spatial or a topical organization when describing objects and people. Consider using a temporal pattern when describing events and processes. Let's say you want to describe the layout of

The two most engaging powers of an author are, to make new things familiar and familiar things new.
—SAMUEL JOHNSON

Do the lecturers you prefer follow these principles for informative speaking? Can you give specific examples of how they follow these rules?

What other topics would be appropriate for speeches of description?

the Museum of Modern Art. You might use a spatial pattern and start from the first floor and work up to the top floor. To describe the inventions of Thomas Edison, you might select three or four major inventions and discuss each equally, using a topical pattern.

If you were describing events leading to the tearing down of the Berlin Wall, you might use a temporal pattern, starting with the earliest and ending with the most immediate. A temporal pattern would also be appropriate to describe how a hurricane develops or how a parade is organized.

2. Use a variety of categories to describe the object or event. Use physical categories and ask yourself such questions as: What color is it? How big is it? What is it shaped like? How much does it weigh? How long or short is it? What is its volume? How attractive or unattractive is it?

Also, consider social, psychological, and economic categories. In describing a person, for example, consider friendliness-unfriendliness, warmth-coldness, rich-poor, aggressive-meek, and pleasant-unpleasant.

3. Consider using audiovisual aids. Show pictures of the brain, the inside of a telephone, the skeleton of the body. In describing an event or process, create a diagram or flow chart to illustrate stages: in buying stock, in publishing a newspaper, in putting a parade together.

**What descriptive categories might you use to describe this book? Does this book have psychological as well as physical characteristics that might be useful in describing it?**

### Developing the Speech of Description

Here is how you might construct a speech of description. In this example, the speaker describes the four steps in reading a textbook. Each main point covers one of the major steps. The organizational pattern is a temporal one. The speaker discusses the main points in the order they would normally occur. The outline form for the body of such a speech might appear like this:

SPECIFIC PURPOSE: to describe the four steps in reading a textbook.

THESIS: You can increase your textbook reading effectiveness.
*(How can you increase your textbook reading effectiveness?)*

 I. Preview the text.

 II. Read for understanding.

 III. Read for retention.

 IV. Review the text.

In delivering such a speech a speaker might begin:

There are four major steps you should follow in reading a textbook. Preview the text, read for understanding, read for retention, and review what you have read. Let's look at each of these steps in more detail.

The first step is to preview the text. Start at the beginning and look at the table of contents. How is the book organized? What are the major parts? Each part consists of several units. Let's look at how a unit is organized.

**How would you outline a speech of description about the way the earth is structured?**

## The Speech of Definition

What is leadership? What is a born-again Christian? What is the difference between sociology and psychology? What is safe sex? These are all topics for informative speeches of definition.

A definition is a statement of a concept's or term's meaning. Use definitions to explain difficult or unfamiliar concepts or to make a concept more vivid or forceful.

In defining a term or giving an entire speech of a definition you may focus on a term, system, or theory, or the similarities and differences between them. The subject may be new to the audience or a familiar one presented in a new and different way. Here are some examples:

**Defining a Term**

What is a bull market?

What is drug addiction?

What is censorship?

**Defining a System or Theory**

What is terrorism?

Confucianism: its major beliefs

The cultivation theory of mass communication

**Defining Similar and Dissimilar Terms or Systems**

Communism and socialism: some similarities and differences

What do Catholics and Protestants have in common?

Oedipus and Electra: How do they differ?

## Strategies for Defining

1. Use a variety of definitions. Table 12.1 lists some important ways to define.
2. Use credible sources when defining by authority. When you use an authority to define a term, make sure the person is in fact an authority on that topic. And be sure to tell the audience who the authority is and the basis for the person's expertise.

   In the following excerpt, note how Russell Peterson uses the expertise of Robert McNamara in his definition:

   > When Robert McNamara was president of the World Bank, he coined the term "absolute poverty" to characterize a condition of life so degraded by malnutrition, illiteracy, violence, disease and squalor, to be beneath any reasonable definition of human decency.

3. Proceed from the known to the unknown. Start with what your audience knows and work up to what is new or unfamiliar. Let's say you wish to define *phonemics* (with which your audience is unfamiliar). The specific idea you wish to get across is that each phoneme stands for a unique sound. You might begin your definition like this:

How would you define a computer to people who never heard of one, but who do know about typewriters?

**Table 12.1**
*Types of Definitions*

| Definitions | Meaning | Example |
|---|---|---|
| By Etymology | To explain the term's origin | To define the word "communication," you might note that it comes from the Latin "communis," meaning "common." In communicating, you seek to establish a commonness, a sameness, a similarity with another individual |
| By Authority | To cite some well-known authority | You might use the authority of cynic satirist Ambrose Bierce and define "love" as nothing but "a temporary insanity curable by marriage" and "friendship" as "a ship big enough to carry two in fair weather, but only one in foul" |
| By Operations | To describe how you would construct the object | In defining a chocolate cake operationally, you would provide the recipe |
| By Direct Symbolization | To show your listeners the actual item or a model or picture | To describe clothing through history, you might show actual samples or drawings and photographs of such clothing |

> That which so describes its object as to distinguish it from all others; it is no definition of any one thing if its terms are applicable to any one other.
> —EDGAR ALLAN POE

> Using each of the four types of definitions listed in Table 12.1, how would you define "friendship"? "A healthy diet"? "Teacher"? "Economic recession"?

We all know that in the written language each letter of the alphabet stands for a unit of the written language. Each letter is different from every other letter. A "t" is different from a "g" and a "g" is different from a "b" and so on. Each letter is called a "grapheme." In English we have 26 such letters.

We can look at the spoken language in much the same way. Each sound is different from every other sound. A "t" sound is different from a "d" sound and a "d" sound is different from a "k" sound, and so on. Each individual sound is called a "phoneme."

In this way, you build on what the audience already knows, a useful procedure in all learning.

### Developing the Speech of Definition

Here is an example of how you might go about constructing a speech of definition. The speaker selects three major types of lying and arranges them in a topical pattern.

SPECIFIC PURPOSE: to define lying by explaining the major types.

THESIS: There are three major kinds of lying. (*What are the three major kinds of lying?*)

I. Concealment is hiding the truth.

II. Falsification is presenting false information as if it were true.

III. Misdirection is acknowledging a feeling but misidentifying its cause.

In delivering such a speech, a speaker might begin:

A lie is a lie is a lie. True? Well, not exactly. Actually, there are several ways we can lie. We can lie by concealing the truth. We can lie by falsification—by presenting false information as if it were true. And, we can lie by misdirection—by acknowledging a feeling but misidentifying its cause. Let's look at the first type—the lie of concealment.

How would you outline a speech on the definition of an effective leader?

## The Speech of Demonstration

In using demonstration (or in a speech devoted entirely to demonstration), you show your listeners how to do something or how something works. Here are some examples:

**Demonstrating How to Do Something**

Giving mouth-to-mouth resuscitation

Balancing a checkbook

Piloting a plane

Driving defensively

**Demonstrating How Something Operates**

How the body maintains homeostasis

How a thermostat works

How a heart bypass operation is performed

How stock is purchased

What other topics would be appropriate for speeches of demonstration?

## Strategies for Demonstrating

In demonstrating how to do something or how something operates, consider the following guidelines.

1. Use a temporal organizational pattern (in most cases). Demonstrate each step in the sequence in which it is to be performed. Do not skip steps even if you think they are familiar to the audience. They may not be.

   Connect the steps with appropriate transitions. For instance, in explaining the Heimlich maneuver, you might say:

   Now that you have your arms around the choking victim's chest, your next step is to . . . .

   Label the steps clearly by saying, for example, "the first step," "the second step," and so on.

2. Consider presenting a broad overview and then the individual steps. When demonstrating, it is often helpful to first give a broad general picture and then present each step in detail. For example, let's say you were talking about how to prepare a wall for painting. You might begin by saying:

In preparing the wall for painting, make sure the wall is smoothly sanded, free of dust, and dry.

Sanding a wall is not like sanding a block of wood. So, let's look at the proper way to sand a wall.

In this way, your listeners will have a general idea of how you will go about demonstrating the process.

3. Use visual aids that show the steps in sequence. A good example are restaurant signs demonstrating the Heimlich maneuver. These signs demonstrate each step with pictures as well as words, making it easy to understand this important process.

### Developing the Speech of Demonstration

In this example of a demonstration speech, the speaker demonstrates how to listen actively.

SPECIFIC PURPOSE: to demonstrate three techniques of active listening.

THESIS: We can learn active listening. (*How can we learn active listening?*)

I. Paraphrase the speaker's meaning.

II. Express understanding of the speaker's feelings.

III. Ask questions.

In delivering the speech, the speaker might begin:

Active listening is a special kind of listening. It is listening with total involvement, with a concern for the speaker. It's probably the most important type of listening you can engage in. Active listening involves three steps: paraphrasing the speaker's meaning, expressing understanding of the speaker's feelings, and asking questions.

Your first step in active listening is to paraphrase the speaker's meaning. What is a paraphrase? A paraphrase is a restatement in your own words of the speaker's meaning. . . .

## Amplifying Materials

Once you have identified your specific purpose and your main assertions or propositions (the statements given Roman numerals in your speech outline), devote your attention to amplifying (making more understandable, meaningful, relevant) these assertions. Develop them so the audience will understand each more easily and fully. In this section we explain three ways to amplify your assertions: examples and illustrations, testimony, and audiovisual aids. Another form of amplification—definition—has been explained in our discussion of the speech of definition.

### Examples and Illustrations

Examples and illustrations are specific instances in varying degrees of detail. A relatively brief specific instance is an *example*. A longer, more detailed example told in narrative, or storylike form, is an *illustration*.

---

How would you outline a speech of demonstration on "Registering at College."

---

If this chapter were an informative speech, which type would it be (primarily)? Can you illustrate how this chapter contains elements of all three types of informative speeches?

---

He or she is greatest who contributes the greatest original practical example.
—WALT WHITMAN

---

*What are the major mistakes that speakers make in lecturing? Can you identify specific principles of informative speaking that they frequently violate? What one suggestion for improvement would you offer to a hypothetical college teacher?*

Examples and illustrations make an idea vivid and real in the listeners' minds. To talk in general terms about starvation throughout the world might have some effect on listeners. But an example or illustration of a six-year-old girl roaming the streets eating garbage would make the idea vivid and real.

Examples and illustrations may be factual or imaginary. Thus, in explaining friendship, you might tell about an actual friend's behavior. Or you might formulate a composite of an ideal friend and describe how this person would act in a particular situation. Both types are useful, both effective.

David Rockefeller (1985) uses a particularly effective, real example to illustrate how people can make charitable contributions in creative ways.

> One of the most fascinating ventures along these lines has been the actor Paul Newman's venture into salad oil. Some three years ago—as a lark—he and a friend started a company to market his home-made salad oil and other products such as Newman's Own Industrial Strength Venetian Spaghetti Sauce, and then donate any profits to charity. Last year the company netted some $1.19 million which it gave to support 80 different nonprofit groups!

**How would you illustrate *love*?**

**What examples might you give to amplify the statement "each person makes her or his own happiness."**

## Testimony

Testimony refers to experts' opinions or to witnesses' accounts. Testimony supports your ideas by adding a note of authority. You might, for example, want to state an economist's predictions concerning inflation and recession. Or you might cite an art critic's evaluation of a painting or art movement.

In the following excerpt, U.S. Congresswoman Shirley Chisholm addresses the Independent Black Women's Caucus of New York City and uses the testimony of noted psychologist Rollo May to bolster her argument that black women must assume political power rather than wait for it to be given to them.

> As Rollo May has put it:
>
> Power cannot, strictly speaking, be given to another, for then the recipient still owes it to the giver. It must in some sense be assumed, taken, asserted, for unless it can be held against opposition, it is not power and will never be experienced as real on the part of the recipient.
>
> And those of us in this room know all too well that whatever is given to us is almost always a trap.

You might also consider using an eyewitness's testimony. You might, for example, cite the testimony of an eyewitness to an accident, the inmate who spent two years in a maximum-security prison, or the patient who underwent an operation.

One way to present testimony is to use direct quotations. Although often useful, they can be cumbersome. Therefore, unless the quotation is short, easily understood, and related directly to the point you are trying to make, use your own words. Paraphrase the essence of the testimony. Note, of course, that the ideas are borrowed from your authority or source.

## Audiovisual Aids

When you plan a speech, consider using an audiovisual aid—a visual or auditory means for clarifying important ideas (Kemp and Dayton 1985; Heinrich 1983). At the start, ask yourself if you should use an audiovisual aid. How would the aid make your speech more effective? What type of aid should you use? Charts? Slides? Models? How should you go about creating it? What principles should you follow to make sure your aid helps you achieve your public speaking purpose? How should you use the aid?

Audiovisual aids are not added frills. They are integral parts of your speech and serve important functions. Here are a few of their more important functions.

- Audiovisuals Gain Attention and Maintain Interest. We perk up when the speaker says, "I want you to look at this chart showing the employment picture for the next five years" or "Listen to the way Springsteen uses vocal variety."

- Audiovisuals Add Clarity. Let's say you want to illustrate the growth of the cable television industry in the United States over the last 30 years. You could say, "In 1952 there were 14,000 subscribers,

How would you describe the use of testimonials by advertisers? Do they restrict themselves to experts and eyewitnesses?

What other advantages are there in using audiovisual aids?

in 1955 there were 150,000 subscribers, . . . . " This gets pretty boring and you still haven't covered the sixties, seventies, and the eighties. Note how much easier this same information is communicated in the bar graph in Figure 12.1. At a glance we can see the rapid growth from practically nothing to over 53,000,000 subscribers.

- Audiovisuals Help the Audience to Remember. A great deal of the information we have in our minds is stored in visual form. For example, you probably picture the map of the United States in answering the question, Where is Colorado in relation to California? In a similar way, if you provide your audience with such visual cues, they will be able to more easily recall your speech.

- Audiovisuals Reinforce Your Message. Audiovisuals add the redundancy that listeners need to understand and remember what you have said. An audiovisual aid allows you to present the same information in two different ways—verbally and audiovisually. This one-two punch helps the audience to understand more clearly and to remember more accurately what you have said.

**Figure 12.1**
*Bar Graph of Cable Growth*

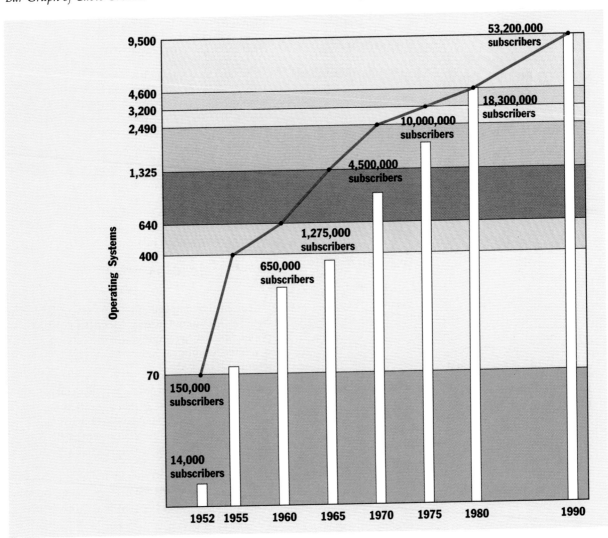

## Types of Audiovisual Aids

Let's say you are convinced of the value of using an audiovisual aid. But what kind? Some of the more popular aids are presented in Table 12.2.

**Table 12.2** *Types of Audiovisual Aids*

| Type | Comments |
|---|---|
| Actual object | The best audiovisual aid; integrate it into your speech if you can |
| Models | Replicas of the actual object are useful when explaining complex structures like the vocal mechanism or the brain. Models help clarify the size of various structures, their position, and how they interface |
| Chalkboard | Useful for recording key terms or important definitions. Be careful not to lose the audience's attention by turning your back |
| Word charts | Help highlight key points (see Figure 12.2) |
| Organizational charts | Show how an organization is structured |
| Flow charts | Help clarify processes like the steps in learning a skill or in performing a complex set of behaviors. Figure 12.3 identifies the stages a child goes through in learning language |
| Flip charts | Large pads of paper mounted on a stand. As you deliver your speech, you flip the pages to reveal visuals |
| Bar, line graphs | Useful for showing differences over time (see Figure 12.1, page 281) |
| Pie charts | Useful for showing how a whole is divided into parts |
| Maps | Useful for showing geographical elements and changes throughout history. Maps can illustrate population density, immigration patterns, economic conditions, and the location of resources |
| Slides and pictures | Useful for showing scenes or graphics you cannot easily describe. They help maintain attention but only if easily seen. Do not pass pictures around the room since they draw your listeners' attention away from what you are saying |
| Records and tapes | Useful for many topics other than music, for example, radio and television advertising, and to present actual excerpts by people you mention in your speech |

What type of visual aid might you develop for a speech on how to make great coffee?

**HOW TO READ A BOOK**

1. Preview
   2. Read for understanding
      3. Read for retention
         4. Review

**Figure 12.2** *Word Chart*

Can you select a speech topic and illustrate how you might use each of these audiovisual aids?

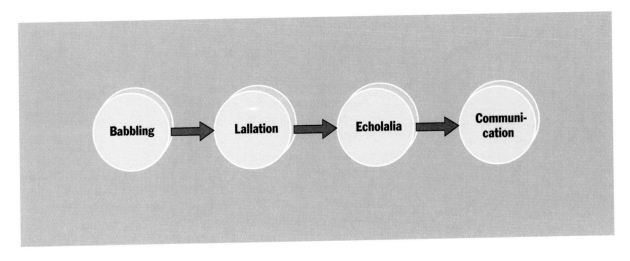

**Figure 12.3**
*Flow Chart on the Stages of Learning Language*

Do your college instructors use audiovisual aids? What suggestions concerning audiovisual aids would you offer them?

### Some Tips on Using Audiovisual Aids

Use the aid only when it is relevant. Show it when you want the audience to concentrate on it and then remove it. If you do not remove it, the audience's attention may remain focused on the visual when you want to continue.

Know your aids intimately. This is especially true when you are planning to use several. Be sure you know in what order they are to be used and what you will say when you introduce them. Know exactly what goes where and when.

Test the aids before using them. Be certain they can be easily seen or heard from all parts of the room.

Rehearse your speech with the audiovisual aids. Practice the actual movements with the actual aids. Decide how you are going to use a chart. Will it stand by itself? Will you tape it to the board (and do you have tape with you)? Will you ask another student to hold it? Will you hold it yourself?

Do not talk to your audiovisual aid. Both you and the aid should be focused on the audience. Talk to your audience at all times. Know your aids so well that you can point to what you want without breaking eye contact with your audience.

By now you should have the informative speech pretty well mastered. The principles of informing will also be useful in your persuasive speeches. The speeches of politicians, advertisers, and religious leaders are perhaps the clearest examples of persuasive speeches. In most of your own speeches, you too will aim at persuasion. You will try to change your listeners' attitudes and beliefs or perhaps change their behaviors.

## Guidelines for Persuasive Speaking

The object of oratory alone is not truth, but persuasion.
—THOMAS BABINGTON MACAULAY

Your success in strengthening or changing attitudes or beliefs and in moving your listeners to action will depend on your use of the principles of persuasion (Smith 1982; Bettinghaus and Cody 1987; Littlejohn and Jabusch 1987). Let's look at three major principles.

## Using Selective Exposure

All audiences follow the "law of selective exposure." It has at least two parts.

1. Listeners actively seek information that supports their opinions, beliefs, values, decisions, and behaviors.
2. Listeners actively avoid information that contradicts their existing opinions, beliefs, attitudes, values, and behaviors.

This principle has an important implication. If you want to persuade an audience that holds different attitudes from your own, anticipate selective exposure. Therefore, proceed inductively; that is, hold back on your thesis until you present your evidence and argument. Only then relate this evidence and argument to your initially contrary thesis.

Let's say you are giving a speech on the need to reduce spending on college athletic programs. If your audience agrees with you and wants to cut athletic spending, you might lead with your thesis. If, however, your audience strongly favors the existing athletic programs, then lead with your evidence and hold off stating your thesis until the end of your speech.

**How do you follow the principle of selective exposure?**

## Using Audience Participation

Persuasion is greatest when the audience participates actively, as in paraphrasing or summarizing. Demagogues who arouse huge crowds often have them chant slogans, repeat catch phrases, and otherwise participate actively.

The implication is simple: persuasion is a transactional process. It involves both speaker and listeners. You will be more effective if you can get the audience to actively participate.

## Using the Magnitude of Change Principle

The greater and more important the change you want to produce in your audience, the more difficult your task will be. The reason is simple: we normally demand numerous reasons and convincing evidence before we make important decisions—career changes, moving our families to another state, or investing our life savings in certain stocks.

**What reasons would you need to decide to change colleges?**

On the other hand, we are more easily persuaded (and demand less evidence) on minor issues—whether to take "History of Television" rather than "History of Film," or to give to the United Heart Fund instead of the American Heart Fund.

**What was the last persuasive speech you heard? Was it effective? Did it follow these principles of persuasion?**

People change gradually and in small degrees. Persuasion, therefore, is most effective when it strives for small changes and works over a period of time.

## Types of Persuasion Speeches

In persuasive speeches, you try to achieve either of two goals. First, you might wish to strengthen (or reinforce) or change your listeners' attitudes and beliefs. Second, you might wish to motivate them to do something.

## Speeches to Strengthen or Change Attitudes or Beliefs

Many speeches seek to strengthen existing attitudes or beliefs. For example, people who listen to religious speeches are usually already believers, so these speeches aim to strengthen their attitudes and beliefs. Here the audience is favorably inclined to the speaker's purpose and willing to listen.

Speeches designed to change attitudes or beliefs are more difficult. Most people resist change. When you try to change beliefs or attitudes, you are fighting an uphill battle.

Depending on the audience's initial position, you can view the following examples as topics for speeches to strengthen or change attitudes or beliefs:

Legalize marijuana.

Television shows are mindless.

Records should be rated for excessive sex and violence.

Make Puerto Rico the fifty-first state.

### Strategies for Strengthening or Changing Attitudes and Beliefs

When you try to strengthen or change attitudes and beliefs, consider the following principles:

1. Carefully estimate the current state of your listeners' attitudes and beliefs. If your goal is to strengthen these attitudes and beliefs, then state your thesis as early in your speech as you wish. Since your listeners basically agree with you, your thesis statement will create a bond of agreement. If, however, you disagree and wish to change their attitudes, then reserve your thesis until after you have provided your evidence.

2. Seek change in small increments. When addressing an audience that opposes your position, limit your purpose to small changes. Let's say, for example, that your ultimate goal is to get an anti-abortion group to favor abortion on demand. Obviously, this goal is too great to achieve in one speech. Therefore, strive for small changes. Try, for example, to get the audience to see that some abortions should be legalized.

3. Give your audience good reasons for believing what you want them to believe. Give them hard evidence and arguments. Show them how such attitudes and beliefs relate directly to their goals and motives.

### Developing the Speech to Strengthen or Change Attitudes and Beliefs

The following speech focuses on attitudes and beliefs. In this example, the speaker uses a problem-solution organizational pattern, first presenting the problems created by cigarette smoking, and then the solution.

SPECIFIC PURPOSE: To persuade my audience that cigarette advertising should be banned from all media.

THESIS: Cigarette advertising should be abolished. (*Why should it be abolished?*)

I. Cigarette smoking is a national problem.

    A. Cigarette smoking causes lung cancer.

    B. Cigarette smoking pollutes the air.

    C. Cigarette smoking raises the cost of health care.

II. Cigarette smoking will be lessened if advertisements are prohibited.

    A. Fewer people would start to smoke.

    B. Smokers would smoke less.

In delivering such a speech, you might begin like this:

I think we all realize that cigarette smoking is a national problem that affects each and every one of us. No one escapes the problems caused by cigarette smoking—not the smoker and not the nonsmoker. Cigarette smoking causes lung cancer. Cigarette smoking pollutes the air. And cigarette smoking raises the cost of health care for everyone.

Let's look first at the most publicized of all smoking problems: lung cancer. There can be no doubt—the scientific evidence is overwhelming—that cigarette smoking is a direct cause of lung cancer.

## Speeches to Move to Action

The persuasive speech designed to motivate a specific behavior may focus on just about any behavior. Here are some examples:

Vote (Do not vote) for Smith.

Give money to the American Cancer Society.

Major in economics.

Buy a Pontiac.

## Strategies for Moving Listeners to Action

When designing a speech to get listeners to do something, keep the following principles in mind.

1. Be realistic about what you want the audience to do. Remember you have only 10 or 15 minutes and in that time you cannot move the proverbial mountain. So, ask for small, easily performed behaviors —to sign a petition, to vote in the next election, to donate a small amount of money.

2. Demonstrate your own willingness to do the same. As a general rule, never ask the audience to do what you have not done yourself.

3. Stress the specific advantages of these behaviors to your audience. Don't ask your audience to engage in behaviors because of only abstract reasons. Give them concrete, specific reasons why they will benefit from the actions.

## Developing the Speech to Move to Action

How would you develop a speech to move to action if your specific purpose was to persuade your listeners to enroll in a course on AIDS education?

Here is an example of a speech to move to action in which the speaker tries to persuade the audience to buy a personal computer.

SPECIFIC PURPOSE: To persuade my audience to buy a personal computer.

THESIS: Personal computers are useful. *(Why are personal computers useful? or How are personal computers useful?)*

   I. Personal computers are useful for word processing.

      A. You can type faster with a word processor.

      B. You can revise documents easily with a word processor.

  II. Personal computers are useful for bookkeeping.

 III. Personal computers are useful for research.

In delivering such a speech, you might say:

> Have you ever added up all the hours spent typing your college papers? Have you ever tried to keep your finances in order only to lose the little pieces of paper you wrote your figures on? And then you had to start all over again. Have you ever gone to our college library and not found what you were looking for?
>
> Typing, bookkeeping, and research are a computer's three greatest strengths. After I show you how a computer can do these things, you'll want to buy a personal computer of your own.

# Thinking Critically About Arguments and Evidence

If your arguments be rational, offer them in as moving a manner as the nature of the subject will admit.
—JONATHAN SWIFT

An *argument* consists of evidence (for example, facts) and a conclusion. *Evidence* together with the *conclusion* that it supports equal an argument. *Reasoning* is the process of forming conclusions on the basis of evidence. For example, you might reason that since college graduates earn more money than nongraduates *(evidence)*, Jack and Jill should go to college if they wish to earn more money *(conclusion)*. Let's look at the four major types of reasoning.

## Reasoning from Specific Instances to Generalizations

Can you give an example of how you recently reasoned from specific instances to a generalization?

In reasoning from specific instances, you examine several items and then conclude something about the whole. This form of reasoning is useful when you want to develop a general principle or conclusion but cannot examine the whole. For example, you sample a few communication courses and conclude something about communication courses in general. You visit several Scandinavian cities and conclude something about all of Scandinavia.

Critically analyze reasoning from specific instances by applying these tests.

  1. Were enough specific instances examined? Two general guidelines will help determine how much is enough.

Can you explain why these two principles for what constitutes "enough specific instances" are true? Can you identify instances where they might be false?

First, the larger the group you wish to cover by your conclusion, the greater the number of specific instances you should examine. If you want to draw a conclusion about your college's entire student body, you will need to examine a much larger sample than if you limit your conclusion to members of your Human Communication class.

Second, the greater the differences among items or people in the group you want to draw a conclusion about, the more specific instances you will have to examine. For example, if you want to draw conclusions about students throughout the world, then your sample would have to be much larger than if you limit your conclusion to students in the United States.

2. Were the specific instances representative? If you want to draw conclusions about your school's student body, you cannot simply survey physics or art majors. Rather, you would have to examine a representative sample.

3. Are there significant exceptions? When you examine specific instances and draw a conclusion about the whole, consider the exceptions. Thus, if you examine a number of Venusians and discover that 70 percent have incomes in the top 25 percent of the galaxy, you might conclude that Venusians are rich. But what about the 30 percent who have incomes in the bottom 10 percent? You have to consider these significant exceptions.

In what way did you last use reasoning from specific instances to a generalization? Did you follow the principles noted here?

## Reasoning from Analogy

In reasoning from analogy, you compare like things and conclude that since they are alike in so many respects, they are also alike in some other respect. Analogies may be literal or figurative. In a *literal analogy* the items compared are from the same class—foods, cars, people, countries, cities, or whatever.

The time to repair the roof is when the sun is shining.
—JOHN F. KENNEDY

In a *figurative analogy*, the items compared are from different classes. These analogies are useful for amplification but are not logical proof. A figurative analogy might compare, for example, children with birds. You might note that, as birds are free to roam all over the world, children need to be free to roam all over their new and unexplored universe.

In critically analyzing the adequacy of an analogy—here of literal analogies—ask yourself two general questions.

1. Are the two cases alike in essential respects? A difference in significant respects will weaken your analogy's strength.

2. Do the differences make a difference? In any analogy, regardless of how literal, compared items will be different: no two things are exactly the same. But in reasoning with analogies, ask yourself if the differences make a difference. Obviously, not all do.

How would you use reasoning by analogy to persuade an audience that college-core requirements should be eliminated?

## Reasoning from Causes and Effects

You may either reason from cause to effect or from effect to cause. Causal reasoning goes like this:

*X* results from *Y*

since $X$ is undesirable

$Y$ should be eliminated

In an actual speech, the reasoning might be presented like this:

All the available evidence shows unmistakably that cancer [$X$] results from smoking [$Y$]. Smoking is personally destructive [$X$]; we have no choice but to do everything we can to eliminate smoking entirely [$Y$].

Alternatively, of course, you might argue that $X$ results from $Y$; and since $X$ is desirable, $Y$ should be encouraged. In a speech, you might say:

We know that general self-confidence [$X$] results from positively reinforcing experiences [$Y$]. Therefore, if you want to encourage the development of self-confidence in your children [$X$], give them positively reinforcing experiences [$Y$].

In critically analyzing reasoning from cause to effect or from effect to cause, ask yourself these questions.

1. Might other causes be producing the observed effect? If you observe a particular effect (say, high crime), ask if causes other than the one you are postulating might be producing it. Thus, you might assume that poverty leads to crime, but other factors might be actually causing the high crime rate. Or poverty might be one cause but not the most important.

"'The subway was late' is an excellent excuse for tardiness, however, there are no subways in Iowa!"

CARTOON BY ART BOUTHILLIER

2. Is the causation in the predicted direction? If two things occur together, it is often difficult to determine which is the cause and which the effect. For example, we often see in the same person a lack of interpersonal intimacy and of self-confidence. The person who lacks self-confidence seldom has intimate relationships—but which is the cause and which the effect? The lack of intimacy might cause low self-confidence. However, low self-confidence might also cause a lack of intimacy. Or, maybe some other cause (a history of negative criticism, for example) is producing both.

3. Is there evidence for a causal rather than merely a time-sequence relationship? Although two things might occur together, they may not be related in a cause-effect relationship. Divorce frequently results after repeated infidelities, but infidelity itself may not be the cause. Rather, some other factor (for example, boredom or the desire for change) may be leading to both infidelity and divorce.

How would you use cause-effect reasoning to show that learning a foreign language is financially beneficial?

## Reasoning from Sign

Medical diagnosis is a good example of reasoning by sign. The general procedure is simple. If a sign and a condition are frequently paired, the sign's presence is taken as proof of the condition's presence. Thus tiredness, extreme thirst, and overeating are signs of hyperthyroidism since they frequently accompany the condition. When these signs (or symptoms) disappear after treatment, it is taken as a sign that the thyroid disease is arrested.

Critically analyze reasoning from sign by asking yourself:

1. Do the signs necessitate the conclusion? Given the extreme thirst, overeating, and the like, how certain can you be of the hyperthyroid conclusion? With most medical and legal matters you can never be absolutely certain. You can only be certain beyond a reasonable doubt.

2. Are there other signs that point to the same conclusion? In the thyroid example, other factors could have caused the extreme thirst and similarly, the overeating. Yet taken together they pointed to only one reasonable diagnosis. Generally, the more signs that point toward the conclusion, the more confidence you can have that it is valid or correct.

3. Are there contradictory signs? Let's say, for example, that Higgins, suspected of murder, had a motive and a history of violence (signs that support the conclusion that Higgins was the murderer). But if Higgins also had an alibi for the time of the murder (a contradictory sign), the conclusion of guilt would have to be discarded.

The whole of science is nothing more than a refinement of every-day thinking.
—ALBERT EINSTEIN

Can you describe a recent instance in which you reasoned from sign?

To reason correctly from a false principle is the perfection of sophistry.
—DELOS CARLETON EMMONS

## Critically Analyzing Fallacies in Reasoning

We discussed the various forms of reasoning, especially the tests for assessing their validity, from the point of view of a speaker using them in a speech. But, these forms of reasoning and tests are equally valuable for the listener. That is, not only must you analyze the validity of the reasoning when you are the speaker, but also when you are the listener.

We should also guard against these additional fallacies of reasoning, both as speakers and as listeners. These seven major fallacies were originally identified for the Institute for Propaganda Analysis (Lee and Lee 1972), but are now recognized as common to all forms of persuasion (Albrecht 1980; Ruggiero 1990).

**Name Calling:** the speaker gives an idea, a group of people, or a political ideology a derogatory name ("anti-labor," "atheist") thus trying to make us condemn the idea without analyzing the evidence and argument.

**Glittering Generality:** the opposite of name calling. Here the speaker tries to gain our acceptance of some idea by associating it with things we value highly ("democracy," "Americanism"). By using "virtue words"—those that denote highly respected qualities—the speaker tries to persuade us to ignore the evidence and simply approve the idea.

**Transfer:** the speaker associates his or her idea with something we respect to gain our approval ("the proposal is in the best tradition of equality and democracy") or with something we dislike to gain our rejection ("the proposed change is another form of apartheid").

**Testimonial:** the speaker uses the authority of some person to gain our approval (if we respect the person) or our rejection (if we do not respect the person). Advertisers use this technique in testimonials by famous and well-liked people to convince us to buy everything from toothpaste to cereal to designer jeans.

**Plain Folks:** the speaker identifies himself or herself and the proposal with the audience. The speaker and the proposal are good—the "reasoning" goes—because they are of the people, just "plain folks," like the rest of us.

**Card Stacking:** the speaker selects only the evidence and arguments that build a case (even falsifies evidence and distorts the facts). Although there is a deliberate attempt to distort, the "evidence" is presented as being fair and unbiased.

**Band Wagon:** the speaker tries to persuade the audience to accept or reject an idea or proposal because "everybody is doing it," or the "right" people are doing it. The speaker attempts to convince us to jump on the band wagon.

## Psychological Appeals

When you use psychological appeals, you aim at your listeners' needs and desires. Psychological appeals focus on motives—those forces that energize a person to develop, change, or strengthen particular attitudes or behaviors. Some of the motives to which you might address your appeals are:

### Power, Control, and Influence

We want power, control, and influence. We want power over ourselves and others, to control events and things in the world, and to be influential. You will motivate your listeners when you enable them to increase these factors by learning what you have to say or doing as you suggest.

---

> When dealing with people, let us remember we are not dealing with creatures of logic. We are dealing with creatures of emotion, creatures bustling with prejudices and motivated by pride and vanity.
> —DALE CARNEGIE

> Can you describe recent advertisements that use any of these seven fallacious reasoning techniques?

> What motives are most effective in persuading you? Why are these motives more effective than others?

> We would frequently be ashamed of our good deeds if people saw all of the motives that produced them.
> —LAROCHEFOUCAULD

In a commencement address at Ohio University, Vincent Ryan Ruggiero (1987) appeals to his listeners' desire to control their lives more efficiently:

> People often ask me how I have managed to stay abreast of the research in several disciplines, write articles and books, and maintain an active speaking and consulting schedule, usually while teaching a full course load. . . .
>
> I decided that by being thrifty with time and investing it with the same care wealthy people exercise in investing their money, I could, in effect, *lengthen my life*. So I set about developing some rules that would help me live more efficiently. I'd like to share with you the six I have found most helpful.

## Self-Esteem and Approval

We all want to see ourselves positively, in the best possible light. We want to see ourselves as worthy and contributing human beings. Inspirational speeches—of the "you are the greatest" type—never seem to lack receptive audiences. In relating to your audience's desire for approval, avoid being too obvious. Few people want to be told that they need or desire approval.

> To please people is the greatest step toward persuading them.
> —LORD CHESTERFIELD

> What slogans might you offer the Big Deal Cereal Company that would appeal to the desire for power? For self-esteem or approval? For achievement? For financial gain?

"I *like* it, Ridgely!"

CARTOON BY CHARLES S. RAY

## Achievement

We want to achieve. As students you want to be successful. As a teacher and writer I too want to be successful. We want to achieve as friends, as parents, as lovers. This is why we read books and listen to speeches that tell us how to be more successful.

To use the achievement motive, explicitly state how your ideas and recommendations will contribute to the listeners' achievements. If you tell your listeners how they can increase their potential, earn better grades, secure more prestigious jobs, and become more popular with friends, you will have a highly motivated audience.

## Financial Gain

The desire for financial gain motivates many people. If you show an audience that what you advocate will make them money, they will listen with interest.

In a speech designed to motivate action against certain proposed budget cuts, Cyril F. Brickfield appeals to the financial motive of his senior citizen audience:

> Congress is now considering freezing Social Security COLA's [cost-of-living adjustments]. Congress is willing to force more than a half million of us into poverty. But the defense budget is exempt from any freeze.
>
> Ladies and gentlemen, let me ask you, is it *fair* that older Americans must lose their inflation protection while the Pentagon doesn't?

## Credibility Appeals

How believable are you as a speaker—apart from any evidence or argument you might advance? What is there about you as a person that makes others believe or not believe you? We call this believability quality *speaker credibility* (McCroskey 1982; Riggio 1987).

Credibility is important to the politician because it influences how people vote. It is important in education, since it influences a teacher's impact on a class. Credibility influences every communication situation.

We can identify three major qualities of credibility: *competence*, the knowledge and expertise the audience thinks the speaker has; *character*, the speaker's intentions and concern for the audience; and *charisma*, the speaker's personality and dynamism. We consider each of these characteristics and ways you may effectively demonstrate them as a speaker.

Figure 12.4 presents a sample rating scale as a visual summary of some of the more essential qualities of credibility.

## Competence

The more knowledge and expertise the audience perceives you to have, the more likely they will believe you. For example, you believe a teacher to the extent that you think he or she is knowledgeable on the

Other motives frequently mentioned as effective in persuasion are altruism, fear, individuality and conformity, love and affiliation, and status. How might these be used in a speech on "Helping the Homeless"?

There is one principal 'credibility blunder' in most interracial situations: the how-do-you-feel or what-do-you-think syndrome. . . . The 'credibility blunder' assumes that the other communicator is omniscient on matters relating to his own ethnic group. This means, in the mind of the communicator initiator, that there should be nothing the ethnic person should not know about any other person from that ethnic group.
—MOLEFI ASANTI

| Knowledgeable | 7 | 6 | 5 | 4 | 3 | 2 | 1 | Unknowledgeable |
|---|---|---|---|---|---|---|---|---|
| Experienced | 7 | 6 | 5 | 4 | 3 | 2 | 1 | Inexperienced |
| Confident | 7 | 6 | 5 | 4 | 3 | 2 | 1 | Not confident |
| Informed | 7 | 6 | 5 | 4 | 3 | 2 | 1 | Uninformed |
| Fair | 7 | 6 | 5 | 4 | 3 | 2 | 1 | Unfair |
| Concerned | 7 | 6 | 5 | 4 | 3 | 2 | 1 | Unconcerned |
| Consistent | 7 | 6 | 5 | 4 | 3 | 2 | 1 | Inconsistent |
| Similar | 7 | 6 | 5 | 4 | 3 | 2 | 1 | Dissimilar |
| Positive | 7 | 6 | 5 | 4 | 3 | 2 | 1 | Negative |
| Assertive | 7 | 6 | 5 | 4 | 3 | 2 | 1 | Unassertive |
| Enthusiastic | 7 | 6 | 5 | 4 | 3 | 2 | 1 | Unenthusiastic |
| Active | 7 | 6 | 5 | 4 | 3 | 2 | 1 | Passive |

**The first four qualities refer to *competence*; the second four to *character*; the last four to *charisma*.**

**Figure 12.4**
*Rating Scale for Evaluating a Speaker's Credibility*

> You will always find a few Eskimos ready to tell the Congolese how to cope with the heat.
> —STANISLAW LEC

subject. Here are some methods to demonstrate your competence to your audience.

1. Tell the audience of special experience or training that qualifies you to speak on this specific topic. At the same time, do not call attention to your inadequacies or to any gaps in your knowledge. Avoid such statements as "I know I'm not expert, but . . . ."

2. Cite a variety of research sources. Make it clear that you have thoroughly researched the topic—mention books you have read, persons you have interviewed, articles you have consulted. Weave these throughout your speech.

3. Stress particular competencies of your sources if your audience is not aware of them. Instead of saying, "Senator Smith thinks . . . ," establish the senator's credibility early by saying something like: "Senator Smith, who headed the finance committee for three years and was formerly professor of economics at MIT, thinks. . . ."

If you were Surgeon General Antonia Novello's speech advisor, what kinds of persuasion appeals (logical, psychological, or credibility) would you suggest she emphasize in a speech to your class on the need for increased funding for AIDS research? What would you advise if she were addressing Congress on this same topic? If she were addressing the leaders of major private funding agencies?

> What you are speaks so loud, I cannot hear what you say.
> —RALPH WALDO EMERSON

> Before you try to convince anyone else, be sure you are convinced, and if you cannot convince yourself, drop the subject.
> —JOHN H. PATTERSON

## Character

Character concerns the speaker's honesty and basic nature. We want to know if we can trust the speaker. We believe a speaker we trust. As a speaker, demonstrate qualities of character that will increase your credibility. Here are some suggestions.

1. Stress your fairness. When delivering a persuasive speech, stress that you have examined both sides of the issue and that your presentation is accurate and fair.
2. Stress your concern for enduring values. Make it clear to the audience that your position—your thesis—is related to higher-order values. Show them exactly how this is true.

Notice how President George Bush (1988) stressed his concern for such enduring values as family, religion, tradition, and individual power in his speech accepting the Republican nomination:

At the bright center is the individual. And radiating out from him or her is the family, the essential unit of closeness and of love. For it is the family that communicates to our children—to the twenty-first century—our culture, our religious faith, our traditions and history.

How would your class evaluate your credibility in general? Your competence? Character? Charisma?

*"I promised there wouldn't be any new taxes. I said nothing about the old ones getting bigger and bigger."*

CARTOON BY BOB SCHOCHET

From the individual to the family to the community, and so out to the town, to the church and school and, still echoing out, to the country, the state, the nation—each doing only what it does well, and no more. And I believe that power must always be kept close to the individual, close to the hands that raise the family and run the home.

3. Stress your similarity with the audience, particularly your beliefs, attitudes, values, and goals. The more similar you are to your listeners, the more likely they will perceive you as credible. At the same time, make it clear that the audience's interests are foremost in your mind.

## Charisma

We favor the dynamic speaker over the hesitant, nonassertive one. We perceive the shy, introverted, soft-spoken individual as less credible than the extroverted and forceful individual. Some suggestions for demonstrating charisma are:

1. Demonstrate a positive attitude to the entire speech encounter. Stress your pleasure at addressing the audience. Stress hope rather than despair, happiness rather than sadness.

2. Demonstrate assertiveness. Show the audience that you are a person who will stand up for your rights. Show them that you will not back off simply because the odds may be against you.

3. Be enthusiastic. The lethargic speaker who plods through the speech is the very opposite of the charismatic speaker. Try viewing a film of Martin Luther King, Jr. or Billy Graham speaking. They are totally absorbed with the speech and the audience. They are excellent examples of the enthusiasm that makes speakers charismatic.

Which of these three credibility qualities would most influence you in buying a new car? In choosing a doctor? In selecting a graduate school? In choosing a relationship partner? Why?

Who would be credible sources to your class members for a speech on "Making Big Money"? For a speech on "Staying Healthy"? For a speech on "How to Develop a Loving Relationship"? Why?

# FEEDBACK

In this chapter we covered the nature of the informative and of the persuasive speech and ways we can most effectively communicate information and change attitudes and behaviors.

1. Three general **types of informative speeches** are **speeches of description, speeches of definition,** and **speeches of demonstration.**

2. In preparing informative speeches, observe the **guidelines for informative speaking:** limit the amount of information, stress the information's usefulness, relate new information to information the audience already knows, and present information through several senses.

3. Use amplifying materials to make your ideas clear to your audience: **examples and illustrations, testimony,** and **audiovisual aids.**

4. The major types of **persuasive speeches** are (1) those that aim to strengthen or change attitudes or beliefs and (2) those that aim to actuate or move the listeners to action.

5. In preparing your persuasive speeches, consider the following **guidelines for persuasive speaking:** the selective exposure principle, the audience participation principle, and the magnitude of change principle.

6. **Argument** refers to a reason or series of reasons that lead to or support a conclusion. **Evidence** plus the conclusion it supports equal an argument.

7. In **reasoning from specific instances to a generalization,** we examine several specific instances and then conclude something about the whole.

8. In **reasoning from analogy,** we compare like things and conclude that since they are alike in so many respects, they are also alike in some unknown or unexamined respect. Analogies may be literal or figurative.

9. In **reasoning from causes and effects,** we may go in either of two directions: We can reason from known or observed cause to unobserved effect, or from observed or known effect to some unobserved cause.

10. In **reasoning from sign,** we deduce that if a sign and an object, event, or condition are repeatedly or frequently paired, the sign's presence is taken as evidence or proof that the object, event, or condition is present.

11. In critically analyzing reasoning fallacies be alert to such techniques as **name calling, glittering generality, transfer, testimonial, plain folks, card stacking,** and **band wagon.**

12. **Psychological** or **motivational appeals** are directed at an individual's needs and desires such as fear; power, control, and influence; self-esteem and approval; achievement; and financial gain.

13. **Credibility** refers to the persuasiveness quality that depends on the audience's perception of the speaker's character. Three dimensions of credibility are *competence, character,* and *charisma.*

Effective public speakers need to master a variety of informing and persuading skills. Check your own use of these skills. Use the following rating scale:

1 = almost always,   2 = often,   3 = sometimes,
4 = rarely,   5 = hardly ever.

_____ 1. In my informative speeches, I follow the principles of informative speaking: limit the amount of information, stress its relevance and usefulness to the audience, and relate any new information to what the audience already knows.

_____ 2. In my informative speeches, I select a variety of amplifying materials: examples, illustrations, testimony, and audiovisual aids.

_____ 3. In my persuasive speeches, I apply (where relevant) the principles of persuasion: selective exposure, audience participation, and magnitude of change.

_____ 4. In my persuasive speeches, I critically analyze reasoning from specific instances to generalizations, analogy, causes and effects, and sign.

_____ 5. In listening to persuasive attempts, I detect such fallacies as name calling, glittering generality, transfer, testimonial, plain folks, card stacking, and band wagon.

_____ 6. To motivate my audience I use psychological appeals—for example, fear; power, control, and influence; achievement; and financial gain.

_____ 7. In my speeches, I seek to establish my credibility by displaying competence, stressing my character, and acting dynamic (charismatic).

# SKILL DEVELOPMENT EXPERIENCES

## 12.1 AMPLIFYING STATEMENTS

Here are some rather broad statements. Select one and amplify it using at least three different methods of amplification. Identify each method used. Since the purpose of this exercise is to provide greater insight into amplification forms and methods, you may, for this exercise, invent facts, figures, illustrations, examples, and the like. In fact, it may benefit you to go to extremes in constructing these forms of support.

1. Significant social and political contributions have been made by college students.
2. The Sears Tower in Chicago is the world's tallest building.
3. Dr. Kirk is a model professor.
4. My grandparents left me a fortune in their will.
5. The college I just visited seems ideal.
6. The writer of this article is a real authority.
7. I knew I was marrying into money as soon as I walked into the house.
8. Considering what that individual did, punishment to the fullest extent of the law would be mild.
9. The fortune-teller told us good news.
10. The athlete lived an interesting life.

## 12.2 GAINING COMPLIANCE

Here are six compliance-gaining strategies—techniques to get others to do as we want (Marwell and Schmitt 1967; Miller and Parks 1982).

### Strategies

1. **Promise.** Pat promises to reward Chris if Chris complies with Pat's request.
   Pat: *I'll give you anything you want if you will just give me a divorce. You can have the house, the car, the stocks, the three kids; just give me my freedom.*
2. **Threat.** Pat threatens to punish Chris for non-compliance.
   Pat: *If you don't give me a divorce, you'll never see the kids again.*
3. **Expertise.** Pat promises that Chris will be rewarded for compliance (or punished for non-compliance) because of "the nature of things."
   Pat: *If you don't listen to the doctor, you're going to wind up back in the hospital.*
4. **Self-feelings.** Pat promises that Chris will feel better if Chris complies with Pat's request and worse if Chris does not.

Pat: *You'll see. You'll feel a lot better if you donate blood during the blood drive.*
5. **Altercasting.** Pat casts Chris in the role of "good" person (or "bad" person) and argues that Chris should comply because a person with "good" qualities would comply while a person with "bad" qualities would not.
   Pat: *Any intelligent person would vote additional funding for the homeless.* or *Only a cruel and selfish tightwad would deny the homeless additional funding.*
6. **Esteem.** Pat tells Chris that people will think more highly of Chris (relying on our need for approval) if Chris complies with Pat's request or people will think less if Chris does not comply.
   Pat: *Everyone will respect your decision to volunteer at the Homeless Shelter.* or *Everyone will think you're lazy and selfish if you don't volunteer your free time.*

State how you would use at least one of the strategies to persuade others and accomplish each of the following goals.

1. You want your friend to go with you on a ski-weekend instead of studying for finals.
2. You want your relationship partner to be more complimentary toward you.
3. You want an instructor to let you enroll in Intercultural Communication even though you do not have the prerequisites.

## 12.3 CONSTRUCTING ARGUMENTS

Construct an argument (from specific instances to generalizations, analogy, causes and effects, and sign) for or against any one of the following propositions. Since the purpose of this experience is to familiarize you with constructing arguments, use hypothetical (even fanciful) data to build your arguments.

1. AIDS Prevention should be (should not be) a required course in colleges.
2. Tenure for college teachers should be (should not be) abolished.
3. Church property should be (should not be) taxed.
4. The death penalty should be (should not be) abolished in all states.
5. Records, tapes, and cassettes should be (should not be) labeled for sexual content and violence.

## 12.4 CONSTRUCTING MOTIVATIONAL APPEALS

The *New York Post* (September 17, 1979, p. 19) reported that, according to "exhaustive studies," the ten greatest sources of fear, in order of importance, are:

1. Fear of losing money or not making enough; 80 percent noted this financial fear.
2. Fear of losing their jobs; 74 percent noted this.
3. Fear of ill health; 69 percent cited fear of real or imaginary ailments.
4. Fear of negative personal appearance; 59 percent feared that their personal appearance might handicap their chance for success.
5. Fear of political developments; 56 percent cited the fear of taxes and various government trends.
6. Fear of incompatability; 44 percent feared marital difficulties and general incompatability.
7. Fear of lack of self-confidence; 40 percent feared not having enough self-confidence.
8. Fear of religious confusion; 37 percent worried about what they should believe in terms of religious and philosophical convictions.
9. Fear of sexual matters; 34 percent worried about sexual temptations or transgressions.
10. Fear of trouble with relatives; 33 percent feared difficulties with relatives.

Select one of the specific purposes and audiences noted below and develop a motivational appeal based on one or more of these fears. After constructing these appeals, share your results with others, either in small groups or the class as a whole. In your discussion you may wish to consider some or all of the following questions.

1. Why did you select the specific motivational appeal(s) you did?
2. Why did you assume that this (these) appeal(s) would approve effective with the topic and the audience selected?
3. How effective do you think such an appeal would be if actually presented to such an audience?
4. Might some of the appeals backfire and stimulate audience resentment? Why might such resentment develop? What precautions might be taken by the speaker to prevent such resentment?
5. What ar the ethical implications of using these motivational appeals?
6. What appeals to fear might prove more effective than the ten noted here?
7. Where in the speech do you think you would place this (these) appeal(s)? In the beginning? Middle? End? Why?

### Purposes

1. Marijuana should (not) be made legal for those over 18 years of age.
2. Cigarette smoking should (not) be banned in all public places.
3. Capital punishment should (not) be law in all states.
4. Social Security benefits should be increased (decreased) by at least one-third.
5. Retirement should (not) be mandatory at age 65 for all government employees.
6. Police personnel should (not) be permitted to strike.
7. National health insurance should (not) be instituted.
8. Athletic scholarships should (not) be abolished.
9. Property taxes should be lowered (increased) by 50 percent.
10. Required courses in college should (not) be abolished.
11. Teachers should (not) be paid according to performance; they should (not) be paid according to seniority, degrees earned, or publications.
12. Divorce should (not) be granted immediately when the parties request it.

### Audiences

1. Senior citizens of Metropolis
2. Senior Club of your high school
3. Small Business Operators Club of Anytown
4. American Society of Young Dentists
5. Council for Better Housing
6. Veterans of Vietnam
7. Los Angeles Society of Interior Designers
8. Catholic Women's Council
9. National Council of African-American Artists
10. Parent-Teachers Association of elementary schools in your community
11. Midwestern Council of Physical Education Instructors
12. Society for the Rehabilitation of Former Drug Addicts

## 12.5 THE ONE MINUTE CREDIBILITY BUILDER

Write a brief introduction (approximately one minute in length) about yourself for someone else to use in introducing you and your next speech. Mention at least three specific details that would help establish your competence, character, and/or charisma.

# CHAPTER 13

# Style, Delivery, and Criticism

ORAL STYLE

WORD CHOICE
- Clarity
- Vividness
- Appropriateness
- Personal Style
- Forcefulness

SENTENCE CONSTRUCTION
- Favor Short over Long
- Favor Direct over Indirect
- Factor Active over Passive
- Favor Positive over Negative
- Vary the Type and Length

TRANSITIONS
- Internal Summaries

METHODS OF DELIVERY
- The Impromptu Method
- The Manuscript Method
- The Extemporaneous Method

VOICE
- Volume
- Rate
- Pitch
- Articulation and Pronunciation
- Pauses

BODILY ACTION
- Eye Contact
- Facial Expression
- Posture
- Gestures
- Movement

REHEARSAL: PRACTICING AND IMPROVING DELIVERY
- Rehearse the Speech as a Whole
- Time the Speech
- Approximate the Actual Speech Situation
- See Yourself as a Speaker
- Incorporate Changes and Delivery Notes
- Rehearse Often

EVALUATING THE SPEECH
- Guidelines for Speech Criticism
- The Speech Critique
- Expressing Your Evaluations

FEEDBACK

SKILL DEVELOPMENT EXPERIENCES

## Goals

After completing this chapter, you should be able to

1. identify at least three suggestions each to achieve clarity, vividness, appropriateness, personal style, forcefulness, and effective sentence structure in public speaking style

2. define the three general methods of delivery

3. identify four guidelines for using notes while delivering a speech

4. define volume, rate, pitch, articulation, and pronunciation and the problems associated with each

5. explain the general guidelines for a public speaker's use of eye contact, facial expression, gestures, movement, and proxemics

6. explain the major goals of public speaking rehearsal and some specific rehearsal suggestions

7. explain the guidelines for expressing critical evaluations

*How should you phrase your speech?* ■ *What kind of language should you use?* ■ *Should you use simple or complex words?* ■ *Should you memorize your speech?* ■ *How can you increase your vocal effectiveness?* ■ *What about pausing during the speech?* ■ *How can you use notes effectively?* ■ *What should you do with your hands?* ■ *How should you stand?* ■ *How can you best rehearse your speech?*

In this chapter we consider style and delivery in public speaking. In looking at style, we focus on the speech's oral style and provide guidelines for selecting words and constructing sentences. In looking at delivery, we focus on delivery methods, guidelines for using your voice and body to best advantage, and offer some suggestions on how to rehearse your speech. Last, we combine all factors and consider how to evaluate the speech.

## Oral Style

> No style is good that is not fit to be spoken or read aloud with effect.
> —WILLIAM HAZLITT

You do not speak as you write. Words and grammatical constructions differ in written and spoken language. The major explanation is that you compose speech instantly. You select words and construct sentences as you think. When you write, however, you compose your thoughts after considerable reflection. Even then you may rewrite and edit as you go along.

Another explanation for the differences between speaking and writing style is that the listener hears a speech only once; therefore, it must be instantly intelligible. The reader can reread an essay or look up an unfamiliar word. Temporary attention lapses may force the reader to reread a sentence or paragraph, but the listener can never make up for such lapses.

Researchers who have examined a great number of speeches and writings have found several important differences (DeVito 1965, 1981; Akinnaso 1982). Generally, spoken language consists of shorter, simpler, and more familiar words than does written language. There is more qualification in speech than in writing. For example, speakers make greater use of such expressions as *although, however,* and *perhaps.* Writers probably edit these out before their work is published.

Spoken language also contains a greater number of self-reference terms—"I," "me," "my." And, it contains more expressions that incorporate the speaker as part of the observation (for example, *it seems to me that. . .* or *as I see it . . .* ).

> A good style should show no signs of effort.
> —W. SOMERSET MAUGHAM

Retain this oral style in your public speeches. But, since you will compose your speech much as you write an essay—with considerable thought, deliberation, editing, and restyling—you will have to pay special attention to choosing your words and phrasing your sentences.

> What other differences do you notice between speech and writing?

These specific suggestions will help you style a speech that will retain the best of the oral style while maintaining comprehension and persuasion. First, we offer suggestions for selecting words to achieve an effective speech style. Second, we offer suggestions for styling sentences to give them greater clarity and force.

# Word Choice

Choose words to achieve clarity, vividness, appropriateness, personal style, and forcefulness.

## Clarity

Clarity in speaking style should be your primary goal. Here are some guidelines to help you make your speech clear.

### Be Economical

Don't waste words. Two important ways to achieve economy are to avoid redundancies (unnecessary repetition) and meaningless words. Notice the redundancies in the following expressions and how a more economical and clearer style results when you eliminate the italicized terms:

*more* unique

at 9 a.m. *in the morning*

we *first* began the discussion

the full *and complete* report

I *myself personally*

blue *in color*

*over*exaggerate

you, *members of the audience*

*clearly* unambiguous

about *approximately* nine inches *or so*

cash *money*

Eliminate meaningless phrases. Instead of saying "would seem to indicate," say "indicates." Instead of saying "the function of this plug is to connect. . . ," say "this plug connects . . . ." Instead of saying "for the reason that," say "because."

CARTOON BY LEN SPENCER

## Use Specific Terms and Numbers

Picture these terms:

- living thing
- animal
- dog
- poodle

Notice that as the terms get more specific, the picture gets clearer and more detailed. Be specific so your audience will see what you want them to see. Don't say *car* when you want them to picture a limousine, and don't say *movie* when you want them to think of *Cape Fear*.

The same is true of numbers. Don't say "earned a good salary" if you mean "earned $90,000 a year." Don't say "taxes will go up" when you mean "taxes will increase 22 percent." Don't say "their defense budget was enormous" when you mean "the defense budget was $17 billion."

## Use Guide Phrases

Help your listeners move from one idea or piece of evidence to another with guide phrases. Use "now that we have seen how . . . ," "let us consider how . . . ," and "my next argument . . . ."

Terms such as *first, second, also, although,* and *however* also help the audience follow your line of thinking. Our discussion of transitions elaborates on this important guiding function.

## Use Short, Familiar, and Commonly-Used Terms

Favor the short word over the long, the familiar term over the unfamiliar. Here are a few examples:

| Poor choices | Better choices |
|---|---|
| innocuous | harmless |
| elucidate | clarify |
| utilize | use |
| ascertain | find out |
| erstwhile | former |
| eschew | avoid |
| expenditure | cost, expense |
| assist | help |
| indicate | show |

## Use Repetition, Restatement, and Internal Summaries

Repetition (repeating something in exactly the same way), restatement (rephrasing an idea or statement), and internal summaries (summaries or reviews of subsections of your speech) all help the listeners follow what you are saying.

True eloquence consists in saying all that should be said, and that only.
—LaRochefoucauld

Are you impressed by speakers who use words you don't understand? If so, would you suggest revising what is said about using short, familiar, and commonly-used terms?

A simple style is like white light. Although complex, it does not appear so.
—Anatole France

How might your instructors achieve greater clarity? Politicians? Doctors?

"YES," SHE MUMBLED?...SIGHED?... MUTTERED?...SNARLED?... HISSED?...GROWLED?...

DRAWING BY C. BARSOTTI; 1981 THE NEW YORKER MAGAZINE

### Vividness

Select words to help make your ideas come alive in the listeners' minds.

### Use Active Verbs

Favor verbs that communicate activity rather than passivity. The verb *to be*, in all its forms—*is, are, was, were*, and *will be*—is relatively inactive. Try replacing such forms with action verbs. Instead of saying "Management will be here tomorrow," consider "Management will descend on us (or jets in) tomorrow."

### Use Strong Verbs

The verb is the strongest part of your sentence. Carefully choose verbs so they work hard for you. Instead of saying "He *walked* through the forest," consider *wandered, prowled, rambled, roamed*. Consult a thesaurus to replace any verb you suspect might be weak.

### Use Figures of Speech

One of the best ways to achieve vividness is to use figures of speech. Table 13.1 presents a few you might use.

| Figure | Definition | Examples |
|--------|-----------|----------|
| Alliteration | Repetition of the same initial consonant sound in two or more words close to one another | Fifty Famous Flavors |
| Hyperbole | Use of extreme exaggeration | I'm so hungry I could eat a cow. |
| Metaphor | Comparison of two unlike things | She's a lion when she wakes up. He's a real bulldozer. |
| Metonymy | Substitution of a name for a title with which it is closely associated | City Hall issued the following new release ("City Hall" is used instead of "the mayor" or "the city council") |
| Personification | Attribution of human characteristics to inanimate objects. | This room cries for activity. My car is tired and wants a drink. |
| Rhetorical question | A question used to make a statement or produce some desired effect rather than to secure an answer, since the answer is usually obvious | Do you want to be popular? Do you want to get well? Do you want to pass the next exam? |
| Simile | Comparison of two unlike objects using the words "like" or "as" | He takes charge like a bull. The teacher is as gentle as a lamb. |

**Table 13.1**
*Figures of Speech*

## Use Imagery

Appeal to the audience's senses, especially their visual, auditory, and tactile senses. Make them see, hear, and feel what you are talking about.

VISUAL IMAGERY. Describe people or objects to create images the audience can see. When appropriate, describe visual qualities such as height, weight, color, size, shape, length, and contour. Let your audience see the sweat pouring down the faces of coal miners, and the short, overweight executive in a pin-striped suit smoking an enormous cigar.

AUDITORY IMAGERY. Use terms that describe sounds to appeal to the audience's sense of hearing. Let listeners hear the car *screeching*, the wind *whistling*, the bells *chiming*, and the angry professor *roaring*.

TACTILE IMAGERY. Use terms referring to temperature, texture, and touch to create tactile imagery. Let listeners feel the cool water running over their bodies, the fighter's punch, the rough-as-sandpaper clothing, and a lover's soft caress.

> **How would you use imagery to describe your college to someone who has never seen it?**

## Appropriateness

Here are some guidelines to help you choose appropriate language.

### Speak at the Appropriate Level of Formality

Although public speaking usually takes place in a relatively formal situation, relatively informal language seems to work best. One way to achieve an informal style is to use contractions: *don't* instead of *do not*, *I'll* instead of *I shall*, and *wouldn't* instead of *would not*. Contractions give a

> **A good style must, first of all, be clear. It must not be mean nor above the dignity of the subject. It must be appropriate.**
> **—ARISTOTLE**

public speech the sound and rhythm of conversation—a quality to which listeners generally react favorably.

Avoid written-style expressions such as "the former" or "the latter" as well as such expressions as "the argument presented above." These make listeners feel you are reading to them rather than talking with them.

Use personal pronouns instead of impersonal expressions. Say "I found" instead of "it has been found." Say "I'll present three arguments" instead of "Three arguments will be presented."

### Avoid Unfamiliar (and Hence, Inappropriate) Foreign and Technical Terms, Jargon, and Acronyms

Be careful to avoid terms the audience does not know. Avoid foreign and technical terms unless you are certain the audience is familiar with them. Similarly, avoid jargon (the technical vocabulary of a specialized field) unless you are sure its meaning is clear to your listeners. Some acronyms (NATO, UN, NOW, and CORE) are probably familiar to most audiences; most, however, are not. When you use these words, explain their meaning.

### Avoid Slang and Vulgar Expressions

Be careful not to offend your audience with language that embarrasses or makes them think you have little respect for them. Although your listeners may use such expressions, they generally resent their use by public speakers.

### Avoid Offensive Terms and Expressions

Avoid terms that might be interpreted as sexist, heterosexist, or racist (Bate 1988; Thorne, Kramarae, and Henley 1983). Do not use the masculine pronoun to refer to all persons. That is, do not use *he* or *him* generically. Change your sentences so you can use the plural *they* or *them*, or say *he and she* or *her and him*. Do not refer to professions or positions by masculine names. Avoid *chairman*, *policeman*, and *repairman* when applied to both sexes. Substitute *chair* or *chairperson*, *police officer*, and *repairperson*. Similarly, avoid using *man* when referring to the human race. *Human* serves as well and is more descriptive.

Don't imply that the hypothetical doctor or lawyer is male by using sex identifiers such as "woman doctor" or "female lawyer." Similarly, do not imply that all couples or relationships consist of a man and a woman. Avoid qualifying terms indicating affectional orientation, as in "the lesbian psychiatrist" or "the gay athlete."

### Personal Style

Audiences favor speakers who use a personal rather than an impersonal style—who speak *with* them rather than *at* them.

How might you make more vivid such bland sentences as "The children played in the yard," "The soldiers took the hill," and "The singer sang three songs"?

Would you be offended by slang and vulgar expressions if you overheard strangers in the street use them? If your instructor used them? If students gave speeches using them? Under what circumstances, if any, would it be acceptable to use these expressions?

[The eloquent speaker] can treat subjects of an humble nature with delicacy, lofty things impressively, and moderate things temperately.
—CICERO

Why are such expressions as "female physicist" or "gay doctor" offensive? What do such expressions imply? What impression do you get of a speaker who uses such expressions?

## Use Personal Pronouns

Say *I, me, he, she,* and *you.* Avoid such expressions as the impersonal *one* (as in, "One is led to believe that . . ."), "this speaker," or "you, the listeners." These expressions distance the audience and create barriers rather than bridges.

## Direct Questions to the Audience

**Personal style is not always the most effective style to use. When might a more formal, impersonal style be more effective?**

Involve the audience by asking them questions. With a small audience, you might even briefly take responses. With larger audiences, you might ask the question, pause to allow the audience time to consider their responses, and then move on. When you direct questions to your listeners, they feel part of a public speaking transaction.

## Create Immediacy

*Immediacy* is a connectedness, a relatedness, and a oneness with your listeners. Immediacy is the opposite of disconnectedness and separateness. Create immediacy by using the "you approach." Say "you'll enjoy reading . . ." instead of "everyone will enjoy reading . . . ."

**How might you communicate immediacy nonverbally?**

Refer to commonalities between you and the audience. Say, for example, "We are all children of immigrants" or "We all want to see our team in the playoffs." Refer also to shared experiences and goals. Say, for example, "We all need a more responsive PTA." Finally, recognize and refer to audience feedback. Say, for example, "I can see from your expressions that we're all here for the same reason."

## Forcefulness

To achieve your purpose, whether it be informative or persuasive, direct the audience's attention, thoughts, and feelings with forceful language (Bradac, Bowers, and Courtright 1979).

**Style is effectiveness of assertion.**
—GEORGE BERNARD SHAW

### Eliminate Weakeners

Eliminate phrases that weaken your sentences, such as those italicized in the following examples:

> *It seems to me that* Mike Swazey is the best candidate for the job.

> *I'm not sure about this but* my research shows that movie attendance has declined in the last several years.

Rewrite to make sentences more forceful. Eliminate phrases that water down your meaning. Don't say "There are lots of things we can do to help." Say "We can do lots of things to help." Don't say "It should be observed in this connection that, all things considered, money does not produce happiness." Say "Money doesn't bring happiness."

### Avoid Bromides and Clichés

*Bromides* are sentences that are trite—worn out by constant usage: "Honesty is the best policy," "If I can't do it well, I won't do it at all," and

"I don't understand modern art, but I know what I like." When we hear bromides, we recognize them as unoriginal and uninspired.

*Clichés* are overused phrases that have lost their novelty and part of their meaning; they call attention to themselves because of their overuse. Some clichés to avoid are these:

in this day and age

sweet as sugar

happy as a lark

tell it like it is

free as a bird

no sooner said than done

to all intents and purposes

it goes without saying

few and far between

from the ridiculous to the sublime

**Hush little bright line
Don't you cry . . .
You'll be a cliché
Bye and bye.**
—FRED ALLEN

**What impression would you get of a person who frequently used clichés?**

*Leo Buscaglia, popular author and lecturer, is much in demand, in part because his language is clear, vivid, appropriate, personal, and forceful. How would you describe your own speaking style? What is your greatest strength? Your greatest weakness? How might you correct this weakness?*

# Sentence Construction

Effective public speaking also requires careful attention to the construction of sentences. Here are some guidelines.

## Favor Short over Long

Short sentences are more forceful and economical. They are easier to understand and to remember. Listeners do not have the time or inclination to unravel long and complex sentences. Help them to listen more efficiently: Use short rather than long sentences.

## Favor Direct over Indirect

Direct sentences are easier to understand. They are also more forceful. Instead of saying "I want to tell you of the three main reasons why we should not adopt the Bennett Proposal," say "We should not adopt the Bennett Proposal. Let me give you three good reasons."

## Favor Active over Passive

Active sentences are easier to understand. They also make your speech livelier and more vivid. Instead of saying "The lower court's original decision was reversed by the Supreme Court," say "The Supreme Court reversed the lower court's decision." Instead of saying "The proposal was favored by management," say "Management favored the proposal."

## Favor Positive over Negative

Positive sentences are easier to comprehend and to remember (DeVito 1976; Clark 1974). Notice how sentences (A) and (C) are easier to understand than (B) and (D).

(A) The committee rejected the proposal.

(B) The committee did not accept the proposal.

(C) This committee works outside the normal company hierarchy.

(D) This committee does not work within the normal company hierarchy.

## Vary the Type and Length

The advice to use short, direct, active, and positive sentences is valid most of the time. But, too many sentences of the same type or length, will make your speech boring. Use variety while generally following the guidelines.

# Transitions

Connect parts of your speech to each other so their relationships are clear to you *and* to the audience. Remember, your audience will hear your speech only once.

*Transitions* are words, phrases, or sentences used to connect the various parts of your speech. They provide guideposts that help the audience follow the development of your thoughts and arguments.

Use transitions in at least the following places:

- between the speech's introduction and its body
- between the body and the conclusion, and
- between the speech's main points

Some examples of transitional expressions you may find useful are:

My next point . . .

A second example (argument, fact) . . .

By way of introduction . . .

If you want further evidence, consider . . .

First, . . . , second, . . . .

Furthermore, . . .

But, as we will see . . .

So, as you can see . . .

Given this situation, what should we do?

How, then, can we deal with these three problems?

It follows, then, that . . .

Not only should we . . . , but we should also . . . .

Now that we understand the basic structure of X, let us look into its basic functions.

In contrast, consider/think . . .

The other side of the issue is this: . . .

What transitions might be appropriate for going from one argument to another? From the introduction to the body of your speech? From problem to solution? From one example to a second example?

Also make use of "nonverbal transitions." For example, pause between main points; move to the other side of the room; step forward or backward; stand still if you are moving or move if you are standing still; or lean forward. These movements, especially when combined with verbal transitions, will help signal that you are going from one idea to another.

What kinds of transitions do stand-up comics use as they shift from one joke to another?

### Internal Summaries

Closely related to the transition is the *internal summary*—a statement summarizing what you have discussed, usually a major subdivision of your speech.

Incorporate internal summaries into the transitions connecting the major arguments or issues. Here's one example:

Now that we've seen how a college education will help you get a better job, let's look at how college can increase your personal effectiveness.

Do your instructors use transitions and internal summaries in their lectures? Might they profit from the advice given here?

Internal summaries remind your listeners of what they have just heard *and* preview what they will hear. The clear connection that internal summaries create will help listeners follow your speech despite any lapses in attention or noise.

# Methods of Delivery

Speakers vary widely in delivery methods. Some speak "off-the-cuff" with no apparent preparation. Others read their speeches from manuscript. Others construct a detailed outline and compose the speech at the moment of delivery. These represent the three general methods of delivery: impromptu, manuscript, and extemporaneous.

## The Impromptu Method

The impromptu method involves speaking without preparation. You and the topic meet for the first time, and the speech begins.

On some occasions, you cannot avoid impromptu speaking. In a classroom, you might be asked to comment on the speaker and speech you just heard: in effect, you give an impromptu speech of evaluation. At meetings, people are often asked for impromptu comments on various issues. You can greatly improve impromptu speaking by cultivating public speaking ability in general. The more proficient you are as a speaker, the better you will be impromptu.

> The best impromptu speeches are the ones written well in advance.
> —RUTH GORDON

## The Manuscript Method

In the manuscript method, the speech is written out and the speaker reads it. This is the safest method when exact timing and wording are required. It could be disastrous if a political leader did not speak from manuscript on sensitive issues. An ambiguous word, phrase, or sentence that proved insulting, belligerent, or conciliatory might cause serious problems. With a manuscript speech, the speaker can control style, content, organization, and all other elements. In fact, a great advantage is that speech advisers can review it and suggest resolutions to any potential problems.

A variation of the manuscript method involves writing out the speech and then memorizing it. You would then recite the entire speech from memory, much as an actor recites a part in a play.

## The Extemporaneous Method

Extemporaneous delivery involves thorough preparation—memorizing the main ideas, the order in which they will appear, and perhaps the first and last few sentences. There is, however, no commitment to exact wording. This is the method we recommend you use to deliver your public speeches.

### Advantages

> To make others feel we must feel ourselves; and to feel ourselves we must be natural.
> —BENJAMIN DISRAELI

The extemporaneous method is useful when exact timing and wording are not required. Good lecturing by college teachers uses this method. They have prepared thoroughly, know what they want to say, and have the lecture's organization clearly in mind. But they are not committed to exact wording.

This method allows greater flexibility for feedback. Should a point need clarification, you can elaborate when it will be most effective. It is also easy to be natural, because you are being yourself. And, you may move about and interact with the audience.

### Disadvantages

The major disadvantage is that you may stumble and grope for words. If you have rehearsed the speech several times, however, this is unlikely. While you cannot give the precise attention to style that you can in the manuscript and memorized methods, you can memorize certain key phrases.

### Guidelines for Speaking Extemporaneously

Clearly preferring the extemporaneous method, we do suggest you memorize three parts of such a speech: (1) your opening lines—perhaps the first two or three sentences; (2) the major propositions and the order in which you will present them; and (3) your closing lines—perhaps the last two or three sentences.

Memorizing the opening and closing lines will not only free you to focus completely on the audience, but will put you more at ease. Memorizing your main ideas and their order will give you a feeling of control and will allow you to make your main points without referring to notes. After all, if you expect your audience to remember these points, you should remember them as well.

### The Delivery Outline

In using the extemporaneous method, you need a delivery outline to assist you in delivering the speech. Do *not* use your preparation outline as you may read from the outline which is not an effective way to give a speech. Instead, construct a brief delivery outline. Here are some guidelines.

BE BRIEF. This outline is to help you communicate your ideas to your audience. It should not stand in the way of speaker-audience contact. Therefore, be brief. Do not use full sentences. Use key words to trigger in your mind the ideas you wish to discuss.

BE DELIVERY-MINDED. This is your outline, constructed to help you deliver your speech most effectively. Therefore, include any delivery guides you might wish to remember while you are speaking. For example, you might note when you will use your visual aid and when you will remove it. A simple "Show VA" and "Remove VA" should suffice.

REHEARSE YOUR SPEECH WITH THIS OUTLINE. In your rehearsals, use this outline only. Do not rehearse with your full-sentence outline. This is simply a specific application of the general rule: Make rehearsals as close to the real thing as possible.

Why is it dangerous to memorize your entire speech? What are some of the problems that memorizing a speech may create?

What advantage is there to rehearsing with a delivery outline over rehearsing with a more complete, full sentence outline?

*A Sample Delivery Outline*

Note the list of features of the following sample outline.

1. It is brief enough so that you will be able to use it effectively without losing eye contact with the audience. It uses abbreviations (SD for self-disclosure; C for communication) and phrases rather than complete sentences.

2. It is detailed enough to include all essential parts of your speech, including transitions.

3. It contains delivery notes specifically tailored to your own needs, for example, pause suggestions, terms to be emphasized, and guides to using visual aids.

4. It is clearly divided into introduction, body, and conclusion (though to save space, lines are used instead of the labels) and uses the same numbering system as the preparation outline.

How would you construct a delivery outline for the speech given on pp. 331–333?

PAUSE!

LOOK OVER THE AUDIENCE!

    I. Get to know self: SD

        A. Research supports: feel better

        B. *BUT*, problems too

        C. Understanding SD: effectiveness

PAUSE—SCAN AUDIENCE

    II. Immerse self in SD

        A. As student

        B. As researcher (SHOW BOOKS ON SD)

        C. As writer

    III. Understanding SD

WRITE 2 TOPICS ON BOARD

        A. SD: form of C

        B. SD: rewards and problems

[Let's examine SD as a form of C]

    I. SD: form of C

        A. Type of C

        B. *NEW* (not *OLD*) in formation

        C. Hidden information

[Now that we know what SD is, let's look at some rewards and problems]

    II. SD: rewards *AND* problems

TAPE REWARDS/PROBLEMS VISUAL AID CHART TO BOARD

        A. Rewards: know self better, deal with problems, release energy

[*BUT*, there are problems too]

        B. Problems: personal, professional, social

PAUSE

STEP FORWARD

[Let's review what we now know about SD]

    I. SD: unique form of C

    II. SD: most significant form of C

    III. Get to know self: SD

PAUSE!

ASK FOR QUESTIONS

### Using Notes

In speaking extemporaneously, you will use notes when delivering your speech. A few simple guidelines may help you avoid some common errors (McCroskey 1982; Kesselman-Turkel and Peterson 1982).

KEEP YOUR NOTES TO A MINIMUM. Usually, the fewer the better. Do not bring your entire speech outline. You may be tempted to rely on it and not speak directly to the audience. Instead, compose a delivery outline, using only key words, and bring this to the lectern. One side of a three-by-five-inch index card, or at most an 8½-by-11-inch page, should be sufficient for most speeches. This will relieve anxiety over forgetting your speech but not be extensive enough to prevent meaningful speaker-audience interaction.

KNOW YOUR NOTES INTIMATELY. Rehearse at least twice with the same notes you will take to the speaker's stand.

USE YOUR NOTES WITH "OPEN SUBTLETY." Don't make them more obvious then necessary, but don't try to hide them. Don't gesture with your notes in your hand, but don't turn away from the audience to steal a glance at them, either. Use them openly and honestly but gracefully, with "open subtlety."

YOUR NOTES SHOULD NOT PREVENT YOU FROM SPEAKING DIRECTLY TO YOUR AUDIENCE. When referring to your notes, pause to read, then regain audience eye contact and continue your speech. Do not read from your notes, just take cues from them. Exceptions to this are an extensive quotation or complex set of statistics that must be read. Then, almost immediately, resume direct eye contact with the audience.

What major problems do you notice when speakers use notes?

## Voice

Your voice is your major tool in delivering your message. Let's look at how to use your voice more effectively. We distinguish five voice dimensions: volume, rate, pitch, articulation and pronunciation, and pauses. Manipulation of these elements will enable you to control your voice to maximum advantage.

REPRINTED WITH SPECIAL PERMISSION OF NORTH AMERICAN SYNDICATE, INC.

## Volume

*Volume* refers to the voice's relative intensity (loudness or softness). In an adequately controlled voice, volume varies according to such factors as the distance between you and your listeners, the competing noise, and the emphasis you wish to give an idea.

An obvious problem is a voice that is too low. If listeners have to strain to hear, they will soon tire of listening. On the other hand, a too loud voice will prove disturbing because it intrudes on the listeners' psychological space.

Vary your volume to best reflect your ideas—perhaps increasing volume for key words or phrases, lowering volume when talking about something extremely serious. Be especially careful not to fade away at the ends of sentences.

## Rate

*Rate* refers to the speed at which you speak. About 140 words per minute is average for speaking as well as for reading aloud. Speaking too fast, too slow, or with too little variation are the problems of rate . If you talk too fast, you deprive your listeners of time they need to digest what you are saying. If your rate is too slow, your listeners' thoughts will wander to unrelated matters. Therefore, speak at a pace that engages but doesn't bore and allows listeners time for reflection.

Vary your rate during the speech. Variations call a listener's attention to certain points and add variety. If you are interested in what you are saying, your rate variations should flow naturally and effectively.

## Pitch

Pitch refers to the relative highness or lowness of your voice as perceived by your listeners. Pitch results from the rate at which your vocal cords vibrate. If they vibrate rapidly, listeners will perceive a high pitch. If they vibrate slowly, listeners will perceive a low pitch.

Changes in pitch often signal changes in meanings. The most obvious is the difference between a statement and a question. Thus, the difference between the declarative sentence, "So this proposal represents our best interests" and the question "So this proposal represents our best interests?" is inflection, or pitch.

Problems of pitch include levels that are too high, too low, or too predictable. Neither of the first two is common in speakers with otherwise normal voices.

With practice, you can correct a pitch pattern that is too predictable or monotonous. Also with practice, pitch changes will come naturally from the sense of what you are saying. Because every sentence is different, there should be a normal variation—one that results from the meanings you wish to convey to the audience, not from some predetermined pattern.

How effective is your voice? What might improve it?

## Articulation and Pronunciation

Articulation and pronunciation are similar in that both refer to the way in which you produce sounds and words. *Articulation* refers to movements of the speech organs as they modify and interrupt the air stream you send from the lungs. Different movements (for example, of the tongue, lips, teeth, palate, or vocal cords) produce different sounds. *Pronunciation* refers to the production of syllables or words according to some accepted standard, such as that of a dictionary.

Our concern here is to identify and correct some of the most common problems associated with faulty articulation and pronunciation.

Everyone who speaks American English speaks a dialect (regional or social variety) of that language.
—ROBERT G. KING AND ELEANOR M. DIMICHAEL

### Articulation Problems

There are three general articulation problems: omission, substitution, and addition of sounds or syllables.

ERRORS OF OMISSION. Omitting sounds or even syllables is a major articulation problem but one easily overcome with concentration and practice. Here are some examples:

| Incorrect | Correct |
|-----------|---------|
| *gov-a-ment* | *gov-ern-ment* |
| *hi-stry* | *hi-sto-ry* |
| *wanna* | *want to* |
| *fishin* | *fishing* |
| *studyin* | *studying* |
| *a-lum-num* | *a-lum-i-num* |
| *hon-orble* | *hon-or-able* |
| *comp-ny* | *comp-a-ny* |
| *vul-ner-bil-ity* | *vul-ner-a-bil-ity* |

What articulation errors do you often hear in your classes?

ERRORS OF SUBSTITUTION. Substituting an incorrect sound for the correct one is also easy to correct. Among the most popular substitutions are [d] for [t] and [d] for [th]. Here are a few examples:

| Incorrect | Correct |
|-----------|---------|
| *wader* | *waiter* |
| *dese* | *these* |
| *ax* | *ask* |
| *undoubtebly* | *undoubtedly* |
| *bedder* | *better* |

Other types of substitution errors include:

| Incorrect | Correct |
|-----------|---------|
| *ekcetera* | *etcetera* |
| *ramark* | *remark* |
| *lenth* | *length* |

ERRORS OF ADDITION. These errors involve adding sounds where they do not belong. Some examples include:

| Incorrect | Correct |
|-----------|---------|
| *acrost* | *across* |
| *athalete* | *athlete* |
| *Americer* | *America* |
| *idear* | *idea* |
| *filim* | *film* |
| *lore* | *law* |

If you make any of these errors, you can easily correct them by following these steps:

1. Become conscious of your own articulation patterns (and the specific errors you are making).
2. Listen carefully to the articulation of prominent speakers (for example, broadcasters).
3. Practice the correct patterns until they become part of your normal speech behavior.

### Pronunciation Problems

Among the most common pronunciation problems are accenting the wrong syllable and adding sounds that do not belong.

ERRORS OF ACCENT. The following words are often accented incorrectly:

| Incorrect | Correct |
|-----------|---------|
| New Orleáns | New Órleans |
| ínsurance | insúrance |
| orátor | órator |

ERRORS OF ADDING SOUNDS. For some words, many people add sounds that are not part of the acceptable pronunciation. In the first three examples, the error is pronouncing letters that are a part of the word but should remain silent. In the last three examples, sounds are inserted where they do not belong.

| Incorrect | Correct |
|-----------|---------|
| *homage* | *omage* |
| *Illinois* | *Illinoi* |
| *evening* | *evning* |
| *athalete* | *athlete* |
| *airaplane* | *airplane* |
| *burgalar* | *burglar* |

**What words are you not sure about how to pronounce?**

The best way to correct pronunciation problems is to check a word's pronunciation in a dictionary. Learn to read your dictionary's pronunciation key.

### Pauses

Learn to pause...or nothing worthwhile will catch up to you.
—Doug King

There are two basic types of pauses: filled and unfilled. Filled pauses are those in the stream of speech that you fill with vocalizations such as *-er*, *-um*, and *-ah*. Even expressions such as *well* and *you know*, when used just to fill up silence, are filled pauses. These pauses are ineffective and weaken the strength of your message. They will make you appear hesitant, unprepared, and unsure.

Unfilled pauses, silences interjected into the stream of speech, can be especially effective if used correctly. Here are a few examples of places where unfilled pauses—silences of a few seconds—should prove effective.

**Why do you suppose speakers underuse the pause? In what ways is the pause overused?**

- Pause at transitional points. This will signal that you are moving from one part of the speech or from one idea to another. It will help listeners separate the main issues you are discussing.

- Pause at the end of an important assertion. This will let the audience think about its significance.

- Pause after asking a rhetorical question. This will give the audience time to think about how they would answer.

- Pause before an important idea. This will help signal that what comes next is especially significant.

In addition, pause before you begin your speech and after you finish it. Before beginning, pause to scan the audience and gather your thoughts. After your last sentence, pause to allow your speech to sink in. Don't give the audience the impression that you are anxious to leave them.

## Bodily Action

Your body is a powerful instrument in your speech. You speak with your body as well as with your mouth. The total effect of the speech depends not only on what you say but also on the way you present it. The five aspects of bodily action especially important in public speaking are eye contact, facial expression, posture, gestures, and movement.

## Eye Contact

Avoid the major eye contact problems: not enough and eye contact that does not cover the audience fairly. Speakers who do not maintain sufficient eye contact appear distant, unconcerned, and less trustworthy than speakers who look directly at their audience. And, of course, without eye contact, you will not be able to secure that all important audience feedback.

Maintain eye contact with the entire audience. Communicate equally with members on the left and on the right, in the back and the front.

## Facial Expression

Facial expressions are especially important in communicating emotions. If you believe in your thesis you will probably display your meanings appropriately and effectively.

Nervousness and anxiety, however, can prevent you from relaxing enough so that your emotions come through. But time and practice will allow you to relax, and your emotions will reveal themselves appropriately and automatically.

## Posture

When delivering your speech stand straight but not stiff. Try to communicate a command of the situation but not any nervousness you may feel.

Avoid putting your hands in your pockets. Avoid leaning on the desk, the podium, or the chalkboard. With practice you will feel more at ease and will communicate this in the way you stand before the audience.

## Gestures

Gestures help illustrate your verbal messages. We do this regularly in conversation. For example, when saying "Come here," you probably motion the listener in your direction with your head, hands, arms, and perhaps your entire body.

To be effective, bodily action should be spontaneous and natural. If you feel relaxed and comfortable with yourself and your audience, you will generate natural bodily action without conscious and studied attention.

## Movement

Movement keeps the audience (and you) more alert. Even when standing behind a lectern, you can give the illusion of movement. You can step back or forward or flex your upper body so it appears you are moving more than you are.

Avoid these three problems of movement: too little, too much, and too patterned. Speakers who move too little may appear fearful or distant. Too

How would you describe Arsenio Hall's delivery style? How would you describe your own? What would you like to improve? How might you make these improvements?

much movement may lead the audience to concentrate on the movement itself, wondering where you will wind up next. With too patterned movement, the audience may become bored.

Use greater movements to emphasize transitions and to introduce important assertions. For example, when making a transition, you might step forward to signal that something new is coming. Similarly, use this type of movement to signal an important assumption, bit of evidence, or closely reasoned argument.

## Rehearsal: Practicing and Improving Delivery

I am the most spontaneous speaker in the world because every word, every gesture, and every retort has been carefully rehearsed.
—GEORGE BERNARD SHAW

Effective delivery does not come naturally. It takes practice. Learn how to use your practice time effectively and efficiently. The goal is for you to develop a delivery that will help you achieve the purposes of your speech. Rehearsal should enable you to see how the speech will flow as a whole and to make any necessary changes and improvements. It will also enable you to time your speech so that you stay within the allotted time.

The following procedures should help you use your rehearsal time most effectively.

### Rehearse the Speech as a Whole

Rehearse the speech from beginning to end rather than in parts. Be sure to include all the examples and illustrations (and audiovisual aids if any).

### Time the Speech

Time the speech during each rehearsal. Adjust your speech—both what you say and your delivery rate—on the basis of this timing.

### Approximate the Actual Speech Situation

Rehearse the speech under conditions as close as possible to those under which you will deliver it. If possible, rehearse in the room in which you will present the speech and in front of a few supportive listeners. Get together with two or three other students in an empty classroom where you can each serve as speaker and listener.

### See Yourself as a Speaker

Rehearse the speech in front of a full-length mirror to help you see how you will appear to the audience. This will be difficult at first, and you may have to force yourself to watch yourself. After a few tries, however, you will begin to see the value of this experience. Practice your eye contact, your movements, and your gestures in front of the mirror.

### Incorporate Changes and Delivery Notes

Make any changes in the speech *between* rehearsals. Do not interrupt your rehearsal to make notes or changes. Insert pause notations, "slow down" warnings, and other suggestions into your delivery outline. If possible, record your speech (ideally, on videotape) so you can hear exactly what your listeners will hear.

### Rehearse Often

Rehearse at least three or four times or as long as your speech continues to improve.

## Evaluating the Speech

You will learn public speaking techniques largely from preparing and delivering speeches and from evaluations and feedback from others. In this section we consider some evaluation guidelines. First, what do we look for when evaluating a public speech? Second, how can we can best express our evaluations?

> The clock is always slow; it is later than you think.
> —ROBERT W. SERVICE

> It is necessary to have something more than knowledge of the subject. You must have earnestness in its presentation. You must feel that you have something to say that people ought to hear.
> —WILLIAM JENNINGS BRYAN

> What additional suggestions would you offer for effective speech rehearsal?

> [Criticism is] disinterested endeavour to learn and propagate the best that is known and thought in the world.
> —MATTHEW ARNOLD

## Guidelines for Speech Criticism

As a beginning guide to speech criticism, focus on the following questions which come from topics covered in this chapter as well as in Chapters 11 and 12. You can use these questions to check your own speeches as well as a guide to evaluating the speeches of others.

### The subject and purpose

1. Is the subject worthwhile?
2. Is the subject relevant and interesting to the audience and to the speaker?
3. What is the speech's general purpose (to inform, to persuade)?
4. Is the specific topic narrow enough to be covered in some depth in the time allotted?
5. Is the specific purpose clear to the audience? Is this clarity (or lack of it) appropriate to this speech for this audience?

### The audience

6. Has the speaker considered the age; sex; cultural factors; occupation, income, and status; and religion of the audience? How does the speech deal with these factors?
7. Is the topic appropriate to the general context?

### Research

8. Is the speech adequately researched?
9. Do the sources appear reliable and up to date?
10. Does the speaker seem to thoroughly understand the subject?

### The thesis and major propositions

11. Is the speech's thesis clear and limited to one main idea?
12. Are the speech's main propositions clearly related to the thesis?
13. Are the thesis and the major propositions clear to the audience?
14. Are there an appropriate number of major propositions in the speech (not too many, not too few)?

### Supporting materials

15. Is each major proposition adequately supported?
16. Are the supporting materials appropriate to the speech and to the propositions?
17. Do the supporting materials amplify what they purport to amplify? Do they prove what they purport to prove?
18. Are a variety of supporting materials used?
19. Are enough supporting materials used to clearly and forcefully present each of the major propositions?

## Organization

20. How is the body of the speech organized? What is the organization pattern?
21. Is the organization pattern appropriate to the speech topic? To the audience?
22. Is the organization pattern clear to the audience? Does it help the audience follow the speech?

## Style and language

23. Does the language help the audience to understand clearly and immediately what the speaker is saying? For example, are the words simple rather than complex, concrete rather than abstract? Are terms and sentence patterns personal and informal? Are sentences simple and active?

## The conclusion, the introduction, and transitions

What other questions would serve as useful guidelines to speech criticism?

24. Does the conclusion effectively summarize the speech's main points?
25. Does the conclusion effectively wrap up the speech and provide a recognizable closure?
26. Does the introduction gain the audience's attention?
27. Does the introduction provide an adequate and clear orientation to the subject matter?
28. Are there adequate transitions? Do the transitions help the audience better understand the speech's development?

## Delivery

What do you believe is the single most important factor in evaluating a public speech? Why?

29. Does the speaker maintain eye contact with the audience?
30. Are there any distractions (of mannerism, dress, or vocal characteristics) that will divert attention from the speech?
31. Can you easily hear the speaker?
32. Are the volume and rate appropriate to the audience, occasion, and topic?
33. Are the voice and bodily actions appropriate to the speaker, subject, and audience?

## The Speech Critique

How do you feel about receiving criticism of your speaking efforts?

It is helpful to have a form to record your evaluation of a particular speech. Here we present a critique form that is open ended and encourages comment on the effectiveness of the various steps. While providing some reminders of areas to look at, it also provides a rating system for evaluating essential areas and some reminders of areas to work on.

## Speech Critique Form

*EVALUATION KEY:*  1 = excellent;  2 = good;  3 = fair;  4 = needs improvement;  5 = needs lots of improvement

*CIRCLE* or *UNDERSCORE* items the speaker needs to *Work on;* write in additional items requiring attention.

SPEAKER _____  DATE _____

SPEECH _____

_____ **Subject and purpose**
*Work on:* selecting more worthwhile subject, relating to audience, clarifying purpose, making purpose clear to audience

_____ **Audience Analysis and Adaption**
*Work on:* Relating topic and support to specific audience, occasion, and context

_____ **Research**
*Work on:* doing more extensive research, using more convincing sources, integrating sources into speech.

_____ **Thesis and Major Propositions**
*Work on:* clarifying your thesis, stating propositions more clearly, relating propositions to thesis

_____ **Supporting Materials**
*Work on:* using more support, using more varied support, relating support more directly to your propositions, establishing your credibility

_____ **Organization**
*Work on:* using a clear thought pattern, making pattern clear to audience

_____ **Style and Language**
*Work on:* clarity, vividness, appropriateness, personal style, forcefulness

_____ **Conclusion**
*Work on:* summary, closure

_____ **Introduction**
*Work on:* gaining attention, orienting audience

_____ **Transitions**
*Work on:* including more transitions, integrating transitions more smoothly into speech

_____ **Delivery**
*Work on:* volume, rate, pitch, quality, articulation, pronunciation, pauses, eye contact, facial expressions, posture, gestures, movement

_____ **General Evaluation**

## Expressing Your Evaluations

The major purpose of classroom evaluation is to improve your public speaking technique. Through constructive criticism you, as a speaker and as a listener-critic, will more effectively learn the principles of public speaking. You will be shown what you do well and what you can improve.

For all its benefits, however, we often resist critical evaluations. The main source of resistance seems to be that evaluations are often expressed in a manner that encourages defensiveness. Criticisms often appear as personal attacks. We offer the following suggestions to make critical evaluations a more effective part of the total learning process.

SAY SOMETHING POSITIVE. Egos are fragile and public speaking is extremely personal. Recall that part of your function as a critic is to strengthen the already positive aspects of someone's public speaking performance. Positive criticism is particularly important in itself, but it is almost essential as a preface to negative comments. There are always positive characteristics, and it is more productive to concentrate on them first.

BE SPECIFIC. Criticism is most effective when it is specific. Statements such as "I thought your delivery was bad" or "I thought your examples were good" are poorly expressed criticisms. These statements do not specify how the speaker might improve delivery or capitalize on the examples. In commenting on delivery, refer to such specifics as eye contact, vocal volume, or whatever else is of consequence. In commenting on the examples, tell the speaker why they were good. Were they realistic? Were they especially interesting? Were they presented dramatically?

In giving negative criticism, specify and justify—to the extent that you can—positive alternatives. Here is an example:

> I thought the way you introduced your statistics was vague. I wasn't sure where they came from or how recent or reliable they were. It might have been better to say something like 'The 1990 U.S. Census figures show that. . . .' In this way we would know that the statistics were recent and the most reliable available.

BE OBJECTIVE. In criticizing a speech, transcend your own biases as best you can. See the speech as objectively as possible. Assume, for example, that you strongly support women's right to abortion. You encounter a speech diametrically opposed to your position. In this situation, you would need to take special care not to dismiss the speech because of your own bias. Examine the speech from the point of view of the (detached) critic. Evaluate, for example, the validity of the arguments and their suitability to the audience, the language, the supporting materials. Analyze, in fact, all the ingredients that went into the speech's preparation and presentation.

Conversely, take special care not to evaluate a speech positively *because* it presents a position with which you agree. Submit this speech to the same objective evaluation. Similarly, when evaluating a speech by a

I love criticism just as long as it's unqualified praise.
—NOEL COWARD

What principle for expressing critical evaluations do you most often see violated? What effect does such violation have on the speaker? On the audience?

What additional principles would you suggest for effectively expressing critical evaluations?

Do not use a hatchet to remove a
fly from your friend's forehead.
—CHINESE PROVERB

What guidelines would you offer
a speaker for receiving the critical evaluations of classmates?

speaker you feel strongly about—whether positively or negatively—be
equally vigilant. A disliked speaker may give an effective, well-con-
structed, well-delivered speech. And, a well-liked speaker may give an
ineffective, poorly constructed, poorly delivered speech.

BE CONSTRUCTIVE. Criticism should be constructive. Do not use criticism to demonstrate your own expertise or to air your personal views.
Certainly there is no need to hide your knowledge of the subject. Nor is
there a need to hide opposing views. However, your primary goal
should be to provide the speaker with insight that will prove useful in
future public speaking transactions.

REMEMBER THE IRREVERSIBILITY OF COMMUNICATION. Communication is irreversible. Once something is said, it cannot be unsaid.
Remember this when offering criticism, especially when it may be too
negative. If in doubt, err on the side of gentleness.

# FEEDBACK

In this chapter we looked at effective public speaking style and delivery.

**1.** The preferred style in public speaking is **oral style.** Compared with written style, oral style contains shorter, simpler, and more familiar words; greater qualification; and more self-referential terms.

**2. Clarity** may be best achieved by being economical and specific. Use guide phrases; short, familiar, and commonly-used terms; and repetition, restatement, and internal summaries.

**3. Vividness** may be best achieved by using active verbs, strong verbs, figures of speech, and imagery.

**4.** Make your style **appropriate** to your audience by speaking on a suitable level of formality, and by avoiding unfamiliar, foreign, and technical terms, jargon, acronyms, slang and vulgar terms, and offensive expressions.

**5. Personal style** may be best achieved by using personal pronouns, asking questions, and creating immediacy.

**6. Forcefulness** may be best achieved by eliminating weakeners, avoiding bromides and clichés, and varying intensity as appropriate.

**7.** In **constructing sentences** for public speeches, favor short, direct, active, and positively phrased sentences. Vary the type and length.

**8.** There are three general **methods for delivering public speeches:** impromptu, manuscript, and extemporaneous.

**9.** The **impromptu method** involves speaking without any specific preparation. The **manuscript method** involves writing out the entire speech and reading it to the audience. The **extemporaneous method** involves thorough preparation, and memorizing the main ideas and their order of appearance, but no commitment to exact wording.

**10.** Adjust your **volume** on the basis of the distance between you and your audience, the amount of competing noise, the room's acoustics, and the emphasis you wish to give certain ideas.

**11.** Adjust your **rate** on the basis of time constraints, the speech's content, and the listening conditions.

**12.** Adjust your **pitch** (the relative highness or lowness of the voice) on the basis of the meanings you wish to communicate.

**13.** Avoid the major **problems of articulation and pronunciation:** errors of omission, substitution, addition, accent, and adding sounds.

**14.** Use **pauses** to signal a transition between the major parts of the speech, to allow the audience time to think, to allow the audience to ponder a rhetorical question, and to signal the approach of a particularly important idea.

**15.** Effective **bodily action** involves maintaining eye contact with your entire audience, allowing your facial expressions to convey your feelings, using your posture to communicate command of the public speaking interaction, gesturing naturally, and moving around a bit.

**16.** Use **rehearsal** to time your speech; perfect your volume, rate, and pitch; incorporate pauses and other delivery notes; and perfect your bodily action.

**17.** In **expressing critical evaluations** try to say something positive, be specific, be objective, be constructive, and remember the irreversibility of communication.

Several significant skills for style and delivery were stressed in this chapter. Check your mastery.

_____ 1. I word my speech so that it is (1) clear, (2) vivid, (3) appropriate, (4) personal, and (5) forceful.

_____ 2. I construct sentences that are short, direct, active, and positive and vary the type and length of sentences.

_____ 3. In general, I use the extemporaneous method of delivery.

_____ 4. I vary my vocal volume, rate, and pitch so as to best reflect and reinforce my verbal messages. I avoid the common problems with volume, rate, and pitch.

_____ 5. I avoid the articulation and pronunciation errors of omission, substitution, addition, accent, and pronouncing sounds that should be silent.

_____ 6. I use pauses to signal transitions, to allow listeners time to think, and to signal the approach of a significant idea.

_____ 7. During the speech delivery, I maintain eye contact with the entire audience, allow my facial expressions to convey my feelings, gesture naturally, and incorporate some general body movements.

_____ 8. I rehearse my speech often, perfect my vocal and bodily delivery, rehearse the speech as a whole, time the speech at each rehearsal, approximate the specific speech situation as much as possible, see and think of myself as a public speaker, and incorporate any delivery notes that may be of value during the actual speech presentation.

_____ 9. In expressing critical evaluations of the speeches of others I try to say something positive, be specific, be objective, be constructive, and remember the irreversibility of communication.

# SKILL DEVELOPMENT EXPERIENCES

**13.1  BE SPECIFIC**

One of the major skills in public speaking is learning to make your ideas specific so that your listeners will understand exactly what you want them to understand. Rewrite each of the following ten sentences to make the italicized terms more specific.

1. The *woman* walked up the *hill* with her *children*.
2. The *teacher* was discussing *economics*.
3. The *player scored*.
4. The *teenager* was listening to a *record*.
5. No one in the *city* thought the *mayor* was doing anything useful.
6. The *girl* and the *boy* each received lots of *presents*.
7. I read the *review* of the *movie*.
8. The *couple* rented a great *car*.
9. The *detective* wasn't much help in solving the *crime*.
10. The *children* were playing an old *game*.

**13.2  CLIMBING UP AND DOWN THE ABSTRACTION LADDER**

The "abstraction ladder" shows that there are degrees of verbal abstraction.

Notice in the chart that as we go from "animal" to "pampered white toy poodle" we are descending to lower levels of abstraction; that is, we are getting more and more specific. And as we do so, we communicate our meanings more clearly and hold the listener's attention more easily.

For each term listed, indicate at least four possible terms that indicate increasing specificity.

| Level 1 | Level 2 more specific than 1 | Level 3 more specific than 2 | Level 4 more specific than 3 | Level 4 more specific than 4 |
|---|---|---|---|---|
| animal | dog | poodle | toy poodle | pampered white toy poodle |
| house | | | | |
| goal | | | | |
| desire | | | | |
| car | | | | |
| toy | | | | |
| machine | | | | |
| message | | | | |
| sports | | | | |

## 13.3 THE IMPROMPTU SPEECH

The following experience may prove useful as an exercise in delivery. Students should be given three index cards each. Each student should write an impromptu speech topic on each card. The cards should be collected and placed face down on a table. A speaker, chosen randomly, selects two cards, reads the topics, selects one and takes approximately one minute to prepare a two- to three-minute impromptu speech.

A few guidelines follow:

1. Do not apologize. Everyone will have difficulty with this assignment, so there is no need to emphasize any problems you may have.
2. Do not express verbally or nonverbally any displeasure or any negative responses to the experience, the topic, the audience, or even to oneself. Approach the entire task with a positive attitude and appearance. It will help make the experience more enjoyable for both you and your audience.
3. When you select the topic, jot down two or three subtopics you will cover and perhaps two or three bits of supporting material you will use to amplify these subtopics.
4. Develop your conclusion. It probably will be best to use a simple summary conclusion in which you restate your main topic and the subordinate topics you discussed.
5. Develop an introduction. Here it probably will be best to simply identify your topic and orient the audience by telling them the two or three subtopics you will cover.

Topics for impromptu speaking should be familiar but not clichés. They should be worthwhile and substantive, not trivial. They should be neither too simplistic nor too complex. Here are some sample topics to use in lieu of the above procedure.

1. The values of a college education
2. What makes someone attractive
3. How to meet another person
4. What is love
5. What is friendship
6. How to resolve conflict
7. How to communicate with your family
8. What is success
9. What makes a person happy
10. Places to visit
11. Things to do
12. An ideal day
13. An ideal relationship
14. An ideal occupation
15. An ideal lover
16. An unusual pet
17. Tough decisions
18. My favorite movie
19. My favorite television show
20. My favorite sport
21. My favorite meal
22. My favorite character from literature
23. Unusual pastimes
24. An important moment from history
25. A current national concern
26. My hero
27. What I hate most
28. The type of person I dislike
29. What to do on a Saturday night
30. How not to be a good student
31. How to survive in college
32. How to say "I love you"
33. How to hurt someone you love
34. Body language
35. Contemporary music
36. Dreams
37. Happiness is…
38. How to say "no"
39. If I had three wishes
40. College life in the year 2000

## 13.4 ANALYZING A SPEECH

The following speech provides you with an opportunity to apply the principles and insights learned in these three chapters on public speaking. Analyze this speech, considering some or all of the following questions:

1. What type of speech is this? Informative? Persuasive?
2. What is the speech's specific purpose?
3. What is the thesis?
4. What is its organizational pattern?
5. What functions does the introduction serve?
6. What functions does the conclusion serve?
7. What types of amplifying materials are used? Are they appropriate? Do they help the speaker achieve her purpose? How might they have been improved?
8. What kinds of reasoning does this speaker use? Does the reasoning pass the tests for critically analyzing reasoning discussed in Chapter 12?
9. What kinds of psychological appeals are used? Are they effective? How might they have been made more effective?

10. What kinds of credibility appeals does the speaker use? Are they effective? How might they have been made more effective?
11. Describe the style of this speech? What style qualities can you identify? How might the style have been improved? What would you title this speech?
12. Assume that this speech was delivered in your class. Was the speaker's audience analysis and adaptation effective? How might the speaker have more closely adapted the speech to your specific class?

**Persuasive Speaking Final Round Winner***

Recently, I saw a commercial on television for a major pest control company. The commercial depicted a young couple frantic that their home would be consumed by termites. So, like many Americans they called the Terminix man who came to their house, killed the termites, and saved the day. As I watched the commercial though, I thought about Beatrice Nelson. Beatrice Nelson, a middle-aged Colorado housewife, found herself lost and disoriented one evening two years ago. Her husband rushed her to a nearby emergency room where she was examined by toxicologist, Dr. Daniel Tautlebaum.

Tautlebaum found that Beatrice was so confused that she could not remember days of the week or the names of any U.S. Presidents. He was bewildered until he was told that a month earlier Beatrice had an exterminator at her house to spray for termites, as she puts it, just to be safe. Ironically, the result of that action made Beatrice anything but safe. The exterminator used a nerve-damaging pesticide called chlordane, which was not only effective in ridding the home of termites, but in robbing Beatrice of part of her mind. Even now, Bea cannot pass simple neurological tests, or remember simple details of her life.

Unfortunately, Bea is not alone. In fact, the Environmental Protection Agency Hotline, which is an 800-number set up for reporting complaints, problems, and illnesses associated with pesticides, received over 7,500 phone calls concerning chlordane last year alone. And, according to the National

*Speech by Jan Moreland. From 1987 *Championship Debates and Speeches* ed. by John K. Boaz and James R. Brey, American Forensic Association, 1987. Reprinted by permission.

Coalition Against the Misuse of Pesticides, or N-CAMP, there are currently eighty-four cases in litigation against the manufacturers of chlordane and the pest control companies who use it.

Obviously, the problem of chlordane poisoning is not a small one. But what is more frightening is that there is nothing being done to prevent exterminators from using the chemical around our homes. Now, the impact of chlordane poisoning cannot be fully understood until we first look at the problem surrounding the chemical, then, examine why it's still on the market, and, finally, discuss some solutions that prevent any further harm.

Perhaps the director of the citizens group People Against Chlordane, Pat Manichino, said it best when he said, "The problem is not the use or application of the chemical. The problem is chlordane, and until we face that fact, the problem will never be solved. You see, chlordane is a termiticide that attacks the central nervous systems in termites. Unfortunately, it can have the same effect on human beings as well."

The chemical is so dangerous, in fact, that in 1982 the National Academy of Sciences conducted a study for the United States Air Force to determine the level of chlordane contamination in their own base homes. The study's finding, there is no level below which no adverse biological effects will occur. And the study went on to say that at a level of only five micrograms per cubic meter of air, a home should be evacuated. Now the frightening fact here is that according to a January 1987 report on National Public Radio, over three-hundred thousand homes will be treated with chlordane this year alone. Three-hundred thousand homes treated with a chemical that is unsafe at any level.

Now, the EPA disputes this evidence, and believes that proper training of exterminators and proper application of the chemical would prevent contaminations. But the EPA should have done their homework. Four years ago, health officials in New York and Massachusetts were so concerned about chlordane poisoning that they placed several restrictions on the chemical's use and application. But, according to Nancy Ridley of the Massachusetts Health Department, none of the restrictions were effective. She said, "We had just as many cases reported and our restrictions were much tighter than the ones the EPA is proposing."

In addition, the Belsicoff Corporation, the manufacturers of chlordane, stated in a June 1984 issue of *Pest Control Technology* that, "It is impossible to eliminate risks, spills, or accidents on any given job using chlordane." And there's a catch. Even when the chemical is applied properly, contaminations occur.

According to a study conducted by Ross Lighty, chemist at North Carolina State University, air samples were taken in homes where the application of chlordane was strictly supervised and label instructions were followed to the letter. The air samples revealed levels approaching five micrograms per cubic meter, the same level at which the NAS recommends evacuation. Pat Manichino states that any regulation that allows for the use and application of the chemical cannot prevent spills or accidents and, therefore, they are all inadequate.

Manichino's point is well taken. The continued use of chlordane has prompted thousands of phone calls yearly to organizations such as the EPA hotline and N-CAMP complaining of adverse symptoms from chlordane. For example, Kelly Purdell of Houston, Texas began to feel so confused and, well, "crazy" as she puts it, that she was ready to admit herself to a psychiatric ward before officials found high levels of chlordane in her home and condemned it. The home of the Delaney family was so contaminated that Charleston officials condemned it as well. But perhaps the worst example is that of Charles Hanson. When his home became contaminated two years ago, he and his family were forced to evacuate, forced to live in rented houses and motels. They're still making mortgage payments on their contaminated home.

You see, what we need to understand is that when a family evacuates their home, they are likely never to return. According to a 1983 publication entitled "EPA Facts," published by the EPA, once a home is contaminated with chlordane, it cannot be decontaminated until the chemical dissipates which can take 20 to 25 years.

Well, now that we know that we are dealing with such a dangerous chemical you might be asking yourself, "Why is it still on the market?" Good question. And the EPA believes they have an answer. EPA official Doug Camp states that there is not enough evidence to suggest that enough people have been harmed. Good answer, Doug. But, in defense of the agency, it is important to understand that evidence is not always readily available, because the public is generally uninformed. For example, when was the last time you asked your Orkin representative what he uses to kill termites? Or better yet, when was the last time you suffered a headache, sore throat, sinus problems, or any number of other minor ailments and attributed them to your exterminator? It never comes to mind, does it? And, according to Diane Baxter of N-CAMP, that's part of the problem. She states that some of the symptoms can begin so subtly, that we don't even consider the idea that we may have been poisoned.

Now, at this point it is important for me to tell you that no deaths have been linked to chlordane so far. And according to Leah Wise of the Massachusetts Health Department, that's another reason the chemical hasn't been removed from the market. She says, "In this country we tend to be more concerned with mortality than morbidity, so if people are just getting sick we don't pay too much attention."

The scope of the chlordane problem has become too broad for any of us to ignore any longer. Especially when we consider that homes have been contaminated to the point of condemnation and people have suffered permanent neurological damage while the EPA sits by and watches. Well, they say there is not enough evidence to suggest that enough people have been harmed. Until, and if that evidence is found, the EPA will not ban chlordane. Not enough evidence? How many people have to suffer permanent neurological damage before we have enough evidence?

Now, at this point it should be obvious that some kind of a solution needs to be found. Perhaps a solution like the one implemented by New York, Massachusetts and the Federal Government of Japan: ban chlordane. But we have already heard the EPA's answer to that request. So, it appears then that we are faced with two choices. Either run the risk of termites eating us out of house and home so to speak, or endangering our health in an effort to stop them. Well, lucky those are not our only two choices. Since their banning chlordane in 1984, New York and Massachusetts have been using a new chemical called Dursban. Now Dursban is as effective as chlordane, but doesn't produce the same devastating effects.

Well, it seems these two states are on the right track, but the EPA is standing firm. As consumers, though, we don't have to remain passive victims of chlordane poisoning. There are solutions we can actively pursue now without waiting for the EPA.

Of course, each one of us has already taken a step toward one solution: we are informed. It is now our responsibility to inform others. Make your family and friends aware that their health may be in danger every time an exterminator comes to their home.

The second solution. As responsible consumers we need to be aware of the steps that we can take to protect ourselves against poisoning. The first is to call an exterminator before he comes to your home and ask him if he uses chlordane or if we have a choice as to which chemical he will use around our home. If the exterminator tells you he uses chlordane, tell him you will not patronize his services for that reason. If pest control companies become aware that they are losing business because of chlordane, they may stop using it.

Also, we need to make agencies such as the EPA aware when we do experience problems with a chemical. They want evidence, let's give it to them. We can do this by notifying the Environmental Protection Agency Hotline. Now, if you would like that phone number I will be available after this speech to give you that number and the numbers of N-CAMP and People Against Chlordane. These can get you in touch with someone who can help you if you feel that you or someone you know has been poisoned. Also, if you have any questions about the chemical. The final step that we as individuals can take is to ask our local health departments to check any home that we are considering to buy or rent for high levels of chlordane.

The use of chlordane must be stopped. And the responsibility lies with us. A combination of the individual steps that we can take and the national level steps the EPA should take, can prevent our families, our friends, and ourselves from ever suffering the painful consequences from chlordane poisoning. Yes, as that commercial depicted we may be frantic over the fear of termites, but perhaps we should be afraid of the exterminator as well.

## 13.5 ANALYZING A SPEECH OUTLINE

Here is a full sentence speech outline. Analyze this outline against the organization standards that were considered throughout the public speaking discussion (Chapters 11-13). Does the outline follow the suggestions? How might you improve the outline? What other information should the outline contain?

Some instructors want preliminary information to be included in the outline. For example, it is often helpful, as a preface to the outline, to identify the general and specific purposes and the thesis. After reading the outline, how would you identify the general purpose? The specific purpose? The thesis?

You may find it helpful to review the outline and indicate the specific function that each item serves, for example, to gain attention, to orient, to summarize, to state major proposition, to support the first major proposition, and so on.

## Revealing Yourself to Others

### Introduction

I. If you want to get to know yourself better, reveal yourself: Self-disclose.

    A. This may sound peculiar, but it is supported by much scientific research.

    B. Self-disclosure can lead you to feel better about yourself but can also lead to many problems.

    C. Understanding self-disclosure can help you make the most effective use of this most important communication form.

II. In order to understand self-disclosure, we need to focus on two aspects.

    A. Self-disclosure is a form of communication in which you reveal information about yourself that is normally kept hidden.

    B. Self-disclosure involves both rewards and problems.

[Let's consider first the definition of self-disclosure.]

### Body

I. Self-disclosure is a form of communication in which you reveal information about yourself that is normally kept hidden.

    A. Self-disclosure is a type of communication.

        1. Self-disclosure includes overt statements.

            a. An overt confession of infidelity to your lover is self-disclosure.

            b. A letter explaining why you committed a crime is self-disclosure.

        2. Self-disclosure includes slips of the tongue and other unintentional communications.

a. A slip of the tongue in which you reveal that you are really in love with your best friend's spouse is self-disclosure.

b. An uncontrollable rage in which you tell your boss all the horrible things you've kept inside is self-disclosure.

3. Self-disclosure is not noncommunication.

a. Writing personal thoughts in a diary that no one sees is not self-disclosure.

b. Talking to yourself when no one overhears is not self-disclosure.

B. Self-disclosure involves information about the self not previously known by the listeners.

1. Telling people something about someone else is not self-disclosure.

a. Self-disclosure involves the self.

b. Self-disclosing statements begin with "I."

2. Telling people what they already know is not self-disclosure.

C. Self-disclosure involves information normally kept hidden.

1. Self-disclosure does not involve information that you do not actively keep secret.

2. Self-disclosure involves only information that you work at to keep hidden, that you expend energy in hiding.

[This, then, is what self-disclosure is; now let us focus on what self-disclosure may involve.]

II. Self-disclosure involves both rewards and problems.

A. There are three main rewards of self-disclosure

1. First, you get to know yourself better.

a. Talking about my fear of snakes led me to understand the reasons for such fears.

b. Results from studies show that persons who disclose have greater self-awareness than do those who do not self-disclose.

2. Second, you can deal with your problems better.

a. Dealing with guilt is a prime example.

b. Studies conducted by Civikly, Hecht, and me show that personal problems are more easily managed after self-disclosure.

3. Third, you release a great deal of energy.

a. It takes energy to keep secrets.

b. After self-disclosure, people feel more relaxed, sleep better, and have a higher energy level than before self-disclosure.

B. There are three major dangers of self-disclosure.

1. First, self-disclosure may involve personal problems.

a. The fear of rejection may be more damaging than retaining the secrets.

b. Self-disclosure may bring to the surface problems that you are not psychologically ready to deal with.

2. Second, self-disclosure may involve professional problems.

a. A number of ex-convicts who disclosed their criminal records have been fired.

b. Persons who revealed they were treated by psychiatrists have had their political careers ruined.

3. Third, self-disclosure may involve social problems.

a. Peer groups will often withdraw social support.

b. Friends and even relatives may reject you.

[Let me summarize some of what we now know about self-disclosure.]

## Conclusion

    I. Self-disclosure is a unique form of communication

        A. Self-disclosure is a form of communication in which you reveal information about yourself that is normally kept hidden.

        B. Rewards and problems await self-disclosure.

    II. So, if you want to get to know yourself better, self-disclose.

### 13.6 THE SKELETAL OUTLINE

Here is a skeletal outline—a kind of template for structuring a speech. This particular outline would be appropriate for a speech using a time, topical, or spatial organizational pattern. Note that in this skeletal outline there are three major propositions (I, II, and III in the Body). These correspond to the II A, B, and C in the introduction where you would orient the audience and the I A, B, and C in the conclusion where you would summarize your major propositions. The transitions are signaled by square brackets.

    Construct a similar skeletal outline for a speech using one of the other organizational patterns discussed in Chapter 11: problem-solution pattern, cause-effect/effect-cause pattern, or the motivated sequence pattern.

---

**Introduction**

    I. _____.

    II. _____.

        A. _____.

        B. _____.

        C. _____.

[                             ]

**Body**

    I. _____.

        A. _____.

        B. _____.

[                             ]

    II. _____.

        A. _____.

        B. _____.

[                             ]

    III. _____.

        A. _____.

        B. _____.

[                             ]

**Conclusion**

    I. _____.

        A. _____.

        B. _____.

        C. _____.

    II. _____.

# PART TWO
# CRITICAL THINKING
# PERSPECTIVES AND
# REVIEW

In this end-of-the-part summary we continue to identify and highlight the communication principles that are especially relevant to critical thinking. Recognize that the principles noted here, although discussed under headings of interpersonal, small group, or public communication, apply to all forms of human communication. Thus, for example, although we discuss the fallacies of reasoning in the public speaking chapters, they are relevant to interpersonal and small group communication as well. Similarly, the principles of mindfulness and flexibility discussed in the interpersonal section are also relevant to small group and public communication.

## Critically Assess and Use Interpersonal Communication Strategies

For interpersonal communication to be effective, its principles must be applied mindfully and flexibly. Because each communication event is unique, you need to be flexible. However, strategies that proved effective in one situation might prove ineffective in another (Chapter 6).

In regulating openness, empathy, supportiveness, positiveness, equality, confidence display, immediacy, interaction management, expressiveness, and other-orientation be sensitive to the specific elements making up the unique communication situation (Chapter 6, Skill Development Experience 6.1, 6.2). Be aware that members of different cultures would respond differently to these qualities and would display them with different verbal and nonverbal behaviors.

Develop awareness of how others try to persuade you to do as they wish (compliance-gaining strategies, SDEx 12.2) or to like them (affinity-seeking strategies, SDEx 7.2). Critically assess these strategies to avoid appeals that may convince you

to do things against your wishes or to believe things that are not true.

## Critically Analyze Interpersonal Conflict

Conflict is inevitable. Thinking critically about conflict, and particularly those strategies you and others use to resolve it, can turn a potentially damaging experience into a positive and productive one (Chapter 6, SDEx 6.3, 6.4, 6.6).

Avoidance, force, minimization, blame, silencers, gunnysacking, manipulation, and personal rejection will almost always prevent meaningful conflict resolution. Analyze the consequences of such strategies and recognize them in your own behaviors as well as in others (SDEx 6.7).

Instead fight above the belt, fight actively, take responsibility for your thoughts and feelings, be direct and specific, and use humor for relief never for ridicule.

## Critically Analyze Problems

Problems are best analyzed and eventually resolved by following a logical sequence of steps (Chapter 9, SDEx 9.1) These same steps are also useful in dealing with and resolving interpersonal conflicts (Chapter 6).

1. Define and analyze the problem. For example, use the six hats techniques—fact, feeling, negative argument, positive benefits, creative new idea, and the control of thinking hat (Chapter 9).
2. Establish criteria for evaluating solutions.
3. Identify possible solutions. Use the suggestions for brainstorming (Chapter 9).
4. Evaluate solutions.
5. Select the best solution.
6. Test the selected solution.

*Although many have spoken for women's rights throughout history, the contemporary women's movement began largely in response to Betty Friedan's* The Feminine Mystique *(1963). She challenged assumptions about women's roles that most had simply accepted and raised issues that are still being debated. She thus helped us to think differently about women as well as about men and about female-male relationships. If you were to write a book in a similar tradition, what existing assumptions (about women and men, race, national and international relations, education, sexual behavior, religion, etc.) would you challenge? What arguments might you offer to support your challenge?*

## Critically Assess Information

You can't think about very much without information, so part of the process of critical thinking involves accumulating and critically assessing information. Not all information is equally relevant or equally valid. Thinking critically about information will help you separate the valuable from the irrelevant.

Secure information from a variety of sources (Chapter 11, SDEx 11.5, 11.6). For example, this

textbook—as all textbooks—summarizes and develops research and theory applications. In its summary function, it is a secondary source. Although textbook authors try to be both thorough and objective, there is much we are forced to omit. Similarly, like anyone else, we have biases that influence the topics we include and exclude, the research and theory we present, and the emphasis we give to the topics. Recognize that textbooks are subjective presentations. When you come upon a topic particularly important to you, seek out additional sources of information. Insofar as possible, avail yourself of the primary source material as well, for example, the research studies and theories cited throughout the text.

While you're looking up primary source material, familiarize yourself with your library. Learn where the reference materials you will need most are located; about interlibrary loans and how to use the materials on film. Similarly, learn how to access relevant data bases, either through your own computer or one at school.

Talk with those who know what you want to know. Whether it's the secrets of popularity or the reasons for the recession, someone will have worthwhile information that is easily available. Your college faculty is probably the most concentrated group of knowledgeable individuals that you will ever come across. Use them and appropriate others.

## Critically Evaluate the Validity of Persuasive Appeals

Persuasive appeals come in three major forms: credibility, emotional and logical. *Credibility appeals* present the speaker or advocate as competent, moral, and charismatic; in short, as believable (SDEx 12.5). *Emotional appeals* are directed to people's basic needs and desires, for example, their desire for wealth or status or their fear of failure (SDEx 12.4). Although both credibility and emotional appeals are effective in motivating people to believe or to do certain things, they do not constitute proof; they are not evidence.

*Logical appeals* are proof; they offer evidence. These are the only valid appeals. Many arguments, however, may seem to offer logical proof but are actually fallacious. Generally, support should be as recent as possible and corroborated by other sources, if possible. It should emerge from sources that are unbiased (SDEx 12.3).

In using and in listening to arguments, use your critical reasoning abilities. Apply the tests discussed here (Chapter 12) for reasoning from specific instances to a generalization, from analogy, from cause and effect, and from sign.

Also, become alert to the common reasoning fallacies of name calling, glittering generality, transfer, testimonial, plain folks, card stacking, and band wagon (Chapter 12).

Mastery of these ten critical thinking principles (the five covered here and the five covered in the Part I summary) represents a major step in your developing these important skills. As already noted, these principles are not limited to communication and, in fact, will prove useful in all your activities and throughout your personal, academic, and professional lives.

Here are some suggested readings to help you continue your study of critical thinking. They expand and add to much that we covered.

Albrecht, Karl. *Brain Power: Learn to Improve Your Thinking Skills.* Englewood Cliffs, NJ: Prentice-Hall [Spectrum], 1980.

Allen, Steve. *Dumbth and 81 Ways to Make Americans Smarter.* Buffalo, NY: Prometheus Books, 1991.

Gross, Ronald. *Peak Learning.* Los Angeles: Jeremy P. Tarcher, 1991.

McCarthy, Michael J. *Mastering the Information Age.* Los Angeles: Jeremy P. Tarcher, 1991.

Ruchlis, Hy. *Clear Thinking: A Practical Introduction.* Buffalo, NY: Prometheus Books, 1990.

Ruggiero, Vincent Ryan. *The Art of Thinking: A Guide to Critical and Creative Thought,* 3rd ed. New York: HarperCollins, 1990.

---

## Critical Thinking Experience

### Thinking Critically about the Contexts of Human Communication

The objectives of this exercise are (1) to provide practice in applying critical thinking skills to the analysis and evaluation of a variety of assertions about interpersonal, small group, and public communication and (2) to provide a useful procedure for reviewing some of the major propositions about human communication covered in Chapters 6 through 13.

Presented are 40 assertions about the contexts of human communication. In small groups or with the class as a whole, analyze and evaluate each statement. Here are a few questions that might prove useful in your analysis:

1. Is the statement suitably qualified? Or, for example, is it too general? Does the statement—for example, "All relationships pass through the same stages"—take into consideration relevant cultural, gender, and situational differences? What changes will make it more accurate?

2. Is the statement adequately supported by research evidence? For example, is there evidence to support the statement "Emotional appeals are more effective than logical appeals"?

3. Does the statement assert that a causal relationship exists when there is no evidence? For example, the statement "Democratic leadership results in greater productivity of the group" asserts a causal relationship—that democratic leadership causes greater productivity.

#### Interpersonal Context

1. (*attraction*) The more we reward people, the more they will like us; similarly, the more we reward people, the more we will like them.

2. (*attraction*) Opposites attract and birds of a feather flock together.

3. (*matching hypothesis*) People date and mate those who are about as physically attractive as they are.

4. (*depth and breadth in interpersonal relationships*) Developing relationships increase in breadth and depth while deteriorating relationships decrease in breadth and depth.

5. (*reasons for interpersonal relationships*) All relationships are designed or entered into to lessen loneliness.

6. (*stages in interpersonal relationships*) Initiating a relationship is the most difficult of all the stages.

7. (*openness in interpersonal relationships*) The more open and honest people are, the better and more satisfying their relationships will be.

8. (*interpersonal relationships*) The more positive a person is in a relationship, the more satisfying the relationship will be.

9. (*self-monitoring in interpersonal relationships*) People who self-monitor in close relationships are being dishonest and are violating the principles of openness.

10. (*interpersonal relationships*) We develop and maintain relationships in which the rewards are greater than the costs and do not develop or maintain (or even exit) relationships in which the costs are greater than the rewards.
11. (*interpersonal conflict*) Remaining silent in an interpersonal conflict will aggravate the conflict.
12. (*interpersonal conflict*) A partner in a relationship who fights fairly while the other fights to win will soon lose the respect of the other and perhaps even self-respect.
13. (*interpersonal conflict*) Gunnysacking will damage an interpersonal relationship.
14. (*interviewing*) An interviewee should never answer questions that are technically illegal.
15. (*interviewing*) It is best for the interviewee to come to the job interview with clearly defined answers to anticipated questions.

### Small Group Context
1. (*small group norms*) Members should always discover and follow the norms of the group they will work in or with.
2. (*problem solving groups*) Members should always establish criteria for evaluating solutions *before* they identify possible solutions.
3. (*personal growth groups*) Members who enter personal growth groups must commit to total honesty at all times and on all topics.
4. (*small group formats*) The panel or round table format is the best for sharing information.
5. (*small group roles*) Group task and group building and maintenance roles are always productive in small group communication.
6. (*small group roles*) Individual roles always hinder the group's productivity and morale.
7. (*groupthink*) Groupthink will eventually demoralize members and destroy the group.
8. (*leadership*) All groups need and function best with a clearly defined leader.
9. (*leadership style*) Democratic leaders are more effective than authoritarian leaders.

10. (*leadership functions*) Group leaders should focus equally on productivity (or task) and morale (or people).

### Public Speaking Context
1. (*topics and audiences*) All speech topics should be derived from a careful analysis of the audience.
2. (*purposes*) Effective public speeches are exclusively informational or persuasive; speeches that mix the two are almost always ineffective.
3. (*topics*) Topics such as "how to save time while grocery shopping" or "how to style hair effectively" or "how to change a tire" are simply inappropriate for public speeches.
4. (*research*) An effective speech must rely on extensive library research.
5. (*apprehension*) Apprehension is always detrimental to effective public speaking.
6. (*language*) The more understandable the language of the speech, the more persuasive it will be.
7. (*methods of presentation*) Memorized or manuscript speeches are less effective than extemporaneous speeches.
8. (*thesis*) It is best to tell your audience your thesis at the beginning of your speech.
9. (*main points*) Four main points is the maximum that a speaker should cover in a single speech.
10. (*introductions*) Public speaking introductions should always contain a section that orients the audience.
11. (*conclusions*) The conclusion to a public speech should always summarize its major points.
12. (*style*) A personal, informal style is more effective than an impersonal, formal one.
13. (*delivery*) The fewer notes a speaker uses, the more effective the speaker will be.
14. (*rehearsal*) The more rehearsal, the more effective the presentation will be.
15. (*credibility*) The more competent the speaker, the more credible or believable the speaker will be.

# GLOSSARY

A word is dead
When it is said,
Some say.
I say it just
Begins to live.
—EMILY DICKINSON

Included here are definitions of the major concepts covered in *Essentials of Human Communication*. Also defined are additional terms that may logically be used throughout an introduction to communication course. For a more extensive glossary see Joseph A. DeVito, *The Communication Handbook: A Dictionary* (HarperCollins 1986).

**Abstraction** A general concept derived from a class of objects; a part representing some whole.

**Abstraction process** The process by which a general concept is derived from specifics; the process of the senses perceiving some (never all) characteristics of an object, person, or event.

**Accent** The stress or emphasis placed on a syllable when pronounced.

**Acculturation** The processes by which contact with or exposure to another culture modifies or changes a person's culture.

**Active listening** A process of combining into some meaningful whole the listener's understanding of the speaker's total message—verbal and nonverbal, thoughts and feelings.

**Adaptors** Nonverbal behaviors that serve some kind of need and occur in their entirety when emitted in private or in public without being seen—for example, scratching one's head until the itch is eliminated.

**Adjustment principle** The principle of verbal interaction that claims communication can take place only to the extent that the communicating parties share the same system of signals.

**Affect displays** Movements of the facial area and body that convey emotional meaning such as anger, fear, and surprise.

**Affinity-seeking strategies** Behaviors designed to increase your interpersonal attractiveness and make another person like you more.

**Agapic love** Compassionate, self-giving, spiritual, and altruistic love.

**Allness** The assumption that all can be known or is known about a given person, issue, object, or event.

**Altercasting** A statement that places the listener in a specific role for a specific purpose and asks that the listener consider the question or problem from this role's perspective.

**Ambiguity** The condition in which a word or phrase may be interpreted as having more than one meaning.

**Appeals for the suspension of judgment** A type of *disclaimer* in which the speaker asks listeners to delay their judgments until they have heard the entire message.

**Appraisal interview** A type of interview in which management or more experienced colleagues assess the interviewee's performance.

**Arbitrariness** The feature of human language that refers to the fact that there is no real or inherent relationship between a word's form and its meaning. If we do not know anything of a particular language, we could not examine a word's form and discover its meaning.

**Argot** A kind of "sublanguage," generally of an underworld or criminal class, which is difficult and sometimes impossible for outsiders to understand.

**Articulation** The physiological movements of the speech organs as they modify and interrupt the air stream emitted from the lungs.

**Artifactual communication** Communication that takes place through the wearing and arrangement of various artifacts—for example, clothing, jewelry, buttons, or the furniture in your house and its arrangement.

*Assertiveness*   A willingness to stand up for your rights but with respect for the rights of others.

*Assimilation*   The process of message distortion in which you rework messages to conform to your attitudes, prejudices, needs, and values.

*Attention*   The process of responding to a stimulus or stimuli.

*Attitude*   A predisposition to respond for or against an object.

*Attraction*   The state or process by which you are drawn to another, by having a highly positive evaluation of that other person.

*Attractiveness*   The degree to which one is perceived to be physically attractive and to possess a pleasing personality.

*Attribution*   A process through which you attempt to understand the reasons or motivations for the behaviors of others (as well as your own).

*Audience participation principle*   The principle of persuasion that states persuasion is achieved more effectively when the audience participates actively.

*Authoritarian leader*   A group leader who determines group policies or makes decisions without consulting or securing agreement from members.

*Avoidance*   An unproductive conflict strategy in which you take mental or physical flight from the actual conflict.

*Barriers to communication*   Those factors (physical or psychological) that prevent or hinder effective communication.

*Behavioral synchrony*   The similarity in the behavior, usually nonverbal, of two people. Generally, behavioral synchrony is an index of mutual liking.

*Belief*   Confidence in the existence or truth of something; conviction.

*Beltlining*   The unproductive conflict strategy in which one person hits another with insults or attacks below his or her level of tolerance—that is, below the belt.

*Blame*   The unproductive conflict strategy in which the conflict's cause is attributed to the other person; the concentration on discovering who is the cause of a conflict or difficulty, and the avoidance of confronting the issues causing the conflict.

*Blindering*   A misevaluation in which a label prevents you from seeing as much of an object as you might; a process of concentrating on the verbal level while neglecting nonverbal levels; a form of *intensional orientation*.

*Blind self*   The part of yourself that contains information about you that is known to others but not to you.

*Boundary markers*   *Markers* separating territories—such as the armrests in a theater that separate one person's space from another's.

*Brainstorming*   A technique for generating ideas among people.

*Breadth*   The number of topics about which individuals in a relationship communicate.

*Bypassing*   A pattern of misevaluation in which people fail to communicate their intended meaning. Bypassing may take either of two forms: (1) when two people use different words but give them the same meaning, resulting in apparent disagreement that hides the underlying agreement; and (2) when two people use the same words but each gives them different meaning, resulting in apparent agreement that hides the underlying disagreement.

*Cant*   A kind of *sublanguage*; the conversational language of any nonprofessional (usually noncriminal) group, which is generally understood only by members of that culture; distinguished from *argot*.

*Central markers*   A type of *marker* which consists of an item placed in a territory to reserve it—for example, a jacket left on a library chair.

*Certainty*   An attitude of closed-mindedness that creates a defensiveness among communication participants; opposed to *provisionalism*.

*Channel*   The vehicle or medium through which signals pass.

*Cherishing behaviors*   Small behaviors that you enjoy receiving from a relational partner—for example, a kiss, a smile, or a gift of flowers.

*Chronemics*   The study of the communicative nature of time—how you treat and use time to communicate. Two general areas of chronemics are: *cultural time* and *psychological time*.

*Civil inattention*   Polite ignoring of others so as not to invade their privacy.

**Clichés** Overused phrases that have lost their novelty and part of their meaning, and that call attention to themselves because of their overuse.

**Closed-mindedness** An unwillingness to receive certain communication messages.

**Code** A set of symbols used to translate a message from one form to another.

**Cognitive disclaimer** A disclaimer in which the speaker seeks to confirm his or her cognitive capacity, for example, "You may think I'm drunk, but I'm as sober as anyone here."

**Cohesiveness** The property of togetherness. Applied to group communication situations, it refers to the mutual attractiveness among members; a measure of the extent to which individual group members work together.

**Colloquy** A small group format in which a subject is explored through the interaction of two panels (one asking and one answering questions) or through panel members responding to questions from audience members.

**Communication** (1) The process or act of communicating; (2) the actual message or messages sent and received; and (3) the study of the processes involved in the sending and receiving of messages. The term *communicology* (q.v.) is suggested for the third definition.

**Communication network** The pathways of messages; the organizational structure through which messages are sent and received.

**Communicology** The study of *communication*, particularly that subsection concerned with human communication.

**Competence** In communication, the rules of the more social or interpersonal dimensions of communication, often used to refer to those qualities that make for effectiveness in interpersonal communication.

**Complementary relationship** A relationship in which one person's behavior stimulates complementary behavior in the other; in complementary relationships, behavior differences are maximized.

**Compliance-gaining strategies** Tactics that are directed to gain the agreement of others; behaviors designed to persuade others to do as you wish.

**Compliance-resisting strategies** Tactics used to resist or refuse to do as asked. Nonnegotation,

negotiation, identity management (positive or negative), and justification are four types of compliance-resisting strategies.

**Confidence** The absence of social anxiety; the communication of comfortableness in social situations. One of the qualities of effective interpersonal communication.

**Confirmation** A communication pattern that acknowledges another person's presence and communicates an acceptance of the person, the person's definition of self, and your relationship as defined or viewed by this other person. Opposed to *disconfirmation*.

**Conflict** A disagreement between or among individuals.

**Connotation** The feeling or emotional aspect of meaning, generally viewed as consisting of evaluative (for example, good-bad), potency (strong-weak), and activity (fast-slow) dimensions; the associations of a term. See *denotation*.

**Congruence** A condition in which both verbal and nonverbal behaviors reinforce each other.

**Consensus** A principle of attribution through which you attempt to establish whether other people react or behave in the same way as the person on whom you are now focusing If this is so, then you seek reasons for the behavior outside the individual; if the person is not acting in accordance with the general consensus, then you seek reasons that are internal to the individual.

**Consistency** (1) A perceptual process that influences you to maintain balance among your perceptions; a process that influences you to see what you expect to see and to be uncomfortable when your perceptions contradict your expectations; (2) a principle of attribution through which you attempt to establish whether a person behaves the same way in similar situations. If there is consistency, you are likely to attribute the behavior to the person, to some internal motivation; if there is no consistency, you are likely to attribute the behavior to some external factor.

**Contamination** A form of territorial encroachment which renders another's territory impure.

**Content and relationship dimensions** A principle of communication that messages refer both to content (the world external to both speaker and listener) and to relationship dimensions (the relationship existing between the individuals interacting).

*Context of communication* The physical, social-psychological, cultural, and temporal environment in which communication takes place.

*Controllability* One of the factors you consider in judging whether or not a person is responsible for his or her behavior. If the person was in control, then you judge that he or she was responsible.

*Conversational turns* The changing (or maintaining) of the speaker or listener role during a conversation. These turns are generally signaled nonverbally. Speaker cues include turn-maintaining cues that allow the speaker to maintain the speaker role and turn-yielding cues that let the listener know the speaker wishes to give up the speaker role. Listener cues include turn-requesting cues that let the speaker know the listener would like to speak, turn-denying cues that let the speaker know the listener does not wish to say anything, and backchanneling cues that communicate agreement or involvement in the conversation without any desire to exchange speaker and listener roles.

*Cooperation.* An interpersonal process by which individuals work together for a common end; the pooling of efforts to produce a mutually desired outcome.

*Cooperation, principle of* An implicit agreement between speaker and listener to cooperate in trying to understand what each is communicating.

*Counseling interview* A type of interview in which the interviewer tries to learn about the interviewee in an attempt to provide some form of guidance, advice, or insight.

*Credentialing* A type of *disclaimer* in which the speaker acknowledges that what is about to be said may reflect poorly on himself or herself but will say it nevertheless (usually for quite positive reasons).

*Credibility* The degree to which a receiver perceives the speaker to be believable.

*Cultural time* The communication function of time as regulated and perceived by a particular culture. Generally, the three types of cultural time are: *technical time* referring to precise scientific time; *formal time* referring to a culture's divisions of time (for example, dividing a semester into 14 weeks); and *informal time* referring to the loose use of such time terms as *immediately, soon,* and *right away.*

*Cultural transmission* The feature of language referring to the fact that human languages (at least in their outer surface form) are learned. Unlike various forms of animal language, which are innate, human languages are transmitted traditionally or culturally. This feature does not deny the possibility that certain language aspects may be innate. Also referred to as *cultural transmission.*

*Culture* The relatively specialized life-style of a group of people—their values, beliefs, artifacts, ways of behaving, and ways of communicating—that is passed from one generation to the next.

*Culture shock* The psychological reaction you experience when placed in a culture very different from you own or from what you are used to.

*Date* An extensional device used to emphasize the notion of constant change and symbolized by a subscript: for example, John Smith $_{1972}$ is not John Smith $_{1993}$.

*Decoder* That which takes a message in one form (for example, sound waves) and translates it into another code (for example, nerve impulses) from which meaning can be formulated. In human communication, the decoder is the auditory mechanism; in electronic communication, the decoder is, for example, the telephone earpiece. See *encoder.*

*Decoding* The process of extracting a message from a code—for example, translating speech sounds into nerve impulses. See *encoding.*

*Defensiveness* An attitude of an individual or an atmosphere in a group characterized by threats, fear, and domination; messages evidencing evaluation, control, strategy, neutrality, superiority, and certainty are assumed to lead to defensiveness. Opposed to *supportiveness.*

*Democratic leader* A group leader who stimulates self-direction and self-actualization of members.

*Denial* One of the obstacles to expressing emotion; the process by which you deny your emotions to yourself or to others.

*Denotation* Referential meaning; the objective or descriptive meaning of a word. See *connotation.*

*Depenetration* A reversal of penetration; a condition where the *breadth* and *depth* of a relationship decreases.

**Depth** The degree to which the inner personality—the inner core of an individual—is penetrated in interpersonal interaction.

**Dialogue** A form of communication in which each person is both speaker and listener; communication characterized by involvement, concern, and respect for the other person; opposed to monologue.

**Disconfirmation** A communication pattern in which you ignore the other person as well as this person's communications. Opposed to *confirmation.*

**Distinctiveness** A principle of attribution in which you ask whether a person reacts in similar ways in different situations. If the person does, there is low distinctiveness and you are likely to conclude there is an internal cause or motivation for the behavior; if there is high distinctiveness, you are likely to seek the cause in some external factors.

**Double-bind message** A particular kind of contradictory message possessing the following characteristics: (1) The persons interacting share a relatively intense relationship; (2) two messages are communicated at the same time, demanding different and incompatible responses; (3) at least one person in the double bind cannot escape from the contradictory messages; (4) there is a threat of punishment for noncompliance.

**Dyadic communication** Two-person communication.

**Dyadic consciousness** An awareness of an interpersonal relationship or pairing of two individuals, distinguished from situations in which two individuals are together but do not perceive themselves as being a unit or twosome.

**Dyadic effect** The tendency for the behavior of one person in a dyad to influence a similar behavior in the other person. Used most often to refer to the reciprocal nature of self-disclosure.

**Ear markers** A type of *marker* consisting of identifying marks that indicate that the territory or object belongs to a particular person—for example, initials on an attaché case.

**Effect** The outcome or consequence of an action or behavior; communication is assumed always to have some effect.

**Emblems** Nonverbal behaviors that directly translate words or phrases—for example, the hand signs for *okay* and *peace.*

**Empathy** A quality of effective interpersonal communication that refers to the ability to feel another's feelings as that person does and to communicate that similarity of feeling.

**Employment interview** A type of interview in which the interviewee is questioned to ascertain his or her suitability for a particular job.

**Encoder** Something that takes a message in one form (for example, nerve impulses) and translates it into another form (for example, sound waves). In human communication, the encoder is the speaking mechanism; in electronic communication the encoder is, for example, the telephone mouthpiece. See *decoder.*

**Encoding** The process of putting a message into a code—for example, translating nerve impulses into speech sounds. See *decoding.*

**Enculturation** The process of transmitting culture from one generation to another.

**E-Prime** A form of the language that omits the verb *to be* except when used as an auxiliary or in statements of existence. Designed to eliminate the tendency toward *projection,* or assuming that characteristics that one attributes to a person (for example, "Pat is brave") are actually in that person instead of in the observer's perception of that person.

**Equality** A quality of effective interpersonal communication in which personalities are recognized as equal, and both individuals are seen as worthwhile, valuable contributors to the total interaction.

**Equity theory** A theory claiming that you experience relational satisfaction when rewards and costs are equally distributed between the two persons in the relationship.

**Erotic love** A sexual, physical love; a love that is ego-centered and given because of an anticipated return.

**Etc. (et cetera)** An extensional device used to emphasize the notion of infinite complexity; since you can never know all about anything, any statement about the world or an event must end with an explicit or implicit *etc.*

**Ethics** The branch of philosophy that deals with the rightness or wrongness of actions; the study of moral values.

**Ethnocentrism** The tendency to see others and their behaviors through your cultural filters, often as distortions of your behaviors; the tendency to evaluate the values and beliefs of your culture more positively than those of another culture.

*Euphemism*   A polite word or phrase substituted for a more direct, but taboo or otherwise offensive, term.

*Evaluation*   The process of placing a value on some person, object, or event.

*Exit interview*   A type of interview designed to establish why an employee (the interviewee) is leaving the organization.

*Expressiveness*   A quality of effective interpersonal communication referring to the skill of communicating genuine involvement in the interpersonal interaction.

*Extemporaneous speech*   A speech that is thoroughly prepared and organized in detail and in which certain aspects of style are predetermined.

*Extensional devices*   Linguistic devices proposed by Alfred Korzybski for keeping language as a more accurate means for talking about the world. The extensional devices include the *etc.*, *date*, and *index*—the working devices; and the *hyphen* and *quotes*—the safety devices.

*Extensional orientation*   A point of view in which the primary consideration is given to the world of experience and only secondary consideration is given to the labels. See *intensional orientation*.

*Fact-inference confusion*   A misevaluation in which you make an inference, regard it as a fact, and act upon it as if it were a fact.

*Factual statement*   A statement made by the observer after observation, and limited to the observed. See *inferential statement*.

*Fear appeal*   The appeal to fear to persuade an individual or group of individuals to believe or to act in a certain way.

*Feedback*   Information given back to the source. Feedback may come from the source's own messages (as when you hear what you are saying) or from the receiver(s) in the form of applause, yawning, puzzled looks, questions, letters to a newspaper editor, increased or decreased magazine subscriptions, and so forth.

*Feedforward*   Information sent prior to the regular messages telling the listener something about future messages.

*Field of experience*   The total of your experiences, which influences your ability to communicate. In some communication views, two people can communicate only to the extent that their fields of experience overlap.

*Force*   An unproductive conflict strategy in which you attempt to win an argument by physical force or threats of force.

*Forum*   A small group format in which group members answer questions from the audience; often follows a *symposium*.

*Free information*   Information about a person that you can see or that he or she drops into the conversation, and that can serve as a topic of conversation.

*Friendship*   An interpersonal relationship between two persons that is mutually productive, established and maintained through perceived mutual free choice, and characterized by mutual positive regard.

*General semantics*   The study of the relationships among language, thought, and behavior.

*Group*   A collection of individuals related to each other with some common purpose and structure.

*Groupthink*   A tendency in some groups to make agreement among members more important than the issues at hand.

*Gunnysacking*   An unproductive conflict strategy in which you store up grievances against the other person and unload them during a conflict encounter.

*Haptics*   Touch or tactile communication.

*Hedge*   A type of disclaimer in which the speaker disclaims the importance of what he or she is about say.

*Heterosexist language*   Language that assumes all people are heterosexual and thereby denigrates lesbians and gay men.

*Hidden self*   The part of yourself that contains information about you that is known to you, but unknown to and hidden from others.

*Home field advantage*   The increased power that comes from being in your own territory.

*Home territories*   Territories for which individuals have a sense of intimacy and over which they exercise control—for example, a child's club house.

**Hyphen** An *extensional device* used to illustrate that what may be separated verbally may not be separable on the event or nonverbal level; although you may talk about body and mind as if they were separable, in reality they are better referred to as body-mind.

**Illustrators** Nonverbal behaviors that accompany and literally illustrate the verbal messages—for example, upward motions that accompany the verbalization "It's up there."

**"I" messages** Messages in which the speaker accepts responsibility for personal thoughts and behaviors; messages in which the speaker's point of view is stated explicitly. Opposed to "you" messages.

**Immediacy** A quality of effective interpersonal communication referring to a feeling of togetherness and oneness with another person.

**Implicit personality theory** A personality theory that each individual maintains, complete with rules or systems, through which others are perceived.

**Inclusion, principle of** In verbal interaction, the principle that all members should be a part of (included in) the interaction.

**Impromptu speech** A speech given without any prior preparation.

**Index** An *extensional device* used to emphasize the notion of nonidentity (no two things are the same) and symbolized by a subscript—for example, politician$_1$ is not politician$_2$.

**Indiscrimination** A misevaluation caused by categorizing people, events, or objects into a particular class and responding to specific members only as members of that class; a failure to recognize each individual as an individual and unique; a failure to apply the *index*.

**Inevitability** A communication principle referring to the fact that communication cannot be avoided; all behavior in an interactional setting is communication.

**Inferential statement** A statement that anyone can make at anytime, and is not limited to the observed. See *factual statement*.

**Information** That which reduces uncertainty.

**Informative interview** A type of interview in which the interviewer asks the interviewee, usually a person of some reputation and accomplishment, questions designed to elicit his or her views, predictions, perspectives, and the like on specific topics.

**Information overload** That condition in which the amount of information is too great to be dealt with effectively; or the number or complexity of messages is so great that the individual or organization is not able to deal with them.

**In-group talk** Talk about a subject or in a vocabulary that only certain people understand, often in the presence of someone who does not belong to this group and therefore does not understand.

**Inoculation principle** A persuasion principle that states persuasion will be more difficult to achieve when previously challenged beliefs and attitudes are attacked, because the individual has built up defenses in a manner similar to biological inoculation.

**Insulation** A reaction to *territorial encroachment* in which you erect some sort of barrier between yourself and the invaders.

**Intensional orientation** A point of view in which you give primary consideration to the way things are labeled and only secondary consideration (if any) to the world of experience. See *extensional orientation*.

**Interaction management** A quality of effective interpersonal communication referring to the ability to control the interaction to the satisfaction of both participants.

**Interaction process analysis** A content analysis method that classifies messages into four general categories: social emotional positive, social emotional negative, attempted answers, and questions.

**Intercultural communication** Communication between persons of different cultures or who have different cultural beliefs, values, or ways of behaving.

**Interethnic communication** Communication between members of different ethnic groups.

**International communication** Communication between nations.

**Interpersonal communication** Communication between two persons or among a small group and distinguished from public or mass communication; communication of a personal nature and distinguished from impersonal communication; communication between or among intimates or those involved in a close relationship;

often, intrapersonal, dyadic, and small group communication in general.

*Interpersonal conflict*  A conflict or disagreement between two persons; a conflict within an individual caused by his or her relationships with other people.

*Interpersonal perception*  The perception of people; the processes through which you interpret and evaluate people and their behavior.

*Interracial communication*  Communication between members of different races.

*Interview*  The interpersonal communication in which two persons interact largely by question-and-answer format to achieve specific goals.

*Intimate distance*  The shortest proxemic distance, ranging from touching to 6 to 18 inches.

*Intrapersonal communication*  Communication with yourself.

*Irreversibility*  A communication principle referring to the fact that communication cannot be reversed; once something has been communicated, it cannot be uncommunicated.

*Invasion*  The unwarranted entrance into another's territory that changes the territory's meaning. See *territorial encroachment*.

*Jargon*  A "sublanguage," often of a professional class, which is unintelligible to individuals not belonging to the group; the "shoptalk" of the group.

*Kinesics*  The study of the communicative dimension of face and body movements.

*Laissez-faire leader*  A group leader who allows the group to develop, progress, or make mistakes on its own.

*Leadership*  That quality by which one individual directs or influences the thoughts and/or the behaviors of others. See *laissez-faire leader*, *democratic leader*, and *authoritarian leader*.

*Leveling*  A process of message distortion in which a message is repeated, but the number of details is reduced, some details are omitted entirely, and some details lose their complexity.

*Level of abstraction*  The relative distance of a term or statement from the actual perception; a low-order abstraction would be a description of the perception, whereas a high-order abstraction would consist of inferences about inferences about descriptions of a perception.

*Linguistic collusion*  A reaction to *territorial encroachment* in which you speak in a language unknown to the intruders and thus separate yourself from them.

*Listening*  The process of receiving, understanding, remembering, evaluating, and responding to a message.

*Looking-glass self*  The self-concept that results from the image of yourself that others reveal to you.

*Loving*  An interpersonal process in which you feel a closeness, caring, warmth, and an excitement for another person.

*Ludus love*  Love as a game, as fun; the position that love is not to be taken seriously and is to be maintained only as long as it remains interesting and enjoyable.

*Magnitude of change principle*  The persuasion principle that the greater and more important the change desired by the speaker, the more difficult it will be to achieve.

*Manic love*  Love characterized by extreme highs and extreme lows; obsessive love.

*Manipulation*  An unproductive conflict strategy which avoids open conflict; instead, attempts are made to divert the conflict by being especially charming and getting the other person into a noncombative frame of mind.

*Manuscript speech*  A speech designed to be read verbatim from a script.

*Markers*  Devices you use to signal others that a particular territory belongs to you; three types of markers are usually distinguished: *boundary*, *central*, and *ear markers*.

*Mass communication*  Communication addressed to an extremely large audience, mediated by audio and/or visual transmitters, and processed by gatekeepers before transmission.

*Matching hypothesis*  The assumption that persons date and mate people who are approximately the same in terms of physical attractiveness.

*Meaningfulness*  A perception principle that refers to your assumption that people's behavior is sensible, stems from some logical antecedent, and is consequently meaningful rather than meaningless.

*Mere exposure hypothesis* The theory that repeated or prolonged exposure to a stimulus may change the attitude toward the stimulus object, generally in the direction of increased positiveness.

*Message* Any signal or combination of signals that serve as *stimuli* for a receiver.

*Metacommunication* Communication about communication.

*Metalanguage* Language used to talk about language.

*Metamessage* A message that communicates about another message.

*Micromomentary expressions* Extremely brief movements that are not consciously perceived and that are thought to reveal a person's real emotional state.

*Mindfulness and mindlessness* States of relative awareness. In a mindful state, you are aware of the logic and rationality of your behaviors and the logical connections among elements. In a mindless state, you are unaware of this logic and rationality.

*Minimization* An unproductive conflict strategy in which you make light of the other person's disagreements or of the whole conflict.

*Model* A physical or verbal representation of an object or process.

*Motivated sequence* An organizational pattern for arranging the information in a discourse to motivate an audience to respond positively to your purpose.

*Monologue* A communication form in which one person speaks and the other listens; there is no real interaction among participants; opposed to *dialogue.*

*Negative feedback* Feedback that serves a corrective function by informing the source that his or her message is not being received in the way intended. Negative feedback serves to redirect the source's behavior. Looks of boredom, shouts of disagreement, letters critical of newspaper policy, and the teacher's instructions on how to better approach a problem are examples of negative feedback See *positive feedback.*

*Neutrality* A response pattern lacking personal involvement; encourages defensiveness; opposed to empathy.

*Noise* Anything that distorts or interferes with the message in the communication system. Noise is present to the extent that the message sent differs from the message received. *Physical noise* interferes with the physical transmission of the signal or message—for example, the static in radio transmission. *Psychological noise* refers to distortions created by such processes as prejudice and biases. *Semantic noise* refers to distortions created by a failure to understand each other's words.

*Nonallness* An attitude or point of view which recognizes that you can never know all about anything and that what you know, say, or hear is only a part of what there is to know, say, or hear.

*Nonnegotiation* An unproductive conflict strategy in which the individual refuses to discuss the conflict or disagreement, or to listen to the other person.

*Nonverbal communication* Communication without words.

*Olfactory communication* Communication by smell.

*Openness* A quality of effective interpersonal communication that refers to the willingness (1) to engage in appropriate self-disclosure, (2) to react honestly to incoming stimuli, and (3) to own your feelings and thoughts.

*Open self* The part of yourself that contains information about you that is known to you and to others.

*Oral style* The style of spoken discourse that, when compared with written style, consists of shorter, simpler, and more familiar words; more qualification, self-reference terms, allness terms, verbs and adverbs; and more concrete terms and terms indicative of consciousness of projection—for example, *as I see it.*

*Other-orientation* A quality of effective interpersonal interaction referring to your ability to adapt to the other person's needs and desires during the interpersonal encounter.

*Other talk* Talk about the listener or some third party.

*Owning feelings* The process by which you take responsibility for your feelings instead of attributing them to others.

*Panel or round table* A small group format in which participants seated together speak without any set pattern.

*Paralanguage* The vocal (but nonverbal) aspect of speech. Paralanguage consists of voice qualities (for example, pitch range, resonance, tempo), vocal characterizers (for example, laughing or crying, yelling or whispering), vocal qualifiers (for example, intensity, pitch height), and vocal segregates (for example, *uh-uh* meaning "no," or *sh* meaning "silence").

*Passive listening* Listening that is attentive and supportive but occurs without talking or directing the speaker in any nonverbal way; also used negatively to refer to inattentive and uninvolved listening.

*Pauses* Silent periods in the normally fluent stream of speech. Pauses are of two major types: filled pauses (interruptions in speech that are filled with such vocalizations as *-er* or *-um*) and unfilled pauses (silences of unusually long length).

*Perception* The process of becoming aware of objects and events from the senses.

*Perceptual accentuation* A process that leads you to see what you expect and want to see; for example, you see people you like as better looking and smarter than people you do not like.

*Personal distance* The second-shortest proxemic distance, ranging from 18 inches to 4 feet.

*Personal rejection* An unproductive conflict strategy in which the individual withholds love and affection, and seeks to win the argument by getting the other person to break down under this withdrawal.

*Persuasion* The process of influencing attitudes and behavior.

*Persuasion interview* A type of interview in which the interviewer attempts to change the interviewee's attitudes or behavior.

*Phatic communion* Primarily social communication designed to open the communication channels rather than to communicate something about the external world; "Hello," and "How are you?" in everyday interaction are common examples.

*Pitch* The highness or lowness of the vocal tone.

*Polarization* A form of fallacious reasoning that considers only the two extremes; also referred to as "either-or" thinking.

*Positive feedback* Feedback that supports or reinforces behavior along the same lines as it is proceeding—for example, applause during a speech See *negative feedback*.

*Positiveness* A quality of effective interpersonal communication referring to the communication of positiveness toward the self, the other, and the communication situation generally, and willingness to stroke the other person as appropriate.

*Pragmatic love* Practical love; love based on compatibility; love that seeks a relationship that will satisfy each person's important needs and desires.

*Primacy effect* The condition by which what comes first exerts greater influence than what comes later.

*Primary affect displays* The communication of the six primary emotions: happiness, surprise, fear, anger, sadness, and disgust/contempt. See *affect displays*.

*Process* Ongoing activity; nonstatic; communication is referred to as a process to emphasize that it is always changing and in motion.

*Productivity* The feature of language that makes possible the creation and understanding of novel utterances. With human language you can talk about matters you have never talked about before, and understand utterances you have never heard before. Also referred to as *openness*.

*Progressive differentiation* A relational problem caused by the exaggeration or intensification of differences or similarities between individuals.

*Projection* A psychological process whereby you attribute your characteristics or feelings to others; often used to refer to the process whereby you attribute your faults to others.

*Pronouncements* Authoritative statements that imply that the speaker is in a position of authority and the listener is in a childlike or learner role.

*Pronunciation* The production of syllables or words according to some accepted standard, such as in a dictionary.

*Provisionalism* An attitude of open-mindedness that leads to the creation of *supportiveness*; opposite to *certainty*.

*Proxemics* The study of the communicative function of space; the study of how people unconsciously structure their space—the distance between people in their interactions, the organization of space in homes and offices, and even the design of cities.

*Proximity* As a principle of perception, the tendency to perceive people or events that are physically close as belonging together or representing some unit; physical closeness; one of the qualities influencing interpersonal attraction.

*Public communication* Communication in which the source is one person and the receiver is an audience of many persons.

*Public distance* The longest proxemic distance, ranging from 12 to more than 25 feet.

*Public speaking* Communication that occurs when a speaker delivers a relatively prepared, continuous address in a specific setting to a relatively large audience.

*Punctuation of communication* The breaking up of continuous communication sequences into short sequences with identifiable beginnings and endings, or stimuli and responses.

*Pupillometrics* The study of communication through changes in the size of the pupils of the eyes.

*Psychological time* The importance that you place on past time, in which particular regard is shown for the past and its values and methods; present time, in which you live in the present for the enjoyment of the present; and future time, in which you devote your energies to planning for the future.

*Purr words* Highly positive words that express the speaker's feelings rather than refer to any objective reality; opposite to *snarl words.*

*Pygmalion effect* The condition in which you make a prediction and then proceed to fulfill it; a type of self-fulfilling prophecy but one that refers to others and to your evaluation of others rather than to yourself.

*Quotes* An extensional device used to emphasize that a word or phrase is being used in a special sense and should therefore be given special attention.

*Racist language* Language that denigrates a particular race.

*Rapid fading* The evanescent or impermanent quality of speech signals.

*Rate* The speed with which you speak, generally measured in words per minute.

*Receiver* Any person or thing that takes in messages. Receivers may be individuals listening to or reading a message, a group of persons hearing a speech, a television audience, or a machine that stores information.

*Recency effect* The condition in which what comes last (that is, most recently) exerts greater influence than what comes first.

*Recurrence, principle of* The principle of verbal interaction that individuals will repeat many times and in many ways who they are, how they see themselves, and in general what they think is important and significant.

*Redefinition* An unproductive conflict strategy in which you give the conflict another definition so that the conflict's source disappears.

*Redundancy* A message's quality that makes it totally predictable and therefore lacking in information. A message of zero redundancy would be completely unpredictable; a message of 100 percent redundancy would be completely predictable. All human languages contain some degree of built-in redundancy, generally estimated at about 50 percent.

*Reflexiveness* The language feature that refers to the fact that human language can be used to refer to itself; that is, you can talk about your talk and create a *metalanguage*—a language for talking about language.

*Regulators* Nonverbal behaviors that regulate, monitor, or control another person's communications.

*Reinforcement or packaging, principle of* The principle of verbal interaction holding that in most interactions, messages are transmitted simultaneously through a number of different channels that normally reinforce each other; messages come in packages.

*Rejection* A response to an individual that rejects or denies the validity of an individual's self-view.

*Relational communication* Communication between or among intimates or those in close relationships; term used by some theorists as synonymous with interpersonal communication.

*Relational deterioration* The stage of a relationship during which the connecting bonds between the partners weaken and the partners begin drifting apart.

*Resemblance*   As a principle of perception, the tendency to perceive people or events that are similar in appearance as belonging together.

*Response*   Any bit of overt or covert behavior.

*Rigid complementarity*   The inability to change the type of relationship between yourself and another even though the individuals, the context, and many other variables have changed.

*Role*   The part an individual plays in a group; an individual's function or expected behavior.

*Selective exposure principle*   The persuasion principle holding that listeners will actively seek out information that supports their opinions, beliefs, attitudes, and values and actively avoid information that contradicts them.

*Self-acceptance*   Your satisfaction with yourself, your virtues and vices, and your abilities and limitations.

*Self-attribution*   A process through which you seek to account for and understand the reasons and motivations for your behavior.

*Self-concept*   Your self-evaluation; self-appraisal.

*Self-disclosure*   The process of revealing something significant about yourself to another individual or to a group—something that would not normally be known by them.

*Self-fulfilling prophecy*   The situation in which you make a prediction or prophecy and fulfill it yourself—for example, expecting a class to be boring and then fulfilling this expectation by perceiving it as boring.

*Self-monitoring*   The manipulation of the image that you present to others in your interpersonal interactions. High self-monitors carefully adjust their behaviors on the basis of feedback from others so that they can project the desired image. Low self-monitors do not consciously manipulate their images.

*Self-serving bias*   A bias that operates in the self-attribution process that leads you to take credit for the positive consequences and to deny responsibility for the negative consequences of your behavior.

*Self-talk*   Talk about yourself.

*Semantics*   The area of language study concerned with meaning.

*Sexist language*   Language derogatory to one sex, generally women.

*Sharpening*   A process of message distortion in which the details of messages, when repeated, are crystallized and heightened.

*Shyness*   The discomfort and uneasiness in interpersonal situations.

*Signal and noise, relativity of*   The principle of verbal interaction that holds that what is signal (meaningful) and what is noise (interference) is relative to the communication analyst, the participants, and the context.

*Signal reaction*   A conditioned response to a signal; the response is immediate rather than delayed.

*Silence*   The absence of vocal communication; often misunderstood to refer to the absence of any and all communication.

*Silencers*   Unproductive conflict strategies that literally silence the other person—for example, crying, or feigning emotional or physical disturbance.

*Similarity*   A principle of attraction holding that you are attracted to qualities similar to those you possess and to people who are similar to you; opposed to complementarity.

*Sin licenses*   A disclaimer in which the speaker acknowledges that he or she is about to break some normally operative rule; the speaker asks for a license to sin (that is, to break a social or interpersonal rule).

*Slang*   The language used by special groups that is not considered proper by the general society; the language made up of the *argot, cant,* and *jargon* of various groups.

*Small group communication*   Communication among a collection of individuals, few enough in number that all may interact with relative ease as both senders and receivers, with members related to each other by some common purpose and some degree of organization or structure.

*Snarl words*   Highly negative words that express the speaker's feelings rather than refer to any objective reality; opposite to *purr words.*

*Social comparison processes*   The processes by which you compare yourself (for example, your abilities, opinions, and values) with others and then assess and evaluate yourself.

*Social distance*   The third proxemic distance, ranging from 4 to 12 feet; the distance at which business is usually conducted.

*Social exchange theory*   A theory claiming that you develop and maintain relationships in which the rewards or profits are greater than the costs.

*Social penetration theory* A theory concerned with relationship development from the superficial to intimate levels and from few to many areas of interpersonal interaction.

*Source* Any person or thing that creates messages. A source may be an individual speaking, writing, or gesturing or a computer solving a problem.

*Speaker apprehension* A fear of engaging in communication transactions; a decrease in the frequency, strength, and likelihood of engaging in communication transactions.

*Speech* Messages utilizing a vocal-auditory channel.

*Spontaneity* The communication pattern in which you verbalize what you are thinking without attempting to develop strategies for control; encourages supportiveness; opposed to strategy.

*Static evaluation* An orientation that fails to recognize that constant change characterizes the world; an attitude that sees people and events as fixed rather than constantly changing.

*Status* The relative level you occupy in a hierarchy; status always involves a comparison, and thus your status is relative only to another's status. In this culture, occupation, financial position, age, and educational level are significant determinants of status.

*Stereotype* In communication, a fixed impression of a group of people through which you then perceive specific individuals; stereotypes are most often negative (Martians are stupid, uneducated, and dirty), but may also be positive (Venusians are scientific, industrious, and helpful).

*Storge love* Love based on companionship, similar interests, and mutual respect; love that is lacking in great emotional intensity.

*Strategy* The use of some plan to control other members of a communication interaction that guides your communications; encourages *defensiveness*.

*Stroking* Verbal or nonverbal acknowledgment of another person; positive stroking consists of compliments and rewards and, in general, behaviors you look forward to or take pride in receiving; negative stroking is punishing and includes criticisms, expressions of disapproval, or even physical punishment.

*Sublanguage* A variation from the general language, used by a particular group of people; *argot, cant,* and *jargon* are particular sublanguages.

*Superiority* A point of view or attitude that assumes that others are not equal to you; encourages defensiveness; opposed to equality.

*Supportiveness* A quality of effective interpersonal communication in which you are descriptive rather than evaluative, spontaneous rather than strategic, and provisional rather than certain.

*Symmetrical relationship* A relationship between two or more persons in which one's behavior stimulates the same type of behavior in the other person(s). Examples include situations in which one person's anger encourages or stimulates anger in another person, or in which one person's critical comment leads the other to respond in like manner.

*Symposium* A small group format in which each member delivers a relatively prepared talk on some aspect of the topic. Often combined with a *forum*.

*Taboo* Forbidden; culturally censored. Taboo language is frowned upon by "polite society." Themes and specific words may be considered taboo—for example, death, sex, certain forms of illness, and various words denoting sexual activities and excretory functions.

*Tactile communication* Communication by touch; communication received by the skin.

*Territorial encroachment* The trespassing on, use of, or appropriation of one's territory by another. The major types of territorial encroachment are *violation, invasion,* and *contamination*.

*Territoriality* A possessive or ownership reaction to an area of space or to particular objects.

*Theory* A general statement or principle applicable to a number of related phenomena.

*Thesis* The main assertion of a message—for example, the theme of a public speech.

*Touch avoidance* The tendency to avoid touching and being touched by others.

*Transactional* The relationship among elements in which each influences and is influenced by each other element; communication is a transactional process, since no element is independent of any other element.

*Turf defense*  The most extreme reaction to territorial encroachment through which you defend your territory and expel the intruders.

*Two-valued orientation*  A point of view in which you see events or evaluate questions in terms of two values—for example, right or wrong, good or bad. Often referred to as the fallacy of *polarization*.

*Universal of communication*  A feature of communication common to all communication acts.

*Unknown self*  That part of you that contains information about you that is unknown to you and to others, but that is inferred to exist on the basis of various projective tests, slips of the tongue, dream analyses, and the like.

*Value*  Relative worth of an object; a quality that makes something desirable or undesirable; ideals or customs about which you have emotional responses, whether positive or negative.

*Violation*  Unwarranted use of another's territory. See *territorial encroachment*.

*Voice qualities*  Aspects of paralanguage, specifically: pitch range, vocal lip control, glottis control, pitch control, articulation control, rhythm control, resonance, and tempo.

*Volume*  The relative loudness of the voice.

*Withdrawal*  (1) A reaction to *territorial encroachment* in which you leave the territory. (2) A tendency to close yourself off from conflicts rather than confront the issues.

*Written style*  See *oral style*.

*"You" messages*  Messages in which the speaker denies responsibility for his or her thoughts and behaviors; messages that attribute what is really the speaker's perception to another person; messages of blame; opposed to "I" messages.

# BIBLIOGRAPHY

It is the vice of scholars to suppose that there is no knowledge in the world but that of books. Do you avoid it, I conjure you; and thereby save yourself the pain and mortification that must otherwise ensue from finding out your mistake continually!

—WILLIAM HAZLITT

Adams, Dennis M. and Mary E. Hamm (1990). *Cooperative Learning: Critical Thinking and Collaboration across the Curriculum.* Springfield, IL: Charles C. Thomas.

Adams, Linda with Elinor Lenz (1989). *Be Your Best.* New York: Putnam.

Addeo, Edmond G. and Robert E. Burger (1973). *Egospeak: Why No One Listens to You.* New York: Bantam.

Adler, Mortimer J. (1983). *How to Speak, How to Listen.* New York: Macmillan.

Adler, Ronald B. (1977). *Confidence in Communication: A Guide to Assertive and Social Skills.* New York: Holt, Rinehart and Winston.

Adler, Ronald B., Lawrence B. Rosenfeld, and Neil Towne (1992). *Interplay: The Process of Interpersonal Communication,* 4th ed. New York: Holt, Rinehart and Winston.

Ailes, Roger (1988). *You Are the Message.* New York: Doubleday.

Akmajian, A., R. A. Demers, and R. M. Harnish (1979). *Linguistics: An Introduction to Language and Communication.* Cambridge, MA: MIT Press.

Alberts, J. K. (1988). An Analysis of Couples' Conversational Complaints. *Communication Monographs* 55, 184-197.

Albrecht, Karl (1980). *Brain Power: Learn to Improve Your Thinking Skills.* Englewood Cliffs, NJ: Prentice-Hall [Spectrum].

Alisky, Marvin (1985). *Vital Speeches of the Day* 51 (January 15).

Allen, Steve (1991). *Dumbth and 81 Ways to Make Americans Smarter.* Buffalo, NY: Prometheus Books.

Altman, Irwin and Dalmas Taylor (1973). *Social Penetration: The Development of Interpersonal Relationships.* New York: Holt, Rinehart and Winston.

Andersen, Peter A. and Ken Leibowitz (1978). The Development and Nature of the Construct of Touch Avoidance. *Environmental Psychology and Nonverbal Behavior* 3:89-106. Reprinted in DeVito and Hecht (1990).

Akinnaso, F. Niyi (1982). On the Differences between Spoken and Written Language. *Language and Speech* 25, Part 2, 97-125.

Argyle, Michael (1988). *Bodily Communication,* 2nd ed. New York: Methuen & Co.

Argyle, Michael and R. Ingham (1972). Gaze, Mutual Gaze and Distance. *Semiotica* 1:32-49.

Arnold, Carroll C. and John Waite Bowers, eds. (1984). *Handbook of Rhetorical and Communication Theory.* Boston: Allyn & Bacon.

Aronson, Elliot (1980). *The Social Animal,* 3rd ed. San Francisco, CA: W. H. Freeman.

Asch, Solomon (1946). Forming Impressions of Personality. *Journal of Abnormal and Social Psychology* 41:258-290.

Authier, Jerry and Kay Gustafson (1982). Microtraining: Focusing on Specific Skills. In Eldon K. Marshall, P. David Kurtz, and Associates. *Interpersonal Helping Skills*: A Guide to Training Methods, Programs, and Resources. San Francisco, CA: Jossey-Bass, pp. 93-130.

Aylesworth, Thomas G. and Virginia L. Aylesworth (1978). *If You Don't Invade My Intimate Zone or Clean Up My Water Hole, I'll Breathe in Your Face, Blow on Your Neck, and Be Late for Your Party.* New York: Condor.

Ayres, Joe (1986). Perceptions of Speaking Ability: An Explanation for Stage Fright. *Communication Education* 35:275-287.

Ayres, Joe and Janice Miller (1986). *Effective Public Speaking,* 2nd ed. Dubuque, IA: Wm. C. Brown.

Bach, George R. and Peter Wyden (1968). *The Intimate Enemy.* New York: Avon.

Bach, George R. and Ronald M. Deutsch (1979). *Stop! You're Driving Me Crazy.* New York: Berkley.

Backrack, Henry M. (1976). Empathy. *Archives of General Psychiatry* 33:35-38.

Bales, Robert F. (1950). *Interaction Process Analysis: A Method for the Study of Small Groups.* Cambridge, MA: Addison-Wesley.

Barker, Larry, R. Edwards, C. Gaines, K. Gladney, and F. Holley (1980). An Investigation of Proportional Time Spent in Various Communication Activities by College Students. *Journal of Applied Communication Research* 8:101-109.

Barna, LaRay M. (1985). Stumbling Blocks in Intercultural Communication. In Larry A. Samovar and Richard E. Porter, eds., *Intercultural Communication: A Reader,* 4th ed. Belmont, CA: Wadsworth, pp. 330-338.

354

Barnlund, Dean C. (1970). A Transactional Model of Communication. *Language Behavior: A Book of Readings in Communication,* comp. J. Akin, A. Goldberg, G. Myers, and J. Stewart. The Hague: Mouton.

Barnlund, Dean C. (1975). Communicative Styles in Two Cultures: Japan and the United States. In A. Kendon, R. M. Harris, and M. R. Key, eds., *Organization of Behavior in Face-to-Face Interaction.* The Hague: Mouton.

Barnlund, Dean C. (1989). *Communicative Styles of Japanese and Americans.* Belmont, CA: Wadsworth.

Baron, Robert A. and Donn Byrne (1984). *Social Psychology: Understanding Human Interaction,* 4th ed. Boston: Allyn and Bacon.

Bartholomew, Kim (1990). Avoidance of Intimacy: An Attachment Perspective. *Journal of Social and Personal Relationships* 7:147-178.

Bate, Barbara (1988). *Communication and the Sexes.* New York: Harper & Row.

Bateson, Gregory (1972). *Steps to an Ecology of Mind.* New York: Ballantine.

Baxter, Leslie A. (1983). Relationship Disengagement: An Examination of the Reversal Hypothesis. *Western Journal of Speech Communication* 47:85-98.

Baxter, Leslie A., and William W. Wilmot (1984). "Secret Tests": Social Strategies for Acquiring Information about the State of the Relationship. *Human Communication Research* 11:171-201.

Beebe, Steven A. and John T. Masterson (1990). *Communicating in Small Groups: Principles and Practices,* 3rd ed. Glenview, IL: Scott, Foresman.

Beier, Ernst (1974). How We Send Emotional Messages. *Psychology Today* 8 (October):53-56.

Bell, Robert A., and Nancy L. Buerkel-Rothfuss (1990). S(he) Loves Me, S(he) Loves Me Not: Predictors of Relational Information-Seeking in Courtship and Beyond. *Communication Quarterly* 38:64-82.

Bell, Robert A., and John A. Daly (1984). The Affinity-Seeking Function of Communication. *Communication Monographs* 51:91-115.

Benne, Kenneth D. and Paul Sheats (1948). Functional Roles of Group Members. *Journal of Social Issues* 4:41-49.

Bennis, Warren and Burt Nanus (1985). *Leaders: The Strategies for Taking Charge.* New York: Harper & Row.

Berg, John H. and Richard L. Archer (1983). The Disclosure-Liking Relationship. *Human Communication Research* 10:269-281.

Berger, Charles R. and James J. Bradac (1982). *Language and Social Knowlege: Uncertainty in Interpersonal Relations.* London: Edward Arnold.

Berger, Charles R. and Steven H. Chaffee, ed. (1987). *Handbook of Communication Science.* Newbury Park, CA: Sage.

Bernstein, W. M., W. G. Stephan, and M. H. Davis (1979). Explaining Attributions for Achievement: A Path Analytic Approach. *Journal of Personality and Social Psychology* 37:1810-1821.

Berscheid, Ellen and Elaine Hatfield Walster (1978). *Interpersonal Attraction,* 2nd ed. Reading, MA: Addison-Wesley.

Bettinghaus, Erwin P. and Michael J. Cody (1987). *Persuasive Communication,* 4th ed. New York: Holt, Rinehart and Winston.

Birdwhistell, Ray L. (1970). *Kinesics and Context: Essays on Body Motion Communication.* New York: Ballantine Books.

Blankenship, Jane (1968). *A Sense of Style: An Introduction to Style for the Public Speaker.* Belmont, CA: Dickenson.

Blumstein, Philip and Pepper Schwartz (1983). *American Couples: Money, Work, Sex.* New York: Morrow.

Bochner, Arthur (1978). On Taking Ourselves Seriously: An Analysis of Some Persistent Problems and Promising Directions in Interpersonal Research. *Human Communication Research* 4:179-191.

Bochner, Arthur (1984). The Functions of Human Communication in Interpersonal Bonding. In Carroll C. Arnold and John Waite Bowers, eds., *Handbook of Rhetorical and Communication Theory.* Boston: Allyn and Bacon.

Bochner, Arthur and Clifford Kelly (1974). Interpersonal Competence: Rationale, Philosophy, and Implementation of a Conceptual Framework. *Communication Education* 23:279-301.

Bok, Sissela (1978). *Lying: Moral Choice in Public and Private Life.* New York: Pantheon.

Bok, Sissela (1983). *Secrets.* New York: Vintage Books.

Borden, Win (1985). *Vital Speeches of the Day* 51 (April 15).

Borisoff, Deborah and Lisa Merrill (1985). *The Power to Communicate: Gender Differences as Barriers.* Prospect Heights, IL: Waveland Press.

Bosmajian, Haig (1974). *The Language of Oppression.* Washington, D.C.: Public Affairs Press.

Boyd, Stephen D. and Mary Ann Renz (1985). *Organization and Outlining: A Workbook for Students in a Basic Speech Course.* New York: Macmillan.

Bradac, James J., John Waite Bowers, and John A. Courtright (1979). Three Language Variables in Communication Research: Intensity, Immediacy, and Diversity. *Human Communication Research* 5:256-269.

Bradley, Bert E. (1988). *Fundamentals of Speech Communication: The Credibility of Ideas,* 5th ed. Dubuque, IA: Wm. C. Brown.

Brickfield, Cyril F. (1985). *Vital Speeches of the Day* 51 (August 1).

Brody, Jane F. (1991). How to Foster Self-Esteem. *New York Times Magazine* (April 28), 15, 26-27.

Brougher, Toni (1982). *A Way With Words.* Chicago, IL: Nelson-Hall.

Bruneau, Tom (1985). The Time Dimension in Intercultural Communication. In Larry A. Samovar and

Richard E. Porter, eds., *Intercultural Communication: A Reader,* 4th ed. Belmont, CA: Wadsworth, pp. 280-289.

Bruneau, Tom (1990). Chronemics: The Study of Time in Human Interaction. In DeVito and Hecht (1990), pp. 301-311.

Buckley, Reid (1988). *Speaking in Public.* New York: Harper & Row.

Bugental, J. and S. Zelen (1950). Investigations into the 'Self-Concept,' I. The W-A-Y Technique. *Journal of Personality* 18:483-498.

Burgoon, Judee K., David B. Buller, and W. Gill Woodall (1989). *Nonverbal Communication: The Unspoken Dialogue.* New York: Harper & Row.

Burgoon, Judee K. and Jerold L. Hale (1988). Nonverbal Expectancy Violations: Model Elaboration and Application to Immediacy Behaviors. *Communication Monographs* 55: 58-79. Reprinted in DeVito and Hecht (1990), pp. 48-62.

Burns, David D. (1985). *Intimate Connections.* New York: Morrow.

Camden, Carl, Michael T. Motley, and Ann Wilson (1984). White Lies in Interpersonal Communication: A Taxonomy and Preliminary Investigation of Social Motivations. *Western Journal of Speech Communication* 48:309-325.

Cappella, Joseph N. (1987). Interpersonal Communication: Definitions and Fundamental Questions. In Berger and Chaffee (1987), pp. 184-238.

Carroll, John B., ed. (1956). *Language, Thought and Reality: Selected Writings of Benjamin Lee Whorf.* New York: Wiley.

Carter, L. F. (1953). On Defining Leadership. In M. Sherif and M. O. Wilson, eds., *Group Relations at the Crossroads.* New York: Harper & Row, pp. 262-265.

Cate, R., J. Henton, J. Koval, R. Christopher, and S. Lloyd (1982). Premarital Abuse: A Social Psychological Perspective. *Journal of Family Issues* 3, 79-90.

Cathcart, Robert S. and Larry A. Samovar, eds. (1988). *Small Group Communication: A Reader,* 5th ed. Dubuque, IA: Brown.

Chesebro, James, ed. (1981). *Gayspeak.* New York: Pilgrim Press.

Chisholm, Shirley (1978). *Vital Speeches of the Day* 44 (August 15).

Cialdini, Robert T. (1984). *Influence: How and Why People Agree to Things.* New York: Morrow, 1984.

Clark, Herbert (1974). The Power of Positive Speaking. *Psychology Today* 8:102, 108-111.

Clement, Donald A. and Kenneth D. Frandsen (1976). On Conceptual and Empirical Treatments of Feedback in Human Communication. *Communication Monographs* 43:11-28.

Cline, M. G. (1956). The Influence of Social Context on the Perception of Faces. *Journal of Personality* 2:142-185.

Cody, Michael J. (1982). A Typology of Disengagement Strategies and an Examination of the Role Intimacy, Reaction to Inequity, and Relational Problems Play in Strategy Selection. *Communication Monographs* 49:148-170.

Cody, Michael J., Peter J. Marston, and Myrna Foster (1984). Paralinguistic and Verbal Leakage of Deception as a Function of Attempted Control and Timing of Questions. In R. M. Bostrom, ed., *Communication Yearbook 7.* Newbury Park, CA: Sage, pp. 464-490.

Collier, Mary Jane (1991). Conflict Competence Within African, Mexican, and Anglo American Friendships. In *Cross-Cultural Interpersonal Communication,* ed. Stell Ting-Toomey and Felipe Korzenny. Newbury Park, CA: Sage, pp. 132-154.

Condon, John C. and Fathi Yousef (1975). *An Introduction to Intercultural Communication.* Indianapolis, IN: Bobbs-Merrill.

Cook, Mark (1971). *Interpersonal Perception.* Baltimore: Penguin.

Cozby, Paul (1973). Self-Disclosure: A Literature Review. *Psychological Bulletin* 79:73-91.

Cragan, John F. and David W. Wright (1986). *Communication in Small Group Discussions: A Case Study Approach,* 2nd ed. St. Paul, MN: West.

D'Angelo, Frank J. (1980). *Process and Thought in Composition,* 2nd ed. Cambridge, MA: Winthrop.

Davis, Flora (1973). *Inside Intuition.* New York: New American Library.

Davis, Murray S. (1973). *Intimate Relations.* New York: Free Press.

Davitz, Joel R., ed. (1964). *The Communication of Emotional Meaning.* New York: McGraw-Hill.

Deal, James E. and Karen Smith Wampler (1986). Dating Violence: The Primacy of Previous Experience. *Journal of Social and Personal Relationships* 3, 457-471.

Derlega, Valerian J., Barbara A. Winstead, Paul T. P. Wong, and Michael Greenspan (1987). Self-Disclosure and Relationship Development: An Attributional Analysis. In Michael E. Roloff and Gerald R. Miller, Eds., *Interpersonal Processes: New Directions in Communication Research.* Newbury Park, CA: Sage, pp. 172-187.

Derlega, Valerian J., Barbara Winstead, Paul T. P. Wong, and Susan Hunter (1985). Gender Effects in an Initial Encounter: A Case Where Men Exceed Women in Disclosure. *Journal of Social and Personal Relationships* 2:25-44.

DeVito, Joseph A. (1969). Some Psycholinguistic Aspects of Active and Passive Sentences. *Quarterly Journal of Speech* 55:401-406.

DeVito, Joseph A. (1965). Comprehension Factors in Oral and Written Discourse of Skilled Communicators. *Communication Monographs* 32:124-128.

DeVito, Joseph A. (1976). Relative Ease in Comprehending Yes/No Questions. In *Rhetoric and Communication,* Jane Blankenship and Herman G. Stelzner, eds. Urbana: University of Illinois Press, pp. 143-154.

DeVito, Joseph A., ed. (1973). *Language: Concepts and Processes.* Englewood Cliffs, NJ: Prentice Hall.

DeVito, Joseph A. (1974). *General Semantics: Guide and Workbook,* rev. ed. DeLand, FL: Everett/Edwards.

DeVito, Joseph A. (1981). *The Psychology of Speech and Language: An Introduction to Psycholinguistics.* Washington D. C.: University Press of America.

DeVito, Joseph A. (1986). *The Communication Handbook: A Dictionary.* New York: Harper & Row.

DeVito, Joseph A. (1986). Teaching as Relational Development. In Jean Civikly, ed., *Communicating in College Classrooms (New Directions for Teaching and Learning),* No. 26 (June). San Francisco, CA: Jossey-Bass, 1986, pp. 51-60.

DeVito, Joseph A. (1992). *The Interpersonal Communication Book,* 6th ed. New York: Harper & Row.

DeVito, Joseph A. (1989). *The Nonverbal Communication Workbook.* Prospect Heights, IL: Waveland Press.

DeVito, Joseph A. (1990). *The Elements of Public Speaking,* 4th ed. New York: Harper & Row.

DeVito, Joseph A. (1990). *Messages: Building Interpersonal Communication Skills.* New York: Harper & Row.

DeVito, Joseph A., Jill Giattino, and T. D. Schon (1975). *Articulation and Voice: Effective Communication.* Indianapolis: Bobbs-Merrill.

DeVito, Joseph A. and Michael L. Hecht, eds. (1990). *The Nonverbal Communication Reader.* Prospect Heights, IL: Waveland Press.

Dindia, Kathryn, and Leslie A. Baxter, (1987). Strategies for Maintaining and Repairing Marital Relationships. *Journal of Social and Personal Relationships* 4:143-158.

Dindia, Kathryn, and Mary Anne Fitzpatrick, (1985). Marital Communication: Three Approaches Compared. In *Understanding Personal Relationships: An Interdisciplinary Approach.* Steve Duck and Daniel Perlman, eds., 137-158. Newbury Park, CA: Sage.

Dodd, Carley H. (1982). *Dynamics of Intercultural Communication.* Dubuque, IA: Brown.

Dodd, David H. and Raymond M. White, Jr. (1980). *Cognition: Mental Structures and Processes.* Boston: Allyn and Bacon.

Downs, Cal W., G. Paul Smeyak, and Ernest Martin (1980). *Professional Interviewing.* New York: Harper & Row.

Dreyfuss, Henry (1971). *Symbol Sourcebook.* New York: McGraw-Hill.

Duck, Steve (1986). *Human Relationships.* Newbury Park, CA: Sage.

Duck, Steve and Robin Gilmour, eds. (1981). *Personal Relationships. 1: Studying Personal Relationships.* New York: Academic Press.

Egan, Gerard (1970). *Encounter: Group Processes for Interpersonal Growth.* Belmont, CA: Brooks/Cole.

Eisen, Jeffrey with Pat Farley (1984). *Powertalk: How to Speak It, Think It, and Use It.* New York: Simon & Schuster.

Ekman, Paul (1965). Communication through Nonverbal Behavior: A Source of Information about an Interpersonal Relationship. In S. S. Tomkins and C. E. Izard, eds., *Affect, Cognition and Personality.* New York: Springer.

Ekman, Paul (1975). The Universal Smile: Face Muscles Talk Every Language. *Psychology Today* 9:35-39

Ekman, Paul (1985). *Telling Lies: Clues to Deceit in the Marketplace, Politics, and Marriage.* New York: W. W. Norton.

Ekman, Paul and Wallace V. Friesen (1969). The Repertoire of Nonverbal Behavior: Categories, Origins, Usage, and Coding. *Semiotica* 1:49-98.

Ekman, Paul, Wallace V. Friesen, and Phoebe Ellsworth (1972). *Emotion in the Human Face: Guidelines for Research and an Integration of Findings.* New York: Pergamon Press.

Ekman, Paul, Wallace V. Friesen, and S. S. Tomkins (1971). Facial Affect Scoring Technique: A First Validity Study. *Semiotica* 3:37-58.

Ellis, Albert and Robert A. Harper (1975). *A New Guide to Rational Living.* Hollywood, CA: Wilshire Books.

Ennis, Robert H. (1987). A taxonomy of Critical Thinking Dispositions and Abilities. In *Teaching Thinking Skills: Theory and Practice,* ed., Joan Boykoff Baron and Robert J. Sternberg. New York: W. H. Freeman, pp. 9-26.

Exline, R. V., S. L. Ellyson, and B. Long (1975). Visual Behavior as an Aspect of Power Role Relationships. In P. Pliner, L. Krames, and T. Alloway, eds., *Nonverbal Communication of Aggression.* New York: Plenum.

Faber, Adele and Elaine Mazlish (1980). *How to Talk so Kids Will Listen and Listen so Kids Will Talk.* New York: Avon.

Filley, Alan C. (1975). *Interpersonal Conflict Resolution.* Glenview, IL: Scott, Foresman.

Fisher, B. Aubrey (1980). *Small Group Decision Making: Communication and the Group Process,* 2nd ed. New York: McGraw-Hill.

Fishman, Joshua A. (1972). The *Sociology of Language.* Rowley, Mass.: Newbury House.

Fiske, Susan T. and Shelley E. Taylor (1984). *Social Cognition.* Reading, MA: Addison-Wesley.

Fitzpatrick, Mary Anne (1983). Predicting Couples' Communication from Couples' Self-Reports. In R. N. Bostrom, ed., *Communication Yearbook 7,* pp. 49-82. Newbury Park, CA: Sage.

Floyd, James J. (1985). *Listening: A Practical Approach.* Glenview, IL: Scott, Foresman.

Folger, Joseph P. and Marshall Scott Poole (1984). *Working Through Conflict: A Communication Perspective.* Glenview, IL: Scott, Foresman.

Freedman, Jonathan (1978). *Happy People: What Happiness Is, Who Has It, and Why.* New York: Ballantine Books.

Frye, Jerry K. (1980). *FIND: Frye's Index to Nonverbal Data.* Duluth: University of Minnesota Computer Center.

Furnham, Adrian and Stephen Bochner (1986). *Culture*

*Shock: Psychological Reactions to Unfamiliar Environments.* New York: Methuen.

Gabor, Don (1989). *How to Talk to the People You Love.* New York: Simon & Schuster.

Galvin, Kathleen and Bernard J. Brommel (1991). *Family Communication: Cohesion and Change,* 3rd ed. Glenview, IL: Scott, Foresman.

Garner, Alan (1981). *Conversationally Speaking.* New York: McGraw-Hill.

Gelles, R. (1981). The Myth of the Battered Husband. In R. Walsh and O. Pocs, eds., *Marriage and Family 81/82.* Dushkin: Guildford.

Gelles, R., and C. Cornell (1985). *Intimate Violence in Families.* Newbury Park, CA: Sage.

Gibb, Cecil A. (1969). Leadership. In G. Lindsey and E. Aronson, eds. *The Handbook of Social Psychology,* 2nd ed., vol. 4. Reading, MA: Addison-Wesley, pp. 205-282.

Gibb, Jack (1961). Defensive Communication. *Journal of Communication* 11:141-148.

Gilmour, Robin and Steve Duck, eds. (1986). *The Emerging Field of Personal Relationships.* Hillsdale, NJ: Lawrence Erlbaum.

Goffman, Erving (1967). *Interaction Ritual: Essays on Face-to-Face Behavior.* New York: Pantheon.

Goffman, Erving (1971). *Relations in Public: Microstudies of the Public Order.* New York: Harper Colophon.

Gonzalez, Alexander and Philip G. Zimbardo (1985). Time in Perspective. *Psychology Today* 19:20-26. Reprinted in DeVito and Hecht (1990), pp. 312-321.

Gordon, Thomas (1975). *P.E.T.: Parent Effectiveness Training.* New York: New American Library.

Goss, Blaine (1989). *The Psychology of Communication.* Prospect Heights, IL: Waveland Press.

Goss, Blaine, M. Thompson, and S. Olds (1978). Behavioral Support for Systematic Desensitization for Communication Apprehension. *Human Communication Research* 4:158-163.

Gratus, Jack (1988). *Successful Interviewing: How to Find and Keep the Best People.* New York: Penguin.

Gronbeck, Bruce E., Raymie E. McKerrow, Douglas Ehninger, and Alan H. Monroe (1990). *Principles and Types of Speech Communication,* 11th ed. Glenview, IL: Scott, Foresman.

Gross, Ronald (1991). *Peak Learning.* Los Angeles: Jeremy P. Tarcher.

Hackman, Michael Z. and Craig E. Johnson (1991). *Leadership: A Communication Perspective.* Prospect Heights, IL: Waveland Press.

Haggard, E. A., and K. S. Isaacs (1966). Micromomentary Facial Expressions as Indicators of Ego Mechanisms in Psychotherapy. In L. A. Gottschalk and A. H. Auerbach, eds., *Methods of Research in Psychotherapy.* Englewood Cliffs, NJ: Prentice-Hall.

Hall, Edward T. (1959). *The Silent Language.* Garden City, NY: Doubleday.

Hall, Edward T. (1963). System for the Notation of Prox-emic Behavior *American Anthropologist* 65: 1003-1026.

Hall, Edward T. (1966). *The Hidden Dimension.* Garden City, NY: Doubleday.

Hall, Edward T., and Mildred Reed Hall (1987). *Hidden Differences: Doing Business with the Japanese.* New York: Doubleday, Anchor Books.

Hamlin, Sonya (1988). *How to Talk so People Listen.* New York: Harper & Row.

Haney, William (1973). *Communication and Organizational Behavior: Text and Cases,* 3rd ed. Homewood IL: Irwin.

Hart, Roderick P, and Don M. Burks (1972). Rhetorical Sensitivity and Social Interaction. *Communication Monographs* 39:75-91.

Hart, Roderick P., Robert E. Carlson, and William F. Eadie (1980). Attitudes Toward Communication and the Assessment of Rhetorical Sensitivity. *Communication Monographs* 47:1-22.

Hastorf, Albert, David Schneider, and Judith Polefka (1970). *Person Perception.* Reading, MA: Addison-Wesley.

Hatfield, Elaine and Jane Traupman (1981). Intimate Relationships: A Perspective from Equity Theory. In Steve Duck and Robin Gilmour, eds., *Personal Relationships. 1: Studying Personal Relationships.* New York: Academic Press, pp. 165-178.

Hayakawa, S. I. and Alan R. Hayakawa (1990). *Language in Thought and Action,* 5th ed. New York: Harcourt Brace Jovanovich.

Hecht, Michael L. (1978a). The Conceptualization and Measurement of Interpersonal Communication Satisfaction. *Human Communication Research* 4:253-264.

Hecht, Michael L. (1978b). Toward a Conceptualization of Communication Satisfaction. *Quarterly Journal of Speech* 64:47-62.

Hecht, Michael L. and Sidney Ribeau (1984). Ethnic Communication: A Comparative Analysis of Satisfying Communication. *International Journal of Intercultural Relations* 8:135-151.

Heinrich, Robert et al (1983). *Instructional Media: The New Technologies of Instruction.* New York: Wiley.

Henley, Nancy M. (1977). *Body Politics: Power, Sex, and Nonverbal Communication.* Englewood Cliffs, NJ: Prentice-Hall.

Hess, Ekhard H. (1975). *The Tell-Tale Eye.* New York: Van Nostrand Reinhold.

Hewitt, John and Randall Stokes (1975). Disclaimers *American Sociological Review* 40:1-11.

Hickey, Neil (1989). Decade of Change, Decade of Choice. *TV Guide* 37 (December 9):29-34.

Hickson, Mark L. and Don W. Stacks (1989). *NVC: Nonverbal Communication: Studies and Applications,* 2nd ed. Dubuque, IA: Wm. C. Brown.

Hocker, Joyce L. and William W. Wilmot (1985). *Interpersonal Conflict,* 2nd ed. Dubuque, IA: Wm. C. Brown.

Hollender, Marc and Alexander Mercer (1976). Wish to Be Held and Wish to Hold in Men and Women *Archives of General Psychiatry* 33:49-51.

Hopper, Robert, Mark L. Knapp and Lorel Scott (1981). Couples' Personal Idioms: Exploring Intimate Talk. *Journal of Communication* 31:23-33.

Huffines, LaUna (1986). *Connecting With All the People in Your Life*. New York: Harper & Row.

Huseman, Richard C. (1977). The Role of the Nominal Group in Small Group Communication. In Richard C. Huseman, Cal M. Logue, and Dwight L. Freshley, eds. *Readings in Interpersonal and Organizational Communication*, 3rd ed. Boston: Holbrook Press, pp. 493-502.

Hymes, Dell (1974). *Foundations in Sociolinguistics: An Ethnographic Approach*. Philadelphia: University of Pennsylvania Press.

Infante, Dominick A. (1988). *Arguing Constructively*. Prospect Heights, IL: Waveland Press.

Infante, Dominick A., Andrew S. Rancer, and Deanna F. Womack (1990). *Building Communication Theory*. Prospect Heights, IL: Waveland.

Insel, Paul M. and Lenore F. Jacobson, eds. (1975). *What Do You Expect? An Inquiry into Self-Fulfilling Prophecies*. Menlo Park, CA: Cummings.

Jaksa, James A. and Michael S. Pritchard (1988). *Communication Ethics: Methods of Analysis*. Belmont, CA: Wadsworth.

Janis, Irving (1983). *Victims of Group Thinking: A Psychological Study of Foreign Policy Decisions and Fiascoes*, 2nd ed., rev. Boston: Houghton Mifflin.

Jecker, Jon and David Landy (1969). Liking a Person as a Function of Doing Him a Favor. *Human Relations* 22: 371-378.

Jensen, J. Vernon (1985). Perspectives on Nonverbal Intercultural Communication. In *Intercultural Communication: A Reader*, 4th ed., ed. Larry Samovar and Richard E. Porter. Belmont, CA: Wadsworth, pp. 256-272.

Johnson, Wendell (1951). The Spoken Word and the Great Unsaid. *Quarterly Journal of Speech* 37: 419-429.

Jones, E. E. and K. E. Davis (1965). From Acts to Dispositions: The Attribution Process in Person Perception. In L. Berkowitz, ed. *Advances In Experimental Social Psychology*, vol. 2. New York: Academic Press, pp. 219-266.

Jones, E. E., et al. (1984). *Social Stigma: The Psychology of Marked Relationships*. New York: W. H. Freeman.

Jones, Stanley (1986). Sex Differences in Touch Communication. *Western Journal of Speech Communication* 50:227-241.

Jones, Stanley and A. Elaine Yarbrough (1985). A Naturalistic Study of the Meanings of Touch. *Communication Monographs* 52:19-56. A version of this paper appears in DeVito and Hecht (1990), pp. 235-244.

Jourard, Sidney M. (1966). An Exploratory Study of Body-Accessibility. *British Journal of Social and Clinical Psychology* 5:221-231.

Jourard, Sidney M. (1968). *Disclosing Man to Himself*. New York: Van Nostrand Reinhold.

Jourard, Sidney M. (1971a). *Self-Disclosure*. New York: Wiley.

Jourard, Sidney M. (1971b). *The Transparent Self*, rev. ed. New York: Van Nostrand Reinhold.

Kanner, Bernice (1989). Color Schemes. *New York Magazine* (April 3):22-23.

Kelley, H. H. (1967). Attribution Theory in Social Psychology. In D. Levine, ed., *Nebraska Symposium on Motivation*. Lincoln: University of Nebraska Press, pp. 192-240.

Kelley, H. H. (1973). The Process of Causal Attribution. *American Psychologist* 28:107-128.

Kelley, H. H. (1979). *Personal Relationships: Their Structures and Processes*. Hillsdale, NJ: Erlbaum.

Kelley, H. H. and J. W. Thibaut (1978). *Interpersonal Relations: A Theory of Interdependence*. New York: Wiley/Interscience.

Kemp, Jerrold E. and Deane K. Dayton (1985). *Planning and Producing Instructional Media*, 5th ed. New York: Harper & Row.

Kesselman-Turkel, Judi and Franklynn Peterson (1982). *Note-Taking Made Easy*. Chicago: Contemporary Books.

Kim, Hyun J. (1991). Influence of Language and Similarity on Initial Intercultural Attraction. In *Cross-Cultural Interpersonal Communication*, ed. Stella Ting-Toomey and Felipe Korzenny. Newbury Park, CA: Sage, pp. 213-229.

Kim, Young Yun, ed. (1986). *Interethnic Communication: Current Research*. Newbury Park, CA: Sage.

Kim, Young Yun (1988). Communication and Acculturation. In Samovar and Porter (1988), pp. 344-354.

Kim, Young Yun (1991). Intercultural Communication Competence. In *Cross-Cultural Interpersonal Communication*, ed. Stella Ting-Toomey and Felipe Korzenny. Newbury Park, CA: Sage, pp. 259-275.

Kim, Young Yun and William B. Gudykunst, eds. (1988). *Theories in Intercultural Communication*. Newbury Park, CA: Sage.

Kleinke, Chris L. (1978). *Self-Perception: The Psychology of Personal Awareness*. San Francisco, CA: Freeman.

Kleinke, Chris L. (1986). *Meeting and Understanding People*. New York: W. H. Freeman.

Knapp, Mark L. (1978). *Nonverbal Behavior in Human Interaction*, 2nd ed. New York: Holt, Rinehart and Winston.

Knapp, Mark L. (1984). *Interpersonal Communication and Human Relationships*. Boston: Allyn and Bacon.

Knapp, Mark L. and Judith Hall (1992). *Nonverbal Communication in Human Interaction*, 3rd ed. New York: Harcourt Brace Jovanovich.

Kochman, Thomas (1981). *Black and White: Styles in Conflict*. Chicago: University of Chicago Press.

Kramer, Ernest (1963). Judgment of Personal Characteristics and Emotions from Nonverbal Properties. *Psychological Bulletin* 60:408-420.

Kramarae, Cheris (1981). *Women and Men Speaking*. Rowley, MA: Newbury House.

LaFrance, M. and C. Mayo (1978). *Moving Bodies: Non-verbal Communication in Social Relationships*. Monterey, CA: Brooks/Cole.

Laing, Ronald D., H. Phillipson, and A. Russell Lee (1966). *Interpersonal Perception*. New York: Springer.

Lambdin, William (1981). *Doublespeak Dictionary*. Los Angeles, CA: Pinnacle Books.

Langer, Ellen J. (1978). Rethinking the Role of Thought in Social Interaction. In J. H. Harvey, W. J. Ickes, and R. F. Kidd, eds., *New Directions in Attribution Research*, vol. 2. J.J. Hillsdale: Lawrence Erlbaum, pp. 35-58.

Langer, Ellen J. (1989). *Mindfulness*. Reading, MA: Addison-Wesley.

Larson, Charles U. (1992). *Persuasion: Reception and Responsibility*, 6th ed. Belmont, CA: Wadsworth.

Leathers, Dale G. (1986). *Successful Nonverbal Communication: Principles and Applications*. New York: Macmillan.

Lederer, William J. (1984). *Creating a Good Relationship*. New York: Norton.

Lee, Alfred McClung and Elizabeth Briant Lee (1972). *The Fine Art of Propaganda*. San Francisco, CA: International Society for General Semantics.

Leeds, Dorothy (1988). *Powerspeak*. New York: Prentice Hall Press.

LeVine, R. and K. Bartlett (1984). Pace of Life, Punctuality and Coronary Heart Disease in Six Countries. *Journal of Cross-Cultural Psychology* 15:233-255.

Light, W. (1984). *Vital Speeches of the Day* 50 (July 15).

Littlejohn, Stephen W. (1989). *Theories of Human Communication*, 3rd ed. Belmont, CA: Wadsworth.

Littlejohn, Stephen W. and David M. Jabusch (1987). *Persuasive Transactions*. Glenview, IL: Scott, Foresman.

Luft, Joseph (1969). *Of Human Interaction*. Palo Alto, CA: Mayfield Publishing Co.

Luft, Joseph (1970). *Group Processes: An Introduction to Group Dynamics*, 2nd ed. Palo Alto, CA: Mayfield Publishing Co.

Lurie, Alison (1983). *The Language of Clothes*. New York: Vintage.

Lyman, Stanford M. and Marvin B. Scott (1967). Territoriality: A Neglected Sociological Dimension. *Social Problems* 15:236-249. Reprinted in DeVito and Hecht (1990), pp. 193-202.

MacLachlan, John (1979). What People Really Think of Fast Talkers. *Psychology Today* 13 (November):113-117.

McCarthy, Michael J. (1991). *Mastering the Information Age*. Los Angeles: Jeremy P. Tarcher.

McCroskey, James C. (1982). *An Introduction to Rhetorical Communication*, 4th ed. Englewood Cliffs, NJ: Prentice-Hall.

McCroskey, James C., Virginia P. Richmond, and Robert A. Stewart (1986). *One on One: The Foundations of Interpersonal Communication*. Englewood Cliffs, NJ: Prentice-Hall.

McCroskey, James C., and Lawrence Wheeless (1976). *Introduction to Human Communication*. Boston: Allyn & Bacon.

McGill, Michael E. (1985). *The McGill Report on Male Intimacy*. New York: Harper & Row.

McLaughlin, Margaret L. (1984). *Conversation: How Talk Is Organized*. Newbury Park, CA: Sage.

McMahon, Ed (1986). *The Art of Public Speaking*. New York: Ballantine.

Malandro, Loretta A., Larry Barker, and Deborah Ann Barker (1989). *Nonverbal Communication*, 2nd ed. New York: Random House.

Malinowski, Bronislaw (1923). The Problem of Meaning in Primitive Languages. In C. K. Ogden and I. A. Richards, *The Meaning of Meaning*. New York: Harcourt Brace Jovanovich, pp. 296-336.

Marshall, Evan (1983). *Eye Language: Understanding the Eloquent Eye*. New York: New Trend.

Marshall, Linda L. and Patricia Rose (1987). Gender, Stress and Violence in the Adult Relationships of a Sample of College Students. *Journal of Social and Personal Relationships* 4, 299-316.

Martel, Myles (1989). *The Persuasive Edge*. New York: Fawcett.

Maynard, Harry E. (1963). How to Become a Better Premise Detective. *Public Relations Journal* 19:20-22.

Medley, H. Anthony (1978). *Sweaty Palms: The Neglected Art of Being Interviewed*. Belmont, CA: Wadsworth Lifetime Learning Publications.

Mehrabian, Albert (1968). Communication Without Words. *Psychology Today* 2:53-55.

Mehrabian, Albert (1976). *Public Places and Private Spaces*. New York: Basic Books.

Mencken, H. L. (1971). *The American Language*. New York: Knopf.

Merton, Robert K. (1957). *Social Theory and Social Structure*. New York: Free Press.

Miller, Gerald R. (1978). The Current State of Theory and Research in Interpersonal Communication. *Human Communication Research* 4:164-178.

Miller, Gerald R. and Malcolm R. Parks (1982). Communication in Dissolving Relationships. In Steve Duck, ed., *Personal Relationships. 4: Dissolving Personal Relationships*. New York: Academic Press.

Miller, Sherod, Daniel Wackman, Elam Nunnally, and Carol Saline (1982). *Straight Talk*. New York: New American Library.

Molloy, John (1975). *Dress for Success*. New York: P. H. Wyden.

Molloy, John (1977). *The Woman's Dress for Success Book*. Chicago: Follet.

Montagu, Ashley (1971). *Touching: The Human Significance of the Skin*. New York: Harper & Row.

Morris, Desmond (1967). *The Naked Ape*. London: Jonathan Cape.

Morris, Desmond (1972). *Intimate Behaviour*. New York: Bantam.

Morris, Desmond (1977). *Manwatching: A Field Guide to Human Behavior.* New York: Abrams.

Morris, Desmond, Peter Collett, Peter Marsh, and Marie O'Shaughnessy (1979). *Gestures: Their Origins and Distribution.* New York: Stein and Day.

Naifeh, Steven and Gregory White Smith (1984). *Why Can't Men Open Up? Overcoming Men's Fear of Intimacy.* New York: Clarkson N. Potter.

Naisbitt, John (1984). *Megatrends: Ten New Directions Tranforming Our Lives.* New York: Warner.

Napier, Rodney W. and Matti K. Gershenfeld (1981). *Groups: Theory and Experience,* 2nd ed. Boston: Houghton Mifflin.

Nichols, Ralph (1961). Do We Know How to Listen? Practical Helps in a Modern Age. *Communication Education* 10: 118-124.

Nichols, Ralph and Leonard Stevens (1957). *Are You Listening?* New York: McGraw-Hill.

Nickerson, Raymond S. (1987). Why Teach Thinking?" In *Teaching Thinking Skills: Theory and Practice,* ed., Joan Boykoff Baron and Robert J. Sternberg. New York: W. H. Freeman, pp. 27-37.

Nierenberg, Gerald and Henry Calero (1971). *How to Read a Person Like a Book.* New York: Pocket Books.

Nierenberg, Gerald and Henry Calero (1973). *Metatalk.* New York: Simon and Schuster.

Oberg, Kalervo (1960). Cultural Shock: Adjustment to New Cultural Environments. *Practical Anthropology* 7:177-182.

Osborn, Alex (1957). *Applied Imagination,* rev. ed. New York: Scribners.

Osborn, Michael (1982). *Speaking in Public.* Boston, MA: Houghton Mifflin.

Patton, Bobby R., Kim Giffin, and Eleanor Nyquist Patton (1989). *Decision-Making Group Interaction,* 3rd ed. New York: Harper & Row.

Pearce, Barnett and Stewart M. Sharp (1973). Self-Disclosing Communication. *Journal of Communication* 23:409-425.

Pearson, Judy C. (1980). Sex Roles and Self-Disclosure: *Psychological Reports* 47: 640.

Pearson, Judy C. (1989). *Gender and Communication.* Dubuque, IA: Wm. C. Brown.

Pearson, Judy C. (1989). *Communication in the Family.* New York: Harper & Row.

Pease, Allen (1984). *Signals: How to Use Body Language for Power, Success and Love.* New York: Bantam Books.

Penfield, Joyce, ed. (1987). *Women and Language in Transition.* Albany: State University of New York Press.

Peplau, Letitia Anne and Daniel Perlman, eds. (1982). *Loneliness: A Sourcebook of Current Theory, Research and Therapy.* New York: Wiley/Interscience.

Perlman, Daniel and Letitia Anne Peplau (1981). Toward a Social Psychology of Loneliness. In *Personal Relationships. 3: Personal Relationships in Disorder,* ed. Steve Duck and Robin Gilmour. New York: Academic Press, pp. 31-56.

Peterson, Russell (1985). *Vital Speeches of the Day* 51 (July 1).

Pfeiffer, J. W., and J. E. Jones (1969). *Structured Experiences for Human Relations Training.* Iowa City, IA: University Associates Press.

Pilkington, Constance J., and Deborah R. Richardson (1988). Perceptions of Risk in Intimacy. *Journal of Social and Personal Relationships* 5:503-508.

Pittenger, Robert E., Charles F. Hockett, and John J. Danehy (1960). *The First Five Minutes.* Ithaca, NY: Paul Martineau.

Qubein, Nido R. (1986). *Get the Best from Yourself.* New York: Berkley.

Rankin, Paul (1929). Listening Ability. *Proceedings of the Ohio State Educational Conference's Ninth Annual Session.*

Reed, Warren H. (1985). *Positive Listening: Learning to Hear What People Are Really Saying.* New York: Franklin Watts.

Reik, Theodore (1944). *A Psychologist Looks at Love.* New York: Rinehart.

Rich, Andrea L. (1974). *Interracial Communication.* New York: Harper & Row.

Richards, I. A. (1951). Communication Between Men: The Meaning of Language. In Heinz von Foerster, ed., *Cybernetics, Transactions of the Eighth Conference.*

Richmond, Virginia P. and James C. McCroskey (1992). *Communication: Apprehension, Avoidance, and Effectiveness,* 3rd ed. Scottsdale, AZ: Gorsuch Scarisbrick.

Richmond, Virginia, James McCroskey, and Steven Payne (1987). *Nonverbal Behavior in Interpersonal Relationships.* Englewood Cliffs, NJ: Prentice-Hall.

Riggio, Ronald E. (1987). *The Charisma Quotient.* New York: Dodd, Mead.

Robinson, W. P. (1972). *Language and Social Behavior.* Baltimore: Penguin Books.

Rockefeller, David (1985). *Vital Speeches of the Day* 51 (September 15).

Rodriguez, Maria (1988). Do Blacks and Hispanics Evaluate Assertive Male and Female Characters Differently? *Howard Journal of Communication* 1: 101-107.

Rogers, Carl (1970). *Carl Rogers on Encounter Groups.* New York: Harrow Books.

Rogers, Carl and Richard Farson (1981). Active Listening. In DeVito, Joseph A., ed., *Communication: Concepts and Processes,* 3rd ed. Englewood Cliffs, NJ: Prentice-Hall, pp. 137-147.

Rothwell, J. Dan (1982). *Telling Its Like It Isn't: Language Misuse & Malpractice/What We Can Do About It.* Englewood Cliffs, NJ: Prentice-Hall.

Rosenfeld, Lawrence (1979). Self-disclosure Avoidance: Why I Am Afraid to Tell You Who I Am. *Communication Monographs* 46:63-74.

Rosenfeld, Lawrence, Sallie Kartus, and Chett Ray (1976). Body Accessibility Revisited. *Journal of Communication* 26:27-30.

Rosenthal, Peggy (1984). *Words and Values: Some Leading*

*Words and Where They Lead Us.* New York: Oxford University Press.

Rosenthal, Robert and L. Jacobson (1968). *Pygmalion in the Classroom.* New York: Holt, Rinehart and Winston.

Ruben, Brent D. (1985). Human Communication and Cross-Cultural Effectiveness. In Larry A. Samovar and Richard E. Porter, eds., *Intercultural Communication: A Reader,* 4th ed. Belmont, CA: Wadsworth, pp. 338-346.

Ruben, Brent D. (1988). *Communication and Human Behavior,* 2nd ed. New York: Macmillan.

Rubenstein, Carin and Philip Shaver (1982). *In Search of Intimacy.* New York: Delacorte.

Rubin, Theodore Isaac (1983). *One to One: Understanding Personal Relationships.* New York: Viking.

Rubin, Zick (1973). *Liking and Loving: An Invitation to Social Psychology.* New York: Holt.

Rubin, Zick and Elton B. McNeil (1985). *Psychology: Being Human,* 4th ed. New York: Harper & Row.

Ruchlis, Hy (1990). *Clear Thinking: A Practical Introduction.* Buffalo, NY: Prometheus Books.

Ruesch, Jurgen and Gregory Bateson (1951). *Communication: The Social Matrix of Psychiatry.* New York: Norton.

Ruggiero, Vincent Ryan (1987). *Vital Speeches of the Day* 53 (August 15).

Ruggiero, Vincent Ryan (1990). *The Art of Thinking: A Guide to Critical and Creative Thought,* 3rd ed. New York: HarperCollins.

Samovar, Larry A., Richard E. Porter, and Nemi C. Jain (1981). *Understanding Intercultural Communication.* Belmont, CA: Wadsworth.

Samovar, Larry A. and Richard E. Porter, eds. (1988). *Intercultural Communication: A Reader,* 5th ed. Belmont, CA: Wadsworth.

Sargent, J. F. and Gerald R. Miller (1971). Some Differences in Certain Communication Behaviors of Autocratic and Democratic Leaders. *Journal of Communication* 21:233-252.

Schaefer, Charles E. (1984). *How to Talk to Children about Really Important Things.* New York: Harper & Row.

Schatski, Michael (1981). *Negotiation: The Art of Getting What You Want.* New York: New American Library.

Scherer, K. R. (1986). Vocal Affect Expression. *Psychological Bulletin* 99:143-165.

Schultz, Beatrice G. (1989). *Communicating in the Small Group: Theory and Practice.* New York: Harper & Row.

Seidler, Ann and Doris Bianchi (1988). *Voice and Diction Fitness: A Comprehensive Approach.* New York: Harper & Row.

Shannon, Jacqueline (1987). Don't Smile When You Say That. *Executive Female* 10:33, 43. Reprinted in DeVito and Hecht (1990), pp. 115-117.

Shaw, Marvin (1955). A Comparison of Two Types of Leadership in Various Communication Nets. *Journal of Abnormal and Social Psychology* 50:127-134.

Shaw, Marvin (1981). *Group Dynamics: The Psychology of Small Group Behaviors,* 3rd ed. New York: McGraw-Hill.

Shimanoff, Susan (1980). *Communication Rules: Theory and Research.* Newbury Park, CA.: Sage.

Silber, John R. (1985). *Vital Speeches of the Day* 51 (September 15).

Sillars, Alan L. and Michael D. Scott (1983). Interpersonal Perception Between Intimates: An Integrative Review. *Human Communication Research* 10:153-176.

Sincoff, Michael Z. and Robert S. Goyer (1984). *Interviewing.* New York: Macmillan.

Singer, Marshall R. (1987). *Intercultural Communication: A Perceptual Approach.* Englewood Cliffs, NJ: Prentice-Hall.

Skopec, Eric William (1986). *Situational Interviewing.* Prospect Heights, IL: Waveland Press.

Smith, Mary John (1982). *Persuasion and Human Action: A Review and Critique of Social Influence Theories.* Belmont, CA: Wadsworth.

Snyder, Mark (1986). *Public Appearances, Private Realities.* New York: Freeman.

Sommer, Robert (1969). *Personal Space: The Behavioral Basis of Design.* Englewood Cliffs, NJ: Prentice-Hall [Spectrum].

Spitzberg, Brian H. and William R. Cupach (1984). *Interpersonal Communication Competence.* Beverly Hills, CA: Sage.

Spitzberg, Brian H. and William R. Cupach (1989). *Handbook of Interpersonal Competence Research.* New York: Springer-Verlag.

Spitzberg, Brian H. and Michael L. Hecht (1984). A Component Model of Relational Competence. *Human Communication Research* 10: 575-599.

Sprague, Jo and Douglas Stuart (1988). *The Speaker's Handbook,* 2nd ed. San Diego, CA: Harcourt Brace Jovanovich.

Steil, Lyman K., Larry L. Barker, and Kittie W. Watson (1983). *Effective Listening: Key to Your Success.* Reading, MA: Addison-Wesley.

Steiner, Claude (1981). *The Other Side of Power.* New York: Grove.

Sternberg, Robert J. (1987). Questions and Answers about the Nature and Teaching of Thinking Skills. In *Teaching Thinking Skills: Theory and Practice,* ed., Joan Boykoff Baron and Robert J. Sternberg. New York: W. H. Freeman, pp. 251-259.

Stewart, Charles J. and William B. Cash, Jr. (1988). *Interviewing: Principles and Practices,* 5th ed. Dubuque, IA: Wm. C. Brown.

Stillings, Neil A., *et al.* (1987). *Cognitive Science: An Introduction.* Cambridge, MA: MIT Press.

Styles, R. P. (1985). *Vital Speeches of the Day* 51 (October 1).

Swets, Paul W. (1983). *The Art of Talking so that People Will Listen.* Englewood Cliffs, NJ: Prentice-Hall [Spectrum].

Taylor, Dalmas A., and Irwin Altman (1987). Communication In Interpersonal Relationships: *Social Penetration Processes*. In *Interpersonal Processes: New Directions in Communication Research*, ed., M. E. Roloff and G. R. Miller, eds., 257-277. Newbury Park, CA: Sage.

Thibaut, John W. and Harold H. Kelley (1986). *The Social Psychology of Groups*. New Brunswick, NJ: Transaction Books.,

Thorne, Barrie, Cheris Kramarae, and Nancy Henley, eds. (1983). *Language, Gender and Society*. Rowley, MA: Newbury House Publishers.

Trager, George L. (1958). Paralanguage: A First Approximation. *Studies in Linguistics* 13:1-12.

Trager, George L. (1961). The Typology of Paralanguage. *Anthropological Linguistics* 3:17-21.

Trenholm, Sarah (1991). *Human Communication Theory*, 2nd ed. Englewood Cliffs, NJ: Prentice-Hall.

Truax, C. (1961). *A Scale for the Measurement of Accurate Empathy*, Wisconsin Psychiatric Institute Discussion Paper No. 20. Madison, WI: Wisconsin Psychiatric Institute.

Tubbs, Stewart L. (1988). *A Systems Approach to Small Group Interaction*, 3rd ed. New York: Random House.

Ullmann, Stephen (1962). *Semantics: An Introduction to the Science of Meaning*. New York: Barnes & Noble.

Valenti, Jack (1982). *Speaking Up with Confidence: How to Prepare, Learn, and Deliver Effective Speeches*. New York: William Morrow.

Veenendall, Thomas L. and Marjorie C. Feinstein (1990). *Let's Talk About Relationships: Cases in Study*. Prospect Heights, IL: Waveland Press.

Verderber, Rudolph F. and Kathleen S.Verderber (1992). *Inter-Act: Using Interpersonal Communication Skills*, 6th ed. Belmont, CA: Wadsworth.

Wade, Carole and Carol Tarvis (1990). *Learning to Think Critically: The Case of Close Relationships*. New York: HarperCollins.

Walster, Elaine, G. W. Walster, and Ellen Berscheid (1978). *Equity: Theory and Research*. Boston: Allyn and Bacon.

Warnick, Barbara and Edward S. Inch (1989). *Critical Thinking and Communication: The Use of Reason in Argument*. New York: Macmillan.

Watson, Arden K. and Carley H. Dodd (1984). Alleviating Communication Apprehension through Rational Emotive Therapy: A Comparative Evaluation. *Communication Education* 33:257-266.

Watzlawick, Paul (1977). *How Real Is Real? Confusion, Disinformation, Communication: An Anecdotal Introduction to Communications Theory*. New York: Vintage Books.

Watzlawick, Paul (1978). *The Language of Change: Elements of Therapeutic Communication*. New York: Basic Books.

Watzlawick, Paul, Janet Helmick Beavin, and Don D. Jackson (1967). *Pragmatics of Human Communication: A Study of Interactional Patterns, Pathologies, and Paradoxes*. New York: Norton.

Weinstein, Eugene A. and Paul Deutschberger (1963). Some Dimensions of Altercasting. *Sociometry* 26:454-466.

Wells, Theodora (1980). *Keeping Your Cool Under Fire: Communicating Non-Defensively*. New York: McGraw-Hill.

Wheeless, Lawrence R. and Janis Grotz (1977). The Measurement of Trust and Its Relationship to Self-Disclosure. *Human Communication Research* 3:250-257.

White, R., and R. Lippitt (1960). *Autocracy and Democracy*. New York: Harper & Row.

Whitman, Richard F. and John H. Timmis (1975). The Influence of Verbal Organizational Structure and Verbal Organizing Skills on Select Measures of Learning. *Human Communication Research* 1:293-301.

Wiemann, John M. (1977). Explication and Test of a Model of Communicative Competence. *Human Communication Research* 3:195-213.

Wiemann, John M. and P. Backlund (1980). Current Theory and Research in Communicative Competence. *Review of Educational Research* 50:185-199.

Williams, Andrea (1985). *Making Decisions*. New York: Zebra.

Wilmot, William W. (1987). *Dyadic Communication*, 3rd ed. New York: Random House.

Wilson, Glenn and David Nias (1976). *The Mystery of Love*. New York: Quadrangle/The New York Times Book Co.

Wolf, Florence I., Nadine C. Marsnik, William S. Tacey, and Ralph G. Nichols (1983). *Perceptive Listening*. New York: Holt, Rinehart and Winston.

Wood, Julia T. (1982). Communication and Relational Culture: Bases for the Study of Human Relationships. *Communication Quarterly* 30:75-83.

Zima, Joseph P. (1983). *Interviewing: Key to Effective Management*. Chicago, IL: Science Research Associations, Inc.

Zimmer, Troy A. (1986). Premarital Anxieties. *Journal of Social and Personal Relationships* 3:149-159.

Zincoff, M. Z., and Robert S. Goyer (1984). *Interviewing*. New York: Macmillan.

# PHOTO CREDITS

# INDEX

Good old index. You can't beat it.
—SHERLOCK HOLMES

Criticism. *See* Evaluation
Critique forms, 229, 235, 324–325
Cues
 backchanneling, 60
 and conversational turns,
  116–117
 interactive strategies and, 55
Culture, 9
 body movements and, 104
 communication skills and, 133
 competence and, 9
 and concept of time, 121
 conflict management and, 150
 and distance, 108–109
 eye movements and, 105
 gift giving and, 113
 implicit personality theory and,
  49, 72
 in-group talk and, 89
 meaning and, 79
 self-disclosure and, 36, 38
 sensitivity to, 133, 151
 spatial distances and, 121
 time and, 118, 127

Databases, 250
Decipher. *See* Decoding
Decision-making, 212
Decoding, 7, 20
Definition. *See* Speeches
Delivery
 extemporaneous, 312–313, 328
 impromptu, 312–313, 328
 manuscript method of, 312–313,
  328
 outline, 313–314
 rehearsing, 321–322, 328
 and using notes, 315
Demonstration. *See* Speeches, informa-
  mative
Denotation, 78–79
Depenetration, 167, 175
Description. *See* Speeches, informa-
  tive
Descriptiveness, 137, 151
Deterioration, 160, 166, 175
Disclaimer, 69–70
Disconfirmation, 91–92, 97
Discovery, 19
Dissolution, 160, 175
Distance, 121
 culture and, 108–109
 influences on, 109
 spatial, 107
Distortion, 63
Dyads, 34, 35, 132

Effects, 11, 20
Emblems, 104, 121
Emotions, 104
Empathy, 135–137, 151
Encoding-decoding, 7, 20
Encounter groups. *See* Groups
Equality
 disconfirmation and, 92
 in interpersonal communication,
  138–139, 151
Equity theory, 163
Ethics, 12, 20, 91
Ethology, 109
Evaluation, 60, 322–327, 328. *See also*
  Interpretation-evaluation
Evidence, 287–291, 297
Examples, 278–279
Expressiveness, 142, 151
Extemporaneous speaking, 312–313
Extensional orientation, 82, 97
Eye contact, 320
Eye movement, 105–107, 121

Facial movements, 103–104, 121,
  320
Fact-inference confusion, 83–84, 97
Feedback
 definition of, 10, 20
 listening process and, 67–68, 72
Feedforward
 definition of, 10–11, 20
 functions of, 69–70
 guidelines for, 70–71
 listening process and, 68–69
Figures of speech, 305–306
Flexibility, 134, 151
Force, 147, 151
Forcefulness, 308, 328
Formality, 306–307

Gender
 self-disclosure and, 36
 sexism, 94–95, 97
 spatial distance and, 109
 word choice and, 307
Gestures, 320
Glittering generality, 291, 297
Gossip, 90–91, 97
Groups
 assertiveness training, 215, 218
 consciousness-raising, 215–216,
  218
 educational, 216–217, 218
 encounter, 215, 218
 formats for, 217, 218
 and group building and maintenance roles, 223, 237

and group task roles, 222–223,
  237
 and groupthink, 227–228, 237
 idea-generation in, 213, 218
 individual roles in, 223–224, 237
 interaction process analysis and,
  224, 237
 leaders in, 228–236
 member participation in,
  225–227, 237
 and personal growth, 215–216,
  218
 problem-solving, 208, 218
 problems of, 236
 small, 206, 218, 222
Groupthink, 227–228, 237
Guide phrases, 304
Gunnysacking, 148–149, 151

Halo effect, 50
Haptics. *See* Touch communication
Heterosexism, 96, 97
Hyperbole, 306

Illustrators, 104, 121
Imagery, 306
Immediacy, 140–141, 151, 308
Implicit personality theory, 49–50
Inclusion, 90
Index, 88
Indiscrimination, 88, 97
Inevitability, 18, 20
Inference. *See* Fact-inference confu-
  sion
Information retrieval, 250
In-group talk, 89–90, 97
Intensional orientation, 81–83, 97
Interaction management, 141–142,
  151
Interaction process analysis,
  224–225
Internal summaries, 304, 311
Interpersonal communication, 4–5
 effectiveness in, 132–143
 interpersonal conflict and,
  143–150
 in interviews, 194–195, 201
 deterioration of, 166–170
 development of, 162–163
Interpersonal relationships
 development of, 162–163
 ending, 173–174
 maintenance of, 164–166
 repair of, 171–173
 stages of, 156–162
Interpretation-evaluation, 47
Interviews, 5